GOING IT ALONE

GOING IT ALONE

Fargo Grapples with the Great Depression

DAVID B. DANBOM

 MINNESOTA HISTORICAL SOCIETY PRESS

www.mhspress.org

The Minnesota Historical Society Press is a member of the Association of American University Presses.

Manufactured in the United States of America

10 9 8 7 6 5 4 3 2 1

♾ The paper used in this publication meets the minimum requirements of the American National Standard for Information Sciences—Permanence for Printed Library Materials, ANSI Z39.48-1984.

International Standard Book Number
0-87351-546-3 (cloth)

Library of Congress
Cataloging-in-Publication Data

Danbom, David B., 1947–
    Going it alone : Fargo grapples with the Great Depression / David B. Danbom.
        p. cm.
    Includes bibliographical references and index.
    ISBN 0-87351-546-3 (hardcover : alk. paper)
        1. Fargo (N.D.)—Economic conditions—20th century.
        2. Depressions—1929—North Dakota—Fargo.
        3. New Deal, 1933–1939—North Dakota—Fargo.
        4. Fargo (N.D.)—Social conditions—20th century.
        5. Fargo (N.D.)—History—20th century.
    I. Title.
HC108.F37D36 2005
330.9784′13—dc22   2005016460

Map on page 2 by Matt Kania, Map Hero, Inc. Photo on page 109 from the State Historical Society of North Dakota. All other illustrations from the Institute for Regional Studies, NDSU Libraries, Fargo.

To the memory of Meyer Nathan,
who showed me what historians do,
and to David Kennedy,
who taught me how to do it.

GOING IT ALONE

ABBREVIATIONS

ADC   Aid for Dependent Children
CCC   Civilian Conservation Corps
CWA   Civil Works Administration
FERA   Federal Emergency Relief Administration
FHA   Federal Housing Administration
NIRA   National Industrial Recovery Act
NLRB   National Labor Relations Board
NRA   National Recovery Administration
NYA   National Youth Administration
PWA   Public Works Administration
RFC   Reconstruction Finance Corporation
VCCC   Veterans' Civilian Conservation Corps
WPA   Works Progress Administration

Going It Alone is an ironic title. No individual, and certainly no community, can be truly independent. We need others, their actions affect us, and our actions affect them. Others feed, clothe, and shelter us. We draw emotional support, love, and even our ideas from one another. The person or community that "goes it alone" in the modern world is an abstraction, and a pernicious one at that.

Yet our emotional health requires that we deny the implications of that reality. Each of us is special in his or her own way, different in some sense from every other person. And what is true of us as individuals is also true of the communities in which we live. Our city or town, however common it might appear on the surface, differs from every other city or town and is, we suspect, better.

Fargo, North Dakota, considered itself to be a special place at the onset of the Great Depression. In the grand scheme of things it was just one more of those regional marketing and service centers that sprang up during the great expansion of commodity agricultural production in North America during the second half of the nineteenth century. But seen through the other side of the microscope Fargo was the major urban place in the Red River Valley region of North Dakota and Minnesota and the largest city in its state. Fargo was the leading retail, wholesale, and service center in North Dakota and, less tangibly, the focus of a disproportionate share of its entrepreneurial energy. Fargo was the biggest success story in a region in which success was not assured, and its success gave it confidence. It was confident it could surmount hard times, even if they originated elsewhere, and it was confident in its continuing growth and bright future. This confidence was not misplaced. While much of the region coped with the problems of contraction, Fargo addressed the problems of growth. At the end of the Depression its regional economic dominance was greater than at the beginning. Fargo was a winner at the beginning of the Depression and a winner at the end, and that fact is an important part of this story.

Like many communities that achieved success, Fargo relied on an array of myths about itself to explain why it was special. When I use the word "myth" I do not mean to suggest a false or fantastical belief, like modern "urban myths," but rather a broadly embraced understanding, rooted in the past but living in the present, that helps shape the ways people interpret events, explain problems, and devise solutions.

At the outset of the Depression Fargoans generally embraced a series of myths that helped shape their response to the economic challenge and the social disruptions that accompanied it. First was the myth of the can-do city, which had the material and especially the moral resources to overcome daunting problems. This myth was related to that of the resourceful and independent community, made up of resourceful and independent people. Then there was the myth of the caring community, which lent a hand to neighbors in need and provided paternal care and supervision for the weak. Another myth embraced by many Fargoans was that of the classless city, in which cordiality reigned between rich and poor and employers and employees. Finally there was the myth of the city of families, characterized by conventional gender relationships and hierarchies and well-behaved children.

Going It Alone is organized around these myths: how they shaped action, how they were challenged, and how they ultimately survived. As a consequence, the chapters that follow mix a chronological organizational scheme with a topical one.

After a short introduction in which I provide a social and economic portrait of Fargo in 1930, "The Depression Comes to Fargo" surveys the onset of economic decline in the city and the effects of deflation, the contraction of credit, and rising unemployment on business, government, homeowners, and workers. While city leaders were confident of Fargo's abilities to survive the downturn and meet human needs, fissures began to appear between classes and a penurious and mean-spirited attitude toward those in need developed where open-handed generosity previously had been the rule.

"Self-Help" examines the numerous ways in which Fargoans demonstrated their can-do spirit in attempting to pull themselves out of the Depression. Self-help endeavors revealed remarkable civic leadership, community confidence, and resourcefulness, but their results were often disappointing. Shortfalls in Community Chest campaigns raised doubts about whether Fargo was truly a caring community. And when the unemployed attempted to help themselves they showed admirable resourcefulness and independence but they also challenged the pretensions of those accustomed to leading and governing the city. Despite the disappointments of self-help endeavors, they were an enduring feature of life in Fargo throughout the Depression.

"Federal Help" is a discussion of the New Deal in Fargo. The federal government played a major role in the city during the Depression, providing infrastructure that helped the city cope with its growth, centralizing and stabilizing the always-troubling transient population, lending money for private construction and renovation, and aiding the aged, single mothers, and others who had previously depended on local taxpayers. Business-minded Fargoans tended to view the federal government as a customer rather than a patron, but its growing presence in local life disturbed those who cherished the city's tradition of self-help and independence.

Of the federal endeavors significant to Fargo none was more troubling than relief for the unemployed. "Relief and Reliefers" examines relief activities and projects in the city, but this chapter focuses especially on local attitudes toward relief and those who received it. Nothing challenged local views regarding independence, resourcefulness, self-help, and the correct relationship among social classes more than did federal relief. And on no other issue did federal and local attitudes diverge so sharply.

Relief contributed to class conflict, including discord between the poor on relief and those off. But relief was hardly the only, or even the primary, locus of class conflict in Fargo during the Depression. "Working" details the ways in which economic hardship sundered cross-class unity and eroded cordial relationships between employers and employees. Increasingly, Fargo workers turned to unionization as an answer to their problems, and employers in the traditionally open-shop city resisted. The struggle between capital and labor, which erupted in violence and death during a coal drivers' strike in 1935, presented the most difficult challenge to the myths by which Fargoans lived. Denying the reality of class struggle and asserting the myth of class harmony became a major rhetorical enterprise among the city's leaders.

Other myths by which Fargoans lived were challenged during the Depression, if not exactly by the Depression. Fargo's self-image was of a city of strong conventional families, yet reality suggested something different. As is detailed in "Women's Work and Women's Lives," Fargo was a city of single women and a city of working wives. These realities not only spawned conflict when women competed for scarce jobs in the thirties but also stimulated debate about the proper role of women in the family and in society. Popular preconceptions about gender roles were further challenged by women who engaged in personal habits and behaviors that were viewed as unladylike by much of the community.

The behavior of children also challenged local conceptions about well-ordered family life. In "Dealing with Disorder," I explain how laissez-faire traditions of child supervision came to be defined as child neglect and how a rising tide of juvenile delinquency led city leaders to embark on a campaign to save the children. Like relations between men and women, relations between adults and children had relatively little to do with the Depression as such, but they preoccupied Fargoans during the 1930s and challenged their accustomed ways of looking at the world.

The experience of Fargo during the Depression was unique in the sense that the experience of every place was unique, but it was not extraordinary. The city confronted new challenges in accustomed ways. Those ways were sometimes found wanting, but their failure did not lead to their abandonment. The values of independence and resourcefulness Fargoans held dear were compromised and even flouted by some, but most continued to cherish them. Traditional agreements about relationships among employers and employees, affluent and impoverished, men and women, and adults and children were called into question, yet all endured, albeit in modified and amended forms.

In the final analysis, what is remarkable about the Depression experience in Fargo is how few and subtle were the changes it brought. Fargo was a dominant city in 1940, as it had been in 1930. Its problems remained the problems of success and growth, not the problems of failure and contraction. Its values, myths, and understandings of human nature and human relationships had sometimes been shaken and sometimes confirmed, but all endured more or less intact. Crises challenge our beliefs, but culture and the understandings and assumptions on which it is based endure.

I was drawn to a study of the Depression in Fargo in part by intellectual curiosity and also by the desire to take part in a rich historical conversation about the Depression and its effects.

In the early years of scholarly examination of the Depression the focus was mainly national and political. The Depression was viewed, reasonably enough, as a national—or, much less often, an international—phenomenon. The American response to it was embodied in Franklin D. Roosevelt's New Deal, which may not have ended the Depression but which made enduring changes in American life, the American economy, and popular American expectations and understandings of the role and function of government. This is a national, Washington-centered story, and it has been told often, most recently and most impressively by David Kennedy in *Freedom from Fear*.[1]

Soon after national stories of the Depression began to appear, scholars started looking at the experience of states and localities. Frequently they focused on the "little New Deals" in progressive states or looked at how federal programs were put into effect at the local level. In the Upper Midwest, works by such historians as D. Jerome Tweton and Michael Johnston Grant explored the operation of federal programs in counties and states, revealing that local preferences, values, and interpretations had much to do with how the New Deal operated. One size certainly did not fit all. The insights and careful investigation of scholars of the local operation of the New Deal have informed and enriched my work.[2]

Over the last generation social history has come to dominate the study of America's past. For a time, social historians were relatively disinterested in the 1930s, apparently assuming that it was an anomalous period in the country's history. More recently, however, such scholars as Lizabeth Cohen and Mary Murphy have integrated the Depression decade into their studies of ethnicity and gender relations. What they have discovered is similar to what Robert and Helen Lynd discovered when they returned to Middletown in 1937—that the Depression challenged values, heightened conflicts, and accelerated change, but it did not alter the trajectory of social and cultural life in a revolutionary way. *Going It Alone* draws heavily on the work of social historians and reflects many of their conclusions about the impact of the Great Depression.[3]

My desire to join this rich historiographical conversation attracted me to this subject, but there is more to it than that. In common with many of my contemporaries in the discipline of history, I have come increasingly to understand the relationship between my commitments and my work—to understand that the personal and the historical are often intertwined.

I was drawn to this period by the experience of my parents, especially that of my mother, who carried habits and attitudes shaped by the Depression and scars inflicted by it throughout her adult life. Any phenomenon powerful enough to mold one's life is worthy of careful attention.

The place I studied was also determined by personal commitments. I have lived in Fargo for more than thirty years. Over that period, but especially in the second half of it, I have become increasingly interested in the city's history. My service on the Fargo Historic Preservation Commission, between 1990 and 1999, was especially significant, teaching me a great deal about the city's past and whetting my appetite for more.

Thirty years in this place have given me an understanding of the city's culture, attitudes, values, and personality. That intimate knowledge of a place is one of the pleasures of doing local history. Another advantage of doing the history of the place in which one lives is that one can *know* the sources and can be immersed in them to a greater degree than someone dropping in for a few weeks or even for a few months to conduct research.

The problem with doing a history of a place about which one cares is similar to the problem with writing a biography. Becoming enamored of the subject, the author loses his or her objectivity and ignores or underemphasizes flaws and weaknesses. The result is a flattering portrait but one that does not do justice to either the author or the subject. I freely and frankly acknowledge my regard for this place. Whether that regard has allowed me to produce a more or less accurate portrayal of its experience in a time of crisis is for the reader to judge.[4]

Fortunately, I did not have to go it alone in writing this book. I benefited from the help of many librarians and archivists, especially John Bye, John Hallberg, and Michael Robinson at the North Dakota Institute for Regional Studies; Lorrettax Mindt, Deborah Sayler, Nellie Vangsness, and Cheryl Zimprich of the North Dakota State University libraries; and Terry Shoptaugh of the Northwest Minnesota Regional Historical Center.

Both my access to records and my understanding of their meaning were immeasurably enhanced by the openness and helpfulness of a number of individuals and agencies in the community. Among those who facilitated my efforts were Kathy Hogan of Cass County Social Services, Tim Mathern of Catholic Family Services, Howard Barlow and Linda Hennings of Lutheran Social Service, Tammy Noteboom of the Village Family Service Center, Shirley Johnson of Fargo Public Schools, Earl Stewart of the Fargo Park Board, and Michael Montplaisir of Cass County. My most cherished sources were the approximately ninety Fargoans and former Fargoans who agreed to be interviewed about their memories of life during the Depression. Not all appear in the book, and I have chosen not to identify some, but they gave me an understanding of life in the city I could not have received by other means. I thank these men and women for sharing their lives with me, and I thank Bob Lind of the *Forum* and Bill Snyder of the *Cynosure* for helping publicize my interviews.

Going It Alone is the beneficiary of close readings by a number of people whose intelligence I admire and whose friendship I cherish. Lois Casavant and Roland Dille shared with me their acute understanding of the city by reading early drafts. Carroll Engelhardt, Barbara Handy-Marchello, Larry Peterson, and Claire Strom are accomplished scholars and specialists in the history of the region who were willing to give me some of their precious time and keen insights. And my mother, Rowene Danbom, read the manuscript with a veteran reporter's eye for errors and infelicities of language. She found many but, alas, probably not all. I also thank the North Dakota Humanities Committee, the Fargo-Moorhead Communiversity, and *North Dakota History* for allowing me to try out some of my ideas on larger audiences. And I thank several score of undergraduate students at North Dakota State University who discussed various portions of my work, albeit under some duress.

This book owes a great deal to Pam Murphy, Reen Kapaun, and especially Terry Jackson, who not only mastered handwriting that becomes murkier with age and emendations that were puzzling and even bizarre but did so with good humor and great efficiency. I cannot overstate their contribution. Finally, I thank Ann Regan and Shannon Pennefeather at Minnesota Historical Society Press for believing in this manuscript, soliciting perceptive readings of it, and improving it in numerous ways. I have never worked with editors more devoted to authors and their work.

Going It Alone is dedicated to the memory of Meyer Nathan and to David Kennedy. It was in Meyer Nathan's "Recent U.S. History" class at Colorado State University that I found my calling in life. He transformed an interest into a passion, and it is one of my regrets that I wasn't able to tell him that before his untimely death. David Kennedy was my advisor at Stanford University. By precept and example he set a standard for rigorous thought, clear expression, and social and professional responsibility that inspires me even now. Perhaps one could have better mentors, but I consider myself most fortunate to have had these two.

GOING IT ALONE

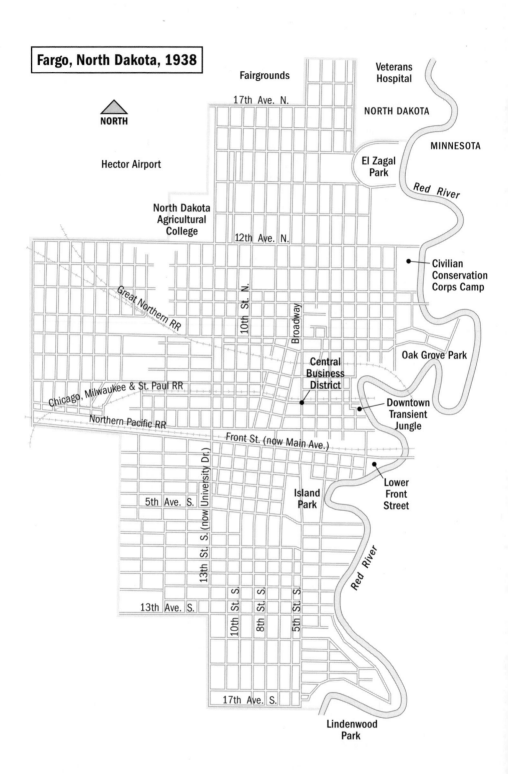

Fargo, North Dakota, 1938

NORTH

Fairgrounds

Veterans Hospital

17th Ave. N.

NORTH DAKOTA

MINNESOTA

Hector Airport

El Zagal Park

Red River

North Dakota Agricultural College

12th Ave. N.

Civilian Conservation Corps Camp

Great Northern RR

10th St. N.

Broadway

Oak Grove Park

Chicago, Milwaukee & St. Paul RR

Central Business District

Downtown Transient Jungle

Northern Pacific RR

Front St. (now Main Ave.)

Lower Front Street

5th Ave. S.

13th St. S. (now University Dr.)

Island Park

Red River

13th Ave. S.

10th St. S.

8th St. S.

5th St. S.

17th Ave. S.

Lindenwood Park

Introduction

"Fargo grows. . . .

"Fargo not only grows, it prospers and progresses . . . and it is so far
from being downhearted that it looks forward to the coming year and
future years with unbounded faith."

Fargo Forum, *January 1, 1932*

NEW YEAR'S DAY is normally a time for optimism, but even so the *Fargo Forum*'s editorial of January 1, 1932, was remarkable. Two years into the most severe depression in the nation's history, with no end in sight, and with wages, prices, and property values still sliding downward, the *Forum* could say "Fargo grows . . . prospers and progresses."[1]

One explanation for the *Forum*'s upbeat outlook was the boosterism woven into the fabric of so many towns and their business communities, especially in relatively young places like Fargo, barely sixty years old in 1932.

But there was more to this optimism than a reflexive denial of reality or an exercise in whistling past the graveyard, though both phenomena were in evidence. The *Forum* was looking forward, but its appraisal of the future was based on its understanding of the past. And what the past revealed was that Fargo had grown—from a tent settlement on the prairie in 1871 to the largest city in North Dakota in 1930. That growth had been the product of luck, to be sure, but also of entrepreneurial vision and energy. And growth was continuing. While North Dakota's farm and village populations had started to decline even before World War I, Fargo had continued to thrive, attracting more and more of the region's sons and daughters and doing more and more of the region's business. Fargo was a winner in an area in which winning did not come easily, and the margin of its victory increased every year.

Growth presented Fargo with problems that other places did not have but wished they did. While others worried about holding population, providing work, and identifying investment opportunities for capital, Fargo was usually preoccupied with housing and serving a growing population, finding adequate workers, and attracting capital. Fargo struggled with such problems as paving streets, putting in sidewalks, laying water and sewer lines, and building schools, parks, and public buildings. That reality did not change during the thirties. Indeed, one of the ironies of the Fargo experience during the Depression was that coping with growth remained a challenge, almost as great as that of coping with hardship.

Fargo's history instilled in it the confidence winners usually have, a confidence reflected in the *Forum* editorial. Fargoans had come to expect that progress and prosperity, while they might be interrupted, were inevitable. Things would generally get better, especially if optimistic and determined people rolled up their sleeves and made it so.

The city's confidence was fed by the civic memory of challenges successfully overcome. In 1893 a fire had destroyed over half of the town, but Fargoans built a bigger and better city on the cinders and celebrated their accomplishment for thirty years thereafter with the annual Fargo Fire Festival. The natural disasters attendant on life on the Northern Plains also came along, including a killer tornado in 1890 and a hundred-year flood in 1897, but the city surmounted all obstacles and pressed ahead.

The Depression was different from these natural disasters in a number of ways, but Fargoans saw no reason why a resourceful community of hardworking, determined, and intelligent people could not overcome it as they overcame the fire. Fargo grew, prospered, and progressed. That was the legacy and the destiny of the city that confronted the Depression.

The Census Bureau counted 28,619 people living in Fargo in 1930. The city fathers, who reckoned the actual population of the city to be somewhere between 34,000 and 35,000, complained of an undercount, but even the lower figure represented a healthy increase over the reported 1920 population of 21,961.[2]

However many people lived in the city, they were concentrated in an area that stretched about thirty blocks north and south along the west bank of the Red River and extended about twenty-five blocks to the west. Front Street— now Main Avenue—divided the city into roughly equal north and south sides. This division was significant to Fargoans, who stereotyped the north side as middle class and common and the south side as elite and arrogant.

That stereotype had some basis in reality. The area of the south side centered on Eighth Street—Fargo's original "great white way"—was the wealthiest in town, inhabited by such civic leaders as former North Dakota governor Louis B. Hanna and bankers E. J. Weiser and Alex Stern. But the north side also contained an elite district, centered on Broadway and stretching north from St. Luke's Hospital. In common with most small, midwestern cities, Fargo had no gated communities or neighborhoods that operated under restrictive covenants. Hence, modest houses could be found even in wealthy neighborhoods, and working-class areas frequently included at least a few impressive dwellings. The city's working-class neighborhoods were clustered in or just to the north and west of downtown, but there were modest enclaves elsewhere, such as the Hollow, which occupied the low, flood-prone area just north of the city water plant on the south side. The lower Front Street area, which was Fargo's original town site, had by 1930 become the city's skid row— or "main stem"—and was largely populated by single resident and transient males and the businesses serving them.

Areas beyond Fargo's city limits were inhabited for the most part by people in modest circumstances who sought to avoid municipal zoning regulations and property taxes and to maintain large gardens and keep animals. Hungry Point, between the El Zagal Bowl and the Veterans Hospital, was one such suburban settlement; another was Golden Ridge, an un-annexed area west of the city dump and the Great Northern tracks that numbered about seventy houses and 300 to 350 people. The city was expanding through annexation of peripheral areas, and the extension of water lines and the laying out and paving of streets in such places as the recently annexed village of North Fargo commanded much of the City Commission's attention during the early 1930s.[3]

Fargo continued to grow during the Depression, reaching a population of 32,580 in 1940. Much of the city's population growth was the result of continuing in-migration from rural areas, especially by single people such as Frieda Oster, who came for business college and stayed on as a bookkeeper at a local clothing store, and Lucille Duval, who came to train as a nurse and married, but also by families such as the Iversons, who moved to Fargo and opened a grocery store after the Kensal grain elevator Ingvold Iverson managed went broke in 1930.[4]

Continuing growth presented the city with challenges that the Depression complicated. The combination of rising population and the virtual end of residential construction meant that housing was scarce and rents were relatively high. City leaders argued that such key municipal facilities as city hall, the library, and the auditorium were inadequate for a modern, growing community and urged that new ones be built. New schools were needed, along with recreational facilities for young people. The city had upgraded its water plant in the 1920s but struggled throughout the drought years of the thirties to secure adequate water to meet public needs. At the start of the Depression the city still dumped raw sewage directly into the Red, an increasingly inadequate expedient with real aesthetic and potential health consequences.[5]

The growing popularity of the automobile further increased burdens on the city. While most people lived close enough to their places of employment to walk to work—as 62 percent reported doing in 1934—automobiles were popular among all classes. The city assessor counted 3,100 automobiles owned by Fargoans in 1931, and a U.S. Department of Commerce survey two years later found that fully one-third of poor families in the city—those earning under $500 per year—owned cars. Moreover, while horses were still used by some lumberyards to deliver coal and building products and while dairies were loath to replace horses trained to stop at each customer's house, the shift to trucks for delivery purposes was well under way by 1930.[6]

The automobile stimulated economic activity and symbolized modernity and prosperity, as illustrated in the 1930 census, which counted sixteen automobile dealers and fifty filling stations and garages employing over six hundred people. But increasing automobility also intensified fiscal pressures on the city. Drivers wanted paved streets and desired that they be cleared of snow in the winter. They complained of inadequate signage, poor street lighting, and a lack of parking, especially downtown. The automobile also posed a law enforcement challenge. People drove carelessly, sometimes damaging property and even causing bodily injury and death. Joy riding became a major juvenile offense, and criminals possessed greater mobility. Drivers refused to obtain licenses for themselves or purchase tags for their vehicles. The failure of traffic violators to stop when hailed by beat policemen forced the city to buy motorcycles and later patrol cars for some of its officers.[7]

The city also struggled to keep abreast of other transportation developments. Fargo owed its existence to the Northern Pacific Railroad's decision to cross the Red there in 1871, and the fact that it was the only city in North Dakota to be served by three railroads gave it superior connections and cheaper freight rates than any would-be rivals. This advantage, strengthened by a favorable rate decision by the Interstate Commerce Commission in 1925, made Fargo the warehousing and wholesaling center of the region. The railroads remained significant, but the Chamber of Commerce, prodded by Secretary W. P. Chesnut and Fargo Aeronautics Club president Murray Baldwin, recognized that air travel was the wave of the future, and it endeavored to obtain regular air service and build a modern airfield for the city. In 1931, Martin Hector, a Fargo pioneer and a leading businessman, gave the city a 160-acre tract north of town for use as a "permanent municipal airport," and Northwest Airways announced that it would begin passenger and mail service to the city. On May 27, five thousand people attended the dedication of Hector Airport and watched Fargo aviatrix Frances Klingensmith fly loops in the spring sky. Air service was correctly viewed as a necessary component of the city's future growth, but providing adequate facilities presented Fargo with a burden that it had not expected and could not easily afford.[8]

In their efforts to meet the challenges of growth and to grasp the opportunities of the modern age, city leaders were handicapped by structural weaknesses in municipal government. The mayor and the city commissioners were all part-time public servants with jobs and businesses that commanded most of their attention, and Fargo lacked any formal planning mechanisms that might help officials manage growth and set priorities. Fiscal operations were informal and sometimes haphazard. Auditors revealed in 1930 that the city lacked an accurate estimate of the value of the property it owned, that its voucher system was lax and subject to fraud and abuse, and that several city departments, including the police, operated without budgets. These revelations led to the first of two attempts by angry taxpayers to recall the City Commission.[9]

Increasing automobility contributed to traffic congestion in Fargo's downtown streets and alleys.

The recalcitrance of citizens further diminished the ability of city government to address problems efficiently. Fargoans sometimes protested the way streets were laid out in new districts, resisted paying for paving and sidewalks, and opposed being hooked up to municipal water and sewer lines. Some continued to keep chickens and even hogs, calling forth neighbors' complaints. And the not-in-my-backyard attitude complicated life at city hall, as in 1931, when neighbors of the City Detention Hospital demanded its removal on the grounds that it depressed property values.[10]

One challenge with which Fargo did not have to cope was pronounced ethnic or racial heterogeneity. Of those Fargoans enumerated by the census in 1930, over 99 percent were white and only 13 percent were foreign born. The latter tended to be older males and were predominantly natives of Norway, with smaller numbers from Sweden, Canada, and Germany. In Fargo's early years divisions and sometimes conflicts between the socially and economically dominant Yankees and the more numerous Norwegians had flared, and during the anti-immigrant hysteria of the World War I era hostility had sometimes been pronounced. Dwindling immigration and continuing assimilation—especially of young people—had reduced divisions substantially, though Norwegians were still believed to favor political candidates whose names ended with "son." Among the non–European Americans, the census found thirty-five African Americans, thirty-five Chinese, and twenty-one Native Americans.[11]

The relatively small number of non–European Americans among them did not prevent Fargoans from exhibiting racial consciousness and bias. Police department arrest records classified those charged as "Colored," "Indian," "Mexican," or "Chinese," with all European Americans identified as "U.S." The *Forum* invariably identified non–European Americans by race and frequently carried pejorative remarks about them. Commenting in 1931 on the closure of a café run and frequented by Chinese Americans, for example, the *Forum* noted, "no more will strains of weird Chinese music be wafted over Broadway. And no more will slant-eyed orientals gather to sing and play the songs of their homeland."[12]

African Americans were commonly objects of either humor or fear in Fargo. Service clubs and organizations frequently staged minstrel shows. In January 1935, the *Forum* noted that the American Legion put on a New Year's Eve party with a "colored" theme, in which the orchestra, dancers, and waiters wore blackface, and that the Elks Band was staging a minstrel show for local orphans. Central High School students marked Costume Day by dressing as "gypsies and Negroes," and school authorities apparently saw nothing inappropriate when "a program of dialect stories . . . and Negro impersonations was presented by Smilin' Bob Briggs in Central high school assembly." Students at the North Dakota Agricultural College were hardly more progressive. The theme of the "Bison Brevities" variety show in 1935 was "Louisiana Swamp Lands." The program featured "a colored chorus, a darky preacher . . . [and] a 'niggah' orchestra leader." Stereotypical blacks sometimes appeared in advertisements, as in one coal company's fair week ad featuring a black man saying, "Boy! Yo' all Miss Dis booth—and ys' done missed de whole Fair!" African American entertainers—and sports teams such as the Harlem Globetrotters—were welcomed in Fargo as long as they behaved in a manner with which whites were comfortable. In July 1930, for example, the Fargo Theater hosted the "Plantation Follies," featuring "'Snake Hips' Earl Tucker" and a "Snappy Creole Beauty Chorus," and in 1934 forty-five "Harlem Gen'men" presented the "Harlem Scandals" at the theater.[13]

African American residents of Fargo came to public attention only when they were beloved figures—such as "Colonel" Frank Plummer, long-time "errand boy" for the prominent Stern family—or when they were agents of disorder. Blacks living in the lower Front Street neighborhood were frequently arrested for gambling, engaging in liquor traffic, and especially prostitution, and police and city officials periodically attempted "clean ups" of the area to drive such blacks as William Darty, "the king of Front Street," away, at least temporarily. African American prostitutes were a source of amusement to some high school students, who would drive down to lower Front to taunt "Nigger Betty," "Snowball," and others. Sometimes racial violence flared. In September 1935, in response to transient Major Evans's boisterous celebration of Joe Louis's knockout of Max Baer, a rock-throwing mob attacked Evans on Front Street. Police rescued Evans from men shouting "let's hang him," arresting him for vagrancy. His attackers were not charged.[14]

Among European Americans religious divisions were notable. Fargo had a Jewish population of at least 350 in 1930. In the city's early decades, Jews had concentrated in the original town site—where they established a synagogue— and had lived by peddling, maintaining second-hand clothing and pawn shops, and engaging in other small-scale retail ventures. Fargo Jews had prospered along with the city, however, and by 1930 the Sterns, Goldbergs, Herbsts, Naftalins, Levitzes, and others were numbered among the city's leading families and were living mainly in the Eighth Street neighborhood on the south side.[15]

Relations between Jews and Gentiles in Fargo were generally cordial. As

Harry Lashkowitz, Fargo lawyer and later assistant U.S. attorney, put it in 1929, "the harmony between the different peoples . . . is still prevailing, and in my humble judgment . . . there will always be a mutual understanding between our people and their neighbors." Certainly such Jews as banker Alex Stern and grain merchant Max Goldberg played an active role in the city, taking the lead in many philanthropic and community development endeavors, and Jews were welcomed into such fraternal organizations as the Elks and the Masons. For about thirty years Stern's son Bill served as Republican national committee-man for North Dakota, an important sign of acceptance in a thoroughly Republican state. Gentiles would occasionally make anti-Semitic remarks or characterizations, but these were usually the product of ignorance rather than malice. And for their parts, Gentile churchmen stressed brotherhood and decried bigotry in their public pronouncements.[16]

At the same time, Jews remembered that Fargo had hosted an active Ku Klux Klan that had once burned a cross on Alex Stern's lawn, and they recognized that some expressions of anti-Semitism were vicious rather than ignorant. One Fargoan remembered that, when it came to resenting Jews, his father "was great for it. When Hitler came along the people who were anti-Jewish were more so. People would say, 'goddamned Jews' . . . it was just resentment." In the mid-thirties the *Forum* began running articles featuring German visitors, or Fargoans who had visited Germany, who emphasized Hitler's popularity and downplayed Nazi anti-Semitism. In 1936, for example, the Reverend W. P. Gerberding of St. Mark's Lutheran returned from Germany to report that "there is no mistaking the genuine enthusiasm that [Germans] feel for the new regime" and to laud "Hitler's fight . . . against communism." Such articles served to remind Fargo Jews that, while they were a part of the community in some ways, in others they were apart from it.[17]

More significant than the differences between Jews and Gentiles were those between Protestants—especially the dominant Lutherans—and Catholics. Lutherans and Catholics tolerated one another, but their relationship was marked by mutual wariness and distrust. The Fargo Klan had been an anti-Catholic organization primarily, and Catholics well remembered its cross-burnings at the state fairgrounds on the north edge of town and at the homes of such prominent Catholic laymen as Central High principal B. C. B. Tighe. Catholics created their own institutional structure, including such organizations as the Catholic Daughters of America and the Knights of Columbus, primary schools in St. Mary's and St. Anthony's parishes, and a high school, Sacred Heart Academy. In addition, Catholics maintained a hospital, orphanage, and welfare agency. Catholic parents were urged to send their children to parochial schools; as a result Catholic and non-Catholic children developed friendship cohorts that were frequently confined to their co-religionists. Tod Gunkleman remembered that in his neighborhood Catholic and Protestant children even formed exclusive teams for pick-up baseball games. Priests and ministers, and presumably parents as well, encouraged separation and especially opposed dating or marriage across religious lines. The result could be anxiety, as when Evelyn Fisher attended the funeral of a Lutheran friend and sat "waiting for God to strike me dead" because her priest had told her that would be the consequence of entering a Protestant church. It is difficult to disagree with the conclusion of one Fargoan that "the Catholic-Lutheran split was a significant part of the culture."[18]

All churches played major roles in the organizational and social lives of Fargoans on the eve of the Depression, but they comprised only one segment of the city's rich institutional culture. Women's clubs were numerous. Some, such as the Fine Arts Club, were devoted to cultural enrichment, while others focused on such recreational activities as gardening and bridge, which was virtually a mania among middle-class Fargoans during the thirties.

In addition, numerous fraternal and patriotic organizations—such as the Shriners, Elks, American Legion, Pythians, Knights of Columbus, and Eagles—and service clubs—such as the Kiwanis, Lions, Rotary, and Quota—served men and sometimes women and even children, especially through their auxiliaries, providing recreation, fellowship, business contacts, and occasionally limited welfare services. Even Depression-era political organizations such as the Townsend Clubs and the Unemployed Men's Club included a strong recreational component.

Fargoans were proud of their commitment to the arts, supporting community theater and a Civic Orchestra. The Amphion Chorus, a men's choir of seventy to one hundred members, was accomplished enough to make a tour of the East in 1937, performing in New York City, Philadelphia, and Washington and on nationwide radio broadcasts. Every summer the park board staged free band concerts in Island Park and sponsored a north side versus south side singing contest. The park board also supervised summer play and winter ice-skating for children and conducted an elaborate Ice Carnival just after New Year's.[19]

Fargoans with time and money could enjoy of a range of commercial recreations, including professional baseball, played by the Fargo-Moorhead Twins, a locally owned minor league team. Several movie houses, ballrooms featuring

Fargo-Moorhead's Amphion Chorus at the Chicago World's Fair in 1933, one of several trips made by the all-male musical ensemble

dancing most evenings, prizefights, and "recreation centers," as pool halls were commonly called, offered further diversions.

The public schools and the North Dakota Agricultural College also provided the community with a range of cultural and sporting events, but that was hardly the principal benefit Fargo derived from education. The 1930 census revealed that less than one-half of one percent of its residents were illiterate and that an astounding 99 percent of children aged seven to thirteen attended school. Even more noteworthy was the fact that 47.8 percent of those aged eighteen to twenty were in school, most probably at the NDAC or one of the city's numerous business, beauty, or nursing schools.[20]

Fargo enjoyed the reputation of being healthy as well as educated. In 1923 the Commonwealth Fund had chosen Fargo as one of its public health demonstration sites and had assigned Kansas physician B. K. Kilbourne to coordinate the work. Kilbourne stressed cooperation with the schools and among hospitals and health professionals to improve sanitation, nutrition, prenatal care, and the early identification and quarantining of people with communicable diseases. Kilbourne was so successful in advancing the health of the city's schoolchildren that Fargo hired him as a full-time public health officer when the Commonwealth money ran out in 1927. By 1930 the city's death rate was barely half the national average.[21]

Fargoans liked to emphasize such sources of pride as high health and education standards, and they tended to mute religious and ethnic differences that could be divisive. They also downplayed class differences, even to the point of denying their existence, but significant variations in income and affluence characterized the city. In 1933 the Commerce Department divided Fargoans into three rough income classes when it noted that 34.4 percent of them made under $1,000 per year, another 54.4 percent earned between $1,000 and $3,000, and slightly over 10 percent made more than $3,000.[22]

Class differences were reflected in housing and creature comforts. The Civil Works Administration survey of 1934 showed just under half of Fargo families with radios and about one-fourth with mechanical refrigeration. The CWA considered 44 percent of Fargo dwellings "spacious" or "very spacious" and 24 percent "crowded" or "very crowded." The CWA noted that 97 percent of homes had electricity, 87 percent had central heat, 86 percent had hot and cold running water, and 80 percent had a shower or bathtub. One interesting revelation in the CWA report for a city that was proud of its strong and stable neighborhoods was that 63 percent of Fargoans rented their dwellings, including the 15 percent who lived in apartments, and that one-third of residents had occupied their present domiciles for eleven or fewer months. This suggests the existence of two Fargos—a stable "community," based on rooted homeowners and long-term renters, and a locale in flux, inhabited by relatively transient individuals and families.[23]

Fargoans of all classes depended on an economy that was normally robust and vital. Fargo was the major retail center in the large and rich Red River Valley region. The 1930 census counted 432 retail stores in the city, employing 2,400 proprietors and workers, or 19.5 percent of all employed Fargoans. Fargo had less than four percent of North Dakota's population but made nine percent of its retail sales. Strong service and finance and banking sectors added to Fargo's status as the major place in eastern North Dakota and western Minnesota, and the city's steady growth helped keep 700 construction workers employed. Fargo's importance as a rail center was reflected in the presence of nearly 500 railroad employees as well as in its strong wholesale sector. Nearly

1,200 Fargoans were employed by wholesale houses, and Fargo did 16 percent of the state's wholesale trade. Fargo's employment profile was as important for what it did not include as for what it included. The city's manufacturing sector was small and oriented mainly to agriculture, and employees were spread among numerous small- and medium-sized firms. As a result Fargo was relatively immune to a severe downturn in manufacturing and the failure of any single firm would not prove economically devastating.[24]

On the eve of the Great Depression Fargo was a growing, prosperous city with a relatively homogenous population and a well-developed social infrastructure. Its main problems were the problems presented by growth and prosperity, which tended to mute its social divisions. Its economy was based in retail, wholesale, and service and was thus buffered to some degree from the devastating downturn in manufacturing and agriculture that the Depression brought. Buffered, but not immune.

1

THE DEPRESSION COMES TO FARGO

"Conditions are bright and not at all depressing."
R. F. Gunkleman, December 12, 1929

"The unemployment situation in Fargo is the worst it has ever been,
Mayor A. T. Lynner told the commissioners today."
Fargo Forum, January 13, 1930

THE ECONOMIC DOWNTURN signified by the collapse of the stock market in
the fall of 1929 did not have an immediate, noticeable impact on Fargo, and
some observers doubted it would have any impact at all. When R. F. Gunkleman of the Chamber of Commerce and Interstate Feed and Grain told the
Forum in December 1929 that "conditions are bright and not at all depressing," he might have been offering a positive interpretation of an uncertain situation, but he was not dissembling.[1]

It soon became apparent, however, that Fargo would not go unscathed.
Within a few weeks of Gunkleman's upbeat assessment, Mayor A. T. Lynner
pronounced the "unemployment situation . . . the worst it has ever been."
Appearing first among those most sensitive to economic fluctuations—the
unskilled—unemployment soon spread to skilled construction workers and
beyond.[2]

Fargo suffered from the three basic, interrelated problems that beset the entire country in the early years of the Depression. First, it experienced a contraction of credit and diminished liquidity as a result of the impact of the stock
market crash on money center banks and the decision of the Federal Reserve
to protect the gold standard by tightening the money supply. Nationally, the
credit contraction was a major factor in the liquidity crisis that resulted in numerous bank failures. No Fargo banks failed during the Depression, but the
credit contraction imperiled all borrowers, including businesses that depended on credit from suppliers and extended credit to customers.

The contraction of credit contributed to—and was in turn exacerbated
by—a deflationary spiral in which falling prices and falling wages fed on one

another. Deflation posed a serious problem for borrowers because their fixed obligations remained the same even as their incomes eroded, further credit was difficult to get in the face of a growing liquidity crisis, and the value of their collateral declined. Fargoans addressed the problems of deflation with a series of voluntary drives, which will be discussed here and in more detail in the next chapter. These activities failed to reverse the deflationary spiral; consequently, debtors were left to work out their own solutions.

The third problem was that of rising unemployment. While the unemployed were encouraged to solve their problems themselves, unemployment was accepted as a subject for public policy to a degree the contraction of credit and deflation were not. In addition to supporting voluntary efforts to relieve unemployment, the city launched a public works program and the county devoted an increasing portion of its budget to relief. By 1932, rapidly rising demand and shrinking resources had created a crisis for local governmental functions generally and for relief particularly.

The struggles with credit, deflation, and unemployment in the early Depression years activated latent social divisions, threatening the community cohesion so prized in Fargo. Property owners, squeezed between falling incomes and fixed mortgage and real estate tax obligations, complained of unfair assessments and profligate government spending and took steps to curb both. And working Fargoans of all classes demonstrated increasing suspicion and distrust for those on relief, who were transformed from neighbors in distress to layabouts, chiselers, and leeches. In the process, a community that had seemed generous and tolerant in 1929 became increasingly penurious and mean-spirited.

I

The stock market crash of the fall of 1929 had little direct impact in Fargo. Despite the entry of small investors into the market during the 1920s—a phenomenon that helped create the bubble that burst in 1929—most Fargoans with money to invest put it into real estate, which was the source of many fortunes in the city. Nor could Fargoans see the implications of the market debacle for the local economy. The *Forum* editorialized on November 24 that "in North Dakota we are about as remote from the effect of the stock market collapse as any section. We are a food producing state and he would be a woeful prophet, indeed, who would say that what has happened on the New York Exchange is going to have any appreciable or sustained effect on the consumption of those staple products which North Dakota produces." Some even believed the crash would be good for the region because, as one commentator put it, "this bond and stock holocaust will undoubtedly re-establish confidence in the basic industry of agriculture, and immediately divert the flow of savings . . . back into farm investments, back into local banks, back into local businesses."[3]

These optimistic projections seemed reasonable, but they ignored softness in the local economy that predated the crash. Agriculture had not shared in the general national prosperity of the 1920s, and in Fargo, as in most of the country, residential and commercial construction had declined from its peak in 1927. Weakness in the local economy showed up first where it always shows up—in unemployment among the unskilled, whose ability to work was directly dependent on the level of business activity. During the 1929 Christmas season adjutant Thomas Leach of the Salvation Army announced, "I have been investigating a few cases in the last few days and I have found conditions that I did not believe existed" and Captain Edith King identified 250 families in need of aid. In January 1930 Mayor Lynner confirmed the seriousness of the situation.[4]

The people on the lower end of the economic scale in Fargo with whom the Salvation Army dealt frequently endured hardship even when times were relatively good, and there was no certainty that their suffering in the winter of 1929–30 would extend to the larger community. However, the nationwide liquidity crisis had a broad impact on the city, touching people with property and steady employment.

In Fargo, as virtually everywhere in the United States, economic activity was sustained by credit. Retailers received credit from wholesalers who in turn got credit from manufacturers. Contractors were carried by lumberyards and other suppliers until they could sell houses. Doctors carried patients; lawyers carried clients. And consumers increasingly purchased goods on time and maintained charge accounts with retailers. Indeed, retailers who did not offer credit found it hard to hold customers. As the *Forum* noted in the fall of 1929, "business firms invite credit accounts. . . . In the olden days a person's reputation for honesty had to be established, before credit was extended, but now most anyone can make purchases on the time payment plan." Surveying the year 1928, the *Forum* noted that 20 million credit purchases had been made in Fargo and in Moorhead, Minnesota, across the Red River, including 90 percent of grocery purchases and 60 to 75 percent of department store purchases.[5]

Credit purchases did not cease with the onset of the Depression—in fact, merchants usually found that they needed to offer credit to do any business at all—but the burdens of carrying debts and debtors became heavy, particularly in some enterprises. In Fargo, the failure of numerous small building contractors left suppliers with the choice of going broke themselves or finishing houses and renting them out until they could be sold. Hence, Interior Lumber and other major yards became reluctant landlords. Consumers struggled to avoid repossession by making their installment payments on cars, radios, and appliances, but in order to do so they frequently had to delay paying their grocery, medical, or legal bills or making payments on their department store charge accounts. The nearly one hundred neighborhood groceries in Fargo were especially hard hit. It was their practice to offer credit and free delivery to customers, and they found it increasingly difficult to collect. They were further squeezed as their suppliers became less lenient with them. Sophie Dizek remembered that when she married in 1942, her husband was still trying to collect grocery bills owed him from the early thirties. Professionals were also hit hard by the liquidity crunch. Lawyers, physicians, and dentists frequently had difficulty collecting and sometimes resorted to barter as an expedient. Jim Pastoret recalled that his father, Al, a dentist, would "pull teeth for a turkey or a chicken or half a cord of wood. We'd keep it in our garage. One winter we heated with wood he got for work." By the time World War II broke out, "he had $15,000 or $20,000 on the books." While professionals might be able to live partially by barter, their institutions and organizations could not. Caught between high fixed indebtedness and declining revenues, St. Luke's Hospital was forced to launch a campaign in 1930 to raise $75,000, a substantial sum. So few attorneys could afford their dues to the American Bar Association that local representative Melvin Hildreth suggested the ABA throw in the towel: "The truth of the matter is, the Bar is broke, the state is broke, and it seems the nation is broke."[6]

The liquidity crisis was soon manifested in declining discretionary consumption, which led to price cuts to reduce inventories, which led in turn to falling profits and wage reductions, making it even more difficult for debtors to meet fixed obligations. These problems fed on one another, with the result that the nation soon found itself in a deflationary spiral that was difficult to reverse. St. Luke's addressed its liquidity problems by dismissing some personnel, reducing the salaries of others, and eliminating "for the time being such expenditures as may be deferred." Bakers and butchers slashed the prices of bread and meat, and union bricklayers voluntarily reduced their hourly wages from \$1.25 to \$1.10, though there was likely precious little work to be had even at the lower rate.[7]

Retailers slashed prices as well, apparently with some effect. Merchants claimed to be satisfied with business in the Christmas season of 1930, and the overall volume of merchandise sold in 1931 was judged to be greater than in any previous year. Speaking on the occasion of the twentieth anniversary of his downtown department store in June 1932, George Black was proud to note that sales volume had increased every year he had been in business. The problem Black faced was that "for the last two years . . . owing to the sharp decline in values, even a materially increased volume of goods sold has not brought increases in the volume of dollar business. Our returns have been smaller but our output much greater during the past two years." For retailers such as Black, who had to meet fixed obligations, shrinking profits created a difficult business environment.[8]

Fargo merchants responded to these challenges with energy and imagination. Retailers pressed their employees to move merchandise, sometimes through promotions and bonuses. Announcing in March 1930 that it was adding three "Climax Days" to its annual anniversary sale, Herbst's declared that every "salesgirl" meeting her quota would receive an extra dollar in her paycheck, and another dollar every time she exceeded her quota by 25 percent: "It's up to you, girls! . . . Sell as you've never sold before. Excel in selling! Here's an opportunity to show the Herbst Store what you can do."[9]

Merchants made heroic efforts to lure shoppers, especially farm families from out of town who were crucial to retail prosperity. Citywide sales were launched on numerous occasions, such as "Peony Days" and "Iris Days" and Spring Cleanup Week in the spring and "Farmers' Month," "Harvest Days," "Turkey Week," and the North Dakota Agricultural College homecoming in the fall. In the summer of 1931 the Chamber of Commerce created a retail section and urged stores to remain open on Saturday nights. That fall the retail section enlisted Boy Scouts to patrol downtown streets, offering directions and assistance to out-of-town shoppers. In May 1932 the chamber suggested that Fargo go on daylight saving time unilaterally to attract evening shoppers. The Fargo Trades and Labor Assembly endorsed this idea as well, but it died amidst doubts as to its legality.[10]

Fargo retailers agreed with the business community nationally that the shock of the stock market crash and the ensuing business downturn had created a "buyers' strike." Commentators in business and government argued that money was being hoarded by consumers anxious about losing their jobs or having their wages cut or hopeful that the deflationary spiral would continue, delivering even lower prices in the future. National publications emphasized that spending was both a patriotic act and an expression of self-interest by consumers, who should take advantage of unprecedented bargains. In November 1930 the *Forum* began running full-page ads urging consumers to buy as a patriotic duty, and early the next year it editorialized that low labor and material costs presented an unparalleled opportunity for home construction or modernization. Early in 1932 President Herbert Hoover appointed Fargoan and former North Dakota governor L. B. Hanna state chairman of his national anti-hoarding campaign. The appointment—ironic in light of Hanna's highly public efforts to reduce government expenditures and public employees' salaries—was ultimately unsuccessful. Rumors of hoarded wealth abounded: one "Fargoan [was] reputed to have some $45,000 in gold in a safety deposit vault," and a Fargo family was believed to hide "$20,000 in $100 bills behind a loose cement block in the basement." The anti-hoarding campaign failed to convince these and other misers to loosen their grips on their funds. The basic problem, of course, was that people whose jobs were in jeopardy, whose incomes were being eroded, and whose fixed obligations were increasingly burdensome were understandably reluctant to spend their money. As one national commentator put it, "if we are to have liberal spending, the one essential requirement is the feeling on the part of the spenders that their income is secure. The destruction of that feeling through the menace of part-time [work] or unemployment is a sufficient explanation" for the buyers' strike.[11]

Merchants beset by shrinking profits and reluctant customers defensively sought to protect their markets from competition. In much of the country small merchants resisted chain stores and lobbied for laws that would shelter them from price competition they could not meet, but in Fargo chains played a minor role on the retail stage. Fargo merchants were more concerned about unfair competition from within their own ranks. In January 1931, for example, complaints by competitors led to the arrest of three grocers for shorting weights of bread and produce, and in June three more grocers were arrested on complaint of the Retail Meat Dealers Association for violating North Dakota blue laws by selling meat on Sunday.[12]

Fargo merchants were also troubled by competition from nonresident peddlers. As early as March 1930, city attorney M. W. Murphy stressed the need to enforce the city's peddler licensing requirement, noting that it had become "almost a 'dead letter.'" In September 1931 the *Forum* made the standard argument against patronizing peddlers, in response to the City Commission's decision to ban itinerant photographers: "Every purchase made from an itinerant merchant is injuring the local merchant who pays taxes to maintain the city, county and state governments, who backs our improvement programs, who supports our schools, and who is called upon to do the hundred and one other things which every businessman is expected to do for the advancement of his community." A few months later the commission passed an ordinance requiring peddlers to pay twenty dollars for every day they did business in the city. This ordinance was aimed mainly at local farmers who sold meat and produce door-to-door. Fuel dealers also complained about itinerants, noting that Minnesotans selling firewood to householders were imperiling their businesses.[13]

Fighting for their own survival, merchants sometimes behaved in petty ways. In 1933 grocers attempted to prevent the opening of Fargo's popular farmers' market but dropped the effort when they appeared mean-spirited. More successful were the druggists, who obtained an ordinance giving them the exclusive right to sell prophylactics in the city.[14]

In the fight to defend their market Fargo merchants were engaging in what was standard practice during the Depression. Americans were urged to buy American, North Dakotans were urged to buy North Dakotan, and Fargoans were urged to patronize Fargo merchants. Businesspeople accustomed to an expanding economy began thinking in terms of a shrinking one, and they feared that a dollar going to someone else was necessarily lost to them. At times the pressure to patronize one's own merchants or even one's own store became oppressive. In March 1932, for example, the retail section of the Chamber of Commerce met with the school board to complain "that some Fargo teachers are making a habit of purchasing in distant cities" and to remind the board "that money raised by Fargo taxpayers should be spent in Fargo stores where possible." And in December 1930 Herbst told its employees to "do your shopping in your *own* store. It is your duty to do this, as much . . . as possible." The siege mentality beginning to appear in business did not bode well for a rapid economic recovery, or for maintaining the cordiality and tolerance of which Fargo was proud.[15]

II

In its annual report for 1930, the Chamber of Commerce was pleased to note that "while the country at large has been laboring under a great disadvantage in having an enormous number of unemployed we are particularly fortunate in

Fargo in that this problem has not been as great as elsewhere." The chamber's assessment of the situation was generally accurate, but misleading. Employment in the retail, wholesale, and service sectors that formed the foundation of the city's economy held up well during the Depression. On the other hand, employment was not expanding—in December 1930 the number of men and women seeking work in the classified section of the *Forum* outnumbered jobs listed by up to 17 to 1—and those who held jobs faced wage cuts of up to 50 percent. So, while retail stores, for example, sought to move merchandise by keeping a full complement of salespeople on the floor, they shaved both hourly wages and commissions in the face of declining dollar volumes. At times, workers would go unpaid because of employers' liquidity problems. Richard Hilber remembered being owed fourteen checks by Crescent Jewelers "because they couldn't get any money to pay the salaries." Underemployment was also a factor in a number of enterprises. Contractors tried to hold crews together by cutting hours and sharing work, the railroad unions accepted a six-hour day to maintain employment levels, and Armour Packing kept its full workforce but put employees on half days.[16]

Unemployment was especially pronounced among two groups of men. Unskilled workers, who had little but muscle to offer employers and whose employment was highly dependent on the business cycle, suffered disproportionately from unemployment. Included in this group were day laborers, warehousemen, construction helpers, and such unskilled rail workers as car cleaners and freight and baggage handlers. Also suffering severe unemployment in Fargo, and elsewhere, were skilled construction workers such as carpenters, bricklayers, lathers, plumbers, electricians, painters, and so forth, of whom there were nearly seven hundred in 1930. These men were usually paid well, sometimes unionized, and normally comfortably circumstanced in a vital and growing city such as Fargo. While construction did not end in Fargo— indeed, a major project was launched in 1930 when George Black built a six-story retail and office building on Broadway—it did decline precipitously. The curtailment of residential construction was particularly pronounced. With equity values shrinking and rents falling, potential investors in new housing chose to sit on the sidelines.[17]

Fargoans were cognizant of the unemployment problem and moved to address it in a variety of ways. In October 1930, Cass County judge A. T. Cole implored Fargoans to hire the unemployed for any "small jobs" they might have around the house, and the Reverend O. E. McCracken, whose Union Mission served many poor Fargoans as well as transients, urged that "work of any kind,

even at reduced wages, will help to tide dozens of families over the forthcom-
ing winter. . . . It will help them keep their self-respect as well as help them keep
their families together." The American Legion also launched a jobs campaign
in the fall of 1930, and the Chamber of Commerce set up a jobs clearinghouse.
At Christmas, postmaster Hugh C. Corrigan announced that fifty more workers would be put on, with preference given to "unemployed men with dependents and no source of income."[18]

These efforts, which were duplicated all over the country, were well inten-
tioned, and even short-term or odd jobs could be significant in the budgets of
the poor. Unemployed and underemployed skilled workers, such as those represented by the Fargo Trades and Labor Assembly, disdained such employment, however, favoring large-scale public construction instead.

Organized labor demanded aid for the unemployed from the City Commission early and often, and it had some success, in part because many of its
endeavors enjoyed Chamber of Commerce support and in part because city finances were generally sound early in the Depression. In November 1930 the
City Commission acceded to a Trades and Labor Assembly plan to have an
employment bureau created by the city and run through the city engineer's office. Two months later the commission followed a union recommendation by
requiring that public work be done by "citizens and residents of Fargo who are
the head of families" and the standard day on such projects be eight hours.
And in April 1931 the commission agreed to reduce the workday of city street
department employees from ten to eight hours and to give preference to local
contractors on public work.[19]

More tangible aid came when the city accelerated some public works projects, raising the south dam on the Red to conserve water and paving and repaving some streets. The commission also wanted to add a bridge across the
Red and replace the Front Street span, but those projects required an agreement between Minnesota and North Dakota that was difficult to obtain. As the
Depression deepened, labor pressures for public works spending intensified.
In February 1932 the Labor Temple hosted a meeting of representatives from
city and county government, the Chamber of Commerce, and the American
Legion. Declaring that between five hundred and six hundred heads of families were unemployed, those in attendance outlined an ambitious public works
program, including construction of a new city hall, fire station, sewage disposal
plant, and two bridges, along with street widenings and airport improvements.
A committee including banker Fred Irish, chamber president Orlando Hegge,
city commissioner W. E. Black, state American Legion adjutant Jack Williams,

Workers rebuilding the south dam in 1930, one of the public works projects instituted by the City Commission to compensate for declining employment in construction

and Trades and Labor president W. W. Murrey was appointed to present these demands to the City Commission.[20]

The City Commission remained sympathetic to labor and the plight of the unemployed, but it was facing growing counterpressures from property taxpayers by the time this ambitious public works plan was developed. Fargoans trying to meet fixed obligations with shrinking incomes demanded that government expenditures be reduced and taxes lowered. The issue of city taxes had flared initially in June 1931, when city assessor John Ness accused the City Commission of undervaluing commercial property downtown and overvaluing residential property for tax purposes. Confronted by angry homeowners, the commission rolled back residential assessments to 1929 levels but also fired Ness. The former assessor launched a drive to remove Mayor Lynner and three of the commissioners, eventually submitting petitions with sufficient signers—mostly from the north side—to force a recall election. Through the use of aggressive challenges and some intimidation, the commission was able to compel enough signers to withdraw to invalidate the petitions, but the episode made it clear that many were genuinely angry with government, taxes, and what they saw as tax favoritism. One reader wrote to the *Forum* complaining, "most of the people we elect to public office seem to forget the poor fellows who are struggling for existence.... They get a mania for appropriating, and spend the people's money like drunken sailors." Another contended, "to wring taxes from some classes of taxpayers without regard for their ability to pay is ruinous."[21]

This local tax revolt was part of a national demand that the state and local tax burden be reduced. As historian David Beito has illustrated, state and local taxes had risen throughout the 1920s, claiming 7.3 percent of national income by 1929. Taxes were not raised dramatically during the early Depression years, but because of the deflation of wages they took an increasing share of income. By 1932 the percentage of national income claimed by state and local taxes had more than doubled, to 16.3, raising anguished cries for lower taxes, reduced governmental expenditures, and diminished valuations on real property, which was, after all, worth much less. Because the problem was state and local taxes, a national movement never developed, but there were few localities in which taxpayer groups did not spring to life.[22]

Fargo tax rebels found their voice in the North Dakota Taxpayers Association and its Cass County affiliate, on whose board of directors sat such prominent local figures as former governor Hanna and T. H. Manchester of Manchester Biscuit Company. The Taxpayers Association attempted to lower valuations, reduce mill levies and other taxes, and consult with public bodies when annual budgets were constructed. In July 1932 the Taxpayers Association won a major victory when voters in the state primary election approved an initiated measure lowering the assessed valuation of real property for tax purposes from 75 percent to 50 percent of true value. Unless the city raised its mill levy, this reduction would lower its revenue by about $100,000, or nearly 25 percent. Revenue would likely be reduced by another $40,000 because of rising tax delinquencies.[23]

While the City Commission could hardly ignore this swelling taxpayer revolt, it continued to be receptive to public works that promised relief for the unemployed and met pressing local needs, budgeting $100,000 for waterworks improvements and moving ahead to consider building a sewage disposal plant. The sewage disposal problem was one that had become a "public scandal" and "a civic disgrace" by 1932. Since the late nineteenth century both Fargo and

Fargo's city hall, which also housed a fire station and the jail, was considered inadequate for a growing city in 1930, but voters refused to pass bond issues to replace it.

Moorhead had dumped raw sewage into the Red. All south side sewage flowed through a main line that emptied into the river just south of Front, and all north side sewage was discharged between First and Second Avenues North. In the summer the stench was intense, especially in the Oak Grove neighborhood just north of downtown, and in the winter sewer pipes would sometimes freeze, pushing raw sewage up into basements all over town. As the city grew, the problem became more serious, and it seemed to reach a crisis in the dry years of the early thirties, when the river flowed at only a trickle and sometimes stopped flowing altogether. As well as being aesthetically displeasing the situation was potentially unhealthy. A physician at Veterans Hospital referred to the river there as "one reeking sewage settling pool, spreading nauseous malodors over a wide area" and suggested that its proximity was harmful to patients. A state sanitary engineer proclaimed the river "a grave menace to health with flies by the millions carrying disease germs from the river," and Seymour Olson, who lived in Oak Grove, remembered that "the sewer rats . . . were as big as wiener dogs!"[24]

City commissioner F. L. Anders suggested building a bypass that would collect all of the city's sewage and deposit it in the Red north of town, but that would anger farmers on the river and would be a short-term solution at best. A modern sewage disposal plant was the unavoidable answer, and most of the significant forces in the city lined up behind it. The chamber endorsed it because it would mean jobs and would make the city more livable. The Trades and Labor Assembly backed it because it would relieve unemployment. The American Legion liked the jobs aspect and thought that patients at Veterans Hospital who had suffered mustard gas in France hardly deserved sewer gas in North Dakota. These groups petitioned a receptive City Commission, which in October asked voters to approve $400,000 in sewer plant construction bonds in the upcoming general election. The city's leaders seriously misjudged the attitude of its taxpayers. The bond issue was defeated overwhelmingly, with just three downtown working-class precincts and the precinct nearest the Veterans Hospital voting in the affirmative. The position of the taxpayers was clear. As one Fargoan put it, "a great many of the taxpayers who voted 'no' on the sewage plant project . . . are no longer in the mood to allow a raid on their pocketbooks through bond issues."[25]

All governmental bodies were pressured by shrinking revenues and angry taxpayers. The Parks Department, managed by an independent park board, levied property taxes to maintain Island and Oak Grove parks, near downtown; Lindenwood, a largely undeveloped park and tourist camp on the south edge of the city; and Edgewood Golf Course, north of town. In addition, the board owned several small properties that were used for ice rinks in the winter, and it was responsible for planting and maintaining trees and shrubs along the boulevards. Pressed by taxpayers who argued that "a park is not a necessity," the board decided in August 1931 "to undertake no new work, so as to reduce the pay-roll and other expenditures as much and as soon as may be." In March 1932, after consulting with representatives of the Cass County Taxpayers Association, the board cut its budget by an additional 15 percent, a move that required salary reductions for supervisors of children's summer recreation programs. Even the trimmed expenditures were too high for some Fargoans, one of whom asked why the park board was "appropriating money to teach children how to play? What child ever needed to be taught to play? Even a puppy knows that."[26]

The school district, which had the largest budget of any governmental unit in the city, was also strained by declining revenues and taxpayer demands for economies. The Depression came at a bad time for the Fargo Public Schools, which were coping with increasing enrollments, especially at the high school level. High school numbers continued to be robust throughout the decade, reflecting dismal employment prospects for adolescents. Early in the Depression the district was able to expand its facilities, most notably by securing voter approval of a bond issue for construction of a new elementary school, Emerson Smith, just west of Central High. But shortfalls in 1931 tax collection forced the board to cut its building fund and freeze teachers' salaries. A year later the revenue situation had deteriorated to the point that the board was compelled to cut teachers' salaries by eight percent, a reduction characterized by the Taxpayers Association as "puny." The board hoped such cuts would be sufficient, but the property tax initiative of June forced more heroic economies. The board considered reducing the length of the school year, but rather than taking a step that might result in the district's loss of its first-class status in the state, it chose instead to eliminate kindergarten and adult education, make no contribution to the building fund, and reduce appropriations for school nurses, books, and supplies. The board also required students in art and manual training classes to purchase their own supplies.[27]

The reduction in teachers' salaries triggered a sharp debate over the relationship between wages and the continuing depression. The Trades and Labor Assembly protested the board's action, noting that "salary slashes mean only reduced buying power." Several Fargoans agreed in letters to the editor of the *Forum,* including one who pointed out that "80 percent of all teachers . . . spend every dollar of their monthly check in Fargo. . . . They pay taxes in Fargo, buy their food and clothes in Fargo. Their medical needs are supplied by Fargo's physicians and druggists, and their amusement is obtained through theaters and other recreation places in Fargo. . . . Considering this, who would suffer most? I would say, the merchants." Defenders of teachers' salaries pointed to a basic paradox in the anti-Depression effort in Fargo, as elsewhere. At the same time city leaders were urging citizens to be confident and to spend, they were accepting, or even initiating, pay cuts for public employees. Still, public officials had little alternative in the face of declining revenues, and taxpayers were more likely to criticize them for cutting too little than for cutting too much. Indeed, while the reductions in teachers' salaries were painful, they were mild in comparison to those suffered by many in the private sector. "Why shouldn't teachers' salaries be cut?" one Fargoan asked. "There are very few working people whose wages have not been reduced, and those who haven't undoubtedly will. . . . As for buying power—how about the taxpayer?"[28]

III

The taxpayer revolt and the deterioration of the local economy, as illustrated by the property tax initiative and by tax delinquency, complicated the efforts of city agencies to carry out their functions, let alone address the challenges presented by the Depression. A more serious problem confronted the Cass County Commission, which was responsible for bearing an increasing relief burden at the very time its resources were shrinking.

In North Dakota, counties were responsible for caring for the indigent. Cass County operated three programs for this purpose. First, it maintained a poor farm north of Fargo. The poor farm housed between eighty and one hundred persons who could not support themselves and who lacked family to support them. Most of the inmates were aged males—commonly farm laborers who had reached the end of their working lives—and people with physical or mental disabilities that precluded self-support. Inmates of the poor farm were expected to labor at the facility, thereby covering a portion of the cost of their care. Second, the County Commission determined eligibility for mothers' pensions under a law passed by the North Dakota legislature in 1915. Under this legislation, designed to prevent family disintegration, mothers with dependent children who were widowed or whose husbands had deserted them and who demonstrated an inability fully to support themselves could receive small monthly pensions to raise their children. Finally, the county provided general assistance to people who were normally self-supporting but whose temporary circumstances were straitened. It was especially common for the county to assist seasonal laborers whose summer savings ran out in the late winter or early spring. This aid usually came in the form of grocery, fuel, or rent vouchers. In addition to these regular relief programs, the county frequently paid the cost of housing Fargoans in orphanages, foster homes, institutions for people with disabilities, and facilities for unwed mothers.[29]

Welfare programs in Cass County had expanded since the mid-teens. As historian Jeff Singleton has shown, such expansion was the rule throughout the country, in part because of the growing public consensus that some groups in the population, such as mothers and minor children, were entitled to aid and in part because the remarkable affluence of the 1920s increased the resources available for all sorts of governmental endeavors. The expansion of national income, as well as rising state and local tax rates, made more funds available for a variety of purposes, including aid for the indigent. In addition, systematic community charitable fundraising, exemplified by the Community Chest idea, further increased resources available to aid those in need. It is never good to be poor in the United States, but it was probably better to be poor in 1929 than ever before.[30]

Unfortunately, professional administration had not kept pace with increasing resources in Fargo or Cass County. None of the Community Chest agencies employed a professional social worker when the Depression began. The County Relief Office had only one professional appointee, Mary McFadgen, but she had no social work training. Systematic administration of relief was further hampered by North Dakota law, which gave individual county commissioners the responsibility for recommending recipients of relief. While this practice probably made sense in rural districts where individuals were well known in the community, the system was potentially inefficient and subject to abuse, especially in cities and at times when hardship was widespread. It was also vulnerable to political manipulation by commissioners who might channel relief to their supporters while ignoring their opponents' needs.

In the first winter after the stock market crash, when Mayor Lynner took note of the high number of unemployed in Fargo, Cass County officials detected a sharp upsurge in the number of indigents seeking aid and consequently in relief expenditures. While the county was willing and still able to fulfill what the *Forum* called its "obligations with respect to . . . indigent residents," officials suspected that much of the upsurge was because the "nonresident poor come in indiscriminately and remain here as charges upon the public funds." In order to discourage this practice, the County Relief Office began an investigation that resulted in the removal of several dozen recipients from the relief rolls and their return to counties where they had established residence. Ferreting out those who did not qualify as residents remained a major job at the County Relief Office throughout the Depression. Naomi Larson, employed as a social worker from 1933 to 1935, recalled that one of her regular jobs was to "go through the hotel registers in the red-light district to try to prove people hadn't been residents too long."[31]

The campaign against nonresidents slowed the growing demand for relief only marginally. In the 1931 fiscal year, county expenditures on poor relief and mothers' pensions were nearly $132,000, a 27 percent increase over the previous year. The County Relief Office and the County Commission responded by looking for economies. In October 1931, the county limited relief families of four or fewer to $3 in groceries per person per month and families with five members or more to $2.50 per person per month. It also imposed a moral means test, expelling those with self-indulgent behaviors from the rolls just as it had started to exclude those who owned radios and automobiles. Visiting one reliefer's apartment, a county commissioner and the county state's attorney "found a woman smoking cigarets [*sic*], three men sitting on a bed drinking and a radio playing." Not only were these layabouts denied further aid, "the group was given 24 hours to leave the county."[32]

The implicit assumption that many relief recipients were morally deficient—an assumption that became more pronounced over time—and the imposition of humiliating means tests undoubtedly kept many of the indigent off the rolls. Proud people were loath to submit to the petty humiliations inflicted at the County Relief Office, and those who cherished the good opinion of their neighbors were understandably reluctant to confess an inability to support themselves. Many Fargoans on the margin scraped along, liquidating resources and stretching pennies through grinding economies, but still the relief rolls lengthened, bringing a crisis in the grim winter of 1931–32.

In early February 1932 the County Commission confronted the sober reality that only $17,000 of the funds budgeted for relief for fiscal 1932 remained unspent. In light of the fact that nearly $14,000 had been expended in January alone, it was virtually certain that the appropriation would be exhausted long before the fiscal year ended on June 30. The commission concluded that a better job of investigating applicants for relief had to be done, but Mary McFadgen indicated that she was "unable to thoroughly investigate all cases and keep records in addition to handling the . . . office." The commission decided to hire Helen Kennedy, a local woman with a college degree and experience in social work, to investigate the relief system and the eligibility of those receiving aid. At a special meeting on February 16, Kennedy revealed that some recipients of county aid owned radios and cars, were habitual drunkards, or were even landlords. She also criticized the county's relief effort for poor record keeping, shoddy investigation, and lack of coordination between the Relief Office and the County Commission. Kennedy was especially critical of the system whereby county commissioners recommended recipients for poor relief. "The trouble with the poor in Cass County," Kennedy contended, "is that they have had things their own way too long and have worked on the sympathy of the county commissioners," with the result that "second generations of families receiving county aid for years are now on the county. Children are being brought up to believe they are entitled to county aid and that the county owes them a living."[33]

The County Commission responded to the fiscal crisis and the Kennedy investigation in three ways. First, the commissioners decided to relinquish their power to place people on relief, at least temporarily, resolving that "all poor cases are to be handled and passed upon by Mrs. McFadgen, County Relief Agent[,] and Mrs. Kennedy, Investigator, and their decision [is] to be final in reference to granting relief."[34]

The second action taken by the commission was to initiate closer cooperation with the Community Welfare Association of Fargo, composed of Community Chest member agencies. Such chest agencies as Catholic Relief, the Union Mission, and the Salvation Army supplemented county efforts by providing about 30 percent of the cost of maintaining indigents in Fargo. In February the Community Welfare Association adopted a plan whereby those requesting aid would be required to do public work such as cutting wood, canning food, and refurbishing clothing. In return for the work the recipient would receive scrip from the association, which he or she could redeem "for food and clothing and other necessities at Fargo stores." The merchant could then redeem the scrip for cash at association offices. This system had at least three benefits. First, as Community Welfare Association president George Hoenck put it, demanding work for aid resulted "in the weeding out of many professional 'bums.'" Second, it produced items that could be used to sustain the poor, such as firewood, canned vegetables, and clothing, thereby reducing the drain on public funds. And finally, it funneled reliefers' business into Fargo stores. The County Commission agreed that recipients of general assistance in Fargo should be compelled to work in return for aid and gave the Community Welfare Association the authority to place them in its work program. Fargo and Cass County embraced work relief relatively late—a number of communities had initiated a work requirement as early as 1930—because it was complicated and usually expensive to administer and because it was not always easy to find projects that did not compete with private enterprise. However, the *Forum* declared the program a success in April, claiming that "the 'I won't work' element among Fargo's beneficiaries of public funds has been subdued and but little in evidence." While the work requirement certainly satisfied those who sought to weed out the "'I won't work' element" and punish those who accepted relief, it failed to achieve its contradictory goal of maintaining recipients' pride and it proved to be expensive and relatively unproductive.[35]

The commission's third response to the crisis was to make a grinding effort to balance the relief budget. Pressed by the Taxpayers Association, county commissioners looked for economies wherever they might be found. In Feb-

ruary they substituted lignite for coal in heating reliefers' homes and urged citizens who knew of "persons . . . 'sponging' on the county and . . . not entitled
to aid" to share information with officials. In March the County Commission
decided to pay only $62.50 for funerals for adult paupers and $30 "for babies,"
despite the fact that undertakers claimed they needed $75. That same month
it agreed to run all relief vouchers through two Fargo storeowners who offered
to provide groceries at five percent above wholesale. In April the commission
engaged in an acrimonious struggle with landlords over reliefers' rents paid by
the county. While the commissioners wanted to lower rents or save money by
"'doubling up' families" in rental units, landlords noted with some justification that their obligations were irreducible and that many were losing money
because they had allowed poor families to stay "in houses for several months
without paying rent." In addition to shaving costs, beginning in early March,
when the relief fund was officially declared to be exhausted, the commission
shifted funds from other budgets to meet relief needs. This proposition was
challenging because other county budgets had already been reduced in antic-
ipation of heavy demands from the unemployed and underemployed.[36]

The county managed to get through the fiscal year but was forced in July to
confront the crisis precipitated by voter approval of the property tax valuation
initiative. Commissioners slashed highway construction and maintenance
budgets, reduced jail expenses from $0.75 per prisoner per day to $0.60, and
cut county salaries, including their own, from 3.5 to 25 percent, depending on
the position. The courts presented a particularly difficult problem. Revenue
from fines had virtually disappeared because so many went unpaid. A mere
three percent of fines for drunkenness, the most common offense in the county,
were paid in 1931. County judges continued to levy fines, however, because jail-
ing offenders would obligate the county to "serve free meals to able-bodied
males and at the same time . . . provide for their families from county poor
funds during the period of incarceration." Allowing men to become scofflaws
appeared preferable. The county did cut witness fees and juror compensation
in half, however, and judges agreed to accelerate trials.[37]

While these reductions helped, the County Commission could not balance
the budget without attacking the cost of poor relief, which was expected to total $150,000 in fiscal 1933. The commission struggled with the issue, pulled
one way by those who believed poor relief must be slashed and the other by
those who stressed that basic human needs must be met. George Hoenck of
the Community Welfare Association urged the county to sell bonds to pay for
poor relief, while W. J. Clapp, another prominent Fargoan, argued that the

poor "must be cared for" even if it meant higher taxes. On the other side were those who wanted to lower relief costs, in part by closer examination and investigation of recipients—which, ironically, involved hiring social workers and paying their expenses, driving the relief budget higher—and in part by making relief harsher and more punitive than it already was. Among the suggestions offered to the commissioners were that single men on relief be housed in barracks, that the poor be fed staples only, and that the poor be removed from Fargo and placed in the countryside where, as Alex Stern noted, "they can raise gardens and where rent is cheap and the privileges are fewer." The general tone of these suggestions was, in the words of sheriff Mark Andrews, that "paupers have no right to live on the same scale as people who pay for their own living and the sooner this fact is made known the sooner we will get rid of a lot of our poor."[38]

The commissioners were not ready to redistribute the poor to the countryside, but they did follow some of the other recommendations they received. County commissioner Garfield Hoglund's idea of building barracks to house single men on relief was tried in the fall of 1932. The county developed a new relief diet which promised to feed one person for $0.65 per week and a family of fifteen for $7.90 per week. The diet featured "oatmeal, prunes, potatoes, dried peas or beans, butter, sugar, eggs, coffee . . . canned milk" and flour. Conspicuous by its absence was meat. In October the county found another way to save when it cut the electricity to families on relief and provided them with kerosene lamps. While it was reducing relief expenses wherever it could, the county also requested help from the city of Fargo in shouldering the burden of caring for the poor. Noting that as many as 85 percent of reliefers lived in Fargo, the county suggested a city appropriation for poor relief. But Fargo was unwilling to infringe on this county responsibility, nor did the city honor a county request to provide free water to reliefers.[39]

As the demand for county aid exploded, the County Commission's attitude toward relief recipients became increasingly callous and suspicious. People in need of public aid had always been subject to moral judgment and had frequently been found deficient. But as demands for aid rose, attitudes hardened dramatically and yesterday's neighbor in need was transformed into today's chiseler and layabout. In one sense, this harsh judgment was puzzling and ironic, coming as it did at a time when the moral and the immoral alike suffered from conditions they had not made and could not rectify. Yet in another way this hard and cruel attitude was necessary to sustain the relief system and to assure that the basic needs of recipients were met. In uncomfortable circumstances themselves, many taxpayers would tolerate a relief system only if they were assured, in Sheriff Andrews's words, that recipients did not "live on the same scale as people who pay for their own living." And the needs of recipients could be met only if relief was made so harsh and degrading that many others in need were deterred from requesting aid. It was a pattern that would continue throughout the Depression in Fargo.[40]

2

"The very independence of our people is best safe-guarded through strong local government and . . . self-help."
  Fargo Forum, *August 24, 1930*

"We are living up to the . . . program of local responsibility, sincerely believing that relief and welfare efforts are local problems which must be shared alike and which demand typical American individualism."
  Ralph Trubey, Community Chest chairman, November 11, 1932

READING THE GENERAL HISTORIES of the Great Depression, which are usually centered on Washington and the dramatic decisions made there, one could get the impression that most Americans, paralyzed by fear, sat around waiting for Franklin D. Roosevelt's New Deal to address their problems. We like stories in which our heroes are heroic and their actions decisive, so we simplify our history, losing some of the nuance, contingency, and complexity that inform real life.

In fact, people throughout the country engaged in a variety of self-help activities between 1929 and 1933 to pull themselves and their communities out of the Great Depression. In embracing self-help, Americans drew on a heritage of strong local government and personal responsibility, on what Ralph Trubey referred to as "American individualism," a faith in the initiative of the individual and his or her willingness to extend a helping hand to neighbors. They also frequently drew on a local history or mythology of communities surmounting crises—in Fargo's case, the devastating fire of 1893. If earlier generations could overcome such crises, they reasoned, surely ours can reverse this economic downturn.[1]

In common with other Americans, Fargoans threw themselves into efforts to overcome the Depression and its effects. A confident, independent local business community led endeavors to restore prosperity and to meet the needs of Fargoans harmed by the economic crisis. A well-integrated and elaborated charitable structure worked to mitigate human suffering. And the unemployed organized to pull themselves out of dire need and to avoid depending completely on relief.

Initially, people did not debate whether to try to address their problems locally or not—they simply assumed that they would. Every town had a core of doers upon whom it could depend, and it did so when anything needed to be done—when war bonds had to be sold or a road had to be paved or a school had to be built or hard times had to be overcome. When the system of local initiative failed, or when it did not work as expected, people did not abandon it. Some held to it tighter than ever, fearing that its failure would mean the failure of America and something essential that America represented. As the *Forum* put it, "the very independence of our people" was tied to localism and self-help. Nor did the onset of the New Deal, with its array of alphabet agencies and its blizzard of programs, stifle local initiative or make local self-help irrelevant. Indeed, the early New Deal in Fargo depended on a network of local activists and a heritage of local self-help for much of whatever success it enjoyed.[2]

Community self-help was customary, necessary, and frequently effective in the United States, but it was not the answer to every problem. Sometimes communities confronted challenges so daunting that they could not be overcome, or localities grappled with problems that had their origins far beyond the city limits. The Depression was not analogous to the Fargo fire. It was an international problem. In addition, self-help depended on a community effort that sometimes flagged or was lacking. Some people were unwilling to sacrifice, to be stewards for their neighbors, or to fulfill their commitments. Called upon to demonstrate generosity and magnanimity, they sometimes demonstrated selfishness and fear instead. Along with the problem of those who failed to exhibit the proper self-help spirit there were problems with some of those who embraced the self-help ideal but refused to follow those who were accustomed to leading. Rather than accepting customary social arrangements, they challenged long-standing ideas of capitalism and class deference and hierarchy.

The result was that the self-help ideal was seriously strained by the Depression experience in Fargo. It was rejected by some, and those who continued to embrace it were less idealistic and innocent and more cynical, suspicious, and manipulative than they had been before. That it survived at all—let alone that it continued to play a vital role in the life of the city—was tribute to its resiliency and to the devotion of its champions to what it meant.

I

Leadership in Fargo's self-help efforts during the Depression was based in the business community. This is not to say that all businesspeople took part in self-help efforts, nor that the city's most prominent business figures played an active and public role, because they did not. But the leadership in anti-Depression campaigns and in such ameliorative activities as Community Chest drives came from within the business community, which also provided leadership for the city's churches, lodges, and service clubs.

Leadership came from such people as Harry Alsop, owner of Interior Lumber, a small chain of yards headquartered in Fargo. Alsop chaired the school board for a time, was secretary-treasurer of the Community Chest, was active in the Chamber of Commerce and the Masons, served as treasurer for the Florence Crittenton Home, and took leadership positions in the Episcopal Church in Fargo and at the statewide level. Another leader was Charles Dawson, who owned an agency specializing in hail insurance for farmers. Dawson was an active Kiwanian and Presbyterian, and in 1932 he served as grand potentate of the Shrine. Dawson took the lead in traffic safety campaigns in Fargo—among his other accomplishments was getting the city to equip police cars with radios—and eventually served as mayor. He was also active in the Community Chest, exhibiting a special interest in such character-building organizations as the Boy Scouts and the YMCA. Ralph Gunkleman, one of the owners of Interstate Seed and Grain, was another person who played a multi-faceted leadership role. He was one of the organizers of the Community Chest and the Kiwanis. He was a leader in the Grain Dealers Association and the Shippers Board. Gunkleman was an active Mason and a dedicated Baptist layman who held leadership positions in the North Dakota Council of Churches. He sat on the boards of several philanthropic or charitable agencies, including the YMCA and the Union Mission.[3]

Alsop, Dawson, and Gunkleman were part of what Gunkleman's son Tod referred to as the "network," an informal, interlocking directorate of about two dozen men who assumed leadership positions in combating and alleviating the effects of the Depression in Fargo as well as in doing numerous other things for community and institutional betterment. The network functioned effectively in part because Fargo was small enough that the major figures in the business community were well acquainted and had a good understanding of the strengths, weaknesses, and inclinations of their peers. As Tod Gunkleman put it, "those people all knew each other and knew each other well. If there was something to be done in the community, someone would step forward and organize the others."[4]

An established position in the Fargo business community was not the only characteristic shared by members of the network. In a city that was predominantly Norwegian, they tended to be Yankees, and they were more often members of one of the old-line Protestant churches than of the Lutheran or Catholic churches to which most Fargoans belonged. They were the same sorts of people who had dominated the city and its economy and had shaped its institutions since it was founded and who assumed leadership in other cities in the Midwest and on the Great Plains.[5]

To note that Fargo's network came from the business community and that it shared certain ethno-religious characteristics explains some of its assumptions and provides clues regarding why it was willing to undertake some activities and not others. What cannot be explained is why some men played an active role in a range of community enterprises while other affluent and established Fargoans—such as Louis B. Hanna—did not. Economic self-interest likely was a factor in some of their activities. Membership in the Masonic Or-

Fargo was a major distribution point for goods of all kinds and a national center for the marketing of agricultural implements.

der, for example, was and always had been valuable for men courting business success in Fargo. Moreover, one could argue that the philanthropic activities of Alsop, Dawson, Gunkleman, and others like them formed part of a broad outlook that could be termed enlightened self-interest. A more livable, peaceful, orderly, educated, and caring Fargo would be a better community in which to do business. But why did some men believe that boosting Fargo meant making it a more attractive place to live while others apparently did not? One senses that many of these men felt an obligation or even a need to serve the city and to leave it a better place than they found it. Perhaps they were motivated by their religious faith. Perhaps they were inspired by the "service ideal" that developed in the business community nationwide early in the twentieth century and stressed the responsibility of businessmen to be stewards and to use their wealth and talents for community betterment. For whatever reason, these men took on a burden that others were reluctant or unwilling to assume during the Depression. Tod Gunkleman's explanation for his father's activism was that "he was just a committed guy." It is not much of an explanation, but it may be the best we have.[6]

II

Fargo's self-help activities during the Great Depression frequently involved participation in nationwide campaigns or represented local attempts to duplicate endeavors initiated elsewhere. The pattern of national campaigns carried forward by local volunteers had been established during World War I when massive Liberty Loan, Red Cross, and War Chest fund-raising drives had been launched and brought to successful conclusions. It was a pattern with which local people were familiar and comfortable. Beginning in 1931, Fargoans participated in a series of national hiring and anti-hoarding campaigns, sometimes coordinated by the federal government and sometimes under the auspices of the American Legion or some other organization. But the most eventful campaign, and the one that tapped most effectively into the energy of the community, was the War Against Depression in 1932.[7]

The War Against Depression idea was born in Rochester, New York. Its purpose was to shake loose hoarded cash, stimulate business activity, and encourage employment by getting consumers to sign pledges to spend money. Early in 1932 the War Against Depression was launched in numerous cities around the country, including Fargo. A War Against Depression planning committee was formed at a meeting at the Chamber of Commerce on March 5.

The committee drew heavily on the city's service clubs and on the American Legion, which was in the midst of its own national campaign to obtain jobs for one million men. The committee began by mapping a publicity campaign involving printing and distributing 7,500 circulars and purchasing over 1,500 lines of advertising in the *Forum*. Then it organized the "war" along military lines, naming colonels and captains who would solicit pledges from businesspeople, employees, and householders. The campaign began as such enterprises usually did, with a kickoff dinner to energize the troops. The *Forum* lent a hand, highlighting the War Against Depression in a front-page story and editorializing that Fargoans had it in their power to end the Depression if they were so inclined: "You are one of thousands who need something, want something, have means to do it. You have waited until 'business gets better.' . . . Business will get better when you fulfill some of your own needs. Remember, you are not alone in this War Against Depression. What bread you cast upon the waters will be returned to you after not so many days."[8]

Nearly six hundred volunteers followed the March 23 kickoff by canvassing the city, imploring citizens to sign pledges to purchase designated goods and services. Those signing pledges received window stickers featuring blue stars and the words "We Have Enlisted in the War Against Depression." The *Forum* kept a daily tally of the rising pledge total, noting on March 30 that "pledge cards have begun to come in from residential districts calling for dozens of home repair, renovation and lawn jobs, promising employment for a number of men fitted for that sort of work." The next day the *Forum* carried the story of a couple who agreed to buy a car and to adopt a baby "and were checking off a list of baby needs in the shape of a crib, clothes and whatnot, all of which goes to make business for the vendors thereof." On April 11 the *Forum* proudly announced that over $750,000, or $26 per capita, had been pledged, "surpassing by a wide margin Rochester, N.Y., originator of the War Against Depression idea." "Fargo has . . . been accorded national interest as a result of its War Against Depression," the *Forum* claimed, and had defended its honor and the honor of North Dakota in an admirable fashion.[9]

Whether the War Against Depression did any good was another matter. The Depression did not end or even moderate in Fargo, and no effort was made to assure that citizens fulfilled their pledges by actually purchasing goods and services. It was all very well for the *Forum* to compare the "hysteria" about hard times to reactions over "Yellow Perils, food fads, [and] fake healers," but it was difficult to get people to actually spend supposedly hoarded dollars at the very time private employers and public agencies, such as the school board, were cutting salaries and the Community Chest was running out of money to meet basic human needs.[10]

Some contemporary observers were skeptical about the value of campaigns such as the War Against Depression, which consumed a great deal of energy and made promises that could not be kept. A writer in *Harper's Monthly* in May 1932 damned "our American faith in campaigns" as "childlike" and concluded that "the real tragedy of the campaign way of doing things ... is ... that it has shown itself to be utterly futile in the present emergency. We are at the bottom of our bag of tricks." He was right, and it is likely that even among the enthusiastic volunteers in Fargo's War Against Depression there were those who doubted it would work or that it would be sufficient if it did. But self-help campaigns served more than one function. For organizers they were assertions of community leadership and stewardship, and beyond that they allowed local pride and unity to be demonstrated. Moreover, they permitted people who were victims of circumstances they did not control to behave otherwise. By participating in self-help campaigns citizens demonstrated their refusal to be victims and their determination to shape the conditions of their lives. Campaigns such as the War Against Depression were, if nothing else, expressions of the human spirit, and there was something to be said for that. As the *Forum* noted candidly, at least the War Against Depression "is something constructive" and as such "is deserving of honest respect."[11]

Despite its questionable effectiveness, the organized "drive" did not go away or fall into disrepute. Indeed, a local drive played an instrumental role in the launching of the National Recovery Administration program—the means whereby President Franklin Roosevelt's administration hoped to bring recovery from the Depression and return the nation to prosperity—as well as in a number of other federal initiatives. During World War I the federal government compensated for a small and weak bureaucracy by relying on local volunteers to sell bonds, operate the draft, conserve food and fuel, and perform a hundred other tasks. The NRA campaign demonstrated that government reliance on local volunteers continued during the New Deal.

The National Industrial Recovery Act, which created the NRA and which will be addressed in more detail in the next chapter, had three main purposes. First, it aimed to end the deflationary spiral by inducing producers of raw materials, manufacturers, wholesalers, retailers, and providers of services to adopt industry-wide "codes" of competition that stabilized prices. Second, it proposed to improve labor standards and raise wages by committing employers to paying minimum wages and setting maximum hours—forty per week in most cases. By limiting the hours of labor, the NIRA would presumably stimulate the employment of more workers, alleviating the unemployment problem. Finally, the NIRA created the Public Works Administration, which provided loans and grants to localities for the construction of large capital improvement projects. These projects were meant to result in the employment of unemployed workers, especially in construction.

The success of this recovery program depended on the willingness of employers to subscribe to codes and to enter "re-employment" agreements committing them to add workers when hours of labor were reduced. But in order to induce employers to behave contrary to their competitive instincts and to take steps that seemed irrational in light of the economic situation, consumers had to be mobilized and had to agree to patronize only those businesses that complied with the NRA program. Securing these diverse objectives called for just the sort of local volunteer effort at which Fargo was so adept.

Fargo firms began organizing along lines set out by the NRA in July and on August 1, 1933, started filing "certificates of compliance" with postmaster Hugh C. Corrigan. Companies certifying compliance were permitted to display a blue eagle window sticker with the phrase "We Do Our Part." The *Forum* kept a running count of the number of businesses in compliance and optimistically projected the number of jobs that would be added as a consequence. On August 4, Fargo organized its NRA "army" in a meeting at the chamber offices. Mayor Fred Olsen was named "general," and he appointed "colonels" J. F. McGuire of the Union Light and Power Company, attorney George Soule, Ralph Keller of Pierce Printing, and Anna Stevens "of the woman's section of the army." Two weeks later, 250 "rear rank privates" who had enlisted in the "army" gathered at the chamber to learn what their jobs would be in the upcoming canvass of the city. "Colonel" Soule explained that their task was to induce employers "to sign the president's re-employment agreement . . . to get consumer pledges to patronize members of the NRA," and "to list the unemployed for convenience in placing them as jobs open up under the drive."[12]

In order to "stir the people . . . to a high pitch of patriotic fervor, not equaled since the great Liberty Loan drives of the war days," local NRA campaigners staged a huge parade on August 29. Organizers asked firms to excuse workers to allow participation, and Herbst, Manchester Biscuit, and other large employers promised that all of their workers would march. Fargo's NRA parade was a massive success. An estimated seven to eight thousand people—or about one-fourth of the city's population—marched down Broadway to the Armory behind banners emblazoned with employers' names. At the Armory they heard the mayor proclaim, "Fargo will have a definite share in this increased prosperity to the extent that it participates in the plan, so there is a responsibility on every citizen here to co-operate to the utmost to make this gigantic national plan a complete success." It was a stunning response overall, and one the *Forum* believed demonstrated what made Fargo special. "It was something more than a manifestation of the community's support of the NRA program," the newspaper editorialized the next day, "it was a pageant of the city's man power and woman power that moves forward, day in and day out, year in and year out, that has made for Fargo's stability, her achievements in the past, her hope in the future."[13]

Energized by the huge parade and the subsequent rally, four hundred volunteers made a house-to-house and business-to-business canvass of the city in an attempt to secure full compliance with the recovery program and to compile a list of the unemployed for "re-employment" purposes. Employers and consumers signing the agreement received the blue eagle decal to display on their businesses and homes while, the *Forum* noted ominously, "all those who refuse[d] to sign [would] be visited later by another committee."[14]

The National Recovery Administration program represented a departure from the anti-Depression efforts supported by Herbert Hoover in that it was a more centralized and bureaucratically complex response to the national crisis. But the NRA relied on local initiative, on the eagerness of local people to organize themselves and canvass their neighbors, and on the willingness of those neighbors to comply. The parallels between the NRA campaign and the War Against Depression—or the earlier Liberty Loan campaigns—in Fargo are instructive. Voluntarism, boosterism, military terms and organization, appeals to community pride and honor, social pressure to conform exerted on residents, even the stickers that served as tokens of compliance were threads that ran through all of these drives. Small wonder that Fargoans understood the NRA and mobilized for it as if it were just another self-help effort. It may indeed have been true that the American faith in self-help drives was "childlike," but without that faith the NRA never would have got off the ground.

The community spirit exemplified by the response to the National Industrial Recovery Act was also instrumental in advancing other New Deal initiatives in Fargo. In 1934, for example, another volunteer "drive" was launched to induce homeowners to obtain rehabilitation loans under the newly passed Federal Housing Act. Federal relief programs also received a boost from local volunteers, as the response to the Civil Works Administration illustrates.

The CWA was a federal work relief program that operated during the winter of 1933–34. As was the case with most New Deal relief programs, the CWA was designed with male heads of families mainly in mind. Consequently, the beautification, construction, and re-decoration projects it undertook employed men almost exclusively, particularly men in the building trades. Recognizing belatedly that there were also numerous unemployed or underemployed female heads of families, the CWA offered funds to communities that could devise suitable work relief for women. Fargo was allotted $12,000 for its estimated two hundred unemployed female heads of families, and it decided to set up a sewing center—standard in women's work relief programs nationwide—in which they could labor at a task with which they were presumably familiar. The problem was providing adequate fabric and garments for clothing construction and renovation. The Junior Chamber of Commerce (Jaycees) volunteered to procure clothing that could be repaired, remodeled, or transformed into quilts or other useful items.[15]

The Jaycees had some experience with this sort of endeavor. Soon after they organized in Fargo in 1933, they had launched a drive to collect clothing, "furniture, dishes, carpets, rugs, shoes, toys, rags and household articles of various and sundry descriptions, all for use by the Community Welfare Association for distribution to the needy." The Jaycees worked with other service clubs, the Camp Fire Girls, the Boy Scouts, WDAY radio, and the churches to publicize the drive and make collections. The churches were especially supportive of the drive, including notices in bulletins such as this one inserted by Olivet Lutheran on Easter Sunday: "'The Share Your Clothes' campaign . . . will be staged next Sunday, April 23, at 1:00 P.M. Have your bundles of clothes, furniture, dishes, rugs, shoes, etc., and a truck will call for them." Claiming to have visited every home in the city, the Jaycees delivered seventy-six truckloads of material to the Community Welfare Association on the afternoon of collection Sunday.[16]

In conducting the sewing room drive in January 1934 the Jaycees again called on the scouts and Camp Fire Girls, churches, and service clubs. In addition, the American Legion, Red Cross, and Parent Teacher Association lent a hand. The Jaycees divided the city into sixteen districts and used fifty-two donated trucks to gather clothing on Sunday, January 28. Two boxcar loads were collected, more than enough to keep the sewing room busy for as long as CWA funds lasted.[17]

It is clear that the self-help spirit hardly died when the New Deal's recovery and relief programs began operating in Fargo. Indeed, the success of those programs depended largely on the readiness of service clubs and organizations to carry out drives and on the willingness of Fargoans to participate by signing pledges or donating clothing or doing whatever else was requested of them. This dependence on the volunteer drive and the pattern of its execution continued throughout the Depression years.

III

Fargo's rich organizational structure and tradition of self-help activism were also visible in efforts to alleviate the suffering of those at the bottom of the economic scale. Fargoans active in organizations that attempted to aid the indigent generally subscribed to the idea of "cooperative individualism." As articulated by a number of leading Americans—including President Hoover—cooperative individualism was a particularly American belief that individuals should rely on themselves and support themselves. When self-support was impossible, those in need should depend on their local communities for help. Community-based aid presumably bound neighbor to neighbor, and one's desire to maintain the good opinion of his or her neighbors meant that he or she would ask for help only in extreme circumstances and would relinquish aid quickly. The undesirable alternative, to which cooperative individualists directed increasingly strident criticism as the Depression lengthened and deepened, was the British "dole," a centralized, bureaucratized system of relief that supposedly dissolved neighborly ties and sapped the initiative and self-respect of the recipient.[18]

Fargoans were accustomed to meeting the needs of unfortunates through local initiative. The service clubs undertook regular projects on behalf of the disadvantaged, especially at Christmas. The Rotarians put together gift packages for poor children as a yearly Christmas project, and the Lions hosted an annual holiday party for orphans at the North Dakota Children's Home. Some endeavors were cooperative. In 1931 the Kiwanis hosted a free show for one thousand orphans and poor children at the State Theater. The management donated the theater, two union projectionists gave their time, Fargo grocers provided one thousand oranges, and five local amateurs performed a "Scandinavian skit." The holiday activities of the Kiwanians were especially ambitious. Every year they sponsored a citywide toy drive in which Fargoans were asked to donate used or broken playthings. The toys were repaired or refurbished by the Boy Scouts, Camp Fire Girls, and industrial arts classes at Central High, and the renovated items were distributed to needy families. In 1932 the Kiwanis delivered toys to more than 1,400 children in nearly 500 families identified "by the Salvation Army, Fargo Union Mission, the Catholic Welfare Bureau, the Lutheran Aid society, the American Legion and Mrs. McFadgen, county relief agent." The Kiwanis always took care to distribute gifts to parents, rather than to children directly, so as not to undermine parental authority and self-respect. In addition to the Kiwanis drive, the *Forum* and WDAY radio ran an annual campaign to provide food baskets for four to five hundred disadvantaged families at Christmas. In 1931 the basket included one to three chickens along with "bread, butter, coffee, graham crackers, lard, rice, milk, an assortment of canned goods, cabbage, cereal and sugar."[19]

The charitable activities of other organizations were less publicized. Most of Fargo's nearly thirty churches prepared food baskets, donated clothing, or paid for parishoners' medical care. Women's clubs usually made regular contributions to charities and sometimes provided special aid to members in need, as in 1932 when the Round Table gave twenty-five dollars to "Mrs. Stoner . . . who had met with serious misfortunes." Some women's clubs existed exclusively for charitable purposes. The South Side Charity Circle, for example, donated layettes to new mothers who could not afford to purchase them, and in 1931 the Island Park Charity Circle made and distributed 1,466 garments to the poor.[20]

In addition to benefiting from these organizational activities, the indigent enjoyed "the spontaneous, individual relief brought to countless scores through private means." Bakers gave two-day-old bread to the unemployed, and butchers such as Charlie Hauser's father "made up little packages of liverwurst" for poor "women with babies" who would come to the shops begging for food. Union barbers gave free haircuts to orphans, a Fargo restaurateur served one hundred free meals every Christmas day, and, in October 1932, a group of Fargoans took sixty inmates of the county poor farm on a two-hour automobile tour of Fargo-Moorhead.[21]

However neighborly such acts of benevolence might have been, and however satisfying they were to givers and receivers, most disadvantaged Fargoans required more systematic attention. For the day-to-day needs of the poor and unfortunate, Fargo provided a well-developed and articulated organizational structure. Included within this structure were the Florence Crittenton Home and the North Dakota House of Mercy, agencies serving unwed mothers, and a Lutheran home-finding society that placed infants with adoptive parents. It also included two orphanages—St. John's, a Catholic facility maintained by the Presentation Sisters, and the nondenominational North Dakota Chil-

St. John's Orphanage, one of two such facilities in Fargo and part of the Catholic social welfare structure

dren's Home. These institutions served as receiving homes, in which infants and very young children awaiting adoption were held temporarily, but they did much more besides. As several historians have pointed out in recent years, late-nineteenth- and early-twentieth-century orphanages supplemented indigent families and families in crisis in a number of ways, and Fargo's were no exception. St. John's and the North Dakota Children's Home received placements—sometimes temporary and sometimes long-term—from parents who were unable to support their children and from counties that had assumed responsibility for children whose parents or legal guardians had died, deserted them, or were otherwise incapable of providing care. In addition, the North Dakota Children's Home provided lodging for disabled children in town for orthopedic treatment or surgery under a program sponsored by the Elks Lodge.[22]

These institutions were well circumstanced when the Depression began, enjoying supportive boards of directors composed of prominent persons who could raise funds. In addition, all received state appropriations for doing welfare work that would otherwise fall to North Dakota, and counties contributed to the maintenance of residents who required institutional care. The orphanages faced a crisis during the Depression, however, when they were whipsawed between rising demands and declining resources. As early as 1929, superintendent Harold Bond of the North Dakota Children's Home reported a decline in charitable contributions, a problem that worsened over the next few years. At the same time, more parents were using the home temporarily and average stays for children were increasing, both because parents were having a harder time getting back on their feet and because adoptive parents for infants were more difficult to find. Overall residence numbers remained about the same, but only because counties were saving public funds by providing for children locally rather than referring them to the homes. Bond worried that this change might mean "children are permitted to remain under filthy conditions . . . cared for by indecent people in order to save a few dollars for the taxpayer." Intensifying financial pressures on the orphanages was the fact that foster parents, who traditionally supervised many orphans, were increasingly demanding compensation for work that many had done for free prior to the Depression. Bond was proud to note that "while our income from all sources has materially lessened we are glad to report that we have not, as yet, turned back a single case that has been presented to us." Maintaining that service, however, had meant cutting salaries and expenses sharply.[23]

Adults and intact families could seek help from several faith-based agencies that, together, contributed about 30 percent of the cost of caring for Fargo's poor, with the balance coming from Cass County. The most important of these agencies were the Union Mission and the Salvation Army, both of which gave aid to transients, especially meals and lodging, as well as to the resident poor, maintaining free employment bureaus and providing clothing, shoes, furniture, and coal to families in need. The Union Mission was particularly active in caring for the poor in good times and bad, and the Reverend O. E. McCracken, who ran it, was a respected advocate for the city's indigent. McCracken frequently emphasized the duties of the affluent to the less fortunate, sometimes in harsh and uncompromising terms.[24]

The Union Mission enjoyed regular support from several Protestant churches. Jews and Catholics maintained separate relief agencies. The Jewish Welfare Association was mainly concerned with stranded Jewish "wayfarers," but it also paid rent and purchased food and coal for destitute Jewish families in the city. The Catholic Welfare Bureau provided food, coal, clothing, and other items to needy Catholic families. In the mid-thirties its case load averaged eighty to ninety families per month. In common with most of these agencies, the Catholic Welfare Bureau was a labor of love and sacrifice. The director and the case-workers frequently went unpaid, and the bureau lived hand-to-mouth on contributions from wealthy laypeople in space donated by the Knights of Columbus. Father Vincent Ryan of St. Anthony of Padua Church had founded the agency and was its leading light during the Depression. In order to put Catholic Welfare on firmer footing, Ryan developed the "Fargo Plan," which involved the parishes directly in planning the work and raising money. To that end, he instituted "Catholic Action Days" every fall, during which the bureau would explain its endeavors and solicit contributions. While the Fargo Plan was popular locally and caught on around the country, Catholic Welfare still operated "on a shoestring," according to Monsignor Anthony Peschel, who directed the agency in the late thirties.[25]

All of these agencies were included in the Community Welfare Association, which represented Fargo's seventeen charitable, philanthropic, and character-building organizations that were part of the Community Chest. The Community Chest idea, which involved a single fund appeal for a number of charities, had been tried initially in Cleveland in 1913 and had been advanced by the success of the unified War Chest charitable campaigns in 1917 and 1918. By the time Fargo embraced the Community Chest idea in 1927 it had become popular throughout the country. The Community Welfare Association was governed and the chest campaign organized and coordinated by the Community Welfare Board, composed mainly of businesspeople active on the boards of member agencies. The board was very much a business enterprise. Indeed, its office space was in the Chamber of Commerce building, and it cooperated in various business-initiated activities, as in 1932 when it paid printing and advertising costs for the War Against Depression. Businessmen also did most of the campaign work—all 142 male campaigners in 1930 were drawn from the service clubs—which mainly involved soliciting other businesspeople.[26]

The attraction of businesspeople to the Community Chest idea was easy enough to understand. By rolling a number of appeals into one campaign, the chest represented an efficient means of raising money and meeting community needs. Moreover, a governing board dominated by practical businessmen would command respect from people with resources, screen agencies to eliminate unworthy or fraudulent ones, and write an annual, unified charity budget for the city that could be revised when new needs appeared or emergencies arose. The Community Welfare Board also hoped to reform member charities by allowing "business houses" to "check up on efficiency to effect improvements," in the words of J. A. Burger of Northern School Supply. Businessmen active on the board believed they had succeeded in enhancing the efficiency of Fargo's charities. As Ralph Trubey of Guardian Life Insurance put it in his letter transmitting the 1937 budget to contributors, "we believe that you will be pleased with the evidence of sound business practices on the part of the agencies as well as the Chest itself."[27]

While the Community Chest was positive in a number of ways, it guaranteed more than it could deliver. The Community Welfare Association promised efficient charities and implicitly promised that businessmen would reward that efficiency with liberal contributions. The association made guarantees to member agencies, assuring them that they would be treated fairly and that they would have more resources by coming in than they would by staying out. And the association assured the city that it could provide for those suffering from the Depression. All of these promises came into question, and none could be kept fully. Indeed, the failures of the Community Chest during and even prior to the Depression cast doubt on the pretensions of Fargo's business community and on its ability effectively to conduct self-help endeavors.

The chest got off to a good start in the fall of 1927, exceeding its goal and receiving 5,500 pledges, but public support began to wane almost immediately. The 1929 campaign fell more than $8,000 short of its $68,000 goal, despite a fervent appeal by drive chairman Walter L. Stockwell, who argued that "the fair name of this city is at stake." Especially noteworthy was the decline in contributions from businesses, in some cases by up to 40 percent. That disturbing trend continued. The shortfall forced an embarrassed Community Welfare Board to reduce contributions to member agencies, and the failure of large numbers of contributors to fulfill their pledges resulted in further budget cuts.[28]

The Community Welfare Association decided to launch the chest campaign earlier than usual in the fall of 1930 and to redouble efforts to collect unpaid pledges, but again commitments fell short of the goal. Chest workers reported hearing a variety of criticisms that justified failures to contribute. Non-contributors argued that member agencies' liberality had attracted ne'er-do-wells to Fargo, that the association's administrative expenses were too high, or that such member agencies as the Union Mission and the Salvation Army were selling donated items and pocketing the profits—a myth that persisted throughout the Depression.[29]

The declines in charitable giving and in the fulfillment of pledges, in Fargo and elsewhere, were an ominous development in light of the continued deterioration of the economy. National spokesmen in the Hoover administration and the philanthropic community stressed the need for localities to redouble their fund-raising efforts, lest the whole idea of cooperative individualism collapse. As Loring Schuler, editor of the *Ladies' Home Journal,* put it, "failure of this local relief campaign will inevitably bring a federal dole. . . . It is unspeakable that such a system should ever be adopted in the United States."[30]

The Community Welfare Board prepared for the critical 1931 campaign by cutting disbursements once again in response to uncollected pledges and by writing a budget for 1932 that shifted funds away from such "character building agencies" as the Boy Scouts and the YMCA in favor of the "four family relief organizations"—the Union Mission, the Salvation Army, Jewish Welfare, and Catholic Welfare. The board complicated its fund-raising task by agreeing to conduct a special Red Cross campaign simultaneously with its own. The Red Cross was attempting to raise $200,000 statewide to aid drought victims in northwestern North Dakota and had allocated $20,000 of that burden to Fargo.[31]

The Community Welfare Board pressed hard for volunteers, especially in the service clubs. On November 12, the chest campaign was kicked off with a pep rally. "'We want a touchdown!' was the battle cry of the campaign today as the workers were told the drive is a football game between Want and Security, the first coached by Indifference, the second by Good Will," the *Forum* reported, "hunger, cold, sickness and crime are the stars of the challenging team, the citizens of Fargo aided by Unselfishness, Generosity, and Helpfulness, the players on the other." A few days later, the Community Welfare Association staged a large parade featuring a contingent of orphans. Help came from new sources. As part of a national campaign by the motion picture industry, the Fargo, State, New Isis, and Princess theaters all ran benefit performances for the chest and Red Cross, with union projectionists donating their labor.[32]

The Community Chest/Red Cross drive of 1931 appeared to be a stunning success. The Red Cross goal was reached, and the chest was oversubscribed by nearly $20,000. Altogether, more than $99,000 was pledged by Fargoans. This was perhaps the city's finest hour for cooperative individualism and business leadership and a demonstration of the compatibility of a "progressive and modern . . . capitalism" with a "neighborly community." Prominent Fargoans indulged in an orgy of self-congratulation. Community Welfare Association president Burger stated, "we have a right to be proud of Fargo and every Fargoan who was able to give has a right to feel proud of himself." The *Forum* added that "a page in Fargo history where brilliance dims the triumphs of the past and sets a mark for all the future was written by the 1931 campaign." In its annual report, the Chamber of Commerce contended that the drive "is undoubtedly the outstanding accomplishment of the City of Fargo for the en-

tire year" and that "it shows progressiveness and people cannot help but form
good opinions of the citizenry of a community which rises so nobly to an
emergency."[33]

Such euphoria evaporated quickly in the early weeks of 1932. Nationally,
bank deposits fell dramatically in the last quarter of 1931, indicating that the Depression was taking a turn for the worse. Demands on private relief agencies and
on Cass County surged early in 1932 as increasing numbers of unemployed and
underemployed Fargoans exhausted their resources and were forced to appeal
for help. The Community Welfare Association reacted to the unexpected rise
in demands by taking a harsher and more punitive attitude toward those seeking aid, initiating a work requirement for aid recipients in January.[34]

While the rise in demand for aid commanded most of the Community Welfare Association's attention, the shortfall in the supply of funds intensified the
crisis atmosphere and transformed the apparent vindication of cooperative individualism into a bitter joke. An extraordinary number of unfulfilled pledges
forced the board to reduce allocations to member agencies and compelled it to
search for alternative funding sources. In July association officials George
Hoenck and W. P. Shure asked the City Commission to fulfill its "duty" to the
poor with a special $25,000 to $30,000 appropriation. Already coping with angry taxpayers demanding draconian budget cuts, the commission refused.[35]

The Community Welfare Association managed to scrape along in reduced
circumstances, aided in part by the seasonal pick-up in employment in the
spring and summer and by Red Cross donations of clothing and flour. Given
its difficulties, however, the association did not look forward to the upcoming
chest campaign. The fall effort went poorly from the beginning. The number
of volunteers was substantially reduced, and unseasonably cold weather curtailed canvassers' efforts. Regular contributors were resistant, often arguing
that the federal government, which was lending localities relief funds through
the Reconstruction Finance Corporation, was assuming responsibility for the
poor, making the chest superfluous. Others refused entirely. Virtually all faculty at the North Dakota Agricultural College, for example, angered by severe
salary cuts that had been endorsed by the *Forum* and many business leaders,
refused to contribute. The result was a campaign that "was not successful," in
the candid words of Community Welfare Board chairman and Fargo furrier
George Hoenck. Barely $50,000 was pledged, far under the $68,000 budget
set by the board. It got worse. Association treasurer Harry Alsop reported in
May 1933 that barely half of what had been pledged had been paid, a shortfall
that forced sharp reductions in the budgets of member agencies.[36]

The decline in collections and the apparent erosion of support for the whole Community Chest concept led the Community Welfare Board to consider doing away with it early in 1933. Insufficient monies had been pledged to meet stated needs, and the pledges themselves appeared increasingly fanciful. Only the intervention of the federal government, first with the Reconstruction Finance Corporation loans and then with the Federal Emergency Relief Administration and the Civil Works Administration, saved the association the embarrassment that would inevitably accompany its failure to meet its commitments. While the association was pleased that federal help came to Fargo's poor, government intervention cast further doubt on the need to continue the local chest campaign and raised questions regarding what the association's purpose should be.[37]

During the 1933 chest campaign, charitable officials everywhere struggled to justify the continuation of agencies that had addressed the needs of those who were now seemingly being cared for by the federal government. As *Fortune* succinctly put it in a November editorial, "in 1932 there was a moral duty to give for the relief of the unemployed. In 1933 there is no such duty. The government has assumed it." That conclusion was not exactly true, as charity administrators all over the country noted. Federal relief programs mainly covered "employables," which in practice meant married men with dependents. Others continued to rely on county relief and local charitable agencies. Fargo charity leaders also stressed that federal relief was a cooperative endeavor and that local communities must do their part or risk losing aid from Washington. As J. A. Burger explained in an address on WDAY, "the president and his relief administrators have made it perfectly clear . . . that federal relief money is being advanced simply to help out . . . because the financial load is more than the local communities can carry. In order to obtain federal relief funds, therefore, it is necessary for the local community to do its utmost in caring for its own relief needs." But it was not just self-interest that dictated support for the chest. There remained a moral obligation to give. The chest must succeed, Walter Stockwell told another WDAY audience, because it "represents a united community effort. It gives us an appreciation of the fine qualities of our neighbors. . . . It brings us into closer fellowship, one with another." Stockwell concluded with an appeal to the obligations of cooperative individualism and to Fargo's community pride: "We are engaged in a war against loss of morale and those spiritual values which in the last analysis determine the quality of one's manhood and womanhood, and his place in the community life of this fine city. . . . The fair name of Fargo as a public spirited, forward looking city is at stake." Such shopworn appeals were losing their ability to inspire or shame givers by the fall of 1933. The pretense of civic unity was increasingly difficult to sustain, and community pride and the obligations of stewardship, effective in more prosperous times, no longer induced the requisite sacrifices. The 1933 campaign fell short of its goal, leading to another round of budget cuts, the hiring of a collection agency to pursue delinquent pledgers, and the laying off of secretary Rose Horowitz, the association's only salaried employee.[38]

Some member agencies of the Community Welfare Association became restive as a result of disappointing drives and budget cuts, and as early as the fall of 1933 the board recognized that it could not sustain the chest idea if it continued to disappoint them. The board's budgeting process, however businesslike it was portrayed as being, was also a source of complaints. Relatively popular agencies were especially critical, suggesting that they could do better on their own or if chest donors were allowed to designate recipients. In 1936, Harold Bond of the North Dakota Children's Home responded to notification that his agency would receive $3,000 for the upcoming year by complaining pointedly that "the amount is not satisfactory, [and] never has been. . . . We . . . wish to call attention to the fact that we believe that the work we are doing . . . has a much greater appeal to the people of Fargo than any other agency in this city. We believe that we could increase this amount if it were left to the giver to say where he wishes his contribution to go." Bond's suspicion that some agencies might benefit if they stood apart from the association was shared by others. In the fall of 1936 the Red Cross, a popular, high-profile agency, made good on a threat from the previous year and withdrew from the association entirely. It added injury to insult by conducting its campaign just prior to the chest appeal. In 1937 the YMCA asked permission to conduct its own special appeal, as did the Union Mission the next year, and both implicitly threatened withdrawal from the association if they were not allowed to do so. The board had no alternative but to accede to these requests even though they contradicted the whole Community Chest concept.[39]

Of the many disappointments besetting members of the Community Welfare Board during the Great Depression, none was keener than the failure of the business community to support the Community Chest more adequately. Board members agreed that drives fell short because many businesspeople refused to contribute and pledges went unfulfilled because employers failed to press employees to meet their obligations. In 1934 a special board committee investigated the funding problems confronting the chest and noted that, while there were "5500 separate subscriptions or pledges" in 1927, "the number . . .

has been steadily decreasing, until at the present time these pledges number around 4000." The committee blamed the decline on the fact that "less and less attention has been paid to employees [*sic*] cards" and that employers were shirking "the responsibility for seeing that any pledge . . . was paid." The committee concluded, "there are many employers who are still unsold on the work of these agencies and the advantages of the community chest plan."[40]

The committee recognized that the problem was partially organizational. Lacking a professional staff and dependent on volunteers, the Community Welfare Association was letting many employers off the hook and was probably not even approaching others. Moreover, while volunteers could solicit pledges, they could not be expected to assure that pledges were fulfilled. It was also probably the case that some employers were loath to press workers, whose wages they had reduced and whose jobs were often insecure, to make charitable contributions or to fulfill pledges. But some board members identified the basic problem as a moral failure, embodied in an avoidance of responsibility among many businesspeople in the city. In December 1932 George Hoenck was named "Fargo's Outstanding Citizen" and received a Distinguished Service Medal from Cosmopolitan International in recognition of his work on behalf of the Community Chest. In his remarks praising Hoenck, Walter Stockwell suggested that "we are in the confusion of the present day because many of our economic and industrial leaders have not been like George Hoenck, socially minded." At this moment, as both of them contemplated the implications of a disappointing chest campaign, Stockwell concluded pointedly, "the crying need of this critical time is for a greater appreciation on the part of every one of his social responsibility. It is only as our economic and social leaders recognize the right of all men to enjoy life's satisfactions that we can solve the present unhappy situation." Cooperative individualism and communal self-help were being undermined by the very people who should have been leading the community by example.[41]

The Community Welfare Association experimented with a number of devices to secure better cooperation from disinterested and uncommitted members of the business community once it recognized that appeals to pride, duty, and stewardship were insufficient. During the 1933 campaign chest spokesmen suggested that charitable contributions were a means of preventing radicalism, as when Hoenck argued that "support of the Community Chest" was one way of keeping Fargo "free from the unrest evident in so many sections of the United States" and Walter Stockwell contended that "if we hope to preserve even a semblance of the capitalistic theory of economics, if we expect a continuance of the rights of private property, if we hope to develop individual initiative, we must not permit hunger and cold . . . to stalk through our city." In 1934, the association tried another approach, distributing a list of contributing firms to member agencies and urging those agencies to "give them your support in order that as substantial a sum as possible may be returned to them." The association increasingly emphasized the value of the chest to the community in dollars and cents rather than as an expression of values or a moral commitment. As Ralph Trubey put it in a letter to businessmen in 1937, "we believe . . . you will be impressed with the fact that these agencies as a whole constitute a definite business asset to this community." In 1938 the association appealed to the "enlightened self interest" of national retail firms operating in Fargo, arguing that contributions to the chest would improve their public image and thereby help defeat "legislation aimed to curb the operation of chain stores." Over the course of the thirties the chest appeal shifted from an emphasis on moral obligation and city pride to an emphasis on "business assets" and "enlightened self interest." The members of the Community Welfare Board and the chest volunteers may have remained what Stockwell called Hoenck—"socially minded"—but they were under no illusion that the businesspeople to whom they appealed shared that quality.[42]

The struggles of the thirties wore on those involved with the Community Chest, eroding the enthusiasm of volunteers. The special committee of 1934 had recommended a full-time executive secretary be hired to run the chest and collect delinquent pledges. In 1936 the board finally agreed, retaining professional charity manager Richard Sheetz at a salary of $225 per month. While the professionalization of charitable management in Fargo was probably necessary, it further dampened the volunteer spirit on which the chest depended. In 1939 George Hoenck reported that he had been unable to obtain a chairman for the upcoming chest drive "for the very reason that . . . no businessman felt that he could devote 6 weeks . . . to two months of his time to this work, or because of lack of interest of his fellow businessmen getting their pledges in." What had been an honor in the early years of the Community Chest had become an onerous and thankless task a decade later.[43]

The Community Chest survived the thirties, eventually becoming the United Way of Cass-Clay. Part of the reason it survived was because it shifted its emphasis from welfare to "character-building" agencies at a time when there was growing concern about juvenile delinquency in the city, a phenomenon that will be addressed later. This shift was duplicated all over the country as chest organizations came to realize that, whatever the reality might be, the public perception was that the government was now meeting the needs of the poor. Indeed, the general story of the Community Chest in Fargo is similar to the story of that organization in Los Angeles, Seattle, Butte, Montana, and many other places in the United States. Everywhere charities coped with declining resources and increasing demands. Everywhere they struggled to retain support and maintain relevance in their communities. Everywhere their missions and their relationships with clients were complicated by federal relief and welfare programs. Everywhere they had to grapple with the disheartening reality that self-help was insufficient and cooperative individualism inadequate. And everywhere they had to confront the fact that appeals to community pride and stewardship failed to induce much of the business community to assume a leadership role in self-help endeavors. Fargo was not much different from a lot of other places when it came down to it. That must have been a great disappointment to those who believed it was.[44]

IV

Businessmen usually provided leadership in self-help endeavors in Fargo, but the notion that people could and should take action in their own behalf was hardly confined to the business community. Some of the unemployed believed it, too, and acted accordingly.

Formal organization among Fargo's unemployed began in November 1931 when director Leland Scatterday of the YMCA made the facility available to jobless men who desired to meet regularly, exchange employment information, hone job-seeking skills, and share experiences. The initial meeting drew 125 men "from illiterates to college graduates; men past 60 and youths." The evolution of this group over the next year is shrouded in mystery, but in December 1932 what had come to be called the "Unemployed Men's Club" was large enough to be divided into two parts, one for men under twenty-five and the other for older men, and to have its activities coordinated by Fargo attorneys Earl Isensee and Lee Brooks. The *Forum* reported that a meeting of the older men's group was attended by 138 job seekers, mostly married and over forty-five. Most were common laborers, but ten were carpenters, ten were mechanics, nine were salesmen, and eight were clerks.[45]

The Unemployed Men's Club outgrew its quarters at the YMCA building downtown, both because its numbers were increasing and because it was beginning to receive donations of food and clothing. On January 22, 1933, the *Forum* reported that the group had received one thousand articles of clothing and that the Cass County Farmers Holiday Association had donated 4,180 pounds of wheat to be ground into flour. The *Forum* noted further that the group had about 260 members, "most . . . being heads of families." By this point the Unemployed Club had transformed itself into the "Cass County Unemployed Exchange" and was making ready to institute the "Seattle Plan," whereby the jobless could barter work for food, clothing, and other necessities.[46]

The Unemployed Exchange, like most other self-help endeavors in the city during the Depression, was an idea that was born elsewhere and tried in a number of places. Seattle was credited with having the first, and certainly the most fully elaborated, unemployed exchange, and most others followed its general outline. As it was developed in Fargo, the Unemployed Exchange solicited jobs for members, who were paid in cash or with food, clothing, or furniture. Members paid in goods could turn these in to the exchange for scrip, which they could then use to purchase items from the commissary. Stocks in the commissary included both earned and donated goods. Only a few idealists believed the unemployed could actually support themselves through exchanges, but most observers in Fargo and elsewhere applauded the self-help spirit they represented and believed they could provide at least part of what the unemployed needed to live.[47]

In its search for adequate space the Unemployed Exchange approached both the City Commission and the school board about the possibility of occupying Longfellow School, a vacant former elementary school on Tenth Street North, next to the Great Northern tracks. The school board agreed, albeit somewhat reluctantly, and the experiment was launched with good wishes all around, including from the *Forum,* which editorialized condescendingly that "on behalf of these neighbors of ours who, unfortunately and through no fault of their own are out of employment, The Fargo Forum bespeaks a continuation of that fine co-operation which has been accorded them by businessmen and all citizens generally." For its part, the Unemployed Exchange also said the right things, its members assuring the city that "we don't want the taxpayers [*sic*] money spent to feed and cloth [*sic*] us if we can find a better way."[48]

Things went well initially, and aiding the Unemployed Exchange became something of a community project. Beginning in late January, the exchange sponsored a series of dances at the Avalon Ballroom, to which persons contributing food were admitted. The first dance was attended by twelve hundred people who donated "425 tins of canned goods . . . 62 cans of vegetables, mostly home packed . . . 20 pounds of sugar . . . 4 bushels of onions . . . 11 bushels of potatoes . . . [and] 500 pounds of navy beans." A month later, the

Knights of Columbus and the Fargo theaters presented the proceeds from a movie and dance to the exchange. And in April amateur actors staged *The Queen's Husband* at the Orpheum Theater and assigned all of the gate receipts to the exchange.[49]

The exchange's self-help activities were extensive. It collected gifts of food, clothing, and furniture. "Wives of exchange members . . . organized an auxiliary" that transformed irreparable clothes into quilts. Members sold paper flowers on the streets to raise money. The exchange advertised aggressively for jobs, running daily ads in the *Forum* highlighting members' various talents and emphasizing their eagerness to do "spring repair work and spring house-cleaning." The organization also suggested public works projects for the unemployed, urging the County Commission to authorize the laying of drainage tiles in a swampy area at the North Dakota Agricultural College and requesting permission from the park board to cut dead trees in the parks and on the golf course for firewood for their members. This high level of activity was accompanied by rising participation in the exchange by the jobless. From 350 in February membership rose to 450 in April and to nearly 800 in December, a figure that included 100 members of an "Unemployed Ladies Club." If accurate, those numbers represented well over half of the city's unemployed.[50]

All of these activities were certainly within the self-help tradition so prized in Fargo, but there were developments beneath the surface at the Unemployed Exchange that disturbed community leaders. The obliqueness of the public record regarding the exchange makes it impossible to determine exactly what the problem was, but there are clues in the records of the Cass County Welfare Board and elsewhere that suggest why city leaders were uneasy.

From the beginning, the Unemployed Exchange assumed an aggressive posture with local relief authorities, asserting that the unemployed themselves should influence how relief was distributed, who received it, what work projects reliefers undertook, and how much they were paid. In January exchange members lodged "strenuous objection" to county food voucher policies "designating certain stores as the only places where supplies may be obtained" and limiting "the commodities and the amount thereof to which the recipient is entitled." Speaking through one of their sponsors, Earl Isensee, members also complained that married men with dependents were not receiving adequate relief. The exchange appeared to infringe on the prerogatives of relief authorities when it began to suggest projects, how they should be managed, and what compensation should be. When the exchange proposed tree removal on park board property it wanted the work supervised by its own members. That plan disturbed county relief director T. A. Hendricks, Jr., who told the park board that "if such permission be granted it should be done under adequate supervision and control." The park board agreed that the County Relief Office should oversee the work. Two weeks later a dispute erupted over pay for workers on the NDAC drainage project. Exchange representative H. A. Morris wanted workers to receive $0.50 per hour for a six-hour day, while members of the welfare board "felt that this wage scale would be unfair to the farm labor in view of the present scale of wages and hours under which they were working." Morris replied that "farm and other labor were being grossly underpaid." The wage issue arose again at the end of the month, when workers on the county woodpile demanded that their hourly rate be doubled from $0.20 to $0.40. The welfare board refused on the grounds that "it was not a good plan to let the men dictate in the matter."[51]

The irony of the Unemployed Exchange's aggressive attitude was that it developed out of the same pride and dignity that led its members to embrace the self-help ethos in the first place. Those attracted to the exchange were not generally people who had gone through life depending on private charity or county general assistance. They were predominately heads of families who were accustomed to providing for their dependents through their own efforts. The economic crisis made that increasingly difficult, and the attraction of the exchange was that it allowed such people to band together with others like themselves to achieve at least a degree of self-support. Proud people such as these, used to earning their own way, did not passively accept the humiliations that receiving relief in Cass County entailed. They did not consider themselves to be mendicants or second-class citizens, and they did not propose to be treated as such. Their attitude, so threatening to relief officials, became increasingly prominent among Fargo's unemployed as the Depression lengthened.

It is also likely that these proud and traditionally self-reliant people, jobless through no fault of their own and organized with others in the same situation, were receptive to explanations of the Depression that focused on flaws in the structure of the capitalist economic system. Unemployed exchanges in many cities became hothouses for radical thought and activity, and the emergence of H. A. Morris, a prominent local Socialist, as spokesman for the group suggests that may have been the case in Fargo, too. Fargoans applauded self-help as an abstract value, but they were not always comfortable with how it was manifested. In the case of the Unemployed Exchange, self-help was defined and exercised in ways that both disturbed those who dominated the city and challenged their cherished assumptions about property, class, authority, and deference.

In light of the turn the Unemployed Exchange had taken, it is hardly surprising that city officials hastened to cripple it when presented with the opportunity. In November 1933 the Federal Emergency Relief Administration announced that it would establish a Transient Bureau in Fargo if the city could provide suitable quarters. Longfellow School came immediately to mind, and the school board, which had worried as early as February about "the disorderly manner in which some members of [the Unemployed Exchange] were conducting themselves," readily agreed to evict the exchange. The displacement of the Unemployed Exchange was justified on the grounds that most members were working on Civil Works Administration jobs and presumably did not need its services any longer. The exchange protested on two grounds. First, complained Mrs. N. S. Johnson, president of the group's Independent Ladies Club, unemployed women were generally ignored by the CWA and still needed the services provided at Longfellow. And second, "there are about 600 members in the men's club, and while the [CWA] work has been of assistance it will not last forever, and the organization should be kept alive for the future." The city ignored these complaints and was quite content to wash its hands of the whole Unemployed Exchange experiment, launched less than a year before with great fanfare and good wishes.[52]

So the Unemployed Exchange went away. The Independent Ladies Club, however, did not. Nor did the spirit of independence and self-respect among the unemployed that the exchange represented and encouraged. That spirit would continue to devil city leaders and the relief establishment for years to come.

The spirit of self-help and cooperative individualism never disappeared in Fargo and, indeed, reasserted itself periodically throughout the Depression years. But it had reached a crisis by the end of 1933. Despite their best intentions and efforts, Fargoans were unable to pull themselves out of the economic slough through the War Against Depression and similar endeavors. Nor were they able adequately to care for their fellow citizens in need, and their failure to do so raised doubts about the stability of the pillars of business leadership and individual stewardship on which cooperative individualism stood. And when the unemployed responded to the failures of the city's political and economic elite to bring recovery or relieve suffering, their proud and aggressive variety of self-help angered and frightened those accustomed to a deferential working class. Small wonder that all concerned welcomed the growing federal government role in economic recovery and unemployment relief. The conclusion that had been unthinkable in the Depression's early years—that Fargo could not solve its problems—had become an established and widely accepted fact.

3

"The organization has used every effort possible to bring about approval for government projects through PWA, WPA, CCC and others."
Report of the Chamber of Commerce, 1935

"There is an increasing feeling of uneasiness on the part of people generally with reference to the enormous expenditures of the government, and the mounting debt which must ultimately be translated into crushing taxes. People are beginning to say that this cannot continue without grave disaster."
Daniel Heitmeyer to Franklin D. Roosevelt, 1935

INAUGURATION OF Franklin D. Roosevelt's New Deal administration heralded a change in the relationship between states and localities and the federal government, though the dimensions of that change did not become fully apparent for some time. Observers anticipated that the new administration would develop fresh approaches to the problem of economic recovery, and they were correct. Local officials expected that the federal government would continue to assume responsibility for providing funds for relief, as it had since 1932 through the Reconstruction Finance Corporation. They were correct in that assumption, though they did not foresee the conditions under which relief would be offered, the nature of regulations regarding how relief would be dispensed, or the conflicts that would arise between themselves and federal officials over control of relief and relief rules. What they did not generally anticipate was the degree to which localities would come to depend on federal expenditures or the degree to which federal agencies would supplant local ones, fulfilling functions that had traditionally been the exclusive province of states, localities, and private agencies.

The changed relationship between the federal government and localities that eventually emerged from New Deal programs was not clearly foreseen on either Pennsylvania Avenue or Broadway. Fargo, like most of the country, was eager for new economic approaches and was highly receptive to whatever federal aid was available.

Recovery programs, such as those contained in the National Industrial Recovery Act and the Federal Housing Act, were congenial to Fargoans in large part because they emphasized the sort of local self-help and community mobilization strategies with which they were familiar. Nor were Fargoans averse to accepting federal funds. As early as 1930 they had supported cash payment of the bonus to World War I veterans, reckoning that it would stimulate the local economy. During the winter of 1932–33, the Community Welfare Association and Cass County had already compromised their commitment to cooperative individualism by accepting flour and fabric from the Red Cross and by applying successfully for relief funds from the Reconstruction Finance Corporation. Thus it was not surprising that Fargoans welcomed New Deal programs that poured money into the local economy. Every federal agency, from the Agricultural Adjustment Administration to the Transient Bureau, was analyzed by the *Forum* in terms of how many dollars it would put into the pockets of local businessmen. Federal dollars were especially valuable in alleviating the dramatic decline in construction spending in Fargo, a growing city in which building had always helped power the economy. As the Chamber of Commerce implied in its 1935 assurance that it had "used every effort possible to bring about approval for government projects," the federal government had become a key customer and client. Luring it to Fargo was not much different from attracting a large employer or enticing rural shoppers to come downtown.[1]

But it was not just the dollars themselves that were important; it was also what was done with them. Relief funds dramatically reduced the burden on Cass County, and the city government and the park board used federal help to compensate for their serious declines in revenue, thereby relieving local taxpayers. Moreover, federal monies helped the city cope with challenges, such as the transient problem, and to address some of the consequences of its growth.

While they welcomed the boldness, activity, and optimism of the New Deal recovery plan and while they coveted federal funds, Fargoans demonstrated an uneasy ambivalence about government programs that increased as the thirties unfolded. The idea of industrial recovery was unexceptionable, but the details of its execution raised doubts and eventually opposition. Relief funds benefited the community in a variety of ways, but relief regulations diminished local control, violated local understandings of how and to whom public resources should be distributed, and irritated the class frictions that the Depression had stimulated. The city desperately needed the infrastructural improvements the federal government provided, but new facilities entailed financial burdens that local government had to assume. Some Fargoans were humiliated by federal help from the very beginning, believing that the city could and should address its own problems. As Jean-Cameron Shupienis remembered of her mother, Willimina Heller, "mother and her group were horrified when federal relief came into Fargo—they thought they could handle it themselves." By 1935, with the sense of crisis of 1932–33 fading into memory, many more Fargoans were manifesting what Baptist minister Daniel Heitmeyer called "an increasing feeling of uneasiness." While they wanted federal money and recognized what it had done for them, they worried about what it was doing to them, and to the country.[2]

I

The sense of expectation and genuine enthusiasm with which this normally conservative, Republican city greeted the inauguration of Franklin D. Roosevelt reflected the desperation of the winter of 1932–33. Predicting that "Roosevelt's inaugural day" would be "one long to be remembered in the annals of the city," the *Forum* promised a mammoth celebration "to greet the incoming administration with its promise of a 'new deal' for the business life of the nation." The city lined the streets with flags and bunting, and merchants put up patriotic window displays. At 10:00 A.M. on inauguration day "whistles and bells . . . let loose a blast of greeting to the 'new deal'" and signaled the beginning of a massive parade. Never willing to allow a sales opportunity to slip by, merchants advertised "President's Day" and "New Deal" bargains "as their incentive for revival of business and trade."[3]

Even the bank holiday that began on March 6 failed to darken the euphoric mood of merchants and consumers. Theaters, dance halls, and restaurants reported large crowds, with most businesses accepting checks or, in some cases, "I.O.U. slips . . . from patrons." The currency drought was eased somewhat when several large concerns, including the railroads and Armour Packing, met payrolls with cash. Still, some anxiety lurked beneath the surface. Vivian Westberg, who worked at the First National Bank, remembered that "people were so scared—they thought they'd lost everything. We went to work every day, but we didn't do anything—we played cards every single day. It was such a happy day when they opened the doors and people could come in and get some money." All of the Fargo banks, which shared a reputation for prudence and fiduciary responsibility, reopened on March 14. In common with re-opening banks elsewhere, they reported deposits exceeding withdrawals.[4]

Local enthusiasm for the New Deal and affection for President Roosevelt carried beyond early March, in part because there was a noticeable upswing in business and consumer confidence. As the months went by a "New Deal" haberdashery opened and the Heglund Grocery changed its name to the "New Deal" Grocery. On January 30, 1934, two thousand Fargoans celebrated the first of a series of annual birthday balls honoring Roosevelt, with the proceeds going to the Warm Springs Foundation to fight polio. In December 1933 the "Herbstory" newsletter asked employees of Herbst, "Who's afraid of the big bad wolf? The man in the White House isn't! From a few minutes after noon on March 4th, until this very minute he has set an example of fearlessness and faith."[5]

Local enthusiasm for the New Deal was necessary if the recovery program, embodied in the NIRA, was to be implemented. Not only did local volunteers have to march and canvass and induce businesspeople and consumers to sign pledges, but businesspeople of all stripes had to come together to write codes setting minimum prices and wages and defining some conditions of labor, localities needed to form and operate compliance boards, and employers and employees had to abide by the provisions of the codes that were written.

The code-making process got off to a good start in Fargo as groups of businesses agreed to price floors for their goods and minimum wages and maximum workweeks for their employees. In July the bakers agreed to raise the price of a standard loaf of bread from eight to ten cents and adopted a "code of ethics" prohibiting "the sale of baked goods below a minimum price" as well as "secret discounts and rebates of every type." More enterprises followed. Barbers agreed to raise prices of haircuts to $0.50 and to institute a 40-hour week with a $16-per-week guarantee for employees. Cosmetologists wrote a code instituting a 48-hour week and a $14 guarantee. Building contractors set hourly wages for workers, ranging from $1.00 for bricklayers to $0.40 for "helpers and common labor." Coal dealers and photographers wrote codes, and undertakers set the minimum price of a funeral at $50. Even the eleven shoe-shine parlors in town agreed to do their part, setting the price of a shine at $0.15, "black or brown." Large employers also fell into line. Armour subscribed to the national meat-packing code, and most retailers—including all large retailers—agreed to a 40-hour week and a $12 minimum wage for regular employees.[6]

The response to the NIRA was enthusiastic. Merchants proudly displayed the blue eagle, symbolic of their subscription to the code, on their windows and in their newspaper ads, and there was a general "determination to abide by all the price codes." A compliance board dominated by businessmen was appointed, and when labor demanded representation, W. W. Murrey of the Trades and Labor Assembly and Stella Rakow, who worked at Black's department store, were added. The complaints reaching the board came mainly from employees, who protested wage and hour violations or unfair discharge, but the board considered compliance in town to be strong overall.[7]

The effect of the NIRA on labor was less positive than its authors had hoped. Some workers were dubious about the enterprise from the beginning. Reflecting on the grand NIRA kickoff parade, Vivian Westberg remembered that "we had to hurry our work to go march in a parade for shorter hours—then we had to come back and work 'till seven. We always laughed about it afterwards." In the banking business, tellers such as Westberg worked until the books balanced, regardless of what the NRA code might say. Other workers had a more positive experience. Birdie Kerr's husband, a garage mechanic, was supposed to get $15 a week, but only if work came in. Under the NRA code he got that rate whether cars were in the shop or not. The NRA codes were good for workers whose employers could afford to pay the prescribed wages, but many could not, either because of particularly weak conditions in their industries or because they lacked the ability to pass on increased costs to their customers. It was well and good to set bricklayers' wages at $1 per hour, but it did not have much practical effect when most were unemployed at any wage. Sam Paper hired common labor at his scrap metal yard for $9 per week in his highly cyclical business. It was a very low wage, but it was all he could afford to pay. When the NRA code mandated a higher wage, he had no alternative to letting men go. Nor was everyone covered. Teachers, for example, who had suffered salary reductions and would continue to do so, were not included in NRA codes, nor were other public employees.[8]

While the minimum wage provisions of the NRA were designed to raise, or at least stabilize, wages, the hours features of the codes were supposed to spur "re-employment." The thinking of policymakers was that if five forty-eight-hour-per-week workers were cut back to forty hours each, another person would have to be hired to cover the work. This happened in some instances. Armour Packing added forty-five to fifty men, for example, and retailers anticipated putting on another one hundred workers citywide, at least at Christmas. However, there were a number of practical problems with the re-employment theory. First, many workers were already working fewer than forty hours per week; underemployment was a more prevalent problem than overemployment. Second, enterprises that created jobs by cutting hours did not provide employment for those most in need of work. Sam Paper's day laborers were not going to be hired to cut hair, nor were bricklayers likely to take, or be offered, positions in women's ready-to-wear. Finally, cutting workers' hours sometimes reduced their wages, regardless of minimum wage provisions. Retail clerks, for example, who frequently worked at least partially on commission, needed as many hours on the floor as they could get, as did waitresses and others whose compensation came largely in tips.[9]

As Liz Cohen has pointed out in her study of the New Deal in Chicago, the NIRA was not particularly positive for small businesses of the sort that predominated in Fargo, either. Employers were asked to hire more workers and pay higher wages in the hope such action "will increase the buying power—stimulate buying—and, as a result, [employers] will gain sufficient to more than repay [their] temporary additional outlay." An increase in overall buying power might benefit the individual businessman, but if his labor costs rose before that happened, or faster than his profits increased, he ran the risk of going broke. Nonchain retailers also faced the problem that their suppliers raised prices under their codes but when the local merchant tried to pass on increased costs consumers resisted. Finally, in the Northern Plains, the powerful Farmers Holiday Association launched a boycott of NRA code–compliant merchants to protest price increases. Fargo retailers began discreetly discarding the blue eagle from their ads within a few months. The NIRA asked small businessmen to take the same risk they had asked consumers to take in the War Against Depression—to commit resources in the hope that such action would bring recovery. They were willing to do so, to a point, but they were hardly disconsolate when the NIRA was declared unconstitutional in 1935.[10]

Other federal programs enjoyed more enduring public support and popularity in Fargo, particularly when they brought new money into the city. As Dan Dadey, president of the Fargo Chamber of Commerce, put it in 1933, money was flowing out of Washington, and "we've [got] to be ready to cash in right from the opening gun."[11]

Home loan and housing rehabilitation programs were especially welcomed, generating considerable support from banks, business, and labor. The Home Owners Loan Corporation, which purchased troubled mortgages from banks and refinanced them under more attractive terms, was very popular, even among apparently comfortable people. Nils Tronnes, one of the founders of Fargo Clinic, saw his income plummet during the Depression because he could not collect bills and, as his daughter put it, "how could you charge somebody that had a family and needed to eat?" Tronnes was about to lose his ele-

Broadway, looking north from Front Street. The large white building on the left is the Black Building.

gant Broadway home when he was able to obtain refinancing from the Home Owners Loan Corporation. Small wonder he had the opinion that "Roosevelt was a godsend."[12]

The federal government used its financing and refinancing programs to alter the way homes were purchased in the United States. Prior to the government's entry into home financing, a buyer was required to make a large down payment, usually half of the value of the property. The buyer then received a short-term loan, commonly running about five years, on which he or she made payments that covered interest only. At the loan's expiration, the buyer had to either pay the balance of the principal or refinance. In the early years of the Depression it was difficult to do either, with the result that many homeowners defaulted and also lost substantial equity. The federal government improved this system markedly with the Federal Housing Act in 1934. The Federal Housing Administration created under that legislation insured private mortgages, with the condition that the lender require low down payments, allow long loan retirement periods, and adhere to interest-rate ceilings. The FHA revolutionized home buying, facilitating it for both the buyer and the seller. The FHA eventually brought major changes to Fargo, allowing its reality to approach more closely its self-image as a community of stable, homeowning families, though the city continued to have a disproportionate number of renters and apartment-dwellers.[13]

Of more immediate significance to Fargo than the FHA was a provision of the Federal Housing Act offering low-interest loans to homeowners to re-model, renovate, modernize, or beautify their homes. Up to $500,000 was made available for lending in Fargo, and the building trade unions, contrac-tors, lumberyards, and hardware dealers spied an opportunity to pull local construction out of its deep hole. The chamber organized a campaign headed by J. F. McGuire of Union Power and Light to publicize the program, acquaint bankers with the loan provision, and visit "every household in Fargo" in an ef-fort to encourage homeowner participation. Volunteers claimed to have visited every homeowner in town and managed to secure "a total of 715 pledges for $246,426.28 in construction," short of the chamber's goal, but cause for self-congratulation.[14]

Fargoans' desire for federal funds was also demonstrated in their support for cash payment of the bonus to veterans of World War I. Shortly after the end of the war, veterans, led by the American Legion, lobbied Congress for com-pensation for the earnings they lost as a result of their service. In 1924 Congress responded by creating life insurance policies in the form of "adjusted service certificates," maturing in 1945, whose value was set by multiplying the number of days a veteran served in the United States by $1 and the number of days served overseas by $1.25. While the value of these certificates varied consider-ably, they averaged about $1,000.[15]

As early as 1930 Depression-stricken veterans began agitating for the right to cash out their certificates. Congress was unwilling to make a financial com-mitment of this size, but it did agree in February 1931 to make money available to local banks, which were authorized to lend veterans up to half the value of their bonuses at 4.5 percent interest. Numerous Fargoans took advantage of this offer, as did over half of veterans nationally, but the American Legion and other groups continued to agitate for full cash payment. In the summer of 1932 veterans marched on Washington in support of legislation to pay the bonus in cash. This enterprise—which resulted in the expulsion of veterans and their families from the capital by army units commanded by General Douglas MacArthur—was derided as "ill advised" and "fraught with danger" by local Legionnaires, and only a handful of Fargo veterans participated.[16]

It was the marchers' means rather than their ends that drew the objections of Fargo veterans, who continued to support full cash payment of the bonus. Fi-nally, in January 1936, Congress overrode President Roosevelt's veto of a bill providing payment of the bonus in the form of $50 government bonds, with checks covering any amounts in excess of multiples of $50. Veterans could keep the bonds, which would earn three percent interest until 1945, or cash them in at a government "paying center," such as the Fargo post office. After passage of the Bonus Act hundreds of veterans crowded the city auditorium "clutching discharge papers, 'pink slips' or other evidence of their right to share in the bonus." In June, when the bonds and checks were distributed, "war veterans swarmed into the Avalon ballroom ... to get all or part of their adjusted service bonds certified so they could receive checks," and the next day checks totaling $157,400 were distributed to 420 of the city's 1,153 veterans. Money for veterans meant business for merchants. Veterans devoted about 40 percent of their bonuses to paying bills, much to the delight of grocers and clothiers, and spent much of the rest on "new apparel," "used cars," and "jewelry."[17]

Federal money for veterans' bonuses or home loans was as welcome as money from any other source in Fargo, and it did help alleviate problems. Some challenges, however, such as that of the transients, were addressed more directly by the federal government.

II

If there is a universal memory among those who lived in Fargo during the Depression, it is of transients. "The flatcars were full of them," Seymour Olson remembered. "They used to just flop down in Island Park, and around the filtration plant," Vivian Westberg recalled; walking to work she would "step over the bums sleeping there." One of Bill Toomey's vivid memories was of "large clusters of men on lower Front Street and many begging for food door to door and going through garbage cans." The Grabers, who lived near the Great Northern tracks, frequently awoke to "find one sleeping on our porch or in the basement," but even those distant from the railroads have vivid memories of transients. Mary Arvold, who lived on a fashionable block on North Broadway, remembered that "you saw them all around; they'd go by all the time."[18]

Children frequently found transients to be enjoyable companions and romantic characters who seemed to live lives free from the constraints of civilization. Charlie Hauser remembered transients teaching him how to bake a fish by caking it with mud. Sid Cichy, who grew up on a farm south of town, recalled that "for a kid like me ... they broadened my world," but he also noted that "maybe you learned some things from the transients that you shouldn't have learned."[19]

Cichy's remark captures some of the ambivalence with which residents regarded transients. On the one hand, they were pitied because many had fallen on hard times through no fault of their own. "Transients were nice people," Darrow Beaton said, "hard working guys, just looking for something to do." And Avis Gjervold recalled that "they were all pretty good people." Such sympathy was reflected in the willingness of Fargoans, in interviewees' memories, to provide food to beggars or to give a few pennies to panhandlers on downtown streets. But transients stimulated anxiety as well as compassion. Some people feared they might be criminals or radicals: "some were I. W. W.'s —people said they were Communists," Seymour Olson remembered. Fargoans responded to beggars, but was their response grounded in sympathy or fear? "Some looked so desperate you were afraid to have them around but you were afraid to refuse, too," Gladys Welton said in a 1974 interview, and John Carlson believed "people were afraid of them, generally speaking."[20]

Adding to the ambivalence Fargoans felt toward transients was the understanding that they were necessary to the smooth functioning of the regional economy. They were, in the phrase of historian Frank Higbie, "indispensable outcasts." In the Upper Midwest, transient workers had historically provided much of the muscle that mined iron, felled trees, laid track, and raised and harvested crops. The slow decay of the resource-based economy and increased mechanization in much of what was left resulted in diminished employment opportunities for transients, but agriculture remained heavily dependent on them. Some crops grown in the region, such as potatoes and sugar beets, required hand labor for most of the season. More significantly, while grain farmers were increasingly using combined harvester-threshers, the wheat harvest continued to be a labor-intensive operation that depended upon transient workers. Fargo benefited when farmers benefited, but there were other, more direct ways in which transients enriched the city. They helped sustain the numerous temporary employment agencies and other transient-oriented business in the lower Front Street main stem, and when they came back through town after harvest they frequently left at least part of their earnings with legitimate or illegitimate Fargo enterprises.[21]

Transients were part of the Fargo scene the year around, but the seasonality of farm labor meant the bulk of the estimated 30,000 who passed through the city annually were there between early April and the end of September. Itinerants were most numerous in late August and September, when the grain harvest had concluded. Transients who stopped in the city stayed in Front Street flophouses or cheap hotels if they could afford to, though the police also provided free lodging at the jail when room was available. In March 1930, for example, the police reported lodging 623 people. When the weather was good transients slept in the parks or along the river or even on the sidewalks. Fargo also had two large hobo jungles—one downtown south of the Great Northern tracks along the river and the other along the west edge of the city near the Chicago, Milwaukee, St. Paul and Pacific line—that attracted sojourners, but knots of men could be seen wherever there was shade and water. The jungles became semipermanent fixtures in the community. Police reported in 1931 that the downtown jungle featured a sheet metal shack with a "modern fireplace . . . constructed of brick" and "one of the finest kitchens" they had seen. Men in the jungles commonly fixed their own meals, making stews of meat and vegetables they purchased or begged or cooking turtles and fish they caught in the river. Other transients ate at the Union Mission or Salvation Army, begged from householders, or consumed "leavings" from restaurants.[22]

Few transients tarried in town very long. Early in the season they were on their way to employment, which they had sometimes arranged beforehand, and after the harvest they were on their way home. Numbered among the transients were laid-off factory workers and college students seeking summer earnings, but even the unskilled laborers who predominated usually returned to Kansas City, Minneapolis, Chicago, or some other city where they resided through the winter. Only a minority were truly men adrift, with no place to call home. To encourage transients to move along the police conducted "daily 'jungle' cleaning" during the agricultural year, "driving out the 'canned heat' drinkers and others who are merely loafing and have no intention of working." The police also made liberal use of such charges as "riding on trains" and "vagrancy" to limit the transient population. Vagrants usually had jail sentences suspended on condition they leave the city. In 1930 police magistrate F. A. Leonard announced that "floaters" would be given "10 minutes" to leave the city and those not complying would be jailed for thirty days and placed on a regimen of "bread and water."[23]

Police treatment of transients often took the form of petty harassment, but itinerants did represent a significant law enforcement challenge during the 1930s. Most transients were law abiding, and those who ran afoul of the law usually did so for a minor, nonviolent offense such as drunkenness, gambling, or patronizing prostitutes. When transients were involved in more serious crimes they were usually victims—often of one another. Men coming through town after the harvest were tempting targets for thieves. In September 1931 transient Nels Jacobson went drinking with a friend on Front Street and awoke the next morning without $80, "the profits of several weeks of hard labor on farms." In the fall of 1932 Jack Mehl was arrested on suspicion of stealing $114 from another transient in a Fargo café. And in October 1933 Herman Wendt swore out a complaint against five Front Street prostitutes for getting him drunk and relieving him of $75. Assaults, often fueled by alcohol, were also common, as in July 1931 when a brawl in the downtown jungle resulted in a brain concussion for one itinerant and two broken arms for another. And in October 1930 two boys, one sixteen and one eighteen, were killed when other transients pushed them off a freight train west of town.[24]

Sometimes transients victimized residents as well as one another. Itinerants were frequently charged with such offenses as shoplifting, prowling, or petty theft, as in October 1931 when Richard Carey of Richmond, Virginia, was arrested for stealing milk and bread from porches and taking it to the boxcar where he was living. But on occasion transients committed, or were suspected of committing, crimes that shocked the city. In August 1931, for example, a pair of drunken itinerants kidnapped two sisters, aged three and four. The year before it was assumed that a transient had killed Leif Erickson, a collector for International Harvester, in a botched lovers' lane robbery attempt. And in December 1935 transient Charles Marratto was arrested and convicted of shooting grocer Peter Stewart to death during a robbery.[25]

Concerns about transients, expressed frequently in Fargo, intensified during the early 1930s, just as they did in most of the country. As early as March 1930 O. E. McCracken of the Union Mission noted an upsurge in itinerancy. "The transient army this month is the largest I have seen at this time of year in more than 25 years," McCracken claimed. "For the first time in months there is not an overcoat in our stock to be given away. We have been literally stripped of coats, shoes and almost every other article of apparel." More people were on the move in search of work at a time when there was less work to be had, with the result that more transients were getting stranded in town, burdening charities and local authorities. Part of the problem was that an informal system that operated prior to the Depression, whereby stranded itinerants were shipped to their home communities at those places' expense, broke down under the pressure of rapidly rising transient numbers and declining resources everywhere. Cass County and the welfare agencies in Fargo found themselves burdened with unexpectedly high demands from itinerants. Transients had not established residency and were thus ineligible for county general assistance, but when transients died in the county, as did Louis Duffy in July 1930 and Ernest Rodriques in September 1931, both of whom stumbled while trying to board moving trains, the county paid for burials. And when transients became sick, or when they suffered from long-term illness such as syphilis, the county was responsible for providing care.[26]

Transients stuck in Fargo sometimes attempted to obtain employment, which was itself a source of friction because it put them in competition with residents. Many leaned heavily on the Salvation Army and the Union Mission. These agencies could provide a lot of service for little money. In September 1935 the Salvation Army fed transients 332 meals at Otto's Restaurant and the White Front Café for $0.15 apiece and purchased 200 nights' lodging at a Front Street flophouse for $0.15 a bed. But these agencies were caught between shrinking resources and rising demands from the resident poor as well as from itinerants. One answer was for the Salvation Army and the Union Mission to deny aid to transients. They did so on occasion, but then Fargoans complained of increased panhandling and door-to-door begging and blamed the Community Welfare Association for not providing emergency funds. In September 1932 the association instituted a plan to aid worthy itinerants while weeding out "professional bums." The association printed meal tickets, which it sold to businesspeople for a dime apiece. The businesspeople were urged to give meal tickets rather than change to panhandlers. The ticket-holder was entitled to a free meal at the Union Mission, but only after he performed some labor—usually ten minutes of wood chopping. The Union Mission would then redeem the tickets with the association for cash, covering its costs. The plan seemed a stroke of genius. Transients looking to buy "canned heat and other forms of alcohol" would disdain the tickets in the first place, and only energetic, and therefore deserving, ticket-holders would be willing to work for a meal. The plan broke down, however, mainly because a Moorhead printer flooded the town with counterfeit meal tickets. Within a few months, the Union Mission and the Salvation Army had curtailed all aid, and the Community Welfare Association was considering some sort of "Mass Treatment . . . facilities for handling" itinerants.[27]

In 1933 the federal government addressed the transient problem in a way that aided the itinerants and relieved communities struggling with the burden of dealing with them. In December the Federal Emergency Relief Administration announced that it would open centers in areas experiencing high levels of itinerant traffic to provide housing, food, medical care, and work relief for transients. These Transient Bureaus, one of which was planned for Fargo, were ambitiously conceived. FERA hoped first to concentrate and stabilize the transient population. In order to advance that goal, it asked railroads and motorists to stop facilitating transience by allowing free riders and picking up hitchhikers, requested that citizens refer panhandlers and beggars to local centers, and urged the police to enforce vagrancy laws aggressively. Once transients were concentrated and immobilized, FERA hoped to "rehabilitate" them through professional casework, returning them to their families whenever possible. FERA was especially eager to treat young transients, whose growing presence on the road was a matter of increasing national concern. In the words of the *Forum,* which heartily approved the Transient Bureau idea, FERA aimed "to prevent a second generation growing up with ideals of idleness, chiseling and extravagance" that supposedly guided older itinerants. While the process of rehabilitation was going on, Transient Bureau residents would be required to labor on public works projects devised cooperatively by bureau staff and local governments.[28]

Fargo's Transient Bureau got off to a good start. The City Commission and the school board eagerly expelled the Unemployed Exchange from Longfellow School to provide quarters. After one month the bureau had one hundred residents, including three families with seven children, and it continued to grow. In June 1934 the bureau reported providing services to over one thousand itinerants, virtually all single men. Most of those served came from the Midwest, with men from Wisconsin, Minnesota, Illinois, and North Dakota predominating. In accordance with standard bureau practice, the Fargo facility attempted to separate young transients from older ones and maintained separate quarters for families and for women. The *Forum* was generally laudatory, noting in the bureau's early days that "the majority of cases . . . are men who are genuinely interested in obtaining work and establishing their independence." In March a *Forum* reporter, posing as a transient to gain entry to the center, proclaimed that "not in any manner were these men inferior to the average American." The bureau tried to be a good neighbor, undertaking work relief projects and otherwise reaching out to the city. Among other activities, bureau residents presented plays and talent shows for the community and organized a softball team that challenged local groups.[29]

The bureau assured Fargoans they had nothing to fear from its presence in their midst. Speaking to a special meeting of the City Commission in February 1935, Fargo bureau superintendent George Henry noted that 20,000 transients had been served in the previous twelve months and that 500 were in residence. While some clients had been there for more than a year, Henry reassured the commission that residency at the Transient Bureau did not make one a legal resident of Cass County and that his charges intended neither to collect county relief nor to vote. He told the commissioners that "all camps were under strict supervision at all times, watchmen being on duty 24-hours per day to . . . see that transients lived up to the rules laid down to govern their conduct" and "that the Federal Government had no intention of doing anything that would result in a quarrel with, or be objectionable to the residents of Fargo." The Chamber of Commerce certainly did not object, commenting that the Transient Bureau spent "approximately $7,000.00 a month . . . in the City of Fargo for the purchase of supplies, groceries, clothing, etc." The police reported a substantial decline in the number of jailhouse lodgers and "a marked improvement in the local transient situation, with pan-handling and mooching almost eliminated from the streets." And the Salvation Army and Union Mission noted a dramatic reduction in the number of transients seeking aid.[30]

Unfortunately, relations between the city and the Transient Bureau were not always cordial. The bureau wanted free water and the city refused, leading to a long, simmering conflict. The Transient Bureau wanted city government to help it identify work projects, but the City Commission took the position that "so long as there were any unemployed persons in Fargo, any work programs should be reserved for Fargo residents." Other problems arose simply because of the nature of some of the bureau's clients. Police reported that in the winter of 1934–35 one-fourth of arrestees in the city had been residents at the Transient Bureau, and Dr. P. H. Burton of the County Welfare Board suggested "every man in the Transient Bureau should be fingerprinted. They are harboring a lot of [of] men who are fugitives from justice."[31]

There is no question that the bureau was harboring a lot of men, "fugitives from justice" or not. During its first year, the large number of transients clamoring for admission and services forced the bureau to expand by occupying three nearby residences as well as the Zimmerman Hotel on lower Front Street. The bureau also hoped to occupy Dill Hall, on the former Fargo College campus, just south of Island Park. It proposed to spend $10,000 renovating the facility into a 250-bed dormitory and an education and recreation center for younger transients. Residents of the affluent neighborhood south and west of the site protested vociferously on the grounds that the presence of a transient facility would lower their property values, and the City Commission agreed. It was not just transients that these folks wanted to keep out of their neighborhood, however. When the Fargo College facility was subsequently occupied by the Good Samaritan Home for disabled children the neighbors again bemoaned the threat to their property values, especially because "many of the crippled children were allowed to be outside and they wander about."[32]

The Transient Bureau's failure to acquire Dill Hall meant that overcrowding at the main facility would be difficult to alleviate and that the separation of older from younger men would be impossible. In a July 31, 1935, report to FERA officials in Washington, inspector Alice Yonkman reported, "sleeping and eating arrangements are pretty bad. . . . The attic is filled with double deckers, some of them no more than six inches apart. Men all sleep the same way. Metal cots are lodged in wooden framework." Yonkman found that dining facilities were especially inadequate: "While the place feeds about 650 men a day only 76 men can be seated at one time. There are no adequate sterilizing facilities and the dishes are mostly of tin which are very hard to keep sterilized and cleaned." Yonkman pointed out that the crowded conditions prevented the necessary separation of minors from older men, noting that "boys should not be housed with older men," they "should not work in the kitchen with older men and most especially they should not eat with them constantly." Clients echoed Yonkman's concerns, complaining of sleeping "63 men in a room where 12 or 15 men should be enough," of gambling, of "drinking right in the building," and of the sexual exploitation of minors by older men.[33]

Overcrowding restricted the ability of the Transient Bureau to serve new clients. During the 1935 harvest season, there were 100 to 150 new registrants at the bureau every day. In the month of July, the bureau registered more than 3,400 transients and served 64,000 meals, dwarfing anything the Union Mission and the Salvation Army had ever done. On one day, August 4, 969 breakfasts were served. Because the bureau had room for only 500 residents, many registrants received little more than a meal, though that was often enough for men on the move. Superintendent Henry estimated that the turnover of lodgers during the harvest season approached 40 percent per day. By contrast, nationwide turnover at the transient centers was estimated at 100 to 140 percent per month.[34]

The numbers with which the bureau had to cope affected more than just the staff. Householders in the Transient Bureau neighborhood complained that itinerants who arrived after registrations ceased at 11:00 P.M. and before the bureau reopened in the morning slept on their lawns and would "go about improperly clothed in the early morning hours [and] use unseemly language." Henry conceded that this situation existed, but he "pointed out that if registration is stopped or if the bureau is forced to discontinue feeding any large percentage of them, Fargo will have a big problem of panhandling on its hands."[35]

These realities illustrate that the Transient Bureaus worked, but not as they were intended. The itinerant population was not immobilized. Residence in the centers was voluntary, and people left readily when better prospects beckoned. Few transients were able to put down roots in the communities with centers because, as in Fargo, most of those places did not want them to become permanent residents and desired that their own citizens get first crack at whatever jobs and relief opportunities might be available. The numbers and the turnover with which the centers dealt made the social work they tried to undertake virtually worthless. The Fargo Transient Bureau had just one caseworker to serve its 500 residents, effectively limiting attention to just a handful of very young itinerants. Few transients were returned to their home communities or families because those entities frequently did not want them back, or they had no desire to return, or the conditions that had driven them away remained in place. And even if they had been able to work under optimum conditions, the transient centers, which had a capacity of about 300,000 nationwide, could serve only about 20 percent of the country's estimated transient and homeless population of 1.5 million.[36]

In practice, the Transient Bureaus became secular equivalents of the Union Mission or the Salvation Army—places where an itinerant could get a couple of hots and a cot without having to listen to a sermon or sing a hymn. They were, in the words of one observer, "in reality city shelters, better . . . than the old flop-houses, but still with a mass atmosphere." The Transient Bureaus served as a safety net for itinerants, places where those who were not usually eligible for other local or federal welfare services were certain to receive some minimal aid. Ironically and unintentionally, the network of Transient Bureaus around the country might have actually encouraged the transience they were created to deter.[37]

One of the positive aspects of the Transient Bureaus was that they assumed a burden that in their absence would have fallen largely on local communities. That burden shifted back to local communities and the transients themselves in the fall of 1935, when the federal government decided to end registrations in the Transient Bureaus on September 20 and shut them down on November 1. The government was abolishing FERA and turning over its function of providing work relief for employables to the new Works Progress Administration. At the same time, many of those deemed "unemployable" were covered by Old-Age Assistance and Aid for Dependent Children, both of which were created by the Social Security Act. The problem with this scheme was that some people fell through the cracks, a majority of transients included. Most transient center clients were considered employables, but because few had legal residency anywhere it was difficult for them to get WPA work. With no government agencies willing to acknowledge responsibility for them or even to recognize their existence as citizens, transients were thrown back on their own devices and on the tender mercies of the Union Missions of the world. Such was the fate of the lowest of the low during the Great Depression.[38]

III

The Transient Bureau was just a small part of a large and complicated relief structure that operated throughout the United States during the New Deal. The federal government had assumed responsibility for funding unemployment relief when Congress authorized the Reconstruction Finance Corporation to lend money for that purpose in 1932. During the last winter of the Hoover administration, RFC funds covered about 60 percent of the cost of relief nationwide. The RFC loans were understood as an emergency, stopgap expenditure and were not perceived as the basis for a permanent relief structure. In part for this reason, localities were allowed to spend the money pretty much as they saw fit and on whom they wanted, with little direction from Washington.[39]

Harry Hopkins and other New Deal relief administrators did not propose to create a permanent relief structure, either, but they did hope to use federal funds to induce local relief agencies to adopt practices that were standardized, professional, fair, and sometimes—but not always—more humane than those that existed. Their criticism of the RFC program was that it left relief to the discretion of local agencies, which decided for themselves who was worthy and who was not, whether to cover unemployables along with employables, whether to require means tests, and whether to demand work in return for relief. Gently early on, and more forcefully later, national officials attempted to move local relief agencies and administrators toward more modern and scientific relief administration and practices.

Hopkins was head of the most significant relief agency of the early New Deal, the Federal Emergency Relief Administration. Beyond the transient program, FERA had two components that were significant in Fargo. First, the agency provided funds on a matching basis, with one dollar being contributed by the federal government for every two dollars spent at the local and state levels. And, second, FERA made direct cash grants to those states, including North Dakota, where relief needs were great. In addition to FERA funds, the city also received grants and loans from the Public Works Administration to undertake large projects of lasting value, the most important of which was a sewage disposal plant. Fargo was also home to a Civilian Conservation Corps camp, for unemployed young men, located between the river and the Detention Hospital, and a Veterans' Civilian Conservation Corps camp at the state fairgrounds, on the north edge of town. In the winter of 1933–34 Fargo participated in the Civil Works Administration program, which provided work relief for male and female heads of families. In 1935 FERA was replaced by the Works Progress Administration—also headed by Hopkins—a work relief program that operated in Fargo through the balance of the Depression.[40]

As D. Jerome Tweton emphasizes in his study of the operation of the New Deal in Otter Tail County, Minnesota, federal relief programs stressed "grassroots planning, execution, and control," especially in the early years of the Roosevelt administration. Local bodies identified work projects, certified the eligibility of participants, and provided the tools and materials required. The federal government was paying most of the relief bill, but it did not want to offend local sensibilities, and it wanted local people to retain at least a shred of their cooperative individualist faith in community self-help and neighborly aid. The *Forum* wholeheartedly approved the consignment of relief responsibilities to localities, noting in June 1933, "it is generally recognized that, in practically all respects, a local community is better able to soundly and more understandingly give relief."[41]

The local preference in Fargo was for work relief, and the city established a remarkable record of putting FERA clients in jobs. In June 1934, the County Relief Office noted that 88 percent of the employable unemployed in Fargo were on work relief, more than double the percentage in most other places. This showing was a tribute to the energy and efficiency of public agencies and private organizations in identifying projects and providing tools and materials, and a demonstration of Fargoans' desire to use relief money for community betterment.[42]

Federal relief programs had a major impact on employment, business, and public finance in the city and the county. In the winter of 1933–34 nearly 1,600 persons were employed in CWA projects in the county—80 to 85 percent of them in Fargo. The federal payrolls stimulated business, helping give the city a strong holiday shopping season and generally raising morale. Despite a Christmas morning temperature of 31 degrees below zero, there was "cause for rejoicing" because "for scores of Fargo-Moorhead men it was Christmas day with a job to go to Tuesday." There was also cause for rejoicing at the County Commission. In the first eleven months of 1934, nearly $438,000 of the $520,000 expended by the county for relief purposes had come from either FERA or the CWA, significantly relieving fiscal pressures. As Anna Stevens—who served on the County Welfare Board and who, in her words, "detested Roosevelt"—put it, "the people in Cass County . . . were glad there was money coming in that they didn't have to provide." And the money continued to flow, even after the sense of crisis in the early New Deal had passed. Beginning in 1935, federal money came for Old-Age Assistance and Aid for Dependent Children. The WPA, created in 1935, regularly employed 600 to 800 heads of families on work relief in the city. In March 1936 the WPA payroll was running at $1,100 per day. For the year 1936 the WPA and the PWA spent about $350,000 in the city, and the next year federal public works spending outstripped private construction spending by a factor of two to one.[43]

Local government welcomed whatever help it could receive because the revenue situation worsened considerably in 1933. In order to aid beleaguered property owners, especially farmers, the 1933 legislature eliminated penalties on unpaid personal and real property taxes and limited the interest that could be charged on delinquent taxes to a maximum of six percent. This action, when combined with governor William Langer's moratorium on foreclosures of delinquent taxpayers, effectively made "taxpaying an absolutely voluntary matter on the part of the delinquent," in the words of Fargo city auditor Earl Jorgenson. Indeed, the interest rate on unpaid taxes was so low that, in the absence of other penalties, even solvent taxpayers calculated it was to their benefit not to meet their property tax obligation. By 1936 there were 12,000 delinquent personal property and 3,500 delinquent real property taxpayers in Fargo—over one-third of the property owners in the city—who owed about $1.25 million, including $429,000 in special assessments alone.[44]

Governmental units were caught between delinquent-relief legislation and taxpayers' groups on one side and public needs and the demands of clients on the other. In the summer of 1933 the county budgeted $61,000 more than it could raise, the city overbudgeted by $44,000, and the school district's shortfall was nearly $21,000. In terms of budget size, these deficits were 15 percent, 15.4 percent, and 6.2 percent, respectively. Government could and did try to increase revenues by raising mill levies, but as the Cass County Taxpayers Association pointed out, that simply added to the burden on those willing to pay their taxes while allowing delinquents to continue to enjoy a full range of services for free. The alternative was to cut budgets by reducing services, trimming expenditures, and reducing wages. Most agencies of local government did all three.[45]

The city eliminated some positions, reduced salaries of all employees earning more than $100 per month, and introduced a number of other economies, the most controversial of which involved shutting off half of the street lights and illuminating the rest three and one-half fewer hours each night. These actions were too much for the Trades and Labor Assembly and not enough for the Taxpayers Association, but they were insufficient to balance the budget in any case. In October 1933 the city was compelled to issue two-year certificates of indebtedness, which Fargo banks agreed to buy, in order to balance its budget.[46]

The park board, which had trouble balancing its budget even in prosperous times, was in a particularly difficult position. It could not raise its property tax levy, which was limited by law to two mills. For several years the board had followed a risky fiscal strategy in its effort to make ends meet, issuing certificates of indebtedness collateralized by uncollected taxes. Among its other actions, the legislature made this practice illegal, forcing the park board to suspend most of its operations in 1933. No longer able to borrow on the basis of anticipated tax revenues, the board was compelled to cut its permanent staff from fourteen to seven, reduce the salaries of those who remained, end all supervised summer recreation, and even suspend free band concerts at Island Park. The golf course, which paid for itself, remained open, and volunteers agreed to maintain the tennis courts.[47]

The school board was also forced to retrench, and the labor-intensive nature of public education meant that endeavor mainly involved cutting salaries. In March 1933 the board concluded that reductions in teachers' salaries were inevitable, but it was reluctant to ask teachers to take another cut while doing the same amount of work. The board proposed to accompany salary cuts with a reduction in the school year from thirty-eight to thirty-six weeks. Teachers opposed shortening the year because they feared such a step would jeopardize Fargo's status as a first-class district, and they "were thoroughly sold on upholding the standards of the Fargo Public schools," as superintendent James G. Moore observed. In August, however, the board voted to pair a ten-percent salary cut with the two-week shortening. The wage reduction meant that most teachers in the system, including a large majority of teachers in the elementary schools, made under $1,000 annually. The cut was all the more difficult because, as board president Kate Kjorlie noted, the operation of the NIRA had raised prices and "the few dollars they get now will buy much less than the dollars they were getting last year."[48]

Other cuts were more petty—indeed, quite literally so. The board decided to cease paying the salary of a teacher for the unwed mothers at the Florence Crittenton Home, and it doggedly pursued students from homes outside the district who were attending Fargo schools without paying tuition. The board also engaged in a long and acrimonious conflict over free milk for poor children. It had been board policy to charge most children two and one-half cents for a half-pint of milk in order to provide free milk to indigent children, but in December 1932 several paying parents protested what they considered an exorbitant expense. Early in 1933 the board began culling the lists of free-milk recipients and requested that the Red Cross meet the milk needs of poor children. By early 1935 the board was out of the milk business almost entirely and was "depending on relief agencies to furnish it," despite evidence that Fargo milk consumption was 40 percent below what the U.S. Department of Agriculture considered the minimum for an "adequate diet." Neither the milk of human kindness nor milk itself flowed freely at the Fargo Public Schools.[49]

These heroic measures failed fully to close the budget gap, compelling the board to issue $100,000 in warrants at six percent interest early in 1934. The Fargo Clearinghouse, made up of all the banks in the city, agreed to cash the warrants. Then, in August 1934, the board was able to secure overwhelming voter approval for a two-mill increase in the property tax. That action, which the *Forum* editorialized "may be taken as an expression of approval of the manner in which . . . school officials are conducting the city's public educational system," made further serious budget reductions unnecessary.[50]

In the midst of its struggle to balance the budget, the board launched a "Pay Your Taxes Now" campaign, designed to shame delinquent taxpayers into meeting their obligations. In announcing the new initiative, board president Kjorlie noted that delinquent taxpayers "are really accepting services from the county or state—as much as the indigent poor who receive fuel, rent or groceries from the county relief" and contended that delinquency "is unpatriotic. It is shifting our burdens onto other shoulders." The Parent Teacher Associations endorsed the pay-your-taxes campaign, which broadened in 1935 into an effort joined by city government and the park board. Aided by legislation in 1935 that discounted long-standing tax liabilities and forgave interest and by moratoria on various types of penalties by governor Walter Welford, real and personal property tax collections improved, though the problem of delinquency continued to plague public agencies throughout the thirties.[51]

Local government was aided by federal relief expenditures both indirectly and directly during these years of budget stringency. First, federal funds helped compensate for the decline of public and private spending locally, stimulating the economy and promising to increase tax revenues. And, second, because they were usually disbursed to recipients in return for labor, relief monies allowed public agencies to continue to fulfill their purposes and meet public needs.

Early work relief programs were of two types. FERA and the CWA were designed as short-term, emergency programs. Recipients of FERA and CWA relief were usually assigned to projects that were labor intensive, demanded relatively little skill, and could be completed in a fairly brief amount of time. By contrast, the PWA provided work relief on capital projects that were designed to provide long-term benefits to the community. While the PWA endeavored to be as labor intensive as possible, its costs for tools and materials were relatively high and many of its projects employed a disproportionate number of skilled workers. All of these programs were designed to provide employment for residents. The CCC and the VCCC were composed of qualified outsiders, though some local men served in the latter. All relief agencies were limited by the stipulation that they could not put recipients to work doing anything that competed with private industry, lest they impede economic recovery. Rumors swirled that "the Government" planned "to engage in the manufacture of products . . . in direct competition with its citizens," as one Fargo resident wrote to Congressman William Lemke in 1934, and relief agencies took care not to impart substance to such notions.[52]

Most FERA projects in Fargo involved manual labor of some sort. In April 1934, for example, men were employed in the never-ending task of removing debris from the banks of the Red, woodcutting, cleaning the parks, and painting buildings at the fairgrounds. Unemployed female heads of households, some from mothers' pension rolls and some newly indigent as a result of the Depression, were employed in a sewing room, canning project, or nursery school. When it became apparent that the Depression would not go away quickly and that relief for the unemployed would continue to be required, more imaginative projects were developed, including some involving construction. In 1934 and 1935 FERA provided teachers for adult education classes, supplied a nurse to the North Dakota Children's Home, opened a mattress factory, and taught ice-skating to children. FERA workers also installed a lighting system at Hector Field and helped build the Dolve Ski Club's ski jump, located west of the poor farm, the highest artificial ski jump in the United States.[53]

The CWA was an emergency work relief agency that operated for just a few months in the winter of 1933–34. It was the most attractive of the work relief programs for recipients because it paid what were supposed to be prevailing local wages, income was not limited by the family "budgetary deficiency" prin-

WPA workers on a riverfront improvement project during the winter, when WPA work was most plentiful but when projects were difficult to undertake and complete

ciple under which FERA operated, a means test was not imposed, and one did not have to be on the relief rolls to participate. Indeed, of the 1,317 people employed by the CWA at the end of 1933, only 375 had been receiving county relief. The CWA's short duration limited the types of projects it could undertake. Most workers were put to cleaning up the dump grounds and the riverbank, repairing and remodeling garments, painting the interior of city hall, and repairing chairs at the auditorium, but some CWA personnel were used to reassess property for tax purposes and to identify sources of radio interference in the city.[54]

Other relief programs involved projects that provided more enduring benefits to Fargo. The park board was especially alert to the possibilities of using CCC and VCCC labor for park enhancements. The board had more property than it could afford to develop even before the crippling legislation of 1933, and work relief provided the means for maintenance and improvement. In addition to planting, pruning, and cutting trees, CCC and VCCC workers erected entrance gates at Oak Grove Park and the Edgewood Golf Course, "constructed shelters in park areas, built fireplaces for use in the picnic grounds, and constructed two roads." CCC work was especially significant at Lindenwood, on the city's southern edge, the least developed of Fargo's parks.[55]

The Public Works Administration played a crucial role in the construction of capital facilities for the city, spending nearly $1 million in Fargo between 1933 and 1940. The PWA funded capital improvement projects through a combination of outright grants—usually 20 to 40 percent of the cost of the project—and long-term, low-interest loans. In 1934 the city received PWA funds totaling more than $150,000 to replace cedar block paving on Broadway and Fifth Street downtown. This project had been on the city's agenda for some time. The cedar blocks were vulnerable to the weather: in heavy rains some would literally float away, and others would pop out in the spring and fall due to freezing and thawing. Blocks sometimes squirted out from under the wheels of vehicles, as in August 1932 when a passing car inadvertently shot one through the plate glass window of Service Drug on Broadway. In 1935, the city received another $80,000 to repave Eighth Street between Front and Ninth Avenue South.[56]

PWA money was also crucial for construction of a sewage disposal plant, the most significant capital improvement project undertaken in Fargo during the 1930s. Defeat of the sewage bond issue in 1932 no more made the issue disappear than it removed the stench from the Red. In January 1933 Oak Grove residents threatened to sue the city if it continued to dump raw sewage into the river above their homes, and in May farmers living north of Fargo promised court action on the grounds that sewage had so poisoned the Red that they could not water their cattle. The City Commission created a sewage district and proceeded with planning, prodded by the Trades and Labor Assembly but over the protests of such prominent taxpayers as L. B. Hanna and Fargo Laundry owner Orlando Hegge, who argued that the city could not fairly increase the obligations of property owners. The courts forced the city's hand in July. In response to a suit by Oak Grove resident Marvin Jones, judge W. J. Kneeshaw of Pembina gave the city eighteen months to "refrain from further discharging of raw sewage into the Red River."[57]

The City Commission agreed that Kneeshaw's decision settled the issue and requested PWA funds, which were quickly granted. Two problems remained, however. First, the city's preferred location, near El Zagal, was opposed by neighbors who worried the plant would reduce their property values. In March 1934 these opponents secured passage of an initiated ordinance preventing the plant's construction there, forcing the city to settle on a more distant and expensive site, downriver from the poor farm. The other problem was that, when bids were opened in November, the low local proposals exceeded preliminary estimates by more than $60,000, in part because PWA wage scales and work rules drove costs higher, or so city fathers argued. The unexpectedly high bids for the plant set off a bitter debate. On one side were the Chamber of Commerce and the Trades and Labor Assembly, both of which favored proceeding. On the other were organized taxpayers, supported by city commissioner W. E. Black, who favored scrapping the project altogether and defying the court order. The PWA stepped into the dispute, requiring the city to re-advertise for bids and agreeing to allow more money for construction. Eventually, five local firms got the contract for about $663,000, or 30 percent above first estimates and 10 percent above the first bid. Ground was broken for the plant in November 1934.[58]

Construction of the sewage plant was an important and necessary project for Fargo, but it never employed more than a few hundred workers at any given time. Beginning in 1935, most Fargoans on work relief were employed by the Works Progress Administration, which replaced FERA. The WPA was designed to be a permanent work relief provider for the unemployed. Its permanence allowed it to develop imaginative projects fitted to a range of abilities and to execute projects that made a long-term capital contribution to the city.

Some of the WPA's projects in Fargo involved a continuation of FERA work relief. The sewing room, mattress factory, and nursery school all remained in operation, albeit under different auspices. WPA workers supervised recreational activities, just as FERA workers had, running craft shops, teaching ice-skating, organizing singing groups, reading to shut-ins, producing Braille books, and developing junior gardening clubs. The National Youth Administration, a branch of the WPA for high school and college students, supervised summer recreation for children in the parks. Other noteworthy projects included codification of city ordinances and instruction in telegraphy.[59]

While such enterprises were necessary if women and men without abilities as laborers were to be employed, the WPA emphasized construction projects that would provide facilities of permanent value to the city. This dictate placed a burden on local government to plan imaginative ventures beyond the clean-up and fix-up undertakings that had been so characteristic of FERA and CWA work relief. In Fargo, a number of projects of long-term significance were completed by WPA workers. The WPA built a new athletic field for the Fargo Public Schools and a new baseball stadium, Barnett Field, for the Fargo-Moorhead Twins. WPA workers built "a new hanger . . . an administration building, [and] improved runways" at Hector Field. And, most remarkably, the WPA constructed an ice arena and a swimming pool at Island Park.[60]

This recounting of construction projects is impressive, but not as impressive as it might have been. In 1933 the Trades and Labor Assembly presented the City Commission with a wish list of public works projects totaling $1 million. While some were undertaken, many were not. The problem was that all proposed PWA projects, as well as WPA projects involving substantial materials costs, required that voters pass bond issues, and they usually would not. In 1935 voters rejected bond issues for a new city hall and a new library. In 1937, despite a campaign by the American Legion and other patriotic organizations, Fargoans turned back a bond issue for a new convention hall and armory by a vote of 1,891 to 491. And the next year they refused to approve levies for street and sewer repair and for a new firehouse. Vigilant and often angry taxpayers remained a vital presence in the city. As one Fargoan framed their position in a letter to the *Forum* during the city hall/library campaign, "during these trying times, when the ordinary working man is . . . trying so hard to keep within his means and still retain his house—is not time to mortgage the future and burden ourselves with additional taxes."[61]

Taxpayers' resistance to bonded indebtedness, regardless of the benefits to be gained, made it difficult for public agencies to devise worthy projects and meaningful work for relief recipients. Old standbys such as riverbank cleaning and wood chopping came under fire from district WPA director Alvin Arneson, who noted that they should not "qualify for WPA funds" because they did not contribute "something of permanent value" to the community. Exacerbating the problem was the reality that relief needs were highest in the winter, when outdoor building work was difficult, and lowest in the summer, when public works projects were most feasible but when agriculture and private construction absorbed many of the unemployed. As the City Commission noted in December 1937, the WPA required projects of enduring value but "frost and extreme weather made it impossible to carry out many desirable projects, and often the men available could not work on outdoor projects due to the lack of proper clothing." The variant seasonal nature of relief needs and private work meant that projects were started in the winter, only to stand as half-finished eyesores through the summer, awaiting completion the following winter.[62]

In some instances work was not provided because local agencies did not want to create expectations they might one day have to disappoint. In August 1935, for example, the WPA proposed to place twenty women in the public schools, some to help truant officer Mary Maid (yes, that was her real name) but most to work as "charwomen." The school board declined, apparently swayed by the argument of member T. H. Manchester that "it has been my experience that if you put five men to doing the work three have been doing before, when you come to the time that you must make the three responsible for all the work again, you are apt to have considerable difficulty." Relief for the unemployed was well and good, but the school board feared being stuck with the responsibility of hiring or firing the charwomen if and when the federal government stopped paying them.[63]

By the late thirties opposition to the WPA had also developed in the construction industry. In 1938 municipal contractor J. A. Shaw complained to the WPA that "practically all the construction that is being done at the present time is being carried on by your agency." That meant "there is no incentive for any public body to stand on its own feet and do any construction work without accepting Federal Aid," with the result that "legitimate business and legitimate workers are . . . forced into the discard." Many workers apparently agreed. Early in 1939 Fargo locals of the Painters and Decorators and the Bricklayers unions both protested the continuing involvement of the WPA in construction, to the detriment of the "'forgotten man,' who is trying to keep off relief."[64]

Another drawback to work relief was that, while it was preferable to direct relief in terms of maintaining the recipient's morale and returning something tangible to the community, it was expensive for local government. Local agencies had to buy tools for workers and pay workers' compensation, despite the fact that they seldom had budgeted funds set aside for these purposes. The WPA planned and supervised projects, but it would pay for materials equal to no more than ten percent of the cost of labor. For ambitious WPA capital improvement projects this meant that materials costs fell on local citizens and government. The school board needed to spend $7,000 on its new athletic field, and a community fund-raising campaign had to be undertaken to raise the $6,800 necessary for Barnett Field. The Island Park pool required both a Junior Chamber of Commerce fund-raising campaign and a bond issue. Relief facilities also required unexpected support. The park board paid the water, sewage, and power fees for the CCC and VCCC camps. The City Commission provided housing for the Fargo Nursery School and picked up some of its bills. The city even paid half the rental on the WPA's district offices to keep the agency in town.[65]

The expanding public infrastructure that resulted from work relief also increased the responsibilities of local governmental agencies, which were expected to maintain the new facilities. The park board was pleased with the construction completed by relief workers because "most of this work would have been beyond the resources of the Park Board without the aid of the government and the unemployed," but the government worried that the board would be unable to maintain the improvements in light of its uncomfortable fiscal position. In 1935, the CCC asked pointedly whether "the erection of any more buildings would put too severe a strain on the Park Board" and whether the board would be able to maintain them. Later that year the WPA threatened to "abandon the projects" it had undertaken if the "Board found they did not have the funds to carry on."[66]

Aside from burdening public agencies with expenses and responsibilities, facilities constructed by relief agencies were not always built as cheaply or efficiently as some Fargoans preferred. Businessmen frequently grumbled that the government overpaid for labor, and farmers complained that high relief wages upset the local wage scale. In 1933, when the PWA set a minimum wage of $1.20 per hour for skilled and $0.50 per hour for unskilled labor, the Chamber of Commerce and the City Commission protested, with mayor Fred Olsen arguing, "if these wage scales are fixed for this territory the construction of the proposed Fargo sewage disposal plant would be out of the question." When the chamber and the commission asked that minimums be lowered to $1.00 and $0.40, the Trades and Labor Assembly protested vehemently and the PWA scale stood. Another conflict broke out a few months later when the city tried to pay Civil Works Administration workers $0.85 an hour when they were supposed to receive $1.20. FERA and WPA wages were lower, with the former set at a minimum of $0.30 an hour in 1933 and with the latter ranging from $0.48 to $0.77 an hour in 1937, but even that seemed excessive to some employers in a town where unskilled workers were frequently paid $0.25 to $0.30 an hour or even less. Work rules designed to make projects as labor intensive as possible in order to employ the largest feasible number of unemployed contributed further to the impression that government undertakings were expensive and inefficiently built. In 1935 the city accepted work rules proposed by the Trades and Labor Assembly for PWA projects that, among other things, prohibited "portable saws, electric saws [and] electric drills," "paint spray guns," and the use of "steam or gas shovels" for excavation. The rules further required that all plumbers, lathers, and electricians use "only hand tools" and that "all plaster and mortar . . . shall be mixed by hand."[67]

Federal work relief agencies were also criticized for bringing undesirable people to the city. The CCC was undoubtedly the most popular New Deal relief agency and is certainly the most fondly remembered. Yet during the thirties controversies arose about the CCC harboring boys on probation, about assaults, intimidation, and rapes in the camps, and about "food strikes, camp revolts, [and] the discharge of boys for 'communistic and Bolshevistic' plots." The Fargo CCC went out of its way to be a good neighbor, but nobody particularly wanted it in his or her neighborhood. Plans to put the camp at Lindenwood were scrapped when south siders protested, and mothers near its north side location warned their daughters not to walk or ride their bikes nearby. While the nearly three hundred enrollees were no more disruptive or obstreperous than any other three hundred young men in the city, they did occasionally run afoul of the law for drunkenness or joy riding, and CCC boys were arrested on such charges as child molestation, auto theft, and breaking and entering.[68]

New Deal relief agencies and practices drew their share of criticism in Fargo, as they did in most places, but the benefits they conveyed far exceeded their shortcomings. They provided employment, especially in the severely depressed construction industry, albeit not enough to compensate for the decline in private construction spending. They pumped money into the local economy, both through the wages they paid and through their direct spending on materials, buildings, food, and numerous other items. The jobs they offered usually paid at least as well as private-sector employment and allowed reliefers to retain some degree of self-respect. And work relief provided improvements that benefited "the entire population of the city" and helped Fargo cope with the consequences of its growth. The sewage plant was especially significant, but street and airport improvements, park development, and the construction of recreational facilities all helped make the city more livable.[69]

The city's continuing infrastructural shortcomings were certainly not the fault of the federal relief agencies. Fargo suffered from a housing shortage that was serious at the beginning of the Depression and acute at the end. From 1920 through 1931 Fargoans constructed an average of 120 houses per year, but from 1932 to 1935 a total of only 69 houses were built, including just nine in 1933 and ten in 1934. The resulting housing crunch kept rents relatively high and created hardship for the poor especially, but the federal government was unwilling to compete with private builders in meeting this need. The Chamber of Commerce chose to define "the problem of finding suitable housing facilities" as an indication of Fargo's comparative prosperity, which in a sense it was, but it meant inflated rents for people already struggling to live in a low-wage town. Fargo's housing shortage was real and painful, and it resulted from a failure of the capitalist system to meet a human need, not from an abrogation of governmental responsibility.[70]

Important civic needs also remained unmet when the Depression ended. A special planning report produced for the city in December 1939 demonstrated the need for a reliable water supply and for a new city hall, auditorium, fire station, and library. All of those structures could have been built had Fargoans agreed to assume a portion of the burden. As it was, the city had to wait twenty years for capital improvements that had been needed as early as 1930, and then they came as a result of federally sponsored urban renewal. The federal government did a lot for the city, but it could have done even more had the city been willing to do its share.[71]

IV

Federal programs were significant to Cass County mainly for the budgetary relief they provided. The county was caught between rapidly rising poor relief needs and declining tax collections, and the taxpayer alleviation measures passed by the 1933 legislature made a bad situation worse. The Cass County Taxpayers Association, speaking especially for cash-strapped farmers, was particularly aggressive with the County Commission. The association specifically targeted the poor relief budget, which by 1933 had grown to more than 40 percent of county expenditures, opposing the county's application for an RFC loan for relief and suggesting various draconian steps to shave outlays for the poor.[72]

In this painful situation, "federal money was like rain in a drought," allowing the county substantially to reduce its budget for the poor while the federal government picked up most of the tab for relief. The county took full advantage of available funds from such agencies as FERA, the CWA, and the WPA, shifting as many employables and unemployables as possible to FERA and putting most of the able-bodied unemployed on work relief. Nor was the county shy about pressing for more federal money when the opportunity arose. In January 1934 the County Commission requested "the proper agencies of the Federal Government to assume the entire burden of public relief in Cass County" on the grounds that "funds available for county relief are almost exhausted." And that November the commission asked FERA to pay for the medical care of the county's indigents, the cost of which had apparently risen dramatically because of the presence of the Transient Bureau and because "Cass county has been the 'dumping ground' of destitute families from other parts of the state." The federal government refused these requests, but the very fact they were made demonstrated how quickly and easily the county sloughed off the mantle of self-help.[73]

Not only did the federal government help the county meet the challenge of unemployment relief, it also helped Cass fulfill longer-term obligations the county had assumed for indigents defined as "unemployable." Among the unemployables needing county help were aged people who could not support themselves and who lacked family that could or would provide aid. Nationally the number of people over sixty-five rose sharply early in the twentieth century, and even in a recently settled place such as North Dakota, which had become a state only in 1889, older people comprised a growing segment of the population.[74]

It is one of the enduring myths about the United States that, in a more idyllic past, older people who could no longer look after themselves were usually sheltered and supported by children or grandchildren. That was not the case in Cass County, or in most other places in the country either, at least by 1930. Most older people lived alone, and when they were no longer able to do so because of financial or physical circumstances, their children frequently could not be found or, if they were found, refused to take parents in or to contribute to their support. In November 1934 the County Welfare Board discussed the case of Bertrand Nichols, whose daughter and son-in-law both had well-paying jobs but who refused to contribute to his maintenance. Board member P. H. Burton suggested that the board threaten to house him at the poor farm because his children "will not stand for the stigma of sending him to the County Farm." It was not recorded whether this threat brought Nichols's children around, but there was no question that the poor farm was populated mainly by aged indigents or that other elderly people were at least partially dependent upon county general assistance. The Depression exacerbated the plight of the aged, who were among the first to be laid off and the last to be rehired and who were especially vulnerable to bank failures that wiped out the savings of a lifetime. Sensitive to the problems of the indigent aged and of the counties called upon to provide them with some support, the legislature created a modest pension plan in 1933 that provided five to eight dollars per month. By March 1935, 242 Cass Countians—including 152 Fargoans—were receiving these pensions.[75]

Pensions of this size were the best the beleaguered state could do, but they were insufficient by any definition. In place of such penurious outlays, supporters of the Townsend Old-Age Pension Plan favored a liberal pension that would allow the aged to live in dignity while bringing economic recovery. The Townsend Plan was the brainchild of Francis Townsend, a retired physician living in Long Beach, California. Townsend's idea was that every person sixty or older should receive a pension of $200 per month, on the conditions that he or she withdraw from employment and spend the entire pension every month within the United States. The pension feature of the Townsend Plan was especially attractive to the elderly, of course, but younger people saw jobs opening when pensioners withdrew from employment, and many believed the massive economic stimulus entailed by pension expenditures would rapidly end the Depression.[76]

Townsend Clubs, formed by supporters of the plan, sprang up all over the country in 1934 and 1935. In September 1934 an organizational meeting at Island Park drew 800 participants, who were divided into ten clubs. Within a few days Fargo's Townsend Clubs were claiming a membership of 1,500, and in late December a spokesman told the City Commission there were 6,000 members in town—about one-fifth of Fargo's population. These figures were likely inflated, but the plan did generate substantial enthusiasm. When Townsend visited the city in July 1935 he spoke to a large rally at Island Park and then to a crowd that overflowed Central High's 1,500-seat auditorium and spilled into the streets, where "many score stood . . . and heard his address through amplifiers." There were enough Townsendites to command the respectful attention of such local politicians as Congressman William Lemke and of the County Commission and the City Commission, both of which resolved that the Townsend Plan or something similar should be made the basis for a national pension system.[77]

The Townsend Clubs attracted members who did not usually share political positions. One of their leaders was city commissioner W. E. Black, who customarily took a conservative, pro-taxpayer stance on local spending issues, and Townsendites writing to the *Forum* frequently assumed an anti–New Deal position. "We have been living in an age of experimentation and getting nowhere," wrote one Fargo Townsendite, "the ranks of the unemployed are greater now than ever before, the disbursement of relief money is greater than ever, the future taxes will be greater than ever. Therefore as long as we are experimenting and getting nowhere why not try a plan that it is claimed will stimulate business, [and] eradicate to a great extent the government expenditure of taxpayers' money." Another Townsendite claimed, "the Townsend Plan will correct the present abortive morals-destroying method of partial employment in make-believe jobs through state and national welfare agencies." On the other side of the political spectrum were local radicals C. C. Snyder, Lee Brooks, and Quentin Burdick, son of state Farmers Holiday Association leader and western North Dakota congressman Usher.[78]

Congress did not adopt the Townsend Plan or anything close to it, but it did provide funds for a more liberal pension plan than North Dakota's under the Social Security Act in 1935. The Social Security Act was concerned mainly with creating a system of old-age and survivors' pensions financed by workers and their employers, but it also provided for Old-Age Assistance to benefit existing indigent elderly on a matching basis with states. In North Dakota the maximum pension was set at twenty dollars per month, half of which came from the federal government with one-quarter each contributed by the state and the county. These pensions were clearly welfare rather than an entitlement. Applicants had to pass a means test proving that they lacked the resources to support themselves, they had to demonstrate that they had no children capable of caring for them, and they were required to sign their real property over to the county to cover the cost of the aid they received. Welfare officials estimated that no more than 500 people in the county were eligible for the pensions, but despite their humiliating requirements 762 applied in the first five months Old-Age Assistance was available.[79]

The average Cass County pensioner received $17.99 per month, which was not much, and the insufficiency of Old-Age Assistance meant that the Townsend Clubs continued to thrive and to criticize the New Deal's solutions for the problems of the aged. The Townsend movement eventually died out in Fargo, however, in part because of political differences, as in 1938 when several clubs were expelled by the national organization for failing to support the reelection of Senator Gerald Nye. Even though the payments were small and the requirements humiliating, Old-Age Assistance allowed some of the aged to avoid public institutional care and to maintain a life of some independence and a modicum of dignity. As early as 1938 the *Forum* reported that most of the aged had "vacated" the poor farm and were receiving Old-Age Assistance, foreshadowing the demise of an institution that had long provided care to aged indigents.[80]

County finances were further improved by another program created under Social Security, Aid for Dependent Children. Prior to the Depression widowed, divorced, and abandoned women with dependent children could receive mothers' pensions. With the onset of the New Deal, Cass County shifted mothers' pension recipients and most other "unemployables" to FERA relief as a means of diminishing county outlays. In 1935 Congress decided that the relief it would provide in the future would all be work relief under the WPA, with unemployables covered by such Social Security programs as Old-Age Assistance and ADC. One-third of the cost of ADC in North Dakota was paid for by the federal government, with the state and the counties covering the balance.

ADC was similar to Old-Age Assistance in that recipients had to pass a degrading means test and payments were quite low, averaging only $11.62 per child per month in North Dakota in 1939, but the program clearly met a substantial need. In 1940, 535 children in Cass County were receiving ADC, 210 whose fathers were absent and another 181 whose fathers were dead. Despite the illiberality of the program, because of ADC "security has been furnished families on the verge of breaking up, with the consequent elimination of many imminent behavior problems." In October 1938 the County Welfare Board discussed the case of short-order cook Bertha Swanson, who had "always boarded . . . out" her four children but because "we stepped in with ADC" was able to keep them. Swanson's story was hardly unique. The Lutheran Home Society reported in August 1939 that "several children who have been under the care of our society have had the experience of returning to the homes of relatives or have been reunited with a mother through the assistance of the Aid to Dependent Children Program. It gives many children the security and sense of 'belonging' which many children crave and which is their birthright." Skimpy though it was, ADC gave some comfort to the Bertha Swansons of the world and to their children. Not coincidentally, it helped to doom most orphanages in the United States and substantially reduced the burdens on taxpayers in Cass County and elsewhere, who no longer had to pay to keep children institutionalized.[81]

Federal programs contributed a great deal to Fargo during the Depression. FHA loans made property more secure and enhanced the ability of more people to acquire homes. Funds for public works allowed the city to address infrastructural problems. Welfare programs relieved the burdens on property taxpayers and constituted a safety net that benefited many residents.

All of this was positive, but the economic stimulus was most noticeable. In April 1934 the *Forum* attributed a decided upturn in retail trade to "millions in government money pouring into this territory in recent months." In July the newspaper noted that, with 240 federal workers in the city and more being hired every day, the federal building was bursting at the seams. The end of the year saw the "best Christmas trade in years," and it was announced that bank deposits had surged by better than 13 percent in just twelve months. Small wonder that incoming Chamber of Commerce president H. G. Nilles felt confident enough to announce that "we are over the hump, [and] should prepare for increasing prosperity."[82]

"Over the hump," and with the dark days of 1932–33 fading into memory, some Fargoans forgot how they got where they were. It was easy to fall back on

the old bromides of self-help and cooperative individualism and to fashion reassuring myths about recovery. Welcoming President Roosevelt to the state in
August 1936, the *Forum* editorialized that "he will meet with a strong, self-
reliant people." It took a huge dose of self-delusion to believe such a prepos-
terous notion. As Fargoans returned to their comfortable illusions, the federal
programs they had welcomed a few years before seemed overly bureaucratic
and intrusive. They began to worry, as Daniel Heitmeyer worried, about debts
and taxes. And they worried most of all about relief—not about its tangible
products but about the people who depended on it to live. As Fargoans became more comfortable with themselves they became less comfortable with the
New Deal, and the federal introduction with which they were most ill at ease
was relief.[83]

4

"In addition to these tangible, material advantages and results of this [WPA sewing] project, there are those intangible benefits that count for a great deal in life—our president likes to refer to them as spiritual and moral values. Who can not realize that through this project the morale of those employed has been raised by giving them an opportunity to really earn a living by constructive, creative work."

Interested Homemaker, March 28, 1936

"I think a lot of these people who are on relief are better off than we are."

Helen Kennedy, April 11, 1934

RELIEF WAS THE GREAT CONUNDRUM in Fargo during the Depression. Virtually everyone welcomed the federal money that flowed into the city, and the tangible products of work relief enriched the lives of most citizens. Relief met a human need the local community lacked the means to meet, and it reduced the burden on local taxpayers. At the same time, some Fargoans worried about a loss of self-reliance on the part of recipients and the effects of that phenomenon on the community and on society. More disturbing were the attitudes of those seeking relief, which seemed to change in ways that made many uncomfortable. Deferential, humble, and a bit ashamed in the early years of the Depression, indigents had by 1934 become proud, assertive, and even aggressive. As the attitudes of reliefers changed, local disdain for them and the programs that sustained them intensified and fissures opened in the community, along class lines to some degree, but more between those on relief and those off.

In much of North Dakota relief was the normal condition of life in the thirties. The combination of drought and depression put half of the state's heads of families on some form of assistance for parts of both 1934 and 1936, and throughout the decade relief rolls were long. In central and western North Dakota, where yields were relatively low even in normal times and where drought was particularly severe, relief was an especially prominent feature of life.[1]

Cass County was different. Through most of the Depression the percentage of its residents on relief stood at one-half or one-third of the state rate, frequently including under ten percent of families. In August 1937, for example, when nearly one in four people in the state were receiving public assistance, only nine percent of Cass Countians were similarly circumstanced. Four months later, when over 38 percent of North Dakotans were on relief, only 16.4 percent of people in Cass received public assistance. And so it went throughout the thirties. Much of the reason for the disparity can be explained by the fact that farmers in the rich Red River Valley counties were relatively prosperous and made crops even in the driest years. Certainly, the other valley counties were usually clumped with Cass at the bottom of the public assistance lists. Then, too, Fargo enjoyed the most diversified economy in the state and an employment profile disproportionately oriented to the sort of service occupations that were somewhat resistant to the Depression.[2]

But there was more to low participation in relief programs than economics alone. County relief director T. A. Hendricks, Jr., candidly estimated that one-third of Cass Countians were eligible for relief. What kept them off the rolls? Part of the reason for nonparticipation was the stigma that attached to those receiving government aid. "It was a disgrace to go on relief, it really was," one Fargoan remembered in 1974, "people were ashamed of themselves if they went on relief. It was a sin if you had to accept welfare. People were very, very proud." Pride was perhaps as significant as need in distinguishing those who could go on relief and didn't from those who did. Fargoans valued self-reliance and "resourcefulness" and sometimes considered presence on the relief rolls to be evidence of moral weakness. As a result "most people who needed help were too proud to ask."[3]

Stigma and relative need thus worked in tandem to keep Cass relief rolls short. Had need been overwhelming, as it was in the central and western counties, so many people would have been on the rolls that the stigma would have diminished, encouraging still others to overcome their aversion to accepting relief. But with just a small minority on the rolls, the majority opinion held sway, and relief continued to be viewed by many as evidence of characterological inferiority and moral weakness.

The stigma that attached to relief kept most of those who could have been on it off and increased the suspicion directed at those who sought public assistance. While there were those such as "Interested Homemaker" who stressed that work relief raised recipients' morale, the County Relief Office made the process of receiving aid demeaning and humiliating, stimulating conflicts with federal relief officials who sought to preserve relief clients' dignity. The degradations of relief kept some from applying at all and were accepted by others as an inevitable part of the process, but as the Depression wore on recipients increasingly resisted, demanding respectful treatment and claiming relief as their right as citizens. This increasingly prominent attitude further eroded sympathy for reliefers in town and contributed to growing alienation between Fargoans on relief and those off. Men and women who were expected to be grateful and humble were resentful and proud. They wanted to live as well as those who were not on relief, wanted full control of the resources they received, and wanted to direct their own lives according to their own standards rather than the standards set by case-workers or the County Welfare Board. Small wonder that many Fargoans came to believe, with social worker Helen Kennedy, that "these people who are on relief are better off than we are." For Fargoans like Kennedy, relief turned the world upside-down, and they wanted it righted again.[4]

I

Relief burdens and responsibilities overwhelmed the Cass County Commission in the winter of 1932–33. A relief system and bureaucratic structure meant to respond mainly to unemployables in generally prosperous times were found deficient when confronted by the unprecedented calamity of the Great Depression. Poor relief, including mothers' pensions and maintenance of the poor farm as well as county general assistance, was consuming nearly half of the budget. Help came from the Red Cross, in the form of surplus flour and cotton cloth, and the Reconstruction Finance Corporation, in the form of a $40,000 loan under the Emergency Relief and Construction Act, but these resources ironically added to the demands on a County Relief Office that had more than it could manage just investigating applicants for aid.

Criticism of the way the County Commission was handling relief came from several disparate sources, including the Taxpayers Association, the Chamber of Commerce, the Trades and Labor Assembly, the Community Welfare Association, and the *Forum*. In late January 1933 Albert Evans, midwestern director of disaster relief for the American Red Cross, was invited to Fargo by the Community Welfare Association to undertake "a survey of work of relief agencies" and suggest ways "to increase the efficiency of poor relief work in Fargo and Cass county by eliminating duplications and other weaknesses." On February 11, Evans charged that "present administration of poor relief in

Fargo and Cass county is woefully lacking." Specifically, Evans criticized du-
plication of services between private relief agencies and the county, reluctance
on the part of relief agencies to compel clients to engage in self-help activities,
and the tendency to ignore the requirement that recipients work for relief. The
basic problem, in Evans's view, was that no one was responsible. The County
Relief Office was swamped, and neither the Community Welfare Association
nor the County Commission had anyone whose job it was to run an efficient
relief system. His solution was an independent welfare board, a professional
relief administrator, and a corps of trained social workers. At Evans's urging, a
committee of nine was named to look into making these changes.[5]

The County Commission staggered under the growing relief burden, but
it was reluctant to surrender power to an independent board and a professional
administrator. In normal times, county commissioners enjoyed passing relief
out to favored constituents and viewed jobs in the Relief Office as political patronage, and they were understandably averse to taxing and appropriating
money while surrendering control over how it was spent. Pressure was intense,
however, especially from *Forum* editor H. D. ("Happy") Paulson, who was
credited by journalist and New Deal insider Lorena Hickok with leading "the
battle to take control of the relief show away from the county commissioners."
Paulson maintained a steady flow of editorial criticism, arguing that the existing system encouraged "poor relief racketeers" and contending that "poor relief . . . has reached such proportions that it cannot be permitted to move on-
ward and upward without the strictest kind of supervision, without the closest
kind of watching."[6]

The County Commission avoided the inevitable for a few weeks, but on
April 7 it succumbed to the pressure and voted to create a County Welfare
Board of five members representing all of the relief stakeholders, with the significant exception of the clients. Hugh C. Corrigan and Anna Stevens of Fargo
represented the Community Welfare Association, A. L. Engen and P. H. Burton represented the Taxpayers Association, and Joe Runck of rural Cass represented the County Commission. The commissioners urged the board "to
obtain a man to be at the head of the County Relief Office," reflecting the
widely held assumption that a male would be tougher and less kind-hearted
toward recipients than a female. The board got their "man" a month later, appointing Thomas A. Hendricks, Jr., secretary of the "Anti-Begging Committee" of St. Louis. Conveniently enough, Hendricks was recommended highly
by fellow St. Louisian and Red Cross investigator Albert Evans.[7]

The County Commission's apparent surrender of authority to the welfare board and a professional administrator was not enthusiastic, nor did it prevent the commission from meddling in relief administration throughout the balance of the Depression. Clients discontented with the Relief Office or the welfare board found sympathetic ears on the County Commission, which was not notably favorable to reliefers otherwise. In November 1933 the County Commission held a hearing for a number of complainants "protesting some of the work in connection with the relief department" and contending that clients "had been roughly treated and . . . that the poor were not receiving sufficient help." In March 1934 a more serious conflict developed when three hundred angry men, led by L. W. Bray of the Trades and Labor Assembly, crowded into the courthouse to demand that the commissioners dissolve the welfare board, fire Hendricks, and resume control over relief in the county. The petitioners damned Hendricks for unfairness, "inefficiency and incompetency." The commissioners contemplated dissolution of the board but backed off when confronted by the Taxpayers Association, the City Commission, the Chamber of Commerce, and the Community Welfare Association, all of which supported the new arrangement. Further tempering the commission's response was fear that destruction of an independent board, preferred by the federal government, would imperil the flow of relief dollars from Washington.[8]

The ongoing controversy among the commission, the board, and Hendricks flared again in May 1934, when the board requested "that the Cass county board of commissioners submit in writing its sentiment regarding the present relief setup in Cass county and the attitude of the board regarding T. A. Hendricks, relief director." The commissioners answered with detailed criticisms of the board and Hendricks, accusing the latter of ignoring the rural poor, depending too much on inexperienced office help, overstating budgetary savings achieved by his agency, and failing to keep the commission informed regarding relief activities. The commission conceded, however, that "inasmuch as the federal government requires a setup similar to that which we have in Cass county . . . we must, in order to receive these funds, conform as nearly as possible to the federal requirements both as to state and county Welfare Boards, directors, etc."[9]

In 1935 the conflict over control of relief resurfaced when the North Dakota Public Welfare Board suggested that the County Welfare Board be expanded to seven members, while the commission wanted to limit it to five, two of whom were to be commissioners. The Public Welfare Board worried that if the number of commissioners was doubled "the commissioners would tend to be the dominating influence." That was the whole idea, and the commission stood firm for several months, during which time board chairman Hugh Corrigan and relief director Hendricks, both disgusted by commission interference, resigned. But the commission eventually capitulated to the people who paid the piper, in August agreeing to a board of seven, including two commissioners, and in December signing an agreement with the Public Welfare Board "authorizing the county Welfare Board to obligate the county for relief purposes, which in effect virtually makes the Welfare Board entirely responsible for relief work and expenditures."[10]

The County Commission retreated frequently but never surrendered. In April 1936 a bitter controversy broke out between W. F. Sutton and Oscar Covert, county commissioners on the welfare board, and the other members. At Sutton's behest, the board had hired Florence Nelson as purchasing agent, agreeing to pay her $100 per month plus mileage. At the March 3 board meeting, Nelson submitted a mileage bill for $42.85 that P. H. Burton and other board members considered too high. After the board cut Nelson's mileage compensation in half, Sutton attacked Burton, saying he would no longer sit on the board with him. Burton and three other board members responded by resigning because, as he put it, "the commission wants to handle relief under the 'spoils' system, [and] I refuse to be a party to it." The commission won this round, appointing replacements for the protesting four who were acceptable to the state welfare board.[11]

Relations with the County Commission complicated the welfare board's job of administering relief in Cass County. So, too, did relations with the state, where political interference in relief administration was so blatant that the federal government seized control from governor Bill Langer's State Emergency Relief Administration in 1934. The federal government further complicated the work of the welfare board by setting standards and writing regulations with which local relief officials and governments did not always agree, standards and regulations reflecting starkly different views of relief and reliefers than those held locally. Intergovernmental relations made the board's work harder, but they were hardly the only challenges it faced.

II

The functions and responsibilities of the County Relief Office demonstrated the variety and complexity of relief in the New Deal era. The office supported a staff of fifty to sixty-five during the mid-thirties, when it was at its largest, about two-thirds of whom were case-workers. The load varied, but in 1934 the monthly average was a little under 2,900 clients, or about six percent of the county's population. The pool of clients was not stable, however, meaning that over the course of a year as many as one-third of residents had some contact with the office. About three-fourths of the case load was in Fargo, which had a little over half of the county's population.[12]

Welfare board member Anna Stevens said in 1974 that "it was our goal that no one in Cass County should be hungry, in distress, or frightened," and the county had several tools at its disposal to achieve that end. In addition to playing an administrative role in the high-profile federal relief programs, the welfare board continued to maintain the poor farm and the county hospital and to provide general assistance and mothers' pensions.[13]

County general assistance was especially important in supplementing the incomes of seasonal workers or of full-time workers whose jobs paid too little to provide them with the means of self-support. In 1936, for example, the Frank Innis family of six received $70.13 in February and $47.83 in March, but they were off assistance in May and did not need help again until December. In June 1935 the board decided to supplement the income of a mother who was earning $4 a week working in a candy store. And in April 1934 the board voted $0.80 per week to augment the earnings of Wanda Nolan, sixty-eight, who sold flowers on the street. Aid to such persons usually came in the form of rent, grocery, or coal vouchers, though they could also receive surplus commodities, renovated clothing, and other items from a commissary in the basement of Washington School, a lower Front Street neighborhood school closed by the school board during the 1933 budget cutting and turned over to the Relief Office.[14]

The welfare board was also responsible for providing care for orphans and abandoned and illegitimate children, as well as for people with severe mental and physical disabilities who lacked family members willing or able to care for them. In September 1935, for example, the board dealt with the case of Abbie Berenstein, a Russian-Jewish immigrant who was judged insane and who had given birth to a son out of wedlock. The board decided to place Berenstein at the state mental hospital in Jamestown and to board her child with foster parents.[15]

Much of the Relief Office's attention was devoted to maintaining the health of clients. The county provided glasses and dental care for the indigent, though they frequently had to wait months for aid. The county retained a physician, but the $85 per month it paid was insufficient to hold anyone very good. H. M. Knudtson quit in 1934 because of the workload, and the only physician who would take his place was judged to be "drunk three fourths of the time." The board was especially concerned about infant health and high birthrates, which it tried to lower by encouraging birth control. Syphilis was also a major problem, reaching such epidemic proportions in 1937 that the board considered closing the sewing room, where its incidence was judged to be particularly alarming.[16]

The provision of adequate housing was a major challenge for the Relief Office during the Depression. The board agreed in June 1933 to pay no more than $12 per month for rent, but in a city with a housing shortage few livable dwellings were available at that price. Indeed, a Department of Commerce study in 1934 concluded that only five to six percent of the homes in the city could be rented for $12 or less. Some clients were housed in cheap apartments such as the Riverside, at the foot of Second Street North, but Fargo police-woman Alice Duffy and school truant officer Mary Maid protested that the Riverside was little more than a house of ill fame and was especially inappropriate for children. Another possible solution was to house clients in barracks on the grounds of the poor farm, though that idea was eventually dismissed because of its demoralizing effect on family life. Many reliefers, in common with other poor people in Fargo, lived in shacks they erected on vacant land. There were not many options for people with few resources in a city where housing was scarce and expensive.[17]

The poor had always received services and some supervision from the county, but with an independent board and a professional director it was possible for the Relief Office to encourage self-reliance and self-support in a more systematic way. The office taught cooking, canning, and clothing repair and devised menus for clients. Because FERA paid "deficiency wages" covering only the difference between resources and needs, case-workers were required to work with clients to develop strict family budgets. Relief clients were compelled to raise gardens to provide for part of their winter needs; those who refused were "cut off the rolls." In addition, the office maintained large community gardens, whose products were canned and put in the commissary for distribution to recipients of aid. In 1935 the gardening and canning project produced 2,880 cans of vegetables, 4,500 heads of cabbage, and 432 bushels of carrots, which seems impressive until one realizes there were over two thousand clients in Fargo to consume this food. Many relief activities returned relatively little in relation to the effort that went into them. In the fall of 1933 it was reported that the total value of wood produced in the wood-chopping project did not even cover the superintendent's salary and that it would be cheaper for the county to buy firewood from dealers. Other local work relief ideas were somewhat more imaginative and productive. In December 1934 board chairman Hugh Corrigan came up with the idea of having relief recipients repair and/or renovate the houses in which they were living. Corrigan noted that landlords could not afford to maintain dwellings rented at $12 a month, resulting in degradation for both their property and their tenants, but that they might be willing to buy the materials if tenants would supply the labor. FERA allowed more than $26,000 for work relief on this project. A related idea, to have recipients repair the homes of property taxpayers as a return on their investment in relief, was considered but rejected.[18]

In the early phase of the New Deal the Relief Office was mainly responsible for determining relief eligibility, deciding how funds would be distributed, identifying work projects, and supervising clients' work. The federal government had neither the time nor the inclination to create a large relief bureaucracy and write a complex set of rules in 1933, so FERA turned relief responsibilities and funds over to the states, which in turn passed them on to localities. This meant that the welfare board in Cass County, operating through Hendricks's office, set its own standards for relief recipients, mandating residency and a means test. The board decided how clients would be paid, continuing the voucher system with which it was familiar and comfortable. The board and the Relief Office worked closely with public agencies to identify suitable work projects, and the office provided overall supervision of the work.[19]

Because control was local, practices and procedures reflected the attitudes of most Fargo social workers and relief officials—and probably most employed citizens—regarding those on relief. Those in need of aid were frequently viewed as objects of pity or as people with some sort of moral defect that demanded correction. Consequently, the Relief Office supervised clients closely and managed the resources available to them. Federal relief officials, by contrast, tended to view clients as victims of bad fortune or economic maladjustment and to stress that their dignity must be respected and they must control the resources they received. As the Depression lengthened and the federal government assumed a larger role in local relief, this divergence in perceptions became the source of conflicts and alienated many Fargoans not on relief from the system and its clients.[20]

Men on FERA work relief were directly supervised by the city, park board, North Dakota Agricultural College, or some other agency, under county oversight, but the Relief Office itself was in charge of supervising most projects employing women. In June 1933, when it became apparent that there would be a substantial amount of work relief for females, Helen Ewing was hired to do the job of supervising women, a task previously handled by volunteers.

Barnett Field, home of the Fargo-Moorhead Twins baseball team, was built with WPA labor in 1936.

Priority for public employment on most federal relief programs went to heads of families, which were usually men but also included women with dependents who were divorced, widowed, abandoned, or never married at all. Many women in these categories were receiving mothers' pensions in 1933 but were shifted to work relief to ease pressures on the county budget. Additionally, women whose husbands were unable to work could usually get on work relief. Gladys Welton's husband had to leave his WPA job for a time because he was ill, "so I went to work for the WPA on the sewing project. Only one person in the family could work on WPA at a time so I could work only while John was sick."[21]

The sewing room, which employed twenty-five to one hundred women at any given time, depending on the availability of relief funds, was a standard in federal work relief operations for women around the country. The Relief Office also developed a large bookbinding project employing women to repair library materials; a quilt, comforter, and bedding-making project employing about seventy-five women; and a mattress factory which employed men and women. Other female clients did clerical work at the Relief Office, supervised recreation for the park board, taught in the public schools, or were hired as nurses and housekeepers for families on relief. Physical products of work relief such as mattresses, bedding, or garments usually ended up in the commissary for distribution to other clients.[22]

The Relief Office also supported a nursery school that provided day care for children from "relief, WPA, and borderline homes." As historian Elizabeth Rose has demonstrated, such facilities were common throughout the country. The Fargo Nursery School opened in 1933 in temporary quarters in Woodrow Wilson School. After a brief stay at the First Baptist Church, it received a permanent home when the City Commission gave it a house in the lower Front Street neighborhood. The school had a capacity of thirty originally, expanded to sixty in 1937. The Fargo Nursery School advanced work relief in three ways: it was staffed by unemployed teachers, it allowed mothers to take jobs or work relief, and it had men on relief provide transportation for the children enrolled. The school provided medical care and nutritious food for children and, as the *Forum* condescendingly put it, taught "them self help and habits of cleanliness, all of which is hoped will carry over into the home." Even as solicitude for adults on relief flagged, there was great sympathy for poor children in Fargo, presumably because they were pitied as innocent victims of their parents' shortcomings. The Fargo Nursery School thus became a great community project. In addition to the city's contribution of a house, the welfare board provided coal, the Community Chest purchased play equipment, and the Junior Chamber of Commerce and several women's groups raised money for maintenance and remodeling.[23]

With the creation of the Works Progress Administration in 1935 local control over federal relief programs declined precipitously. Unlike the FERA and the CWA, which had been conceived as temporary, emergency programs that would go out of existence when prosperity returned, the WPA was created to be a permanent provider of public employment. It was based on the assumptions that the Depression would probably go on for a long time and that unemployment of employables would be a permanent feature of a mature, slow-growth economy. WPA head Harry Hopkins saw the agency as a public employer rather than an unemployment relief agency. He believed its projects should be of lasting value to the community, its clients should be treated as first-class citizens entitled to public work, and recipients of its relief should earn cash and make their own decisions regarding how to spend it. These ideas were usually sharply at variance with those held by local relief officials, and putting them into effect demanded much greater federal control than had been the case with FERA. Federal eligibility rules were devised that took precedence over local ones, cash payments replaced the voucher system, and WPA bureaucrats undertook supervision of large-scale projects.

The theory of public work and recipient dignity held by Hopkins and his agency was humane and even noble, but practice was something else. As a practical matter, "public employment" was not easily separated from the unemployment relief it supposedly replaced. WPA workers were drawn mainly from local relief rolls. Because WPA employment was sporadic, projects were completed, pay was sometimes inadequate, and family crises arose, clients were periodically back on those rolls, depending on county general assistance and on local charities to supplement their WPA earnings. The welfare board and the Relief Office had a view of clients that differed drastically from that held by the WPA. While the latter treated clients as employees with dignity who should have control over their earnings, local authorities saw them as reliefers with character flaws that needed correction and as irresponsible people likely to waste the resources they received. One result of this divergence was friction between federal and local officials. Another result was a sharp disjuncture in the lives of clients, treated with respect in one setting and humiliated in another. Differences in treatment of reliefers, and differences in their expectations of relief, were most pronounced in the endless controversies over supplementation.

The welfare board and the Relief Office were almost immediately presented with demands for supplementation from families unable to live on the $40 monthly wage for common labor set by the WPA in 1935. In October 1935 the Majewski family complained to the welfare board that the WPA wage was insufficient to support their two adults and six children. The Relief Office initially attributed their problems to character flaws. Relief director Mary McKone, who succeeded Hendricks when he resigned in the summer of 1935, blamed the Majewskis' problems on the fact they were Polish immigrants who did not understand the country, on Mrs. Majewski's "untruthful and vindictive" nature, and on immorality, as evidenced by the presence in the home of an illegitimate five-year-old borne by one of the daughters. Whatever their real or supposed failings, however, the Majewskis were not the only people having trouble making ends meet on WPA wages. Indeed, a group of WPA workers threatened to quit and go back on county general assistance, which better met their needs, until they were dissuaded by the threat that they would be tossed off relief altogether if they left the WPA.[24]

Extraordinary problems further increased demands for supplementation. During the desperately cold winter of 1935–36, when the temperature did not rise above zero for over a month, the Relief Office had to provide coal orders and surplus clothing to WPA families. Supplementation was also necessary when federal checks were late, as was frequently the case. Clients were supposed to reimburse the county when their checks arrived, but they did not always do so. R. M. Parkins, who became relief director in May 1936, explained the problem to the welfare board in January 1937: "Their check is a few days late; we guarantee their grocery and fuel order and they agree to take care of it as soon as their check comes in, and when their check comes they forget all about it. . . . Mrs. Hallenberg [a case-worker] has about 10 or 12 families that have jipped [*sic*] her on guarantees."[25]

Those seeking supplementation from the county and those needing county general assistance to cover gaps in WPA employment were reminded that they were on relief and that relief was humiliating. Getting on relief remained difficult, by design. As the welfare board put it in January 1937, the Relief Office should "make it as tough as possible for them to come on relief." Applicants for relief were required to prove their eligibility. First, they needed to show they had lived in Cass County for at least one year. The welfare board believed, apparently with some justification, that "Cass County has been the Santa Claus county for the west," on which poorer North Dakota counties dumped their indigents. Close investigation of residency limited the problem, though it was never solved entirely. Second, applicants had to pass a means test demonstrating that they lacked property sufficient for self-support, with "at least two visits of investigation" conducted by social workers to uncover any hidden assets. Third, the applicant had to attest that he or she lacked relatives who were willing or able to provide aid. Investigations did not cease once one was certified as eligible to receive relief. Applicants cleared by the Intake Department were assigned case-workers who watched for those secretly holding jobs, receiving aid surreptitiously from Community Chest agencies, or engaging in such underground income-producing activities as bootlegging and prostitution. Those receiving income were quickly purged from the rolls, as in 1936 when thirty-two veterans receiving bonus checks were dropped from relief.[26]

The degradation involved in the process violated all of the WPA's assumptions regarding clients and is difficult to reconcile with Anna Stevens's remarks about the altruistic goals of the welfare board. But Stevens knew that the very survival of county assistance depended on limiting the numbers on the rolls. The humiliations attendant on receiving relief were one of the reasons only a minority of those who qualified for it applied. Those humiliations were also necessary to reassure the working, taxpaying public, which would support relief only if it was reasonably confident that every effort was made to keep the "chiselers" off the lists. One alternative to degrading, humiliating relief was a relief such as that envisioned by Hopkins, one that preserved the recipient's dignity. Another was no relief at all. To the minds of some, relief was not humiliating enough even as it was. In December 1934 welfare board member Joe Runck suggested that "it would be a good plan to publish a list of names of those people on relief. That by doing so, the number of people on relief could be cut down." Bad as it was, it could have been worse, and Anna Stevens and others committed to the poor knew it.[27]

Differences between the federal and the local attitudes regarding clients could be seen not only in the assumptions of relief officials but in the details of disbursement as well. The federal government preferred from the beginning of the New Deal that clients be paid cash for work relief so as to preserve their dignity and self-respect, while Cass County customarily provided vouchers for rent, groceries, coal, and other necessities. The voucher system was at once demeaning for recipients and expensive for the county, due to the record keeping involved, but it reflected the belief that public charges could not be trusted to use public resources wisely. When FERA went into operation in 1933 the Relief Office continued to compensate landlords directly or through rent vouchers and to provide grocery vouchers that could be redeemed at the Central and Waldorf markets, which had agreed to charge just five percent over cost on reliefers' orders. These practices ran counter to federal preference, and the grocery arrangement angered both clients, who wanted to shop around or buy at convenient neighborhood stores, and other grocers, who wanted a piece of reliefers' business. In July the welfare board amended its policies, providing cash for clients to pay rent and allowing grocery vouchers to be redeemed anywhere in town. When the WPA went into effect, workers seeking supplementation got grocery vouchers instead of cash.[28]

The county required that grocery vouchers be exchanged only for items on an approved list, and grocers were responsible for providing detailed bills to the Relief Office demonstrating the rules had been followed. Practice, however, was another matter. Clients sometimes sold "their grocery order" to grocers or others "so they could use the money to buy drinks." More often grocers connived with clients to falsify bills of sale, claiming that reliefers were receiving foodstuffs exclusively when such forbidden items as cigarettes or cosmetics were included in their orders. It was also common for grocers to give change instead of credit, in violation of Relief Office rules. The Relief Office knew that abuses of the voucher system were occurring and vowed to end them.[29]

In January 1937 a Relief Office investigation revealed that twenty-nine of thirty grocers had falsified bills, listing approved items when they had in fact allowed reliefers "to buy tobacco, canned peaches, and other prohibited articles." "The long period of depression apparently has caused a lowering of the morale of many of the people," concluded board member Charles Pollock, who was shocked by the duplicitous behavior of clients and grocers. The possibility that the board's own demeaning policy had turned clients into chiselers apparently did not enter his mind.[30]

There were also differences between federal and local relief authorities over ownership and operation of cars. As relief director Parkins explained it in 1939, the welfare board "did not feel that an automobile was a necessity, and . . . when they are operated by relief clients they use money that should be used for food and clothing for the children." WPA workers were not required to surrender their cars, but when they needed county general assistance they were required to "put it up on blocks and remove tires and wheels, and turn in the license plates to the county welfare office to be considered for direct aid." Some undoubtedly did, but continuing complaints about reliefers with cars indicates that some hid their automobiles or otherwise evaded the humiliating rule.[31]

Unlike the WPA, the Relief Office regularly denied aid to those whose personal behaviors it deemed morally reprehensible, as in February 1939 when it refused a grocery order to Fred Remsberger because he "had been in a pool hall playing the pin ball machines." Use of alcohol by clients was especially abhorrent to local relief authorities. Responding to complaints in the summer of 1936 that a number of "WPA workers were spending much of the paychecks for liquor," the board noted that it lacked authority over workers on WPA projects but that it would deny supplementation to such men if and when they requested it. A few months later two WPA workers who spent their wages on liquor were arrested for nonsupport of their families when their wives requested county relief. Arrest for nonsupport was grounds for removal from WPA rolls, placing these families back on county assistance. Shortly thereafter the City Commission passed an ordinance prohibiting liquor dealers from serving anyone on a "drunkard's directory" composed of fifty-two names from the relief rolls "against whom complaints have been made at some time by members of the family that relief money was spent for liquor while the family went without necessities." Parkins assured the *Forum* that one did not need to be a "habitual drunkard" to be listed in the directory—it was sufficient that someone had complained about him or her at some time in the past. "The Relief Office is not opposed to a relief client having a glass or two of beer . . ." Parkins explained, "but when it comes to a point where relief clients spend a large portion of their relief money for liquor while members of their families either go hungry or are compelled to go to the Relief Office for additional help, drastic steps must be taken." The campaign against alcohol use among relief clients reflected a widely held social perception that immoral behavior was more common among relief recipients than others and that it was probably at least part of the explanation for their need for public aid. In a March 1940 survey of local drinking habits undertaken by the national Women's Christian Temperance Union, one of the questions asked was "To what extent are relief checks cashed in your taverns?" The local WCTU affiliate answered that half to three-fourths of relief checks were cashed in such places and added that "approximately two-thirds of W.P.A. workers (men) drink." Both the question and the answer indicate how pervasive this expectation was.[32]

The practices of the welfare board and the Relief Office in exacting humiliations on recipients, treating them with suspicion, and closely managing their resources and their morals were well within one social work tradition. They were also likely supported by a substantial portion of the local community, those who believed that relief should be humiliating and hard to get, that reliefers should be ashamed, humble, and deferential, and that those seeking aid should not enjoy the same standard of living or the same rights to privacy and self-direction as those who provided the aid enjoyed. Long-time public charges probably accepted the county's rules and petty humiliations as the price that must be paid for help. But others on relief resisted the rules and the assumptions behind them—especially when their contrast with a federal system that stressed recipients' rights and dignity became crystal clear—and their resistance was increasingly organized.

Organization among relief recipients to defend their rights began early in the Depression. Unemployed councils and leagues, usually formed by Communists, Socialists, or other radicals, appeared in major cities as early as 1930. Unemployed exchanges were fertile ground for the organization of reliefers, and, indeed, the Cass County Unemployed Exchange was the first group systematically to assert the rights of the unemployed with local relief authorities. Organization advanced as the Depression deepened and touched families that were not traditional public charges, families that were used to being self-supporting and perhaps owned some property, families headed by men with skills and often some education. This was the conclusion of social scientists Gabriel Almond and Harold Lasswell, who found in 1934 that clients who behaved "aggressively" toward relief authorities were more likely than passive clients to be skilled, educated, young, white, and native born. Such people were more likely than long-term indigents to be proud, self-confident, and resistant to the demeaning treatments and paternalistic attempts to control behavior that were part and parcel of the relief experience in so many places. FERA, and especially the WPA, further encouraged organization among the unemployed, viewing it as one of their rights as American citizens. And as the Depression wore on and relief became a way of life for many of the unemployed, organization made sense as a means of asserting control over what was now viewed both by clients and federal relief officials as regular public employment.[33]

Following the demise of the Unemployed Exchange late in 1933, the task of representing the unemployed was assumed for a time by the Fargo Holiday Association and by the Trades and Labor Assembly, which had many unemployed members. The Holiday Association had apparently been affiliated originally with the Farmers Holiday, a powerful organization in North Dakota, but by early 1934 the two groups had parted company. By that time the Fargo Holiday was exclusively a labor organization, claiming a membership "of nearly a thousand red-blooded American citizens," most of whom were apparently unemployed. "Our physical holiday has been forced upon us," one member wrote the *Forum,* "but mentally we are not taking advantage of a holiday. We are beginning to do our own thinking."[34]

Holiday members, led by Socialist H. A. Morris and laborer Fritz Gransalke, confronted relief director Hendricks and the welfare board frequently and aggressively, especially in 1934. That year throughout the country there was an upsurge in organization and discontent among the unemployed, resulting in part from the jarring disjuncture many reliefers experienced in shifting from the high-paying, un-means-tested, dignity-preserving CWA winter program to locally controlled relief in the spring. Gransalke was especially contentious, demanding more prompt and courteous treatment for relief applicants, more freedom for clients to make their own choices with the resources they received, more liberal county supplementation of federal work relief funds, and inclusion of "a common man" on the welfare board. The tone of his criticism of county relief is nicely captured by this remark he made during an October 1934 meeting of the board: "I believe your relief is rotten. Let me inform you gentlemen of this fact. . . . If you gentlemen want to cooperate with us fine and dandy, but any time this winter a man goes without adequate relief we will . . . go into a store and take it. [We'll] see that this man gets it."[35]

The board, which believed clients should be humble and grateful, was uncertain how to handle Gransalke. Board chairman Corrigan thought Gransalke should be humored and worried that harsh treatment of him would encourage further organization among the unemployed: "If you get too many of these fellows organized you will have difficulty. A few of these fellows like Gransalke if handled properly will not cause trouble. But if you told them to get out of the office, etc., trouble would be started." Members P. H. Burton and Garfield Hoglund, on the other hand, wanted to devise some way to get Gransalke thrown in jail. Hoglund was especially adamant, perhaps because Gransalke had asked Governor Langer to remove him from the County Commission for his role in dismissing a holiday member from employment in the Relief Office. Eventually Gransalke was arrested. In December 1934, when the holiday was supporting workers striking the Knerr Dairy, Gransalke and three other men were charged with assaulting Ed Graunke, a Knerr buttermaker, on his way home from work. After this incident Gransalke slowly faded from the Fargo labor scene, eventually opening a café.[36]

The dairy strike of 1934 and a coal strike that followed early in 1935 were conducted by the "Organized Unemployed and Local Union 173," formed largely through the efforts of Miles Dunne, a Minneapolis Trotskyite. While the union organized dairy and coal drivers, many of its members were unemployed and on relief. In 1935 the union aggressively represented its members and other reliefers with the welfare board and the Relief Office. In January, for example, a conflict between commodity room manager Richard Bostwick and a client was "reported to the Union and Mr. Goldschmitz phoned me at home, want [ing] to know how long I was going to abuse people on relief." In March conflict flared again, when thirty to thirty-five women "marched on the county Relief Office" to protest the quantity and quality of food and clothing clients were receiving. A few days later Hendricks reported meeting with a committee of five from Local 173, who complained about the attitude of case-workers in the Relief Office as well as about some of their decisions.[37]

Beginning in the fall of 1935, reliefers in Fargo were represented mainly by the Workers Alliance, a nationwide union of WPA workers, though the Trades and Labor Assembly continued to appear before the welfare board when it concluded its members had been mistreated. The Workers Alliance focused especially on the supplementation of WPA wages, though it also struggled with the board periodically over whether clients or the board would decide how resources would be used and whether recipients had been mistreated by the Relief Office. In February 1937 the Workers Alliance presented a petition to the board demanding relief director Parkins's dismissal because "he was incompetent, inefficient, [and] showed partiality." In their detailed complaint, members of the Workers Alliance claimed that "the office here is dictatorial, arrogant, and condescending," that "clients come here and . . . they sit here sometimes for days, when they need food, shelter, and clothing," and that "there had been considerable discrimination."[38]

Parkins had a reputation for treating relief clients harshly. As relief director in Eddy County, he had crossed swords with the Farmers Holiday Association, which had complained about him to Senator Lynn Frazier and Congressman Usher Burdick and had demanded his removal. It is reasonable to assume that the Cass County Welfare Board, which had its hands full of aggressive and confrontational clients, got what it wanted when it hired Parkins. He certainly did not mellow when he came to Cass, and complaints about him continued, as in July 1940 when Harriet Davis wrote Burdick that she had pawned her washing machine and her husband's shotgun "and have sold dishes and my curtains out of my house" but that Parkins would not put her back on relief in the sewing room: "I have asked him to please put me back to work and he says to Hell with me."[39]

Removing Parkins was high on the Workers Alliance agenda, but it was not the only item. Repeating a demand that other advocacy groups had made, the Workers Alliance argued that labor and the unemployed should be represented on the board and among case-workers. There was no "genuine and sympathetic cooperation between the client and the social worker" because the latter lacked understanding of the former. "These caseworkers should be taken from the ranks of the people that are on relief," the Workers Alliance said, "because . . . they were better qualified to understand the needs of the client." On March 10 the board answered the Workers Alliance—though none of its members were allowed in the meeting room—by affirming its support for Parkins and endorsing the operations of the Relief Office.[40]

In 1935 an examination of organization among reliefers concluded that there was a fundamental conflict between relief unions, which wanted relief to be more secure, and relief authorities, who did not want people to become too comfortable on relief. That was certainly true in Fargo, but the differences between the organizations and relief authorities were far more fundamental and profound. The Holiday Association and the Workers Alliance believed that relief recipients were citizens in no way inferior to other citizens, that they deserved to be treated with dignity and respect, that they were entitled to the resources they received, and that they should make their own decisions regarding how those resources would be used. The Workers Alliance went beyond being merely an advocacy group, becoming a conventional labor union for its members. By 1939 it was even undertaking strikes in Fargo and Moorhead to attempt to reverse congressional budget cuts and new WPA restrictions. Whether relief unions and advocacy groups truly improved their members' conditions cannot be known, but they certainly upheld clients' morale, which was something the Relief Office and the welfare board claimed they wanted to do, too, their demeaning treatment of reliefers notwithstanding. Relief unions defended reliefers' rights and human dignity, refusing to accept the assumption that those in need and lacking resources were something less than first-class citizens. To relief authorities, however, and probably to a large segment of the employed public they represented, clients remained supplicants. They believed that going on relief was humiliating and that it was not necessarily a bad thing to remind recipients of its humiliations. The board and the Relief Office and much of the community believed these groups were made up of potentially dangerous radicals, and the labor activities of Gransalke and Morris and of some Workers Alliance leaders—such as K. J. Diemert, Henry Hitchens, and Hugh Hughes, all of whom had been arrested during the coal drivers' strike—provided support for that belief. So Fargo reliefers were organized, and their organizations may well have provided improvements in their morale and self-image. But organizations of the unemployed did not soften Fargoans' hearts toward those on relief or result in more generous or less demeaning treatment of them. Indeed, the opposite may have been closer to the truth.[41]

III

Relief recipients generally were second-class citizens in Fargo, but there was a clear hierarchy among them. At the top were those, usually men, who supported families. At the bottom were single men.

Single men formed a distinct segment of the city's population during the 1930s. The 1930 census counted 3,407 single men over the age of fifteen in the city, or about 12 percent of Fargo's population. This was likely an undercount, both because of their informal living arrangements and because many were out of town working on farms when the census was conducted. Of those who were enumerated, probably 1,500 were thirty or older.[42]

Fargo had its share of comfortable widowers and eligible bachelors, but most single adult males were unskilled laborers clustered on the bottom rungs of the economic ladder. Fargo's single men were never investigated systematically, but most seemed to fit the profile of the Chicago shelter dwellers studied by Edwin Sutherland and Harvey Locke in 1936: "The typical homeless man ... is a man who secured a meager education, became an unskilled laborer at an early age, and continued that type of labor throughout life." They were also more likely than other Fargoans to be immigrants and had frequently lost contact with, or were alienated from, their families.[43]

The working lives of these single men conformed to broad patterns. During the spring and summer many worked on farms, sometimes in Cass or Clay counties and sometimes farther afield. Others found unskilled labor in town, working construction, doing odd jobs for householders, providing muscle in warehouses and salvage yards, or otherwise scratching out a living, as in the case of Alex Hanson and Ed Indset, who fashioned butcher knives from old saw blades and sold them door-to-door. In the fall those who had worked on farms came back to town and lived on their summer earnings, supplemented by freight handling, snow shoveling, or other day labor. When ends failed to meet they called on the Union Mission or Salvation Army for assistance, and if they could prove residency they were eligible for county general assistance.[44]

Residency was not easy to determine for single men. Many had a mobile lifestyle—indeed, some of Fargo's single men were other towns' transients— and few maintained a legal residence year-round. When they were in town they lived in cheap hotels and rooming houses or in ramshackle shanties, especially in the lower Front Street area, Fargo's main stem, occupied by pawnshops, second-hand clothing stores, cheap cafés, employment agencies, and other businesses catering to the working poor. In the days before strict zoning requirements, shacks that accommodated two to eight people were especially popular among Fargo's single men. Numerous shacks stood behind businesses on lower Front, as well as along the river east of downtown. Salvage yards and contractors sometimes allowed huts to be erected on their property as a means of discouraging prowlers. Shanties were also numerous on the city's under-developed fringe, as in Belmont Park, on the southeast edge of town. The city government was generally indulgent of shack dwellers, regularly granting them permission to erect structures on vacant city-owned lots.[45]

Their employment and residential patterns, class, ethnicity, living arrangements, and lifestyles marginalized single men in Fargo. They usually came to the community's attention when they presented a law-enforcement challenge or died in a particularly degrading manner. As a group they demonstrated behaviors that were at once cause and effect of their single status. They fought, gambled, patronized prostitutes, and drank. Like transients, they were frequently victims and sometimes perpetrators of crimes against persons and property. A perusal of the *Forum* and of police and coroner's records tells the story of lives that were too often disorderly, unhappy, and chaotic. On October 14, 1933, for example, John Worlech, forty-eight, died in a Front Street shanty he shared with Peter Larson and Olaf Johnson from a beating he had received from two transients. Five years later Larson fell asleep while smoking in a barn and burned to death. On August 6, 1935, John Bakke, who shared a shack with Ludwig Nelson on Powers Construction property, was hit by a streetcar while drunk and bled to death on the street. On November 11, 1936, Ernest Stromberg, a sixty-two-year-old laborer and native of Sweden, died of exposure and alcoholism in a Front Street shed he shared with another man. And on February 6, 1938, forty-seven-year-old laborer Lloyd Burley slipped down the bank of the Red while drunk and froze to death when he could not extricate himself from the mud.[46]

Front Street, looking east from the Northern Pacific passenger depot. The building with the turret is DeLendrecie's, a major department store.

The case of Peter Sandberg, a fifty-five-year-old janitor who lived in a shack at Powers Construction, strikingly captures the world in which too many single men lived. Sandberg was found frozen to death next to the Great Northern tracks on New Year's morning of 1935. The autopsy found denatured alcohol in his stomach—he had been drinking since before Christmas—but also a skull fracture that was several days old. His friends offered three possibilities for the injury. In the week before his demise Sandberg had got into a fight at the House of Lords, a notorious Moorhead bar, had been hit with a wrench during an altercation with a garage man near his work, and had fallen violently out of bed in his shanty.[47]

Though single men came to public attention mainly when they misbehaved or died, they were essential to the efficient functioning of the city. They did the necessary but dirty, temporary, demanding, and ill-compensated work that most men avoided. Unfortunately, their jobs were usually highly sensitive to the city's overall level of economic activity, meaning that they were among the first Fargoans to feel the onset of the Depression. As early as March 1930 complaints appeared in the *Forum* that seasonal workers were competing for jobs as cooks, waiters, and countermen in local cafés, depriving "experienced men in this class of the best advantage and [forcing] down the wage scale." Criticized for depressing wages in private employment, single men found public employment hard to get. In January 1931 the City Commission decided to specify in contracts that contractors "will employ on such work only citizens and residents of the city of Fargo who are the head of families." In September the County Commission followed suit, decreeing that contractors "will employ ... only citizens of Cass County who are the heads of families."[48]

Single men who believed the onset of federal work relief would improve their situations were soon disabused of that notion because FERA, the CWA, and the WPA all gave priority to heads of families. This preference reflected the belief that relief funds would be more beneficial if distributed to several persons rather than just one, but it also demonstrated a commitment by government at all levels to maintain and uphold families. Public agencies saw families as the building blocks of society and family life as the correct way to live. By those standards, single men were not only less needy but also less morally deserving. They were shirking their responsibilities as men and were thus relegated to a secondary position when desirable relief was available.

Single men protested the injustice of their situation, but to no avail. In December 1933 one hundred single men crowded into the Relief Office, demanding Civil Works Administration employment from T. A. Hendricks, Jr., but their protest was insufficient to change government policy. On those rare occasions when they did get work relief, they were expected "to save part of their earnings to tide them through the winter" and were denied county aid if they failed to do so. And when single men got relief, or even were rumored to be getting relief, needy married people who were not on the rolls protested, as in 1935 when a Fargo woman complained that FERA was "hireing [*sic*] single men . . . and the married man with a family can sit home."[49]

As a practical matter, most resident single men in need of public aid were on county general assistance, both before and after the New Deal began, and the county did not suffer them graciously. Indeed, they were commonly viewed as parasitic layabouts who squandered the largesse the public provided for them. Arguing in February 1932 that "many did nothing but loaf around pool halls" while on county aid, county commissioner Garfield Hoglund suggested housing single men in barracks outside of town, "where pleasures they now enjoy would not be available," instead of keeping them in cheap lodgings on the main stem. In that way, Hoglund concluded, "we can rid ourselves of many of the men who hang around Fargo during the winter and 'sponge' off the county." The County Commission agreed with this idea and that fall constructed barracks for sixty-five to seventy men at the county poor farm. Conditions there were apparently so Spartan as to be punitive. The men were required to chop wood and do other manual labor, were fed "salt pork, beans and plenty of vegetable stew," and slept on "straw mattresses" with "no springs."[50]

The barracks experiment was not repeated the next year, apparently because of discontentment and disorder among the men there. As Hendricks put it in 1934, "the barracks idea is in opposition to the best social work practice. Regardless of care they do get to talking. We do not like to congregate." Instead of placing them in barracks, the Relief Office kept single male clients in boarding houses in the winter of 1933–34 at a maximum of $0.40 a day. As Hendricks admitted, though, "this proved to be very unsatisfactory . . . as the men were forced in many instance to occupy unsanitary rooms and were fed largely on donuts and coffee." The next winter the Relief Office doubled up single men in rooms renting for $1.50 a week. Kathryn Tharalson of the county FERA office characterized these quarters as "unsanitary in the extreme, foul with vermin and other filth."[51]

Despite treatment that was callous at best and quarters that were abysmal, as many as three hundred single men applied for county relief every winter. They had once been self-supporting, and most continued to work in the summer, but they were no longer able to support themselves the year around. As case-worker James Thompson explained the situation to the welfare board in January 1935, "during the summer the wages are so small and they spend what money they make; in the winter they have no money saved up." Not only were many of these men dependent on work in the depressed agricultural sector, they were further frustrated by the reality that farm mechanization was diminishing the number of available jobs, meaning that "there has been an excess of unskilled labor in urban areas and the farm laborer has become a chronic reliefer due to conditions over which he has no control." Exacerbating the situation was the fact that, of Thompson's case load of 210 men, "most . . . are from 55 to 83 years of age" and thus frequently too old to compete successfully against younger workers for jobs. In addition to being aged and having few resources, they had "no relatives to whom they may turn," as another case-worker explained.[52]

The sober demographic and economic realities confronting single men on relief did not soften the heart of the welfare board toward them. It continued to consider them layabouts and chiselers and to cut off their relief at the slightest hint of employment. The board was especially taken with the idea of placing single men with farmers who would supply them with room and board in return for their labor. "As far as I'm concerned, I would not give a single man a pleasant look," P. H. Burton said in 1934, "any single man can go to the country and work for his board." In November 1938 relief director Parkins informed the board that the Relief Office was offering single men to farmers who agreed to provide "room and board, clothing and tobacco money," but he had few takers.[53]

By the fall of 1936 the welfare board and the Relief Office had concluded that a more permanent and systematic solution had to be found for the persistent problem of indigent single men. At that time the Relief Office created a "Men's Bureau," housed in Longfellow School, which had been occupied until the previous November by the Transient Bureau. The Relief Office required single men on county assistance to move there, anticipating about two hundred residents over the winter. Seventy-five to one hundred single men refused to go or left soon after arriving, which pleased the Relief Office because they could be cut from the rolls entirely for nonparticipation. The inmates of the Men's Bureau lived under a strict regimen. They were put to work shoveling snow and chopping wood. They were prohibited from having liquor, though they did receive a dime's worth of tobacco or candy bars each week. In November 1936 the Relief Office estimated the cost of maintaining the Men's Bureau at $0.68 per man per day, but by January 1939 the 178 men in residence were being kept for $0.25 per man per day. The Relief Office recorded its costs and savings closely. Gustav Lundberg had cost the county $4 a week when it was keeping him at a rooming house on Front Street, but he cost the taxpayers only $2.65 a week at the Men's Bureau in 1936–37. And Harold Youngquist could be kept at the bureau for $8.50 a month, substantially less than the $18 he had received when he was lodging on NP Avenue. The taxpayers saved, but their savings came at the expense of the dignity of Lundberg, Youngquist, and their fellows, if indeed these men retained any of that precious quality by the time they entered the Men's Bureau.[54]

It was appropriate that Gustav Lundberg and Harold Youngquist and other single men ended up at the old Transient Bureau. They were just a step above transients in the eyes of the welfare board and the Relief Office, and not a long step at that. They were mostly marginal men—uneducated, unskilled, and frequently immigrants. They lived in the community but were not accepted as a legitimate part of it. And their lifestyles and single status brought them disdain in a place that considered itself highly moral and family oriented. With the exception of the CWA protest in December 1933 they were unable to organize themselves. Only rarely would anyone of influence say a word for them. Responding to Senator James Byrnes's 1938 request for an appraisal of the relief situation in the state, Fargoan and North Dakota State Federation of Labor president William Murrey complained that "only men with families are certified, which in my opinion is wrong as we have a number of single men who are able-bodied and should be certified to WPA and given the chance to earn their livelihood rather than being forced upon direct relief. . . . There should be no discrimination shown upon a work program of this kind." But Murrey's was a voice in the wilderness, and similar opinions were not expressed. Even progressive or radical organizations, such as the labor unions, the Holiday Association, and the Workers Alliance, put their first priority on relief for heads of families. If reliefers in Fargo could be said to be pariahs, then surely the single men were pariahs' pariahs.[55]

IV

In Fargo, as in most of the country, an apparent contradiction was noted in 1934 and 1935. The economy seemed to be improving, yet the relief rolls were expanding. It was obvious, as Hendricks noted in November 1934, that "a much higher proportion of the unemployed are now receiving relief than received relief one year ago." Hendricks and the welfare board believed the explanation was that "even though general employment conditions may be better, these people have exhausted their resources and although they may have been unemployed throughout the depression only now are being forced to apply for relief." Another possible explanation was that drought and depression on area farms had driven rural people to the cities, where they arrived without the resources and skills for self-support. These were plausible explanations for the rising relief population, but they were not the only ones. An increasingly popular argument in Fargo and elsewhere was that swelling relief rolls were an indication of demoralization among the unemployed, that relief had become too easy to get, and that people were too eager to get it.[56]

In the summer of 1935 journalist Hubert Kelley detected a disturbing trend during his visit to several midwestern states. At the beginning of the Depression, one relief administrator told him, those suffering were so proud that "we made them take the money." But "the next year they were taking relief gladly," and "this year they are demanding it." The result, Kelley believed, was that "a well-defined class of pensioned loafers" had developed. People who had once cared for yards, washed windows, or collected junk did so no longer—"all are on relief." Relief officials in Fargo also sensed a changing attitude among reliefers, not only manifested in such organizations as the Holiday Association but also seen in the behavior of individuals. In July 1934, for example, the welfare board discussed the case of Ole Arnegard, who supposedly quit a $95-a-month job at the Shotwell greenhouses because he could get "a full living from the county." "Think of a man quitting a $95 job when he has not another job, just because he could live on the County," P. H. Burton reflected. In January 1935 the board discussed the Martin family. Mrs. Martin demanded money for silk stockings for her daughter because "the girl . . . don't want to go to high school without silk stockings." "That case is surely a puzzle," Anna Stevens concluded, "they are not doing right by their children; they are bringing the children up to be chiselers. They live on relief and it is not necessary."[57]

The worthiness of relief recipients was widely questioned in the community. One woman, remembering a neighbor on relief, concluded that "the husband never could seem to find a job. I don't think he was very ambitious." A man whose father refused relief because of the humiliation of the means test remembered resenting people driving "their cars down to pick up surplus food." And a mother who could not afford oranges for her children recalled reliefers having citrus along with other surplus foods: "People who were getting commodities . . . really and truly, they were so wasteful with them." Naomi Larson perceived a change over time, as did many others: "People were getting too smart, and some were on welfare who shouldn't be. We who lived here knew a lot of these people, but we had to keep still. A lot of people thought 'What is he getting relief for? Why is he getting coal?' but they didn't say anything." People who believed they should be on relief but had been denied were frequently the harshest critics of those who were. In a rambling 1939 letter to Franklin and Eleanor Roosevelt, a Fargo woman turned down by the Relief Office complained of wasted surplus food, of "people who have steady work" being on relief, of reliefers who received clothes and then "pawned it at the Jew's store," and of "women who have young men who earn good money" receiving relief. Such anecdotes were repeated and embellished, becoming urban legends and providing support for the belief that reliefers generally were lazy, parasitic, and morally deficient.[58]

Fargoans valued pride and resourcefulness and praised neighbors who demonstrated those characteristics. The resourcefulness and energy of many Fargoans during the thirties was indeed remarkable. Most householders had gardens and canned extensively. Children took jobs selling newspapers or magazines, collecting bottles, babysitting, housecleaning, delivering groceries, or caddying. Families took in boarders, a good way of supplementing incomes in a city where housing was tight. June Dobervich's father, Walter Probstfield, was a housepainter who supplemented his income with farm work and odd jobs. Her mother, Lillie, canned, put up sauerkraut, and took in boarders and roomers. The children helped with odd jobs, including selling squash to NDAC fraternities for two cents a pound. Still, ends barely met. Dobervich did not get her first new coat until she was a sophomore in high school, and "we ate a lot of cornflakes and oatmeal. When we had meat it was hamburger." Mavis Nymon's mother, Clara, canned, and her father dried meat for family use. Both of her sisters worked at the NDAC bakery, and she labored as a housekeeper "12 hours a day, 6 days a week, for $3 a week" to supplement her father's income as an auto mechanic whose customers frequently failed to pay. "You had less, you *really* had less," Nymon concluded. People who could not earn the necessities would barter for them, as when the proprietor of the Butler Beauty Shop offered to "exchange permanent wave for butter, eggs, chickens, or turkeys."[59]

Those too proud to go on relief were much admired. In February 1935 the welfare board praised a former social worker who had fallen on hard times, noting "she is taking in washing. She refuses to apply for relief." In 1936, the *Forum* lauded the men living in a shack colony at the Johnson brothers' salvage yard who eked out a living doing odd jobs and seasonal labor. "While hundreds of others ask relief or seek government jobs, these men want private employment," the *Forum* noted, conveniently ignoring the bleak and degrading relief available for single men forced to ask for aid. The next month the *Forum* carried a glowing story about elderly people who turned down Old-Age Assistance under Social Security when they discovered it was welfare rather than a pension: "Although sadly in need of help, many old timers . . . have refused to accept it. . . . Pride, more than ability to provide for themselves, has kept them off relief rolls to date and they have no intention of going on relief now." The *Forum* concluded that the elderly had "a greater sense of personal pride than the younger generation," which had "developed the idea that the world owes them a living." The *Forum* failed to mention that unexpectedly high numbers of aged indigents were clamoring for public assistance. Nor did the *Forum* or many people in the community for which it spoke consider the possibility that relief clients might be proud and resourceful, too, but had reached the point where those qualities were insufficient to sustain a decent life. Instead, many of those too proud or not destitute enough to seek relief, struggling to make ends meet, scraping by, doing without, and living by barter or on credit, concluded that reliefers were "sitting pretty" and even that, in Helen Kennedy's words, "these people who are on relief are better off then we are."[60]

Their supposed lack of resourcefulness and pride was only one of the moral shortcomings of relief clients in Fargoans' eyes. Others could be identified when clients were examined closely. In 1934 Fritz Gransalke of the Holiday Association complained to Congressman William Lemke and President Roosevelt that five men had been denied aid unjustifiably by Cass County. FERA demanded an extensive report on each of these cases, providing a glimpse at some of the people who suffered unemployment and sought relief.

One of the men, Frank Ramsey, was a disabled veteran of the Spanish-American War. He and his wife had both been married previously, and the first three of their four children had been born out of wedlock. Ramsey had a solid employment history but had been fired by the Northern Pacific Railroad for suing the company when he was injured in a wreck. Clarence Kellogg had been thrown off relief for refusing a farm job. He was divorced and had held four jobs in three years. Thomas Stanton was born in Ohio and had held numerous jobs in several states. He had a son who was living with his dead wife's parents in South Dakota, and an illegitimate daughter in Fargo. Olaf Carlson, who eked out a living delivering handbills, lived with his wife in a shack on lower Front. Carlson was divorced and had two children from a previous marriage.

Most interesting was the case of Vernon Nelson. Nelson was put off the relief rolls for quitting his job sorting beans for a nickel an hour and for refusing a job as a Great Northern section hand because "I might look like a Dago but I don't care to take a Dago job." In the previous two years he had held six different jobs. Nelson had been a vocal member of both the Unemployed Exchange and the Holiday Association and had frequently challenged the Relief Office. For its part, the county accused him of holding a job under an assumed name while collecting relief and contended that his wife had feigned several pregnancies in order to obtain layettes from charity that she presumably sold. The Relief Office further charged the Nelsons with selling grocery vouchers and items obtained from the commissary "to go to the movies."[61]

Unemployment was not like rain. It did not fall evenly on people of all classes, races, occupations, and conditions. It was most severe for those who did not have any particular skills, who were disabled, who were black or brown, who were very young or very old, or who were not firmly established in a community or a job. Perhaps it fell more heavily on those with difficult or even chaotic family lives than on those who were more emotionally secure. Perhaps it was more pronounced for those who did not suffer the petty indignities of work in silence than for those willing to defer to the boss. Perhaps it was just a matter of bad luck, of being in the wrong place at the wrong time, or of working for the wrong employer. But to many Fargoans—most of whom were employed even during the depths of the Depression—unemployment was frequently the sign of a flawed character. One was a poor husband or father; one was not a hard worker or a loyal employee; one drank or was addicted to other pleasures; one was a radical, a chiseler, or a cheater. And the most severe character flaw of all was revealed when one asked for relief. To the modern sensibility Ramsey and Nelson and the others were victims of bad luck or a bad system, and they deserved pity. To many Fargoans in 1934 they were victims of themselves, and they deserved contempt.

Contributing to the negative image of relief recipients was the widespread belief that once people got on relief they were reluctant to take private employment. In 1935 complaints reached the welfare board that potential employers "can't get men to do any work" because "men [are] not asking for jobs and [are] living better on relief than they were before." The idea that relief workers rejected private employment became something of self-fulfilling prophecy. Assuming that reliefers were poor workers and layabouts, employers were reluctant to hire them. William Murrey claimed that even public contractors doing Public Works Administration jobs were "very antagonistic toward the relief workers and . . . [were] opposed to using such labor on contract jobs. . . . Once [WPA workers] become a certified case, most contractors hesitate to employ them."[62]

Farmers were especially critical of relief, agreeing that it had dried up the pool of agricultural labor available at a price they were willing and/or able to pay. In response to farmers' concerns, the welfare board decided in April 1935 that any man turning down private employment, "regardless of price," would be removed from relief. A week later U.S. attorney P. W. Lanier and state FERA administrator E. A. Willson announced a war on "chiselers" aimed at purging from the relief rolls people who refused farm work. "The time has come when the people of North Dakota interested in the state's future well-being should take steps to begin cutting down the relief rolls rather than increasing them," Lanier said. "Altogether too many people in the state who have been receiving relief are taking the attitude the government owes them a living."[63]

In order to further assure an adequate supply of farm labor, the welfare board ended all relief payments to single men on July 1. Later that month the state FERA office ended most construction projects to free still more labor for agriculture. Such draconian measures were necessary because there was no independent incentive for relief workers to pursue farm work. Fargoans would have to leave their families and labor at jobs with which many were unfamiliar for a low wage. Farmers were adamant "that they would be unable to pay more than $1.50 per day"—or about $0.15 an hour—while FERA work paid twice that. The Relief Office itself recognized the insufficiency of farm wages for family support when it agreed that "men with families that are unable to care for them through farm work will be given sufficient direct relief, in the form of groceries, rent, etc. to keep the family going."[64]

Complaints from farmers that relief was shrinking the supply of harvest labor were common throughout the Midwest and Great Plains in 1935 and beyond. To some degree it was true that "the government . . . bid against the farmers" for labor, as former welfare board member and Cass County farmer Joe Runck put it in 1936. Unquestionably, relief diminished the vast pool of unskilled laborers who had once been compelled to work at virtually any price, not only on farms but in warehouses, in salvage yards, at construction sites, in laundries, and in private homes. Farmers and others argued that the problem was that the government overpaid. As strong a case could be made that wages in some private endeavors were more abysmal than welfare officials had imagined. Government had long subsidized some employers indirectly by providing general assistance to their underpaid workers in slack times. The difference during the Depression was that work relief programs set a minimum level of compensation to meet basic human needs, a level that went beyond what many private employers could or would pay. In light of that reality, it was hardly surprising that men and women frequently made the rational economic decision to go on relief—even with all of the humiliations involved—rather than to work in jobs such as farm laborer or housemaid, which carried their own humiliations and were paid poorly to boot. In the long run the government-created shortage of low-paid workers contributed to the pressure to mechanize muscle work and household labor. In the short run relatively high relief wages became a lightning rod for employers unhappy with New Deal policies.[65]

In addition to complaining that relief workers would not accept private employment, critics also impugned the quality of the work they did. Relief work was commonly derided as shoddy or haphazard and workers as crude, minimally skilled, and lazy. Reliefers themselves applied self-deprecating sobriquets such as "We Putter Around" to the WPA and talked of goldbricking and leaning on shovels. At the same time, reliefers had their defenders. Glenn Smith, who supervised a number of relief workers at the NDAC, considered them good and conscientious employees. Others emphasized that few relief workers were "shirkers" and accused critics of "ignorance and misunderstanding of the work being done."[66]

Critics of relief work tended to ignore the difficult conditions under which many public relief projects were carried out. Because unemployment was highly seasonal, even during the Depression, relief needs were heaviest at the very time when capital improvement projects such as construction, street paving, and the laying of sewer and water lines were most difficult. Men were required to dig trenches in frozen gumbo soil, attempt to set concrete in temperatures much below those recommended, and undertake carpentry and masonry with fingers and hands stiffened by the cold. Winter construction in North Dakota was difficult under the best conditions. In a period like early 1936, when the state suffered a "continuous period of about six weeks where the thermometer registered below zero," it was "almost impossible to operate out-door projects." Factor in the reality that relief workers were poor men who, as William Murrey noted, "are very poorly clad and suffer from severe weather," and the question becomes not why work was slow or shoddy but how any got done at all.[67]

Still, it was the case that "standards of speed and performance are . . . much lower than in 'regular' jobs," as one observer noted of WPA work in 1936. Public employment was mainly a relief delivery system designed to support the unemployed in a manner that did not demoralize them. The products of work relief were significant but secondary to the main purpose. Workers had little incentive to finish projects quickly, especially when public agencies had such difficulty identifying and funding new ones. Moreover, their tools and work rules did not encourage efficiency, even if they had embraced that ideal. Observers also pointed to the nature of the work relief force. Relief workers tended to be young people who had little experience in private employment or older workers who had passed their prime. Others on work relief were perhaps not as efficient or skilled at their crafts as those who remained employed in the private sector. Employers such as cement contractor Gust Olson and builder John Carlson tried to keep their best men on skeleton crews even at the depths of the Depression. Many of their weaker workers presumably ended up on relief. As the economy began to recover, albeit slowly and incompletely, the better workers on relief were called back to private employment, leaving work relief rolls dominated by the too young, the too old, and the "crippled, lazy, or merely slow." They were not people whose work would be generally respected, especially in a community where the entire enterprise was viewed with suspicion.[68]

V

In 1938 and 1939 the Public Welfare Board of North Dakota conducted a series of discussions on public relief and its significance in the state over the course of the Depression. The board readily conceded that relief funds met a legitimate social need, one that the state could not have met. "The use of public funds for the relief of people who cannot find jobs," the board held, "is unquestionably essential." At the same time, the board noted the "generally expressed opinion . . . that public relief has been administered too expensively, that relief was being made more desirable than private employment, and that there was a vast amount of chiseling by persons receiving relief." As a result of relief programs, the board believed, two ominous and unfortunate attitudes had developed. On the one hand, "part of the dependent population" had "apparently lost interest in being self-supporting," while "the average citizen" had "lost interest in the welfare or well being of those who are without resources."[69]

The decline in public sympathy for those on relief highlighted by the Public Welfare Board could be seen throughout the county by 1935. The nation's partial recovery from the economic depths of 1932–33 led some to believe that relief was no longer necessary. At the same time, the federal government was concluding that the incompleteness of the recovery and the continuing high levels of unemployment made it inevitable that work relief for employables— administered in such a way as to respect the rights and dignity of recipients— would be a permanent fixture of American life. As North Dakota FERA director E. A. Willson put it early in 1935, "the relief load is going to be much larger than normal even when prosperity returns because so many families have lost everything and they will be too old to get a new start." This was not good news to many Americans, including many Fargoans. From the beginning of the Depression on, the *Forum* had warned of "the inevitable breakdown of the morale on the part of some of those who are helped" and their loss of "that fine spirit of independence which is the very backbone of American progress and advancement" and had worried about creation of "a second generation needing county help."[70]

By 1935 those fears seemed to have been realized. A local Relief Office that distrusted clients, managed their resources, and made moral judgments about them warred with a federal relief structure that respected clients, upheld their right to public work, and allowed them to use the resources coming to them as they wished. In place of a humble and deferential group of unemployed people anxious to escape aid as quickly as possible there was now a class of people, led by radicals, who saw relief as their right and who protested loudly when it did not meet their expectations. People had come to see relief as their job, it seemed, and they defended it as such. Critics of relief believed that the morals as well as the morale of the unemployed had been destroyed. The *Forum*'s eagerness to highlight incidents of chiseling and fraud, and the practice of both the police department and the newspaper, beginning in 1936, of identifying as "WPA worker" men and women arrested for drunkenness, disorderly conduct, nonsupport, and other offenses, contributed to an overall picture of moral degradation.[71]

While the *Forum* continued to celebrate the flow of federal relief funds into town and the benefits the projects provided to the city, it increasingly and paradoxically expressed a sense of regret that Fargo participated in federal work relief programs. Praising Traill County in February 1935 for turning down FERA funds, the *Forum* editorialized, "the blight of the Federal relief dole has touched all of the rest of us—but Traill has remained free of its curse. . . . Our hats are off to the people of Traill who, we feel sure, are better citizens, and hold their heads just a little higher than the rest of us, all because they have done the job themselves." A few months later, when Cavalier County decided to forgo federal funds, the *Forum* praised it for having "nipped in its beginning the establishment of a 'permanent' poor relief class whose philosophy was that the 'government owes me a living.'"[72]

As the Public Welfare Board noted in 1939, one unanticipated result of unemployment relief was declining sympathy for those in need. For years the Kiwanis had conducted a Christmas toy drive, in which toys were collected, repaired and refurbished, and then distributed to needy families. In 1935 the toy drive failed, not because it no longer met a need but because of citizen "indifference." The public record is mute on why Fargoans became "indifferent." Did the public believe local needs were now being met by the federal government? Was there anger at the poor after a year of labor strife and relief protests? Had the poor come to be seen as unworthy of sympathy? Were they now proud and demanding, rather than humble and deferential? Had they been transformed from neighbors in need to the Other—an alien presence in the city? Perhaps a bit of each, or something else altogether—we cannot know. What we do know is that the Kiwanis got out of the toy drive business and the WPA took over. Continuing human needs were met, but now meeting them was someone's job rather than an act of charity.[73]

Before the Depression increased their numbers and changed their composition so dramatically, the poor had generally been viewed with a mixture of condescension and affection by comfortable Fargoans. On Christmas Day of 1929, when mayor A. T. Lynner distributed food baskets to three hundred poor families at the Salvation Army, the *Forum* described the scene as one in which "pathos mingled with happiness." Focusing on Bertha Schultz, a seventy-eight-year-old widow living "back under the bridge" on lower Front, the *Forum* noted that "lately things have not been going so good. . . . She is alone, [and] there is no one to send her the greetings a mother loves on the day of Christ's birth." Schultz played her assigned role in this "drama," probably realizing, as the poor usually did, that becoming an object of pity and surrendering one's dignity was the price one paid for help.[74]

Within a few short years the image the public held of the poor had changed significantly. Now the poor were assumed to be lazy, unworthy chiselers with an entitlement mentality, to be derided and perhaps feared. In August 1936, when the *Forum* learned that a relief recipient had been denied a corset by the welfare board, it mockingly launched a "corset fund," urging readers to send donations for the aid of the "suffering sister." Donations came in, frequently accompanied by notes—which the *Forum* approvingly printed—ridiculing the corset requester for her frivolity and her assumption of entitlement. It was all grand fun at another's expense, but at the end of the campaign the *Forum* was embarrassed to report that the garment in question was a "surgical corset" without which the recipient would have been unable to work. Her work relief supported a family of five headed by a man invalided by arsenic poisoning contracted during a grasshopper eradication campaign. "All of which is written to show you folks that your dimes went to a truly worthy cause," the *Forum* meekly concluded. Fewer than seven years separated the stories of Bertha Schultz and Suffering Sister, but in that brief period the relationship between the unpoor and the poor in Fargo had changed dramatically, and the attitude of the former toward the latter had been transformed from maudlin sentimentality to callous and cruel contempt.[75]

5

WORKING

"One's job is the watershed down which the rest of one's life tends to flow in Middletown. Who one is, whom one knows, how one lives, what one aspires to be,—these and many other urgent realities of living are patterned for one by what one does to get a living and the amount of living this allows one to buy."

Robert Lynd and Helen Merrell Lynd, Middletown in Transition, *1937*

"Let's all pause for a moment and just think how lucky we are to have a job. . . .

"Let's show our appreciation, by working harder each day, doing a little more than is laid out for us, proud of our Company that is so much interested in us, and kind to our customers who favor us with their patronage. . . .

"That our chance to show our appreciation to our Company, is here now, we can best demonstrate by deeds, not words; by action, not dreams. Do you appreciate your job? If so, show it!"

A Loyal Fairmont Employee, November 24, 1932

IN FARGO, as in the Lynds' *Middletown,* one's job was an essential component of identity during the Depression, so much so, Darrow Beaton remembered, that it was common to introduce someone by saying, "this is so-and-so, he works at such-and such—it was part of your name." One's job was the major determinant of where and how well one lived, how abundantly one's family would be maintained, and whom one's friends and associates would be. For men, holding a job signified the ability to support a family—to behave in the way adult males were supposed to behave. To some women, holding a job provided a measure of personal independence and family security. For young people, a job was an essential step on the road to adulthood. In a city in which resourcefulness and self-help were highly praised, a job gave one self-respect and gained the esteem of neighbors who tended to measure a person's worth by his or her willingness to work and work hard.[1]

The erosion of employment opportunities during the Depression dramatically increased the value of the job. When popular author and advertising executive Bruce Barton wrote in *American Magazine* in October 1932 that "the *important* fact is that all jobs are a gift from Heaven," he was stating a truism with which most Americans probably would have agreed. When one acquired a job, he or she did not leave it, even when wages were cut, hours were increased, or onerous conditions and demands were attached. Like the Fairmont Creamery worker quoted above, employees worked hard, treated customers well, and demonstrated their appreciation to their employers.[2]

More than ever, workers depended on "our Company that is so much interested in us," on paternalistic employers who took a familial interest in them. The family model of employment was predominant in Fargo during the Depression. Most firms were relatively small and were owner operated. In a small city, employers and employees frequently attended the same churches, sent their children to the same schools, and even lived in the same neighborhoods. Employers and employees regularly developed close relationships that transcended the basic economic connection at the core of labor relations in a capitalist economy. Many employers demonstrated genuine concern for their employees and their families. And many workers reciprocated with hard work and loyalty.

But even as the Depression enhanced the value of personal relationships between employers and workers, it strained those relationships. Even the most well-intentioned employers operated in a capitalist economy, in which the market—not familial love and personal affection—held sway. Margins were narrow, profits easily turned into losses, and credit was tight. Retrenchment was the order of the day, and employees—even cherished ones—sometimes had to be let go, while those who remained coped with the reality of thinner pay envelopes. Nor were all employers caring paternalists. There were undoubtedly employers who did not care about their workers as people and who regarded the labor glut as an opportunity to squeeze employees and to get the upper hand.

The Depression created a situation in which workers clung desperately to jobs that were decreasingly attractive, that did not pay a living wage, and that sometimes were less remunerative even than relief. They witnessed "the much-advertised American standard of living . . . falling to pieces in [their] hands." They lived in fear of wage cuts, of onerous new demands, and of employers whose needs or even whims might make a bad situation worse. But mainly they lived in fear of losing these terrible and insecure jobs and of being thrown on a job market in which new hires were usually less well paid and less well treated than established employees. Most of all, they feared being forced on relief, demeaning, degrading, and stigmatizing their families and advertising themselves as people who could not play the basic role society had written for them.[3]

There were alternatives to depending solely on employers. One could rent out rooms, take in boarders, or put family members on the job market. With a bit of capital, one could strike out on his or her own, opening a small business out of the home or selling door-to-door. Or one could organize with other frightened and insecure workers, building a fraternal rather than a filial relationship in the workplace.[4]

Labor unions had long existed in Fargo, and the railroad workers, the newspaper craft employees, and many in the construction trades were organized. In a city in which retail and wholesale sales and service occupations predominated, however, organized labor was not a major factor in most enterprises. Moreover, in the early years of the Depression, even in the organized trades, the unions could not maintain wage scales. As North Dakota Federation of Labor president Roy G. Arntson put it in his report to the 1933 convention, "the dire need for employment created an atmosphere of self-preservation and selfishness in securing work that has no place in the Trade Union movement." He might as well have said that there was little place for the labor movement in the dog-eat-dog job market of the early Depression.[5]

But this situation was changing by 1934. The Roosevelt administration was supportive of workers who wanted to organize, and throughout the nation established unions expanded and new ones were formed. In Fargo, worker dissatisfaction, heated by wage cuts, autocratic employers, and poor working conditions, boiled over into a series of strikes, most notably among dairy and coal drivers. The latter dispute, which resulted in violent confrontations, mass arrests, and death, deeply shocked a city that imagined relationships between employers and employees to be cordial and itself to be immune to class conflict. In the aftermath of the coal drivers' strike, Fargoans struggled to preserve their self-image as a classless community in the face of a contrary reality.

I

North Dakota's per capita income in 1929 stood at $365, barely half of the national average of $705. In this category it exceeded just six states, all in the former Confederacy. One observer noted in 1933 that income tax records showed only two North Dakotans earning more than $100,000 a year and fewer than fifty earning in excess of $30,000.[6]

Of course, North Dakota was an overwhelmingly agricultural state during the 1930s, and in such places per capita income is not always an accurate gauge of either wealth or standard of living. But even among states in the wheat belt North Dakota was firmly fixed at the bottom, 39 percent behind Nebraska, 33 percent under Kansas, and 12 percent below South Dakota.[7]

As the major place in a large agricultural region, Fargo was a mecca for rural people seeking better pay and a greater range of opportunities than were available in the countryside. Single women, especially, were drawn to a city with numerous retail and service positions of the type that were rare in rural areas. Rural migrants were not usually disappointed. Jobs normally abounded in the growing city, and pay scales were much higher than on the farms and in the rural market towns.

While Fargo pay was good in comparison to that in nearby rural places, the wage scale overall was not impressive relative to that in other cities. In most areas of economic endeavor the city stood at or just below national averages, but the structure of Fargo's economy, with numerous low-paying retail and service jobs and relatively few jobs in manufacturing, depressed wages in the city generally. The available figures demonstrate the modesty of most Fargo incomes. A *Forum* survey of homeowners and house renters in 1935 reckoned the city's per household income at about $1,350 per year, but had those who rented apartments and rooms and lived in shacks been included that figure likely would have been substantially lower. Many Fargoans struggled along on very little. A study by *Business Week* in 1935 showed that only 10.2 percent of Fargo families had incomes in excess of $3,000 per year, while 34.4 percent earned under $1,000.[8]

Fargoans who lived through the Depression had vivid memories of their first jobs and often of their rate of pay. When May Bredeson took a job as a retail clerk at DeLendrecie's in 1938 she was paid $0.25 an hour. Frieda Oster received $45 a month in her first job as a bookkeeper, and Vivian Westberg was paid $65 a month as a savings teller at the First National Bank. Pay for women was usually less than for men, but the latter were not lavishly compensated. Seymour Olson cut ice on the Red for $0.35 an hour. Jack McNair, a 1932 Fargo Central graduate, landed a job at the Red Owl Grocery downtown for $9 a week and was supervised by "a man . . . with a wife and a child [who] made $16 a week." Charlie Hauser, who worked in his father's meat market for $3.50 a week after he dropped out of school in 1936, remembered that "our top butchers got $15 a week."[9]

Relatively low pay was also the rule for many trained professionals. In 1933 T. A. Hendricks, Jr., received just $200 a month to supervise the County Relief Office, though he was much better compensated than most of his social workers, who were paid $85 to $100 per month. In 1935 Hendricks left for a job in Kentucky that offered him a 50 percent raise. Wage cuts from the legislature and an initiated measure in 1933 reduced the annual salary of the North Dakota Agricultural College president to $2,400 and those of his senior faculty to $1,995. Even that sum must have seemed like a king's ransom to public school teachers, most of whom made under $1,000 per year after the 1933 budget cuts. F. A. Leonard, police magistrate, made $1,800 in 1932. And in 1937 St. Luke's Hospital paid its business manager $225 a month, its nursing supervisor $150, and its nursing instructor $95.[10]

The low-wage problem was exacerbated in the early years of the Depression, when employers trimmed salaries and reduced or eliminated Christmas bonuses. Employers argued that the cost of living had declined as well; it had, but not always in step with wages. The *Forum* reported that rents declined 20 percent between 1929 and 1933 but that renters' incomes had dropped by 22 percent. The value of the average owner-occupied home had declined by 15 percent, consuming substantial homeowners' equity, while the typical homeowner's income had dropped by 30 percent.[11]

The fact that wages were declining from already low levels did not go unremarked and sometimes stimulated controversy. Low wages for working women, especially maids, sparked bitter disputes in Fargo in 1931 and 1932. The Trades and Labor Assembly was at the forefront of the struggle to maintain wage rates and to resist cuts for teachers and other public employees. Union members themselves frequently worked below scale, however, because to refuse to do so was to have no work at all. Federal public works and wage-and-hour policies became an issue in a city in which many workers made less than government-mandated minimums. In 1933, when the PWA decreed that skilled and unskilled workers on its projects in the "Northern zone" should receive $1.20 and $0.50 per hour respectively, the Fargo Chamber of Commerce argued that the Northern scale would inflate wage rates in a city where most workers received wages commensurate with those paid in the South. Likewise, minimum wages under the NRA codes sometimes exceeded local wages, with the ironic result that poorly compensated workers were frequently laid off.[12]

City fathers usually defended the low-wage regime and resisted pressures from labor to raise wages. In so doing, the City Commission was presumably speaking for taxpayers, employers, and especially farmers, who strongly opposed any actions that might elevate local wage rates or entice workers to leave the countryside. In 1934, when the Trades and Labor Assembly accused city garbage contractor P. A. Costello of paying his men only $45 a month for working twelve-hour days, the commission answered that "it cannot interfere in the matter of wages paid by him to his employees," even though Costello operated under a city contract. Eventually, however, Costello's employment practices proved to be too much even for the commission to countenance. In 1938 the commission stipulated that the garbage contractor pay his men a minimum of $80 per month because "the men engaged in the work were being paid wages or salaries that were unusually low and far below compensation which would insure them and their families a decent living."[13]

In the absence of strong unions or a local government committed to upholding labor standards, employers had the upper hand during the Depression. They could pick and choose from the large pool of eager, available workers. They could cut wages and reduce whatever benefits they customarily provided. They could demand higher standards from their workers, as in 1935 when the dining room staffs at the Powers and the Gardner hotels were compelled to attend training sessions designed to convert each waitress from being "a hasher" into "a saleslady, merchandising the food listed on her menu." They could even intrude on their workers' personal lives, as the school board did when it demanded that employees live in Fargo and forbade female teachers from smoking.[14]

Most workers enjoyed little leverage in this situation. They lived with less money and fewer benefits, and they satisfied—and sometimes circumvented—the demands that were placed on them. In normal times, the free labor system provides a safety valve for discontented, underpaid, and unappreciated workers—they can quit. But people who had jobs during the Depression did not readily give them up, regardless of how onerous employment might be. Jobs were precious, and few were so undesirable that they could not be easily and quickly filled, usually more cheaply than before. Leaving a job without another in hand was especially foolhardy, because such action might turn one into a dependent, leaning on family or the government for sustenance. This situation existed everywhere, of course, but in places such as Fargo, which valued work and resourcefulness and stigmatized relief, it was especially compelling.[15]

Softening—but also complicating—relationships between employers and employees was the paternalism many of the former displayed toward the latter. Members of employing families vividly recalled close connections with employees and their families. Elizabeth Alsop, whose family owned Interior Lumber, which maintained a string of yards in western Minnesota and eastern North Dakota, remembered, "our employees were there for a long time.... We took a family interest in them." Anna Jane Schlossman contended that her father, George Black, opened the Store Without a Name within months after he sold his share of Black's to Sears because he "was very loyal to his employees," who begged him to go back into retail. People from families of employees also had fond memories of the paternalism displayed by many firms. Darrow Beaton credited the fact that his father was never laid off at Interstate Seed and Grain to the kindness of the Wilk family. Another Fargoan, whose husband was one of about 150 workers in an industrial firm, remembered that the owner's "employees were his family."[16]

In at least a few cases, paternalism was institutionalized into a sort of welfare capitalism. The Herbst Department Store, for example, maintained a "Social and Benefit Club," to which every employee with at least six months of service belonged. One-half of one percent of each employee's salary was assessed to maintain the club, with the company matching the contribution. With these funds, the Social and Benefit Club made donations to the Community Chest, held a monthly "party, picnic, or other entertainment" for employees and their families, and provided flowers in instances of sickness or death. More substantially, the Social and Benefit Club paid a sick benefit of one-half of an ill or disabled employee's salary for up to six weeks and a small death benefit to families of employees.[17]

Herbst also published an in-house newsletter called the "Herbstory," which served several functions. On the one hand, it conveyed gossipy, sometimes teasing news about employees or even managers, along with announcements of personnel changes, engagements, marriages, births, and so forth, all designed to create a familial atmosphere. It also carried information about sales contests, pep talks urging clerks to redouble their efforts, homilies (e.g., "Wisdom flieth out the door when desire comes in by the window"), and advice regarding how employees should treat customers. In December 1933, for example, the "Herbstory" reminded employees that "new customers are just as valuable to us as an old one [*sic*] ... for each new customer is an old one in the making," that "each member of our force is valuable to us only in proportion to his ability to serve," and that retail's mantra, "The Customer Is Always Right," must never be forgotten.[18]

The paternalistic activities of the Herbst Company were more elaborate and formal than those of most employers and were probably shaped at least in part by a shrewd recognition that the firm's predominantly female employees especially cherished the interpersonal and social aspects of work. In most ways, though, the paternalism of the family-run Herbst Company had a simi-

Herbst Store employees—the majority of them women—celebrate the firm's anniversary in 1936.

lar purpose to that displayed by other employers—especially other family-owned firms—in the city. On the one hand, the "Herbstory" and the Social and Benefit Club allowed Herbst systematically to demonstrate its genuine affection and regard for employees. But paternalism could also be good business. It helped create and sustain employee loyalty, allowing the firm to hold its best workers. It gave employees an emotional and material stake in the company and its success. And it allowed the company to shape its employees into the kinds of workers it wanted them to be, which might or might not have conformed to what they themselves wanted to be.[19]

The downside of the paternalistic regime for employers was that it could impede them from doing what had to be done to sustain their enterprises or it could create expectations on the part of employees that could not be fulfilled. In a capitalist system, a business is not and ultimately cannot be a family, regardless of the mutual affection that might develop between employers and employees. Even the most caring and considerate employers might have to reduce wages and benefits or let workers go. At best their decisions might be accepted and understood. One Fargoan who worked as a secretary in a family-owned firm remembered that her boss called all of the employees together to inform them he needed to cut wages, but, she recalled, the employees "knew [the family] would do right by us when they could." Another possibility was that employees of paternalistic employers who were laid off or whose wages were cut would see their bosses as frauds and hypocrites who talked family when it served their purposes but who always attended to the bottom line when push came to shove.[20]

II

Many workers were apparently comfortable with the dominant paternalistic labor regime, but such satisfaction was far from universal. At least some workers in Fargo looked to unionization as an alternative model for relationships with employers. Unions potentially allowed workers to band together and bargain collectively with their bosses. In place of a system that defined wages and benefits as gifts from benevolent employers to grateful employees, unions proposed a relationship in which wages and benefits were a matter of right and justice and were negotiated between business owners and workers, meeting one another more or less as equals.

Organized labor had been a factor in Fargo from the city's earliest days, but unionization had not thrived in a local economy characterized by numerous small family firms and disproportionate employment in retail and service occupations. A major impediment to unionization in the city was employers' strong opposition to collective bargaining. While some of this opposition undoubtedly derived from a belief that unionization would drive wage rates higher, it is also likely that employers feared unions would compromise their ability to control their businesses as they wished or that unions would poison the personal relationships they had with employees. Prior to the Depression, Fargo businesses had taken a strong stand against unions. Organizers from the Industrial Workers of the World had found Fargo a notably inhospitable place before and during World War I, and a successful employer lockout in 1913–1914 devastated unions in the building trades. Hostility to unionization continued in the Depression years as well, as employers maintained informal blacklists of union activists and regularly fired strong union men in their employ or, as one Fargoan put it, "union men fired themselves."[21]

Fargo's anti-union history and unpromising labor climate were insufficient to forestall a surge in organizational activity beginning in 1933. Much of the impetus for unionization both locally and nationally came from a federal administration that was friendlier to organized labor than any in history. The Public

Works Administration favored unions, and the National Industrial Recovery Act guaranteed workers the right to bargain collectively. Responding to the NIRA, the president of the North Dakota Federation of Labor told the group's 1933 convention that deliverance was at hand, noting that "the possibilities for creating new unions are unlimited." When businesses demonstrated reluctance to recognize workers' collective bargaining rights, President Roosevelt created a supportive National Labor Relations Board by executive order in June 1934. Workers throughout the country responded to this favorable environment by organizing, and several spectacular and violent labor conflicts ensued, most notably in San Francisco and Minneapolis in the spring and summer of 1934. Local factors also played a role in the growing desire of workers to unionize. Business activity and employment both increased impressively in 1934, as Fargo and the nation climbed out of the Depression's deepest valley, diminishing workers' fears of unemployment and reducing their willingness to take whatever their bosses dished out.[22]

National trends were significant to Fargo workers, but they were especially attentive to developments in Minneapolis, 250 miles to the southeast. There, an independent union of teamsters enrolled most of the city's truck drivers and launched a series of strikes. As chronicled by Robert Schultz, William Millikan, and others, the Minneapolis strikes resulted in violence and death, but they ultimately forced reluctant employers to recognize the union and bargain with it. Inspired by the Minneapolis teamsters' success in defeating employers in their notoriously open-shop city, Fargoans William Cruden and Austin Swalde, who had been trying to organize local truck drivers since the fall of 1933, asked Minneapolis Teamsters Local 574 for help. The Minneapolis teamsters responded by dispatching a skilled, experienced, and tough organizer, Miles Dunne, to Fargo. Dunne, a Trotskyite, was one of four radical brothers from Little Falls, Minnesota, who played key roles in the Minneapolis strikes. Dunne went to work with a good deal of energy in his capacity as business agent for the Fargo-Moorhead teamsters. By late fall he and local union leaders had organized six to seven hundred drivers and helpers, both employed and unemployed, mostly in the dairy, lumber, coal, ice, and moving and transfer businesses, into Organized Unemployed and Local Union 173. Fargo workers were not the only people in town to draw inspiration and aid from Minneapolis. Employers consulted with members of the anti-union Minneapolis Citizens Alliance. Following its example and advice, more than two hundred businesses formed the Associated Industries of Fargo-Moorhead and hired Eli Weston, a Fargo attorney, as general manager. The Associated Industries was determined to maintain an open-shop town and to assure business unity behind that goal.[23]

The confrontation for which drivers and employers had prepared began on November 4, 1934. Local 173 had been negotiating with the dairies in the city, represented by the Associated Industries, seeking union recognition, a closed shop, and minimum wages of $30 per week plus commissions for drivers and $22.50 per week for "inside workers." When negotiations broke down, a strike was called at 4:00 P.M. on a Sunday. The next twenty-four hours saw a flurry of activity. The American Legion set up a "milk depot" in the City Auditorium, and one hundred "special deputies" were sworn in to help the police maintain order. The police were vague about who these special deputies were, but many were presumably drawn from the American Legion Emergency Corps, which had been created in January 1933 "to perform police, guard, or other duties." Borrowing a tactic used by Minneapolis strikers, dairy drivers formed flying squads to confront scabs on the streets, and on Monday morning five striking "milkmen" were arrested for "rioting" after they stopped a dairy driver on Seventh Street South and threatened to overturn his wagon. Later that morning police arrested Miles Dunne for "directing, advising, and encouraging a riot." Early in the afternoon, however, mayor Fred Olsen, Father Vincent Ryan, state's attorney A. R. Bergesen, and several other prominent citizens negotiated a "truce" under which strikers returned to work for ten days while negotiations proceeded.[24]

During the truce period the two sides made no apparent progress, but they agreed to extend it when requested to do so by North Dakota governor Ole Olson, who stepped in to mediate. On November 18 Olson presented a contract to the drivers and urged them to accept it in the spirit of moderation and compromise. Also urging the union toward moderation were William Ballou, former Unitarian minister and long-time leftist activist, and Herbert Hanson of the North Dakota Agricultural College, who was associated with a number of progressive causes. The next day the union accepted a settlement denying Local 173 a closed shop but raising drivers' pay to about $25 a week and inside workers' pay to $18. Professing satisfaction with the settlement, the Associated Industries' Eli Weston admitted that some increase in wages was probably justified in light of the "improvement in business conditions in the last year."[25]

The peaceful conclusion to the dairy strike and the moderation displayed by the workers did not signal a retreat from what Local 173 perceived as its role of defending the rights of all workers in the city, both employed and unemployed. The union aggressively upheld the cause of the unemployed with the

Relief Office and the welfare board, and it sought to make Fargo inhospitable to nonunion workers. On November 26, six members of Local 173 confronted two nonunion lathers working on the Grand Theater, which was being rebuilt after a devastating fire. A fight ensued in which one of the lathers was badly beaten, and police arrested the union members for rioting.[26]

Nor was the dairy strike over, as far as many workers were concerned. The Frank O. Knerr Dairy Company, run by divorcée Alice Knerr, contended it was not bound by the dairy settlement because its main products were butter and ice cream, rather than milk, a position supported by the Associated Industries. Local 173 disagreed. Union president William Cruden threatened a secondary boycott of dealers handling Knerr products, some Knerr workers walked out, and a picket line was established around the plant. The situation deteriorated rapidly. Nonstriking workers reportedly were menaced, a company delivery truck was overturned by a group of men, someone put sugar in the gas tank of Alice Knerr's car, and she was threatened with bodily harm, leading her to request—and receive—police protection. On December 13, district judge P. G. Swenson of Grand Forks restrained Local 173 from "all forms of picketing intended to interfere with peaceful operation of the Frank O. Knerr Dairy Company." Four days later Swenson extended his injunction to the Fargo Holiday Association after Fritz Gransalke, holiday leader and a forceful advocate for workers and reliefers, was charged with being one of four men who assaulted Ed Graunke, a nonstriking Knerr buttermaker, on his way home from work.[27]

The Knerr conflict simmered on through most of the winter, but it was eclipsed by the much more spectacular coal, ice, and transfer drivers' strike. During the Depression virtually all Fargoans heated their homes and businesses with coal supplied by lumberyards, which marketed the fuel to diminish the seasonality of their primary businesses. Coal was a necessity, so demand for it did not decline substantially when business activity slowed, but householders frequently could not pay for it, or pay for all of it, forcing fuel dealers to extend credit. John Alsop remembered, "you asked for the cash at the time. If you didn't get it . . . you *hoped* you got it before next September. You could say, 'You owe us $100, so you'd better give us $20.' They'd come up with that, but they'd still owe you $80." Diminished cash flow squeezed the yard owners, who responded by laying off workers and cutting wages. Despite the travails of the Depression, however, coal drivers were paid reasonably well by the standards of muscle workers in Fargo, receiving an average of $0.45 an hour, or about $20 a week. The pay was above what the National Recovery Administration code required and "a fair wage under present business conditions" to the thinking of the coal dealers. Still, the work was cold, dirty, physically demanding, and insecure.[28]

While the dairy strike was going on, Local 173 approached the coal dealers, as well as the ice dealers and transfer companies, with a contract that recognized the union as bargaining agent for drivers and helpers, instituted a seniority system, and created a mechanism for arbitration of disputes over wages and work rules. The dairy drivers' strike had taken employers by surprise, but they were ready for the coal drivers and were prepared to make a stand against the rising tide of unionization. When the employers refused to discuss the contract, Local 173 requested that the National Labor Relations Board conduct an election among the workers to determine whether they wanted to be represented by the union. On January 6 the employers rejected NLRB involvement and refused to attend a board hearing, arguing that most of their workers did not desire representation by the union, that their workers were relatively well paid, and that "inasmuch as no controversy exists between ourselves and our employees, the 'public interest' does not require that your board conduct such elections." At the same time, the dealers launched an offensive against union activity in their businesses, with Interstate Lumber firing two workers on January 10 for "union activity."[29]

Faced with the employers' refusal to negotiate, their defiance of the NLRB, and their dismissal of union men, Local 173 concluded that it had no alternative but to strike the coal dealers, along with the ice and transfer firms, which it did on January 22. The union demanded recognition, seniority rights, an arbitration board, and reinstatement of men discharged for union activities. The employers were willing to grant seniority rights and create an arbitration board, but they would not recognize the union or reinstate the workers they had dismissed.[30]

When the coal drivers went out on strike the temperature hovered near 30 degrees below zero, as it sometimes does in January in North Dakota. While striking at such a time was tactically wise—there was no point to striking when people did not need coal—it was a public relations disaster for Local 173. The coal dealers had refused to bargain and had defied the federal government, but it was the strikers who were censured for placing "the public at the mercy of the freezing blasts of winter."[31]

City government moved quickly to assure the availability of coal to protect public health and safety. On January 23 police commissioner W. W. Fuller criticized the strikers for "catching many people unprepared, during the most severe freezing period in several years," and proclaimed that "city and county authorities will exhaust every means at their command to see that deliveries are made." He announced that the police would attempt to protect nonstriking drivers and noted that coal deliveries had already been made to St. John's Hospital and the water plant.[32]

Also on the twenty-third, the Associated Industries condemned the strike at a meeting chaired by Chamber of Commerce president Herbert Nilles and the police announced that they were enrolling "special deputies" because they lacked the manpower to maintain order and insure coal deliveries, a reality underscored by their inability to protect a delivery to Fargo Central High that day. This failure resulted in closure of the school, an outcome protested by few students. Eventually, as many as 250 men were deputized, some from the ranks of the unemployed but many apparently from the coal dealers, the Associated Industries, and the American Legion.[33]

Local 173 suffered a public relations setback for striking in the depth of winter, but that was only one of its difficulties. The dairy drivers had enjoyed some public sympathy, and respected citizens such as George Hoenck and Father Ryan had been willing to defend them. Champions of the coal drivers were conspicuous by their absence. Part of the problem might have been that continuing labor violence at the Grand Theater and the Knerr Dairy—a disturbing development in a city in which public order was prized and conflict stigmatized—had raised suspicions regarding the nature and the purposes of Local 173. The Minneapolis experience, in which a coal driver's strike initiated a process resulting in impressive union gains, was also undoubtedly in the minds of many Fargoans on both sides of the issue. It is clear that the Associated Industries was determined to stand firm against the drivers and that even altruistic citizens such as Hoenck and Ryan were reluctant to question it.

United to a degree that the dairies were not, having the full support of the business community, and allied with the police and city government, the coal dealers enjoyed a position of strength from which they summarily rejected Local 173's offer of a one-day "truce." Contributing to their confidence was the fact that the strike was only partially effective. Only sixty-five of 110 coal drivers went out, and about twenty of them went back to work within a few days. With numerous nonstrikers and former strikers carrying coal under protection of police and special deputies, deliveries returned almost to normal within less than a week. The strikers were reduced to a series of parades to draw public attention to their cause, beginning with one on January 24 in which about two hundred people, including strikers, their families, unemployed men, and supportive NDAC students marched through Fargo and Moorhead, "stopping at some business firms to cheer and at others to 'boo.'" By Sunday, January 27, a "Citizens Committee" was publicly urging the fuel dealers to get back to normal business operations by giving permanent positions to strikebreakers and by filling other jobs by issuing an ultimatum to strikers to "report to duty no later than 8 o'clock Monday morning" if they desired to remain employed.[34]

The coal drivers' strike reached a violent climax on the day the "Citizens Committee" letter appeared in the *Forum*. A group of men from Local 173 went to the Red River at the foot of Thirteenth Avenue South to confront a nonunion crew cutting ice for the Moorhead Ice Company. A pre-arranged signal blast from the whistle at the Moorhead power plant brought rushing to the scene scores of special deputies and policemen who had been positioned nearby. A melee ensued, during which about thirty union men and their supporters were captured while others fled through the trees along the river. State's attorney A. R. Bergesen swore out arrest warrants for thirty-five men, including Dunne, Cruden, and Swalde, charging them with "counseling, advising and abetting a riot." More than two hundred police officers and special deputies, armed mostly with clubs and ax handles, proceeded to Local 173 headquarters at 514½ First Avenue North to serve the warrants. When the police were denied entry, they fired tear gas into the building. About one hundred occupants, some of them women and children, poured into the street, where police arrested sixty-six men and marched them to the Cass County jail, a few blocks away. Police then searched the building, confiscating documents and "a formidable array of weapons," including "sections of iron gas pipe, clubs and rubber hose."[35]

Dunne was not among those arrested at the river or union headquarters, but Cruden and Swalde were. Also jailed were some of the usual suspects who had been involved in violent confrontations on behalf of Local 173 in the past, including Alex Glowka and Hugh Hughes, who had been arrested for confronting the nonunion lathers at the Grand, and William Lind, who was one of those charged with the assault on the Knerr Company buttermaker. Other notables caught in the police net were Jasper Haaland of Hillsboro, who had been the Communist candidate for Congress from the First District of North Dakota in 1934, and O. L. Aasgaard, a Federal Emergency Relief Administration worker who was teaching an American history class at the union hall when the gas attack took place. Police dropped riot charges against him when they concluded he was an innocent bystander.[36]

Sixteen men eventually were tried for "rioting" on "Gas Sunday" in a trial that was at times raucous and disorderly. Local attorneys Lee Brooks and

Quentin Burdick represented the defendants. Focusing on the confrontation at the river and the presence of supposed weapons in the union hall, State's Attorney Bergesen emphasized that "this is not a fight against labor" but a fight for law and order. The defense countered that the police and special deputies had provoked the "alleged riot" and that the "the state's case is part of a deliberate scheme to arrest these men, not because they are guilty of any crime, but because they are laboring men." After deliberating for twenty-one hours, the jury found the defendants guilty. Judge P. M. Paulsen sentenced Cruden, Swalde, and Hughes to six months in jail and the other thirteen defendants to two months apiece. Paulsen told the defendants he had considered suspending their sentences but changed his mind because of continuing strike violence, which he equated with "shouting defiance at the court." The judge also expressed his regret that Miles Dunne, safe from Fargo authorities in Moorhead, was not on trial, noting darkly, "I know there is a man from the outside . . . who should be before this bar of justice and who would be dealt with severely."[37]

As Judge Paulsen indicated, the Gas Sunday arrests and trial did not end strike activity or strike-related violence, both of which continued with some intensity. Addressing a meeting of five hundred strikers and their supporters at Phenix Hall in Moorhead on January 31, Dunne argued that the strike had now become a crusade for "the right of free speech and free assemblage, our right under the Constitution." The strikers in attendance vowed to continue the "fight 'till hell freezes over." The next day a Washburn Coal Company driver making a delivery at the First Baptist Church was assaulted, as was a driver for Adams Transfer. Several more assaults on nonstrikers took place over the next few weeks, strikers began picketing the homes of scabs, and union men set up pickets on highways leading into Fargo "urging people not to patronize a 'scab town.'" There were also incidents of vandalism against coal company property. Bricks were thrown through the windows of the Chesley, Sherwood, and Oscar Kjorlie lumber companies, and vandals emptied 11,000 gallons of fuel oil from a tank owned by the Kjorlie Company.[38]

In addition to heightening the tensions of the strike, the Gas Sunday arrests claimed a life. Early in the morning of February 9, Ernest Falconer, a driver for Washburn Coal and one of the strikers arrested at the union hall, forced his father and his sister out of the house, put a .38 caliber revolver to his head, and pulled the trigger in the presence of his paralyzed mother. Resisting the efforts of coroner Carl Elofson to get them to concede that Falconer's suicide came as a result of pressures from his brother unionists, his parents and friends agreed that he had been unhinged by his arrest and fear of re-arrest. The sole support of two invalided parents, Falconer was apparently anxious about his ability to maintain them in the face of the legal challenges that might confront him. An estimated seven hundred unionists and supporters attended Falconer's funeral on February 12 in Fargo.[39]

The ramifications of Gas Sunday moved beyond the city limits very quickly, much to Fargo's embarrassment. Members of the Langer faction in the state legislature condemned Fargo officials for violating the rights of strikers on Gas Sunday and for using "hired thugs" to break the coal drivers' strike, and they created a special legislative committee to investigate police tactics. Eventually the committee exonerated the city and the police department for their actions on Gas Sunday, but not before coaxing an admission from one Fargo legislator that some of the special deputies "went too far." The events surrounding the strike also drew the attention of the *Nation* and the *New Republic*, national journals of liberal opinion, which condemned the police, the Associated Industries, the special deputies, and the trial held before what critics claimed was a stacked jury.[40]

The coal drivers' strike and Gas Sunday shocked and embarrassed a city that was neither accustomed to nor comfortable with class conflict. Unwilling to abandon the myth of cooperative and congenial labor relations in Fargo, the *Forum*, Judge Paulsen, the Chamber of Commerce, and others sought to fashion another myth to buttress it. Instead of conceding that the coal drivers' strike and its attendant violence were signs of class conflict and resentment in the city, opinion leaders argued that outside agitators with a radical agenda had carried out the strike, poisoning the well of affection from which employees and employers drank and duping the legitimate labor movement as well as the drivers themselves. This exercise in mythmaking involved praising the mainstream labor movement while urging it to disavow the radical forces opinion leaders were demonizing.

The myth repair operation began even as the last whiffs of tear gas dissipated in the winter air. Responding editorially to the actions of police and special deputies at the river and Local 173 headquarters, on January 29 the *Forum* praised the city's established labor movement for its intelligence and moderation and even expressed "the kindliest sympathy for and interest in the welfare of the great bulk of the membership of Local 173," who had "been good citizens in the past, [and] will be good citizens in the future." The *Forum* also praised the employers, most of whom approached their workers "on a basis of fairness and equity." These same employers had helped bring on the strike through their failure to negotiate, but their refusal was justified because, the

Forum concluded, "the real and underlying objective of the Local 173 leadership was not settlement. Rather, the goal at all times has been insurrection—the goal has been the creation of turmoil and warfare." This was the crux of the argument. Gas Sunday was not the work of obdurate employers or bullying special deputies or even of the drivers themselves but of "a certain 'agent' . . . and . . . those who worked with him to arouse the passion of a comparatively small group of men who, left alone, would go about their business peacefully and on good terms with their neighbors and with their employers."[41]

The presence of outside agitator Miles Dunne allowed the *Forum* to argue, in contrast to what seemed to be obvious facts, that industrial relations were actually cordial in the city and class conflict did not exist. Others repeated that theme. Speaking to a joint Methodist, Baptist, and Presbyterian service attended by six hundred people, Daniel Heitmeyer of First Baptist professed sympathy for labor and urged employers and employees to be led by "the Golden Rule, [and] conciliation," but he attributed the coal drivers' strike to "trouble makers" hoping to "bring on the day for the Communist revolution."[42]

In his remarks to the strikers he was sentencing Judge Paulsen also expressed high regard for organized labor, reserving blame for "certain leadership" of Local 173. "Fargo and the officials of this city and county and the court have no quarrel with the union," Paulsen contended. "In fact Fargo is proud of the Fargo Trades and Labor assembly which has been a credit to this community. There is no class distinction here. There is no fight between capital and labor. Here the man who works in the street and at other common labor mingles with the men who work in offices and hold responsible positions." Speaking to the press after the verdict, State's Attorney Bergesen claimed that "this case was in no sense a conflict with organized labor" but was instead "a question of whether we shall have orderly government or mob rule." And the *Forum* added, "this verdict can in no way be regarded as having any bearing on the issue that was raised as between the employees and the employers. Nor can it be accepted nor can it be interpreted as an indictment of organized labor as we have known it in Fargo." The Chamber of Commerce agreed, stating in its 1935 report that the drivers' strike "came about not through the efforts of local people but from outside influences and was very displeasing to both the labor and business interests because Fargo has always had a very good reputation so far as employer and employee relations were concerned."[43]

The picture painted by Paulsen, Bergesen, the *Forum,* and the chamber of a classless city in which harmony characterized the relationship between capital and labor was pleasant but flawed. As long as organized labor was willing to be a junior partner in the economy of the city, it would be viewed as "a credit to this community." And as long as workers accepted a paternalistic relationship with bosses instead of asserting their rights, Fargo's "good reputation so far as employer and employee relations were concerned" would continue. But, as employers made clear in the PWA wage dispute, they were determined that Fargo would remain a low-wage city. And as they showed in the drivers' strike, in which they followed the Minneapolis Citizens Alliance recipe for maintenance of the open shop, while they might show kindness and concern for their employees they had no intention of meeting them as equals or of giving them a formal say in how businesses should be run.[44]

The Trades and Labor Assembly had recognized from Local 173's earliest days that its fight was the fight for all organized labor in the city. The drivers' union stood for dignity and equality for employees and for working-class people generally, as it demonstrated in its confrontations with the Relief Office and the welfare board, even as it threatened the class hierarchy of the city and its paternalistic labor regime. Under the leadership of William Murrey, the Trades and Labor Assembly had supported the dairy drivers and had protested both police protection for Alice Knerr and Judge Swenson's injunction. The Trades and Labor Assembly also stood behind the coal drivers, opposing the appointment and use of special deputies and staging public meetings to protest police actions and the riot trial. The *Forum* admitted as much, noting in its February 21 editorial that the Trades and Labor Assembly "had voted 'moral support' of the strikers while condemning the officials for their actions against the crowd that was jailed," but the newspaper suggested "that the Trades and Labor Assembly action was taken at a time and under circumstances that did not permit a full, free investigation of the facts and calm action thereon."[45]

Over the next few weeks pressure on the Trades and Labor Assembly to sever its relationship with Local 173 intensified, and the organization responded by slowly and reluctantly backing away from the radical union. On March 19 the Trades and Labor Assembly was given the opportunity to dissociate itself entirely from the drivers' union when it received notification from Teamsters' International union president Daniel Tobin that Local 173's charter was being revoked on the grounds that "Communists cannot hold membership in our organization" and "Miles Dunne . . . is an out and out Communist." The Trades and Labor Assembly responded to the Tobin letter by suspending Local 173, Murrey telling the *Forum*, "we are in perfect accord with the rank and file members of Local 173 in their desire to improve their laboring conditions, but they must repudiate that portion of their leadership which has directed them into illegal and reprehensible activities." The *Forum* praised the Trades and Labor Assembly for this action, noting pointedly that it "gives the community new reason for confidence in the regularly constituted labor agencies in Fargo." Others saw the suspension of Local 173 as a cowardly act. Writing to an official of the Trades and Labor Assembly, State Federation of Labor executive secretary Lawrence Mero professed to be "somewhat surprised and at a loss to understand why such action should be taken. . . . It is rather embarrassing for many of us, who took an active part in supporting the Fargo Strikers, to have the Fargo Central Body . . . take such action at this stage of the strike, for if there was any justification for the strike, and I sincerely believe there was, then there is justification to carry it on to a successful conclusion." As for the communism issue, Mero noted that the Trades and Labor Assembly had known all along that Dunne was "somewhat of a Communist" and concluded that "I am as much opposed to Communism as anyone, but it seems when any one [*sic*] gets a little active in the labor movement he is branded a Communist." Mero's points were well argued, but the local atmosphere had become so charged by this point that the Trades and Labor Assembly had apparently concluded that it must disassociate itself from Local 173 or risk severe damage and perhaps even destruction.[46]

The growing consensus that communism, personified by Miles Dunne, was at the root of labor-management conflict in Fargo was reassuring in a sense, but it also contributed to rising anxiety about local radicalism. Even during the depths of the Depression, Fargo was a relatively conservative place, though there was a radical presence in the city. A small but active Socialist party existed, led by William Ballou, a former Unitarian minister whose church was closed under pressure from patriots who objected to his pacifism during World War I. Marion Pressler remembered attending meetings of "a subversive group—they were Socialists," who gathered every two weeks at Ballou's home. Nationally prominent Socialist Party speakers drew some attention, as in 1932 when vice-presidential candidate James Maurer spoke to "several hundred people" at the Labor Temple. In 1935 Ballou hosted presidential candidate Norman Thomas and sixty guests at a tea at his home. Two of the four hostesses assisting Ballou were wives of men arrested on Gas Sunday.[47]

The Socialists were organized well enough to field candidates for local office on occasion, as in 1933 when the party endorsed Howard Morris of the Unemployed Exchange and carpenter Hans Rosenberg for the City Commission. In addition to the Socialists, Fargo was home to other leftist groups, such as the Holiday Association, which attempted to organize the unemployed and aggressively represented reliefers with the County Welfare Board. The Nonpartisan League, Governor William Langer's political machine, also took on a radical hue in Fargo, defending the unemployed and organized labor. Communists were also present, but they were much less numerous. In 1938 the state party held its convention in Fargo, drawing about fifty delegates, and the next year nationally known party leader Elizabeth Gurley Flynn gave a speech in town. Poet Thomas McGrath remembered attending Communist meetings on Front Street and emphasized that the party was especially active in organizing the Workers Alliance.[48]

The church of the left was a schismatic one, composed of numerous sects that were often antagonistic toward one another. Miles Dunne was indeed a "Communist," but as a Trotskyite he was violently antagonistic toward the Stalinist Communist Party USA, which was in turn bitterly hostile toward Socialists such as William Ballou. Fargoans did not usually pay much attention to such distinctions, however, and in the post–Gas Sunday atmosphere virtually anyone who had supported the cause of Local 173 or had even said a kind word for the union could be defined as a "Communist." Anti-communism began to gather steam in March 1935. On the ninth, the *Forum* suggested darkly that Local 173 had received advice and support "from men who live in this community and who . . . while they preach destruction of the government—receive their very livelihood from the government they would tear down." The newspaper's rather opaque reference was clarified on March 11 when the coal companies asked for a court order limiting picketing and "illegal acts" and specifically restraining William Ballou, S. W. Hagan, Local 173 officers Cruden and Swalde, and two union members, Ernest Goldschmidtz and Adam Magloughlin. The most interesting name on the list was Hagan's. The son of North Dakota agriculture commissioner John Hagan, Steve Hagan had been appointed secretary of the North Dakota Agricultural College in 1933 at Governor Langer's insistence. Staffers at the NDAC believed Hagan's mission was to identify and remove from the payroll people who were unsympathetic to the governor and to transform the college into an effective vehicle for Langer's faction of the Nonpartisan League. Hagan played a key role in the identification of seven anti-Langer administrators who were fired in a spectacular "purge" in the summer of 1937. Apparently, though, Hagan was more than a political functionary for the Langer machine, embracing some of the pro-labor principles held by those on the left wing of the Nonpartisan League.[49]

The naming of Hagan drew the attention of red hunters to the NDAC. While the NDAC was at least as conservative as most land-grant campuses, a few faculty had established records as progressives, such as botanist Henry Bolley, education professor Peter Iverson, range scientist Herbert Hanson, horticulturist Clair B. Waldron, and his brother Lawrence, a wheat breeder. In addition, some students and faculty had supported the cause of the coal drivers, marching in their parades and attending protest meetings. That was sufficient evidence for Eli Weston, who told the Kiwanis Club, "Communism is seeping . . . into the North Dakota Agricultural college," adding, "the activities of a group on the payroll of the agricultural college have all the earmarks and resemblances of communism." Weston's accusation was followed by word that the state Board of Administration, responsible for governing state agencies, was investigating charges of communism at the NDAC. "Rumors of Communism at the college have circulated through the state for some years," a board spokesman told the *Forum*, "but became white hot . . . following the Fargo truckers' strike of last winter in which several faculty members of N.D.A.C. are credited with 'counseling and advising.'"[50]

The NDAC had its defenders. On May 4 one of them admitted that "undergraduates and certain . . . young faculty members—have spouted off at times during the Fargo strike" but denied that there was communism at the AC. Another contended that it was only those with "sophomoric minds" and "pedagogical persons, cloistered from the actual realities of the world" who were "tinged with a daub of red." Responding to a charge in 1936 that communism was rife at the NDAC, college president John Shepperd noted that, while "there may be several members of the faculty who are what some people call 'pinks,' . . . the situation in this regard is not nearly so bad as at such institutions as the Universities of Minnesota and Wisconsin." And in October the editor of the NDAC student newspaper was pleased to report to the *Forum* that only seventeen of 823 votes cast in a mock presidential election went to Communist candidate Earl Browder. The board investigation apparently went nowhere, and the charges of communism at the NDAC faded away. In the final analysis, the main effect of the accusations and the investigation was to stifle potential dissent at the NDAC from the emerging consensus about the causes and the nature of the drivers' strike.[51]

Meanwhile the coal drivers' strike and the issues surrounding it slowly petered out. The injunction dramatically limited the effectiveness of the strike, and most of the drivers who were still out sought to return to their jobs. Dunne stayed on for a time, testifying before the North Dakota legislature and directing strike operations from the safety of Moorhead, but he eventually moved on to other work in other places. The state supreme court overturned the convictions of Cruden and Swalde, but they were retried and convicted in March 1936 and served their sentences. In February 1937 Governor Langer gave Cruden a job in the state tax department, and a year later he was an official in the state employees' union, though he continued to dabble in Fargo union affairs. In 1937 Steve Hagan challenged Fred Olsen for the mayoralty, supported by the Workers Alliance, some of the Townsend Clubs, and at least a portion of the Trades and Labor Assembly. Hagan promised municipal ownership of the power plant, enforcement of wage and hour laws, and an ambitious program of public works, but he lost badly to Olsen, carrying only three precincts, all in working-class neighborhoods downtown, and gaining just 27 percent of the vote in a three-man race. The next year he resigned as NDAC secretary.[52]

Local 173 faded from the scene and local radicals were routed, but the self-serving theory that outside agitators had caused Fargo's labor problems was disproved by the dramatic increase in union activity *after* the defeat of the coal drivers' strike. Drawing encouragement from the friendly attitude of the Roosevelt administration, as illustrated especially by passage of the National Labor Relations Act in 1935, workers in Fargo and elsewhere formed and joined unions in large numbers. By 1939, forty-eight unions were operating in Fargo-Moorhead, including organizations among city employees and public school teachers. The largest of these unions was, ironically, the drivers, reorganized in 1936 into Local 116 of the Chauffeurs, Teamsters, and Helpers Union. By the end of that year Local 116 had four hundred members, approaching Local 173's highest total.[53]

Not only did workers join unions, they asserted their positions aggressively, bringing a series of strikes to the city. In 1937 painters, road construction drivers, Western Union messengers, transfer drivers, bakery workers, and barbers all struck. Some of these strikes were lengthy and marked by episodes of violence and intimidation. The barbers' strike, for example, dragged on for half a year. Union barbers set a price of $0.50 for a haircut, but Jack Scheidt of Jack's Barber Shop at 422 Front severely undercut the union by offering haircuts for $0.15. Union barbers picketed Jack's for twenty-four weeks, his windows were broken, and "stench bombs" drove his employees and customers from the shop. Eventually, three other Front Street shops broke the price agreement on the grounds that they could not compete with Scheidt. That defection, along with a court injunction prohibiting picketing at Jack's, effectively broke the strike and led to large-scale defections from the union.[54]

Another protracted and violent strike in 1937 was that of Bakery and Confectionary Workers Local 396, which struck for recognition, a forty-eight-hour

While most Fargoans walked to work, streetcars provided an alternative, especially attractive in the winter.

week, and higher pay. The larger bakeries were willing to negotiate with the union, but the smaller, family-owned firms were not. Union bakers eventually resorted to intimidation in an attempt to bring the bakeries around, and in December police arrested five men, including the ubiquitous William Cruden, for entering Northwest Bakery in Moorhead and threatening two nonstriking workers, Fern Jones and Milton Lee. By that point the strike was collapsing and union members were being arrested for intimidating brother unionists who had returned or who desired to return to work.[55]

Sporadic actions against the bakers continued after the strike was broken, most notably the dumping of kerosene on a load of baked goods being delivered by Twin City Bakery in the lower Front Street area in September 1938. Then, in June 1939, the city was shocked when Milton Lee, the son of Northwest Bakery owner John Lee, was killed by a dynamite bomb when he started his car to go to work. Suspicion fell on the bakers' union because Northwest Bakery had been unwilling to negotiate during the strike, John Lee had received threatening notes and telephone calls that he believed had come from the union, and his plant had been vandalized. Roland Tougas, president of the bakers' union and one of the men arrested for entering the bakery to confront Milton Lee in December 1937, was taken into custody and questioned extensively. Tougas eventually was released, however, and no one was ever charged with Lee's murder.[56]

A 1939 strike at Armour Packing in West Fargo was also marked by violence. In August the company fired two officials of Local 73 of the Packing Workers Organizing Committee, Clarence Wheeler and Mike Jacobson, supposedly for refusing to do work assigned to them. Local 73 contended they were fired for union activity and struck the plant, demanding their re-instatement. The company refused to bargain with the union and also refused arbitration offered by Mayor Olsen and State's Attorney Bergesen. Instead, Armour decided to run the plant with strikebreakers. When scabs entering the plant were confronted by an angry crowd of two hundred that "included many women," Armour decided to house them on company property in Pullman cars. Eventually, the union workers capitulated, agreeing to the dismissal of Wheeler and Jacobson and returning to work with "no seniority rights as far as the regular workers who remained on the job are concerned."[57]

The story of labor conflict in Fargo during the Great Depression demonstrates that union activity did not usually translate into union success. Too often, as in the case of the Armour workers, strikes were broken under humiliating conditions. Even when workers claimed victory, as they did in the dairy drivers' strike and the transfer drivers' 1937 strike, it was only partial, with workers receiving improvements in wages, benefits, and hours but failing to achieve union recognition. Part of the problem lay with the material with which unions had to work. As William Murrey noted in his 1938 presidential report to the North Dakota Federation of Labor, unions had been handicapped because so many members "were new in the movement." New union men were often union men who had a poor understanding of the nature and purpose of the union and a weak sense of loyalty to it. "We do not find it a difficult matter to get a local union set up," Murrey said, "but ... after they [*sic*] are set up and are operating by [*sic*] their own officers ... they begin to be lax in attending meetings and do not seem to have the proper spirit." Small wonder that unionists frequently refused to go out when strikes were called or returned to work before strikes were settled.[58]

Union workers failed to alter Fargo's status as an open-shop city, but their efforts revealed levels of class conflict and employer-employee disharmony that sharply contradicted the city's self-image. Everywhere in the nation class distinctions were more starkly etched during the Depression than before or since, and conflict defined relations between workers and bosses to a remarkable degree. Drawing encouragement from the friendly Roosevelt administration, workers who sought dignity and equality organized, struck, achieved recognition, and inaugurated American labor's golden age.

In Fargo some workers tried to follow the same script, but the play ended differently. Part of the reason was that there were few large industrial employers in Fargo and the small ones who were there organized well to maintain an open-shop city. In that endeavor they enjoyed the support of city government, the police, the courts, and, presumably, much of the public. Not surprisingly, many workers shared the attitudes of their employers and of the community at large. Like the "Loyal Fairmont Employee," many Fargo workers considered themselves "lucky . . . to have a job," and they were unwilling to imperil it by challenging their employers' pretensions or prerogatives. The result was that the paternal model of employer-employee relations survived in Fargo, somewhat battered, to be sure, but unbowed.

6

"Femininity has returned to the feminine world. Just as milady cut her hair, started smoking cigarets [*sic*], drinking hard liquor and wearing trousers a few years ago, now she is hardly in vogue if she isn't knitting . . . crocheting . . . or doing some of the other womanly bits of handicraft we thought had passed. . . . And, wonder of wonders, she likes it and so do the menfolk. Next thing we know they'll be bringing a box of candy instead of a pint of alcohol and the mix, when they come to call."
  Fargo Forum, *February 21, 1934*

"Does not our constitution advocate free and equal rights to all? Why then should a few men . . . bar us from being employed? Are we to believe we are under the rule of Soviet Russia, and not a free country?"
  Mrs. M. C. Osman, June 21, 1932

THE GREAT DEPRESSION took place in the midst of a long and challenging period of change in the Western world in regard to gender relations and men's and women's perceptions of what their respective roles should be. Beginning in earnest in the first half of the nineteenth century, female and male feminists had argued for the economic, social, and political equality of women, usually tempered by their perception that women sometimes required special protections. They had painstakingly achieved some successes, especially regarding women's access to employment and property and—in the entire United States beginning in 1920—the right to vote. However, this was not an uninterrupted advance or a process in which progress was inevitable. Both men and women continued to have social and cultural expectations rooted in a more patriarchal age and reflective of notions of inequality, hierarchy, rights, and obligations that contradicted the republican values guiding civic life. Thus, while such commentators as Mrs. M. C. Osman could, and did, make thoroughly modern, republican arguments for female equality, the *Forum* could simultaneously wax nostalgic about women who thought and behaved in a more traditional manner.[1]

The conflict over gender roles and expectations continued in Fargo during the 1930s. Not surprisingly, in a time of economic stringency the struggle frequently revolved around employment. Some women expected to be employed and believed that their economic rights should be respected, while others entered the job market to support families or maintain a standard of living. They sought to expand the opportunities that modern education and the service-oriented economy had offered to women. At the same time many men, and some women, favored limitations on female employment based on occupation, marital status, or motherhood. They sought to reverse trends in female employment that had appeared prior to the Depression.

While the conflict over women's economic roles took center stage in Fargo during the Depression, it was hardly the only battle in the ongoing gender wars. Fargoans also debated the issue of proper female conduct, focusing especially on personal behavior and sexuality. Increasing numbers of women acted as if they rejected a double standard that prescribed more permissive behavior for men than for women. Yet other women, and many men, believed that women should comport themselves differently from men and that they required special protections—from men and from themselves. At the base of this conflict was the same question that lay at the bottom of the female employment issue: would women enjoy the ability to define and control their own lives, or would they be shaped by others—fathers, husbands, or society generally?

It is clear in retrospect that the ongoing adjustment of women's roles and their relationship to men was not greatly affected by the Depression. It remained the case for individual women in Fargo that class or matrimonial status was more significant than gender in shaping experience. But the Great Depression did heighten sensitivity to issues of employment, family responsibility, the relationship between men and women, standards of behavior, and the nature of gender—issues that are with us still.

I

Fargo liked to portray itself as a city of conventional families, but at the onset of the Depression it could just as accurately have been called a city of unattached women. The 1930 census indicated that 37 percent of the women in the city over the age of fifteen were single and that another 10.4 percent were either widowed or divorced. When allowance is made for women whose husbands had deserted them or were working away from home, were in the service, or were in prison, it is likely that more than half of the women in Fargo in 1930 lived without husbands present.[2]

Many of the young single women in the city were migrants from farms and small towns in eastern North Dakota and northwestern Minnesota. Indeed, it was largely due to the propensity of young rural women to migrate that in Fargo women aged fifteen to twenty-nine outnumbered men in that age group by three to two.[3]

Fargo's educational opportunities attracted some of these female migrants. The North Dakota Agricultural College was located in Fargo, and Moorhead State Teachers College and Concordia College were just across the river. In addition, the city was home to several business and secretarial schools, a number of beauty schools, and nurses' training facilities at St. Luke's and St. John's hospitals and at St. Ansgar's in Moorhead. Harriet Hatfield moved to town from western North Dakota to enroll in the teacher training course at MSTC, Frieda Oster left a southeastern North Dakota farm to take the commercial course at Interstate Business College, and Lucille Duval moved from the nearby farming community of Wild Rice to enter nurses' training. Their stories could be multiplied many times over.[4]

Some single women moved on when their educations were completed and some stayed in Fargo, but few returned to their home communities. Life in small towns and on farms in the Northern Plains could be stultifying even in the best of times, and during the 1930s, when the countryside reeled from the onslaught of drought and depression, it was downright dismal. Rural parents frequently urged daughters to move to places where job opportunities were more plentiful, desirable marriage partners were more numerous, and money could be earned to supplement family budgets. For their parts, dutiful daughters frequently responded to family needs. Myrtle Nymoen sent most of her meager earnings as a housemaid to the family farm near Rothsay, Minnesota, so that her two brothers could remain in school, and Oster somehow managed to build a savings account of $142 out of her paltry bookkeeper's salary to help her father buy cattle.[5]

Single women who stayed in Fargo after completing their educations entered a job market that was relatively vibrant even during the Great Depression, providing employment for 55 percent of single women over the age of fifteen in 1930. It was also a job market that was highly structured along gender lines. Some women worked in manufacturing—especially at food products firms such as the Armour Creamery, the Manchester Biscuit Company, and Cheney-Eberhardt Candy—but most worked in service, clerical, or retail occupations. Indeed, it was the abundance of such pink-collar jobs that made Fargo a powerful magnet for single women. The 1930 census found that of the

4,082 women working in the city, more than two-thirds were employed in one of four categories: "professional and semiprofessional service," which ran the gamut from teaching and nursing to clerical work to cosmetology; "domestic and personal service;" "wholesale and retail trade;" and "hotels, restaurants, and boarding houses."[6]

Some of the most desirable female jobs in the city were available to single women with training or education. The Fargo Public Schools, 170 of whose 216 teachers were women in 1935, required that female teachers be single and dismissed those who married. As career teacher Gladys Carney remembered, "everybody just accepted it," along with rules prohibiting teachers from smoking, living outside of Fargo, or accepting supplementary employment during the school year. Clerical jobs, most of which required business school training or at least a high school degree, were also generally limited to single women. Frieda Oster got work keeping the books in a clothing store, for example, when the previous bookkeeper married and was dismissed. And Irene Fraser lost her job as a "fieldman" at the Armour Creamery when she married in 1938. As she put it, "we knew that was the deal."[7]

Even desirable female jobs did not pay very well, in part because fields dominated by women were so crowded and in part because employers did not believe they needed to pay a family wage to employees who were usually single. After the school board's 1933 cuts, most female teachers made under $1,000 per year and 15 to 20 percent less than males with comparable credentials. In 1937 nurses in supervisory capacities at St. Luke's made between $60 and $95 per month. And in 1936 Cass County relief administrator R. M. Parkins noted that stenographers in his office made $47 to $65 per month while case-workers, most of whom had college training, made $78 to $90.[8]

Single women could support themselves on such wages, but just barely, especially when they were expected to dress professionally and maintain high standards of cleanliness and grooming. A car was usually beyond their means, as was a place of one's own. Relatively affluent single women, like the clerical and retail workers who lived in John Carlson's father's apartment house north of downtown, shared apartments with roommates. Others, such as Oster, took furnished rooms in private homes. Despite her cheap lodgings, Oster had trouble meeting her obligations, confiding to her diary on March 17, 1937, that she had "only 53¢ to live on until 1st." A year later she despaired when she could not pay a nine-dollar grocery bill: "So disappointed. Just cried. So hard to make ends meet."[9]

The situation confronting clerical workers was sobering, but it was far preferable to that facing less skilled service and retail workers such as wait-resses, laundresses, maids, and cashiers. These women held jobs that came under intense competitive pressure during the Depression. Their domestic na-ture and the absence of a perceived need for formal training meant that these jobs could be held by many, many women. Women employed as waitresses or hotel maids found their fields flooded in the Depression's early years by un-skilled rural girls, skilled single women unable to obtain employment appro-priate for their training, wives who needed to help support their families, and high school and college students struggling to pay for educations.

In theory, many less skilled female workers were protected by a minimum wage law passed by the legislature in 1919 and enforced by the state Workmen's Compensation Bureau. The wage floors set by the bureau appeared liberal in light of the economic situation prevailing in the early years of the Depression. Waitresses and counter girls were supposed to earn a minimum of $14.90 per week, mercantile clerks $14.50, chambermaids and kitchen workers $14.20, and laundresses $14.00. In practice, though, there were three problems with this scheme. First, part-timers and "apprentices" could be hired for 15 to 30 percent less than experienced workers. The Workmen's Compensation Bureau had re-quired that no more than one in four workers be a part-timer or an apprentice, but it had removed this ceiling in 1930 at the behest of employers. Second, em-ployers offering "board" were allowed to pay much less per week. Waitresses receiving board, as virtually all waitresses in Fargo did, had their weekly mini-mum wage reduced to $8.90, even though the board they received consisted mainly of what was left over after the last customers had gone. Finally, and most importantly, as the North Dakota AFL put it in 1933, the law "has been openly vi-olated" and "women employees hesitate to report violations through fear of los-ing their jobs and being 'black listed' for future employment."[10]

Pressed by employers who threatened to replace women with men if mini-mum wages were not lowered, the Workmen's Compensation Bureau held hearings around the state in the summer of 1932. It found that the law was be-ing widely ignored. One woman testified in Fargo that dime store clerks were being paid $0.20 an hour when the legal minimum was $0.31 and stated her opinion that "with present wages girls would have to be buried by the county if they were to die tomorrow." And a lower Front Street café owner bragged that he had paid his waitresses only $4 a week plus board since 1929 and that the "girls he employs have been glad to work for the wages he paid." He was very likely right. The Workmen's Compensation Bureau capitulated to em-ployers' demands and reality by lowering minimum wages, though the new minimums were still higher than many bosses, who had learned they could violate the law with impunity, were paying.[11]

At least the state acknowledged responsibility for some female workers. Others—most notably housemaids—were on their own. The 1930 census counted 744 live-in maids employed in Fargo, or about one for every eight households in the city. In affluent neighborhoods, especially on the south side, "everybody had maids," as Ruth Landfield remembered. Maids were drawn overwhelmingly from rural areas, indicating that many country girls were introduced to life in Fargo through this occupation. Fargoans preferred rural maids because they likely had domestic skills and were more tractable than city girls. Rural parents may have desired domestic jobs for their daughters because they would presumably be under family supervision and in safe environments in which their physical needs would be met. Country girls seldom embarked on domestic service as a career. Instead, they used jobs as maids to gain familiarity with the city and its opportunities. A 1939 estimate that the average Fargo maid stayed on the job only three to six months indicates that in normal times many found more desirable employment rather quickly. High turnover meant that employers were frequently in the market for maids, and some went at the task quite systematically. Willimina Heller advertised for maids in rural newspapers and then interviewed prospective employees and their families. Others, such as Lillian Alsop, obtained maids through the YWCA or used the state employment service.[12]

Maids' work was demanding and sometimes degrading. Eva Nelson moved to the city in 1933 from the farming community of Christine, about twenty miles south of Fargo, to work as a maid. She was required to be up by 5:30 to prepare breakfast for the Eighth Street South family that employed her and by 3:30 on Monday—wash day. She prepared all the meals, and because the family was Jewish she had to master the details of kosher cooking. In between meal preparation, serving, and dish washing, she was responsible for house cleaning, silver polishing, washing, ironing, and mending. In the evenings she was expected to be the "companion" of the family's ten-year-old daughter. She had to supply her own maid's dress and was forbidden to enter or exit the house except by the rear door. In compensation she received room and board and three dollars per week.[13]

Away from home for the first time, Nelson suffered intensely from loneliness and isolation. Eventually she developed a friendship with one of the maids who worked nearby, "Helen Kohlhoff, a girl about my age who had come to the 'Big City' from Medina, North Dakota, to find work. . . . I do not know what I would have done without her as I did not know anyone in Fargo." Nelson and Kohlhoff spent what little free time they had together. Fargo maids customarily got Thursday and Sunday nights off, and on "maid's night out" they crowded into downtown movie theaters and ballrooms such as the Avalon and the Crystal, where they were regaled with such clever pick-up lines as "and whose kitchen engineer are you?"[14]

Life as a live-in maid was unattractive in the best of times, but it got much worse in the early years of the Depression. Throughout the country the pool of potential maids grew dramatically as unemployed adult women and students needing board and room competed with traditional domestics for jobs. This situation was a boon to the rich and even the not-so-rich. In December 1932 *Fortune* exulted that "for the first time in a generation, the supply of trained domestic workers is greater than the demand. For the first time, the bargaining power is on the side of the housekeeper." *Fortune* pointed out how this rise in supply had changed conditions of labor: "The whole domestic service situation has been demoralized, both as to wages and to hours. . . . Depression has thrown [domestic servants] into a hectic individual-bargaining stage. This means an unparalleled chance for the housewife."[15]

The implications of this situation for maids in Fargo were revealed in 1931. In March the Community Welfare Association passed a resolution "deploring the attitude of Fargo housewives who have taken advantage of the employment slump among domestic helpers" and noted "that some Fargo housewives had exploited domestic helpers to the extent of drastically cutting the wage scale." The association estimated that because "the supply of domestic help has been swelled" weekly wages for most maids had fallen in a period of two years from $8–12 to $3–7. Further depressing wages was the fact that necessity compelled some women to work for board and room only. Indeed, classified ads placed by women willing to labor under such conditions appeared frequently in the *Forum*. On November 19, 1932, for example, a "Middle-aged widow wants housekeeping . . . for room and board," and three days later "Good dependable Norwegian girl, 34, wants housekeeping or other place. Good home rather than wages in respectable place."[16]

Affluent housewives and their defenders either denied that they were underpaying maids or blamed the victims, suggesting that many seeking domestic positions were not capable. One *Forum* reader argued that many women working as maids "are not worth $3 per week," and the newspaper editorialized that "the incompetent workers—there are far more of them in the field of house workers than usual, because of the lack of employment in other lines—

we have with us always and, naturally, with a great supply, the average paid automatically drops."[17]

Several readers countered by attacking the affluent for taking advantage of those seeking domestic work. One wrote the *Forum* that "if this be true, the condition is to be lamented," and another wondered "how the women of Fargo have the nerve and presumption to expect and ask for a competent maid for such wages as these."[18]

The Community Welfare Association's exposure of the maids' pay situation and the public response to it indicated that many Fargoans felt a paternalistic responsibility toward single women that they did not demonstrate toward older, married women or toward single or married men. That paternalism was reflected institutionally in the three Fargo agencies that provided boarding and employment services to young women new to the city. The Lutheran Inner Mission Society of North Dakota maintained Luther Hall, a boarding house for young single women, just west of downtown. Luther Hall could accommodate up to twenty guests, who received room and board for about $18 per month while they were seeking work. Those without funds could stay for free, and the agency provided "small loans for personal incidentals" and "aid to help them secure passage to their home" if their search for employment proved fruitless. Some years during the thirties Luther Hall registered as many as 230 young women, most of whom also took advantage of an employment bureau that endeavored to find them work, mainly as maids. Fargo Catholics did not have a similar institution, but Catholic Welfare made arrangements for young female migrants to the city to board with Catholic families.[19]

Somewhat larger than Luther Hall was a YWCA facility nearby. The Y boarding home had a capacity of thirty, and in the 1933–34 fiscal year it provided lodging to 454 women new to the city. It also maintained an employment bureau, placing 264 women in 1933–34, mostly in domestic positions. In order to address the need for companionship among lonely young women—albeit on a class-segregated basis—the Y sponsored two "friendship clubs" in 1932, one for domestic servants and another for "stenographers, clerks, and other girls in similar positions." The Y noted that recreational opportunities for women were limited because maids' salaries averaged less than $4 a week and most clerical workers made only $40 to $60 a month.[20]

In addition to these faith-based institutions, the Fargo Women's Boarding Home Association maintained a nonsectarian facility that could house about a dozen residents at 120 Eighth Street South. Like the others, this was a philanthropic endeavor that depended in part on donations and Community Chest support.[21]

Paternalistic attitudes toward single women in Fargo were also noteworthy in the treatment of unwed mothers. Fargo had two institutions dedicated to providing medical and physical care for unwed mothers and their infants, the nonsectarian Florence Crittenton Home and the North Dakota House of Mercy, affiliated with the Norwegian Lutheran Church. Catholics did not maintain a facility for unwed mothers, but they did provide support for pregnant Catholic girls, usually at the Crittenton Home or in their own homes but on rare occasions at the House of Mercy.[22]

The two Fargo homes depended on public and private support. During the 1930s each received a biennial legislative appropriation of $10,000 in return for their services to North Dakota women and children. In addition, each got about $2,000 per year from the Community Chest. The homes charged $20 per month to girls' families or to the counties sponsoring them, but both emphasized that they never turned away a woman lacking support. On the private side, the House of Mercy counted on contributions from Lutheran congregations and laypeople and the Crittenton Home depended on its socially prominent board for backing. Small donations of various types played a minor role in sustaining the institutions. In 1933, for example, the Cass County Commission voted to donate $100 to the Crittenton Home, and in 1935 the Scandinavian Women's Christian Temperance Union gave $2.55 to each institution, along with "canned fruit, jelly . . . and vegetables." In 1934 the *Forum* reported, without irony, that the Fargo Theater had hosted the residents of the Crittenton Home at a showing of *Little Women*.[23]

During the thirties the Crittenton Home and the House of Mercy cared for an average of four to five hundred mothers and infants per year, most on site but a few in their homes. The average stay at a facility was five to six months. The homes preferred that mothers-to-be enter two to three months prior to their due dates, and state law required that they remain in the home, nursing their babies, for three months after delivery. In this relatively brief period, the homes attempted to uplift their charges and turn their lives in a new direction. As superintendent Fannie Brownson of the Crittenton Home put it in 1941, "we feel that the girls who come to us are in need of a different perspective of life than they have had . . . and we try by all means to establish a higher morale among them in such a way that they will be self-supporting, respected citizens." Education was central to this effort. Superintendent Paula Iverson of the House of Mercy explained, "training is given in cooking, plain sewing, fancy work, as well as general etiquette." The House of Mercy also made correspondence courses available through "the Progressive High School at the N.D.A.C.," and the Fargo Public Schools offered classes at the Crittenton Home. Religious instruction was also provided at both facilities. Monsignor Anthony Peschel first became interested in welfare work when Father Vincent Ryan assigned him to teach Catholic doctrine at the Crittenton Home.[24]

The lives of women at the homes were closely directed and monitored. The House of Mercy had more than three pages of rules and regulations—fifty-six in all—covering virtually every aspect of daily life in the facility. Among other things, residents were prohibited from using the staff bathroom, sitting in the kitchen, using the front stairway, turning off the radio when a church service was being broadcast, or reading "True Story, Detective Mystery or Movie Magazines." Nor did attention to women's lives cease when they left the home. As Iverson noted in 1941, "friendly follow-up work giving encouragement, advice, love and corrective criticism is an important part of our work. . . . The aim in our work is to rehabilitate the girls, helping them to face life squarely and to live down the unfortunate experience."[25]

In conformity to the accepted social work practices of the time, the Crittenton Home and the House of Mercy encouraged unmarried mothers to keep their babies. Some did not do so, but one of the effects of the three-month nursing requirement was to strengthen the bond between mother and child. Mothers wishing to keep their children sometimes returned to their home communities but usually did not. Embarrassment, alienation from families, and the lack of employment necessary to support mother and infant turned many into unintentional rural migrants to Fargo. Elizabeth Alsop, who followed her father on the board at the Crittenton Home, remembered, "most of them came from outside of town, but a lot of them would stay in town." In order to help the young mothers, the homes attempted to place them in employment situations in which they could keep their infants. In practice, this meant jobs as maids and sometimes as waitresses. While most rural migrants saw domestic jobs as temporary, they took on more permanent character for women encumbered with infants.[26]

Single rural women migrating to Fargo, whether by choice or by circumstance, could take advantage of the city's paternalism in the form of boarding facilities and homes for the care and education of unwed mothers. These institutions could be and frequently were obtrusive, moralistic, and condescending, and women of independent temperaments undoubtedly chafed under the restraints they imposed, but they did provide a safety net. That safety net was not generally available to homeless women or to transients.

Throughout the country the impact of the Depression on young people was cause for concern generally, but the effects of the crisis on young women were especially noteworthy. In common with many young men, some young women took to the road in the 1930s. Transience remained an overwhelmingly male enterprise, but observers estimated that up to ten percent of itinerants were unattached females, many of them in their teens. Life on the road was very difficult for women. While male transients constituted "a culture and a society of their own" with their own accepted practices and institutions, females were making life up as they went along. Because of their smaller numbers and their gender they were more vulnerable than men to robbery, violence, and sexual exploitation. Local charities were unsure how to handle women unattached to families, and the transient bureaus treated them as afterthoughts. It was difficult for female transients to beg or panhandle, because women approaching men on the streets were likely to be propositioned or arrested for prostitution. On occasion transient and homeless women entered the consciousness of the city, as in 1938 when the *Forum* profiled "Greasy Mary" and "Crook-neck Annie" among a colony of riverbank shack dwellers or the next year when Rita Reyes, eighteen, of Sioux City, Iowa, lost a leg when she fell from a Northern Pacific freight passing through town.[27]

Intentional female migrants new to the city could depend on some institutional support from Fargoans because they were in a well-understood stage of life and they served the city's economic needs. Well before the Great Depression it was accepted—and expected—that young women would leave the homes of their fathers for a relatively brief period of gender-appropriate work, to be ended when they married and formed homes with their husbands. Transient and homeless women were much different and more difficult to understand. Their lives seemed aimless, their family ties were obscure at best, and they did not seem destined for marriage and respectability. Fargoans pitied and perhaps feared them but offered no institutional solutions for their problems.

Also difficult to understand were older, resident females who had failed to marry and who desired to maintain an independent existence. The gender imbalance in Fargo made it inevitable that some women would not marry. Others, such as teacher Gladys Carney, chose not to sacrifice satisfying careers for matrimony. In any event, some women in the city lived lives of independence and self-support that they were loath to surrender. In theory, personal independence was celebrated in a nation founded on principles of individual liberty and self-direction. In practice, however, it was difficult to accept and even understand when applied to women, whose lives had traditionally been defined by their relationships to men on whom they depended and who were expected to have fathers and brothers on whom to lean in times of hardship.[28]

In 1933 the Independent Ladies Club of the Unemployed Exchange noted that seventy-eight women needed work, of whom twenty-one were single. For several years afterward, the Independent Ladies Club ran advertisements like the following one, which appeared in the "Women Want Work" column of the *Forum* in 1934: "Call 3620, the Independent Ladies Club, 1344 Front St. for women to do work of all kinds, unemployed preferring work rather than relief." The idea of the unemployed preferring work to relief undoubtedly appealed to that broad segment of the community that valued pluck, self-reliance, and resourcefulness, but the words "independent" and "ladies" must have seemed dissonant to people whose cultural understandings associated females with dependency. It was, however, a good thing that the Independent Ladies preferred work, because federal relief programs tended to ignore women on their own. The assumption behind work relief programs was that men were usually breadwinners. Women supporting families received consideration as well, but women supporting themselves ran a distant third when they were acknowl-

Egg-breakers at the Armour Creamery, one of few firms—along with Manchester Biscuit and Cheney-Eberhardt Candy—that offered factory jobs to working-class women

edged at all. Beginning in 1935 the Aid for Dependent Children program provided some assistance for mothers and their children, making Washington the patron for substantial numbers of families, but single women still did not fit the social categories the relief bureaucrats devised. In August 1936, a Fargo girl from a family of eight who could not find work after graduation asked the *Forum*, "with the army, navy and CCC camps, the young men seem to have been fairly well taken care of during these hard times, but what is to happen to the girl . . . who cannot find work?" Presumably, she could depend on males in her family. Society offered no other satisfactory answer to her question.[29]

II

The expectation held by most Fargoans that women would be married for at least a portion of their adult lives was fulfilled more often than not. Feminist author Suzanne LaFollette noted in 1926 that, despite the movement for greater gender equality, for a woman marriage remained "a vocation" and the "proper and fitting aim of existence." Marriage was the major marker of a woman's social status. Women who married surrendered their independent identities. Not only did they take their husbands' names, but they were publicly identified as "Mrs. Oscar Kjorlie" or "Mrs. O. A. Stevens" rather than as Kate or Anna. Marriage largely determined who a woman's friends would be, what avocations she would pursue, and what organizations she would join. Marriage opened new options for women even as it closed others, and it was accompanied by an elaborate code of acceptable behavior. Marriage gave women a whole range of concerns and responsibilities single women did not have. And marriage dramatically changed the way women were regarded by the community, by employers, and by government.[30]

A woman's choice of a marriage partner was the most important determinant of the social class in which she would live her life, and in Fargo class went a long way toward defining how one would live. Affluent women had maids, automobiles, and relatively spacious houses. They were likely to be members of the country club as well as of various women's clubs such as the Fine Arts and the Fortnightly. In the summer they would move with their children to Minnesota lake homes. In the dismal year of 1932 the *Forum* interrupted discussions of falling wages, rising unemployment, and shrinking relief budgets to note that many comfortable families were "chucking the family silver out of sight . . . and finally embarking breathlessly on the annual trek to lake homes . . . for summer months of ease and beach activities." When their children left home for college, as they usually did, affluent women and their husbands frequently wintered in California, Florida, or some other pleasant locale. On the day in January 1935 when striking coal drivers and their families were tear gassed, the *Forum* printed a long list of residents who were acting on the "desire to spend the interim between winter and early spring in the bright sunshine or balmy ocean breezes."[31]

While this sounds like a carefree life, reality was often somewhat different. Even with the help of maids, managing households, keeping up appearances, and entertaining were demanding responsibilities. Household work was labor intensive. Ruth Landfield, the daughter of feed and grain merchant and landowner Max Goldberg, recalled that "even though we had a maid there was still a lot to do." Her mother, Ann, "baked all of our bread," and "we were all pressed into service at canning time." Nor were summers at the lake necessarily idyllic. Lake cottages usually did not have electric service or indoor plumbing, meaning that cabins were lighted with kerosene and lacked refrigeration and air conditioning. Surely cleaning lamps and depending on outhouses diminished the allure of "summer months of ease and beach activities." Dirt roads were often impassable after heavy rains, and biting gnats and mosquitoes—the Minnesota "state bird"—added to the discomfort of lake life. Women at the lake were usually alone with children. Husbands came out on the weekends, when they could make it, but maids resisted leaving town. Anna Jane Schlossman, whose father was retailer George Black, remembered that "the lake was work for the maids—they would complain. . . . It was harder and their social life was pretty bad." If they could not find local girls to work, cottage dwellers were on their own.[32]

In addition to maintaining town and lake homes and meeting social expectations, upper-class women helped sustain most of the city's charitable and philanthropic endeavors. Not all affluent women in Fargo had or acted upon a social conscience, and many undoubtedly devoted their free time to shopping, visiting, playing bridge, and other diversions. But it is hard to imagine such agencies as the YWCA, the Crittenton Home, the Red Cross, or the Camp Fire Girls succeeding without the efforts of active and energetic board members who were able to donate time and money and solicit funds from their friends. Nor is it likely that churches would have been as well sustained without the efforts of women with time and money or that the Community Chest would have enjoyed even its qualified success without the aid of 125 female canvassers. Such women as Ada Gunkleman, a lay leader in the Baptist Church and chair of the Fargo Woman's Crusade for the Mobilization of Human Needs, and

Kate Kjorlie, active in Lutheran Social Service and president of the school board, made the voluntary, self-help side of the city work.[33]

Social classes in the United States blend into one another, making it difficult to draw clear boundaries between them. In Fargo, the best way of distinguishing the middle class from the upper class was by indicating what the former normally did not have. Middle-class people did not usually have large homes in affluent neighborhoods, and they were as likely to rent their house as to own it. Most did not have lake cottages. They did not escape the winter weather. Their children usually graduated from high school, but if they received further education it was most often at one of the colleges or business schools in town. They sometimes hired a cleaning lady or gave a college girl room and board in return for help maintaining the house, but they did not have live-in maids. This meant that middle-class women were mainly responsible for their own work—and housework was demanding. "You have no idea what a wife did in those days, jeez," Darrow Beaton remembered, "they did everything the hard way—cooking, canning, sewing, cleaning; they never sat down."[34]

Middle-class women with the time and inclination sometimes worked outside of the home sustaining the city's intricate institutional, charitable, and philanthropic structure. They peopled the women's auxiliaries, the church groups, the sewing circles, the friendship clubs, the PTA, and the youth organizations of the city. They were the muscle and bone of the organizational network that had been central to the idea of cooperative individualism prior to the Depression and that continued to serve the needy, the young, and the vulnerable throughout the thirties.

So middle-class women worked—in the home and in volunteer activities—but they seldom worked outside of the home for wages. Indeed, one of the warmest and most common memories of Fargoans who grew up during the Depression is of stay-at-home mothers. Emily Jackson recalled that "all of the mothers stayed at home. They were too busy—they couldn't have possibly worked outside the home," and Eloise Clower said, "ladies didn't [work] in those days, they just didn't." It was expected that prior to marriage middle-class girls would be employed in order to earn a nest egg for their future homes, gain experience on which they could call in case of divorce or widowhood, meet suitable matrimonial partners, and develop self-confidence. But it was widely understood that they would withdraw from the job market promptly when they married. As Jocelyn Burdick, the daughter of a prominent concrete contractor, put it, "I always expected to work before I was married, but it never occurred to me that I would after." This expectation was rooted partially in the physical demands of keeping house in such a manner as to gain the respect of peers. "If you wanted to maintain a house, you just didn't have the time [for outside work]," Jim Pastoret remembered. "You couldn't have done it and maintain the kind of home you wanted." But there was also a moral dimension to homemaking. Because maintaining a home and raising a family was considered a woman's highest calling, there was seldom any question that she would pour her energies into that endeavor if her husband was able to support her. If she was employed outside the home, she ran the risk of being identified as a poor homemaker, while her husband was stigmatized as an inadequate provider and a weak patriarch. Anna Stevens, who had a master's degree in botany, remembered that leaving her profession "was a very difficult thing indeed," but she noted, "at that time there was no such thing as working after you were married—it was a scandal."[35]

There were exceptions to the rule that middle- and upper-class wives did not work outside the home. Women in such family businesses as jewelry stores, groceries, pharmacies, and cleaning establishments sometimes worked with their husbands, avoiding the morally tricky ground of being supervised by a man other than one's spouse. Moreover, it was understood that divorcées and widows would work to support themselves and their children. Willimina Heller actively managed the family rental portfolio after her husband's death, and Alice Knerr ran the creamery she received in her divorce settlement. Further down the economic ladder, the death of Paul Gallagher's father, Patrick, a buyer for Moody's Department Store, forced his mother to go to work in women's ready-to-wear and sent what had been a middle-class family on a downward spiral that eventually placed them in an efficiency apartment downtown.[36]

It was also common for middle-class women to earn income in their homes. Katherine Burgum recalled neighbors who did "cooking or baking, to earn extra money," and dressmaking, fancy sewing, and hairdressing were also frequently done at home. Warner Litten's mother prepared lunch for teachers from nearby Horace Mann School and made mayonnaise for her children to sell door-to-door. Renting rooms was a profitable enterprise in a city with a chronic housing shortage, and the 1930 census showed that one-sixth of Fargo families did so. Among them were May Bredeson's parents, who maintained a three-room apartment in their home, and Lucille Duval, who hosted as many as seven boarders at a time, mostly migrants from her Francophone home community of Wild Rice. "They got board and room and I washed their clothes for $5 a week," she remembered.[37]

The employment of wives in family businesses or home-centered enterprises was common, venerable, and widely accepted. More controversial—if not
quite a "scandal," in Anna Stevens's terms—was the employment of middle-
class women outside the home, either for wages or in their own businesses.

The early twentieth century was marked by two trends that encouraged
some middle-class wives to swim against the tide of public opinion. First, there
was an explosion of jobs in such female-dominated fields as service, retail, and
clerical work. And, second, there was a growing appreciation among women
of the value of personal independence and a recognition that employment was
a source of self-respect and full citizenship. As Alice Kessler-Harris has noted,
that understanding grew stronger during the Depression, as Social Security
and other entitlements were tied to employment.[38]

These trends were evident even in a small city such as Fargo, distant from
major economic and cultural centers. The city directory listed growing numbers of middle-class wives employed in such enterprises as residential real estate and insurance and in such high-end retailing endeavors as furniture sales.
Apparently, middle-class female consumers found it acceptable and perhaps
even preferable to buy from other middle-class wives. Married women were
also represented in most professions, aside from teaching, and they dominated in nursing, where they were preferred to single women because they
were deemed more stable and less likely to be shocked by the realities of the
human body. The city directory cannot tell us why these women worked, but
self-respect and the desire for independence probably played a role. Certainly
Clara Mason, a court reporter and later a juvenile magistrate who had home-
steaded on her own during World War I, and Winifred Stockman, who became Cass County relief administrator, were motivated by more than money.
Both pursued their chosen professions in the face of social disapproval, despite being married to men able to provide them with comfortable lives.[39]

Employment of middle-class women outside the home was becoming more
common, but it was not yet customary and remained controversial. The employment of working-class women, on the other hand, was so conventional as
to almost be expected.

The 1930 census counted 1,109 "homemakers," representing 17.3 percent
of the city's wives, employed outside the home. While the census did not break
down female employment in class terms, let alone indicate what motivated
women to work, it appears that most of the employed wives were attempting
to supplement low and/or sporadic wages of working-class husbands. They
were most commonly people such as Lila Graber, a mother of seven who

worked in the lunchroom at Armour Packing to augment the income of her husband, John, a butcher, and Ruby Lein, who waited tables while her husband, Henry, worked as a baggage handler for the Great Northern Railway.[40]

Among skilled workers a stigma frequently attached to working wives, just as it did in the middle class. Certainly, the oft-stated demand by unions for a "family wage" contained the unstated implication that men were shamed by the fact that their wives worked outside the home and did not want their families dependent in part on wives' wages. Employers of working-class women, in such businesses as restaurants, hotels, and laundries, however, did not seem to care whether their employees were married or not. Some employers even preferred that workers be married. Clothiers and beauticians, for example, believed that married clerks and cosmetologists could better develop long-term relationships with married customers than could single employees.[41]

Whether they were in the working class or the middle class and whether they were employed outside the home or not, married women came under intense cross-pressures in the early years of the Depression, as Glenna Matthews has demonstrated. Because they were usually assumed to be responsible for managing households, wives were expected to economize in order to match expenditures to breadwinners' reduced salaries. Once again the nineteenth-century domestic values of "skill and frugality" came to the fore. As nationally acclaimed author Mary Roberts Rinehart put it in the *Ladies' Home Journal* in December 1931, "there is only one rule for such periods . . . to cut vigorously, throw pride to the winds, cease to compete with other people, and face the situation squarely."[42]

But at the same time wives were told to retrench they were also urged to consume to pull the country out of the Depression. The month after Rinehart's admonition appeared the *Journal* launched the "It's Up to the Women" campaign, based on the premise that "the purchasing agents of twenty-nine million American families—the women in the homes—can have a lot to do with starting the wheels of progress and prosperity turning." Over the next few months the *Journal* printed articles urging housewives to spend the country out of the Depression, including some by such prominent national figures as businesswoman Elizabeth Arden, suffragist Carrie Chapman Catt, and Eleanor Roosevelt, then first lady of New York State.[43]

Rinehart had the advantage in this argument because most women ranked their duty to the family above their duty to the nation. But the question rose in the Depression whether fulfilling their duty to families might actually compel women to leave their homes, whether meeting their family obligations might require wives to work for wages. Fargoans believed that "a lot of married women tried to go to work" during the early years of the Depression. Whether that perception was accurate or not, it stimulated a debate regarding working wives' motives and the effects of their employment.[44]

Critics of wives who worked or sought employment in Fargo judged them to have selfish or frivolous motives and flawed moral characters. One common criticism of working wives was that their incomes were superfluous to family needs and were thus devoted to fulfilling excessive material desires. One Fargoan, for example, contended that "they must have a car, of course, expensive vacations, fur coats, radios, and other things too numerous to mention," and another added, "the main reason those married women seek employment is because they like to have a new car every year or so, an oriental rug or cottage at the lake." Taking a slightly different tack, one *Forum* reader blamed lazy and self-indulgent husbands—"yellow-fingered sheiks"—for keeping their wives employed so that they could enjoy personal pleasures. More common was the argument that working wives were shaming and imperiling "husband and family" by implying that the primary breadwinner's salary was insufficient to maintain the household. "Husbands resent the fact that their wives are not satisfied to live on what they are making," wrote R.E.C., "they object to coming home to a wife who knows perhaps more about world affairs than they do, and who knows nothing about her own home and children. Thus enters the divorce question." Such criticisms were not unique to Fargo, nor were they confined to the years of the Great Depression. Especially in the 1920s, cultural conservatives had worried about the breakdown in traditional gender and familial roles and had bemoaned rising materialism, individualism, and self-indulgent personal behavior on the part of women. The criticisms lodged against working wives were part and parcel of this ongoing discourse, though the Depression put a special economic edge on them.[45]

Working wives and their motives did not go undefended in Fargo. One woman confronted the issue of materialism, asking, "who, in this great country of ours, is going to take it upon himself to set our standard of living? Should it not be for the married folks themselves to decide if their income is sufficient to allow them to purchase the things they need . . . and live as they see fit?" Others took a strikingly modern, egalitarian line. P. H. Redington contended that "to discriminate against a woman on account of her marriage status is no more fair than to discriminate against a man for the same reason," and Mrs. M. C. Osman asked, "does not our constitution advocate free and equal rights to all? . . . Are we to believe we are under the rule of Soviet Russia, or a free country?" Equal rights–oriented arguments, such as those of Redington and Osman, were firmly rooted in traditional American civic values, but they meant little to cultural conservatives, who defined women's lives in terms of duty, obligation, and sacrifice rather than independence, equality, and self-assertion.[46]

In addition to having their motives impugned, working wives were criticized for the effect of their employment on other, presumably more worthy, participants in the job market. Working wives were frequently accused of taking jobs that men should be holding. In February 1931 a *Forum* reader contributed to an ongoing controversy over working women by claiming that "right now in Fargo there are women holding positions which ex-servicemen with families might fill. . . . In fact, I would be working now if my employer had not hired a woman to fill my position at a cheaper salary." More common, in a city in which single women made up a substantial portion of the population and in which strong paternal feelings existed for them, was the argument that labor by the married choked off opportunities for the unmarried. "Any person who fails to lift up his voice against the practice of business houses, schools, or any public place [hiring] married women, is doing a grave injustice to the young . . . women who are more than willing to fill those places," wrote one Fargoan in March 1932, and a self-described "single girl" added, "every woman that is married, has a home, a family and a husband with a steady income has no business holding down a single girl's job."[47]

Public opinion, ambivalent about the employment of married women in prosperous times, seemed strongly antithetical to the practice during the Depression. Organized labor took an especially strong stand against the employment of wives. Arguing that the available work should go to those who needed it most, the Fargo Trades and Labor Assembly and the North Dakota Federation of Labor urged public employers to dismiss married women, and those agencies usually complied. In 1931–32 both the City Commission and the County Commission acceded to the request of the Trades and Labor Assembly that they discharge all married women on their payrolls, provided those women's husbands were employed and their jobs could be done by someone else. The City Commission went a step further, agreeing to fire male employees if their working wives did not quit the jobs they were holding with private employers. The State of North Dakota did not go to that extreme, but after William Langer attacked the employment of wives in his successful gubernatorial campaign of 1932, the legislature did pass an anti-nepotism law preventing both spouses from working for the state simultaneously. Many other states, along with the federal government, enacted similar legislation.[48]

It is impossible to generalize about the motives of married women who worked and who sought employment in Fargo and elsewhere during the Depression. Certainly such women as Clara Mason and Winifred Stockman, who believed in female equality, opportunity, and independence, would continue to hold and seek jobs regardless of their families' economic situations. Presumably other women worked for social stimulation, a sense of achievement, or even the camaraderie of the shop or office. It is likely, however, that economic need played a major role in pulling women out of the home and into the workplace. National studies demonstrated that women whose husbands were unemployed were 50 percent more likely to work than the wives of employed men. In a city such as Fargo, where relief was stigmatized and self-reliance was celebrated, the desire to stay off the welfare rolls might have moved many wives to seek employment.[49]

It does not necessarily follow, however, that working wives were driven by economic desperation. Even employed husbands were confronted by periodic layoffs or by wage reductions that threatened the family standard of living, especially in households burdened with fixed financial obligations, such as mortgage and installment payments. During the 1920s the material standard of living had advanced impressively in the United States, and many families were reluctant to live lives of diminished abundance just because there was an economic downturn. Presumably, some women entered the job market to maintain a material standard of living to which their families had grown accustomed and to which they believed they were entitled. That does not mean that many women were working to buy "an oriental rug or cottage at the lake," but it does suggest that some, at least, were working so that the family could rent a larger house, buy a car, a radio, or a refrigerator, install a telephone, or keep sons and daughters in high school or college. While some observers might have considered such things luxuries, they were increasingly viewed as necessities in the United States.[50]

While it is difficult to determine the motives of working wives, it is somewhat easier to judge the effect of wives working. There is little evidence to support the charge that married women were taking jobs from married men to any significant degree. Generally, women and men operated in different labor markets in Fargo and throughout the country during the Depression. Women were concentrated in clerical, retail, and service occupations in which few, if any, men could be found. On the other hand, the construction and day labor fields in which unemployment was most pronounced were almost entirely male. The carpenters and masons and freight handlers who were out of work in Fargo

were unemployed because of the cyclical downturn in the economy, not because their employers replaced them with women. Even in occupations held
by both men and women, rigid gender separation was customary. In department stores, for example, saleswomen handled women's ready-to-wear, foundation garments, lingerie, and the like, while men's furnishings, appliances,
and shoes were the province of salesmen. The complaints of displaced men
were valid in a relative handful of occupations in which women were gaining
representation and sometimes a substantial position. Vivian Westberg was the
first female savings teller at the First National Bank, but by the end of the 1930s
female faces were increasingly common in tellers' cages. Likewise, women were
coming to dominate bookkeeping and other low-level white-collar occupations. These displacements, however, represented relatively few jobs overall.[51]

Single women were much more likely than men to suffer from job competition from married women in Fargo. Teaching and some clerical jobs were reserved for single women, but most jobs, and especially those at the lower end
of the employment ladder, were open to both married and single women. Retail clerks, beauticians, laundresses, and waitresses could usually be either married or single. These occupations, which were frequently low paid and low
skilled, were glutted during the Depression by single and married women
alike. The result, as one *Forum* reader put it, was that, even for those who could
find employment, "the wage rate automatically drops." This situation resulted
from a failure in the economic system and was hardly the fault of working wives
or of any other social group. Yet working wives were convenient people to
blame because, by so doing, Fargoans could personalize, moralize, and simplify a complicated economic problem while simultaneously upholding traditional social values.[52]

Employers' attitudes toward the employment of married women had a great
deal to do with the size and composition of the labor pool, though that reality
was generally ignored by Fargoans who preferred to attack job-seeking wives.
In fact, every working wife was hired by some employer, and he probably chose
her over other applicants, including single women. Employers such as Armour
Packing received high praise when they announced that they would no longer
hire married women, but other firms were making different, less-publicized decisions. Because they were usually supplementing another income, working
wives would frequently accept lower salaries than single women needed, and
that was undoubtedly important to employers under economic duress. Businesses might also have determined that married women were more dependable and mature and less likely to leave for another job or resign to marry.

"Married women give more competent reliable service than the young flighty Miss," one subscriber wrote to the *Forum* during the working-wife controversy in 1931. "This is one main reason why employers prefer married women." When bank president Fred Irish of First National hired Vivian Westberg she was engaged, but he went ahead, despite his policy against employing wives, because "you'll be single when we hire you." She was told that, once she married, she would "be the first to go when they let people go," but that never happened. Presumably other employers, acting out of self-interest or principle, were making hiring decisions similar to Irish's.[53]

Even the most severe critics of working wives in Fargo emphasized that their reproaches applied only to women whose husbands were breadwinners. When husbands were unemployed or incapacitated, it was considered acceptable, and even desirable, that wives should support families, regardless of their social class. These unfortunate women were pitied rather than censured. Not only were they compelled to step outside of their prescribed family roles, but they were burdened with husbands who could not fulfill theirs. Fargoans celebrated traditional gender and familial roles, but they also prized independence, hard work, and resourcefulness. The latter usually trumped the former.

The case of Helen Kennedy reveals community attitudes regarding family, class, gender, and responsibility with particular clarity. Helen was the wife of William Kennedy, a member of a prominent family of building contractors in the city. His father, James, had amassed a fortune building many of the most impressive structures in Fargo, including St. Mary's Cathedral, the elegant and graceful headquarters for the Roman Catholic Diocese of Eastern North Dakota. William was also a successful contractor. The 1928 city directory showed him with a downtown office and a residence on an affluent block on Seventh Street South. But by 1932 Kennedy had suffered a sharp reversal of fortune. The city directory identified him as a carpenter in a city filled with unemployed carpenters, and his family was living in a modest bungalow in a lower-middle-class neighborhood. Kennedy's meteoric fall was not confined to the economic realm. In January 1933 he was arrested for public drunkenness on lower Front Street.[54]

The cause of Kennedy's decline is unclear. Quite possibly he was ruined along with other contractors by the collapse of the construction business and the evaporation of credit early in the Depression. Perhaps personal failings, hinted at by his arrest, played a role. In any event, Helen Kennedy was compelled to go to work to help support her family, and in February 1932 she was hired as a social worker by the County Commission.[55]

Kennedy was not hired out of pity—she was a college-trained social worker who had been employed in the field prior to her marriage—but she was clearly pitied. In April 1934 the issue of social workers' pay came before the County Welfare Board. While most case-workers were receiving $80 to $90 per month, Kennedy was paid $100. Board member P. H. Burton justified the disparity on the ground that "Mrs. Kennedy, unfortunately enough has a family to care for. Just a few years ago Bill Kennedy was one of the most influential men in this town, one of the wealthiest, one of the most responsible." The rest apparently did not need to be said. In July the issue resurfaced, and Burton again rose to Kennedy's defense: "If Mrs. Kennedy was single and getting $90 I would say fine and dandy, but some of us fellows have lived here a long time and know the picture.... She is supporting a husband and three children." Kennedy's salary remained at $100.[56]

Burton's remarks and the board's actions in the Kennedy case suggest at least three things. First, in addition to the element of pity for Helen Kennedy there is a degree of contempt for her husband. Because William Kennedy could not or would not fill his familial role, his wife was compelled to step out of hers. Second, the board was willing to help the Kennedys maintain some semblance of a middle-class lifestyle by paying Helen Kennedy more than other case-workers received. But in order to receive the means to maintain her economic status Kennedy had to work outside the home and thus surrender one of the main cultural signifiers of middle-class social status in the community. Her level of pay, elevated though it might be, could not compensate Kennedy for the disgrace of having to support a husband and children, a humiliation that would have been exceeded only by the shame of going on relief. Finally, the Kennedy case demonstrated the mixed blessings of life in a small city. Because P. H. Burton and other prominent people in Fargo knew her family, Kennedy could prevail on their sympathy. But the fact that she was known made her humiliation all the more profound.

What the Kennedy case did not show was that the welfare board had developed an advanced view of acceptable gender roles, or of the propriety of wives working when husbands were able to do so. That became apparent in October 1934, when the board heard the Violet Jeffries case. Jeffries had a work relief assignment as a typist at the Relief Office. Work relief became available for her husband, Thomas, a plasterer, and the office sought to dismiss her and hire him. The Jeffries appealed to the welfare board, arguing that Violet should be allowed to keep working and Thomas should remain at home with their two young children. Violet Jeffries contended that her husband was too old at fifty-

Male and female office workers in Fargo during the 1930s, when the occupation of bookkeeping was being feminized

one for effective labor and that he enjoyed being at home with the kids and taking them to and from school. By contrast, she enjoyed working and "could not get along staying at home." The board was aghast at the reversal of roles the Jeffries were suggesting and unanimously rejected their request. Board member Hugh Corrigan pointed out that "the sentiment of the Board is that the one to earn the living is the husband. . . . The place for Mrs. Jeffries is in the home taking care of the children." And relief director Hendricks added that it was a board rule that the "husband should work and automatically the woman stops work." Ironically, Helen Kennedy was the Jeffries's case-worker.[57]

The Kennedy and Jeffries cases illustrate that traditional understandings of proper gender roles and family organization and hierarchy in Fargo were sometimes bent by extraordinary circumstances, but they did not break. The Depression and the long renegotiation and redefinition of gender roles that had been going on for a century encouraged change, but the change that came was slow, incomplete, and only reluctantly accepted by most men and many women. Currents of culture were deep and strong in Fargo and were modified only modestly even by an economic challenge as significant as the Great Depression.

III

Eva Nelson came to Fargo for work, but there was more to life than labor alone. She and her friend Helen Kohlhoff window-shopped at downtown stores, went dancing, attended movies, and sometimes double-dated. They decided to take up cigarette smoking because the movie stars they admired smoked and they thought it would make them more "sophisticated. . . . We had been brought up to believe that no lady ever indulged in this filthy habit but we were young [and] impressionable . . . and it was easy to convince ourselves that the old teachings were passé. We were now on our own and we must make our own decisions, right or wrong."[58]

Frieda Oster also discovered that there was much more to life in the city than just a job. In addition to attending movies and dances, she learned which liquor stores would sell to minors and which hotels did not inquire too closely about the marital status of guests. Her social life revolved around her lover, a salesman at her store. In June 1939 she confided to her diary that "at noon J & I fun & more to-nite. . . . Went to Fort [Hotel] at 10. Drinking quite a bit. Swell fun though. Slept for a little while. . . . Home at 3:30." But she was not exclusive. Once in 1938 she went out with a traveling salesman who called at the store, recording that he had a "Pontiac car. Rode to Wolverton & back to town. Up back way to hotel room. Had 3 drinks of gin. 1st [drink] my eyes shone[,] 2nd one dizzy[,] and 3rd 1 sleepy. As near tite as I will ever be. . . . Home at 2." And in August 1939 she "went up town with Gil. Went 4 ride. . . . Got ½ pt. Paul Jones [whiskey], Out to Sabin. Played slot machines. . . . Parked, Necked."[59]

William Sherman, one of the deans of North Dakota historians, has written that "North Dakota, even in its 'big towns,' has been marked by the routine and ordinariness of village life. People who wanted 'city life' have had to leave the state to find it." While no one would suggest that Fargo was another Chicago or even Minneapolis, Nelson and Oster and countless other single women found recreations, pleasures, and independence there that were not available in the farm communities from which they came. Oster's life, especially, revolved around movies, dance halls, bars, and roadhouses. Her remarkable diary demonstrates that within a few months she was transformed from an awkward country girl, shy, self-conscious, and uncomfortable with her sexuality, to a sophisticated and streetwise liver of "city life."[60]

Fargo was proud to call itself a city, but Fargoans were wary of some of the components of "city life" and sought to protect young women from them. In addition to its network of social service agencies that existed to shield and shelter young women, the city maintained a policewoman, part of whose job was to look after them. It was appropriate, in light of the city's paternal attitudes toward single girls, that the policewoman also served as juvenile officer. Through most of the thirties the policewoman was Alice Duffy, a University of Chicago–trained social worker who had come to Fargo in 1916. Among her other activities, Duffy met incoming trains and assisted "unaccompanied girls in obtaining proper accommodations in the city," patrolled dance halls to discourage drinking and insure decorous behavior, and provided small loans to "unfortunate girls" to help them return home.[61]

Energetic and dedicated though they were, Duffy's efforts were insufficient to protect all of the city's single women from others or from themselves. Married women, who were expected to be mature, self-disciplined, and homebound and whose husbands were theoretically responsible for overseeing them, were not in her purview at all. On occasion, some event illustrated that not all married women behaved as expected or lived lives of domestic rectitude. In April 1931, for example, Lydia Vikjord, a married mother of five, was struck and killed by an automobile while she and a male companion walked along a country road near Moorhead shortly after midnight on a Sunday morning. Her husband, a sporadically employed carpenter, reported she had taken to attending dances and "picking up men." And in August 1933 Hilda Gray, thirty-one, wife of a Winnipeg hotel manager, left her two daughters with her mother in Moorhead and attended a drinking party at the apartment of D. F. Ellsworth, a federal narcotics agent. Gray passed out on Ellsworth's bed and sometime during the night suffered a fatal blow to the head. The coroner's jury exonerated Ellsworth, surmising that she fell either down the stairs or out of bed.[62]

Shocking events such as these could be dismissed as aberrations. More difficult to ignore was the apparent increase in self-indulgent behavior among women in such areas as cigarette smoking and alcohol use. In their 1935 examination of social change in Muncie, Indiana, *Middletown in Transition*, Robert Lynd and Helen Merrell Lynd reported a pronounced increase in cigarette smoking and alcohol consumption among most people but especially among women. Such seems to have been the case in Fargo as well.[63]

In 1930 a controversy erupted over smoking in cafés. Under North Dakota law, men were prohibited from smoking in restaurants, streetcars, and railway coaches when women were present. The law was usually ignored by authorities, but demands for stricter enforcement early in 1930 brought a stream of commentary, much of it focused on changing mores. One observer noted that "considering the number of women who smoke" it was unlikely the law could be enforced, and another suggested that "there are so many women smoking now that the law should be enforced for the protection of men." The Reverend William Sainsbury of First Methodist stated the traditional view that "there is no such thing as a lady who smokes. No woman who smokes is a lady." Sainsbury was answered in the columns of the *Forum* by a Fargo reader who explained, "I . . . do not smoke, but I number among my friends many splendid women who do. Isn't it rather ridiculous, after all, in this day and age, to bring up the question at all? . . . The smoking ladies will take care of themselves." To some Fargoans, the fact that "ladies" were taking "care of themselves" and making their own behavioral choices was precisely the problem.[64]

Drinking by women was less readily observable than smoking in the early years of the Depression because alcohol use was driven underground by Prohibition. On occasion inebriated women would run afoul of the law, but female drinking was generally hidden from public view. In most of the country Prohibition resulted in changes in traditional drinking practices and the disintegration of long-standing taboos. Pre-Prohibition saloons were, in effect, men's clubs, and respectable women did not enter them. During Prohibition, though, speakeasies were frequented by both sexes. Further "domesticating drink," in Catherine Murdock's phrase, was the Prohibition-era practice of drinking at home and especially the development of the cocktail party as a domestic urban and suburban institution. The degree to which drinking practices had apparently changed in Fargo was graphically illustrated early in 1933. Taking advantage of a new federal law permitting states to legalize 3.2 beer, Minnesota allowed cities to license beer parlors. Moorhead was quick to seize this money-making opportunity, and on April 8 legal beer sales began in that city. Among the hundreds of Fargoans who crossed the river for a legal taste, the *Forum* was surprised to see numerous members of the "fair sex," who entered beer parlors and even sat alongside men at the bar. The *Forum* wondered how establishments catering to mixed crowds could maintain their "respectability," but the times had clearly passed the newspaper by. Whatever their drinking habits had once been, women were in the bars to stay. In March 1940 the Women's Christian Temperance Union of Fargo estimated that fully 40 percent of the city's bar patrons were women.[65]

It also appears that in their sexual behavior young women were following the more permissive trends evident in American society generally. With the exception of sex crimes and periodic campaigns to clean up prostitution or to eradicate syphilis, sexuality was not discussed in the *Forum* or by public agencies in the city. But the sexual practices of young people sometimes came to public attention, usually inadvertently. In June 1930, for example, Leif Erickson, a twenty-six-year-old collector for the International Harvester Company, was shot and killed in a struggle with an armed robber at a lovers' lane near the fairgrounds. Erickson's girlfriend, twenty-year-old Vera Helgerson, told police the couple had spent an hour in the back seat and were preparing to drive back to town when they were accosted by the bandit. Within the next few days several other people reported earlier lovers' lane robberies to police, noting that they had not reported before "due to the natural embarrassment attendant on the circumstances." Lovers' lane robberies, along with harassment of couples by juveniles, continued for several years. In order to discourage parking, the Veterans Hospital erected a tall fence around its grounds and CCC boys planted guard posts to prevent people from pulling off the road at Edgewood Golf Course. In the summer of 1934 the police responded to several lovers' lane robberies and attempted sexual assaults by banning night parking near the fairgrounds and along the river from the Contagion Hospital to the poor farm.[66]

Increased personal and sexual freedom and decreased supervision by parents and communities were undoubtedly thrilling to young women, but freedom was accompanied by greater dangers and intensified pressures for women, and it sometimes presented them with consequences that men did not face. The consequence that came to public attention most frequently was unwanted and/or unplanned pregnancy, which made the news when it resulted in infanticide or abortion.

Instances of infanticide were fairly common in the city. In November 1929, for example, the frozen body of an infant was found wrapped in brown paper in a working-class neighborhood west of downtown. In May 1936 a dead baby boy was discovered on the riverbank, and in March 1937 a group of children found a baby girl's body, wrapped in a towel, at the city dump. Usually the offending mothers were not found, though an eighteen-year-old maid was arrested in March 1930 for leaving an infant under a shed in Island Park, where he died of exposure. Sympathizing with the girl's plight, authorities charged her only with improper burial.[67]

In Fargo abortion was apparently a more popular solution to unplanned pregnancies than infanticide. Over the course of the thirties numerous aborted fetuses were discovered, including several unearthed by relief workers making improvements at Edgewood Golf Course. In 1939 physiotherapist M. W. Dimmick was arrested for performing an abortion on a twenty-one-year-old housemaid who had moved to the city from Aberdeen, South Dakota. Dimmick was exposed when his patient was arrested for stealing a ring from her employer. She told police she sold it and used the proceeds to pay for the operation.[68]

Birth control was also available. On occasion the *Forum* would advertise birth control devices, including abortifacients. In July 1933, for example, "Bornlucke Laboratories" of Minneapolis advertised, "married women don't worry for monthly delay. Be wise and keep your beauty, use our relief tablets. Harmless and effective in most unusual cases. Relief obtained 3 to 5 days." Still, birth control remained an embarrassing subject for many, and one often shrouded in mystery. Frieda Oster was a sexually active woman who solicited birth control advice from friends because she could not depend on her partners to take precautions. She had at least one pregnancy scare that sent her to the doctor for an examination. When she asked him about birth control, he "advised me against intercourse." That advice did not take, and unfortunately he provided her with nothing more helpful.[69]

None of this demonstrates that the behavior of all, or even most, women was changing or that most men's expectations had been altered substantially. Still, the Depression took place in the midst of a long period of redefinition and renegotiation of proper gender roles and behaviors by both men and women. Generally, women anticipated being more independent and self-directive than their mothers and grandmothers had been. By 1930 it was widely expected that, while they might continue to enjoy some of the protections provided by familial or communal paternalism, single women would enjoy at least a brief period of adult life in which they were not under the supervision and direction of fathers or husbands. That meant, in Eva Nelson's words, that they "were on our own and . . . must make our own decisions, right or wrong." While the community supported some of those decisions, particularly those pertaining to employment, it was less comfortable with decisions reflected in behaviors that were self-indulgent or that violated traditional expectations of what proper women should do.

Expectations regarding marriage, the relationship between spouses, and their respective roles were also changing. To a greater extent than ever before, women entered marriage with some education and employment experience. Living in a culture that increasingly equated consumption with happiness, they had material expectations that exceeded those of their mothers. And they were more likely to marry because of romantic attraction and to expect husbands to be loving companions rather than domineering patriarchs. The problem was that expectations have a way of going unfulfilled, and wives sometimes discovered that the roles they believed they and their husbands would play or the benefits they hoped to receive from marriage did not come to pass. When that happened, women were better prepared than their mothers had been to leave disappointing or dangerous marriages, in part because they had abilities and self-confidence their mothers lacked and in part because the legal dissolution of marriage had become more common and acceptable. The result was a rising divorce rate, nationally and in Fargo, where it was reported in 1930 that, while the number of marriages had stood steady at about 190 per year since 1910, the number of divorces had tripled, reaching 101 in 1929. The epidemic of divorce was cause for great concern, and it was usually wives, with their independent spirits and their enhanced expectations for marriage, who were blamed. Commenting on what might be perceived as the shortcomings of modern girls, Cass County judge P. M. Paulsen urged the boys of Interstate Business College to marry homely women because they "have a tendency to adjust themselves a little better to married life." Paulsen's assumptions about women and their responsibility for marital difficulties were hardly unique.[70]

Social and cultural discourse during the 1930s frequently assumed a conservative tone. It was common, especially among religiously oriented observers, to claim that the Depression was divine retribution for the self-indulgence and materialism of the twenties. And public debates, such as that over the propriety of wage work for wives, were characterized by the expression of traditional views regarding the roles and responsibilities of men and women. Still, social conservatives could not reverse, or even slow appreciably, the tendencies of the modern age. Single women still cherished their independence, and brides continued to carry high expectations into married life. In some ways the Depression accelerated behavioral changes. The economic and personal failures of the William Kennedys of the world demonstrated that women must be prepared to lead families and be breadwinners. By 1935 no less a paragon of middle-class respectability than the *Ladies' Home Journal* was endorsing the idea that married women must have the tools to be independent. Even the *Forum*, which usually took a conservative position on gender roles and relationships, celebrated modern, self-reliant Fargo girls such as aviatrix Frances Klingensmith and actress Virginia Bruce. And in September 1937 it printed menus for "the woman who has two jobs to hold—the woman who is an efficient business person during the day and a homemaker out of office hours." This hardly represented an embrace of modernity in gender relations, reflecting as it did the social assumption that even working women were primarily responsible for keeping homes and nurturing families. But it demonstrated a major shift from the celebration of "femininity" and "womanly bits of handicraft" that had appeared in the newspaper just three years before. In its expectations regarding men and women Fargo was changing, in spite of itself and perhaps even unbeknownst to itself.[71]

7

DEALING WITH DISORDER

"It is significant that augmented leisure and legalized liquor are entering the social fabric at the same time. Activities which degrade personality, lower the moral tone of a community, and destroy bodily health and vigor must be prevented from excessive growth, since to hope that they may be abolished is vain."
Fargo Forum, *March 21, 1934*

"The neglected home is responsible for 90 per cent of all crime. That neglect applies to all homes, rich and poor."
Usher L. Burdick, August 10, 1936

FARGO CONSIDERED ITSELF to be a law-abiding community in the 1930s, and the available statistics generally support that belief. The city suffered relatively little violent crime and in 1930 spent only $2.51 per capita on police protection, far below the national average of $5.47 for cities of its size. Most Fargoans seemed to enjoy a physically secure existence in a city proud of its strong families, numerous churches, and well-developed social service infrastructure.[1]

But a secure community was not always an orderly one, and Fargo was vexed by public disorder throughout the 1930s. Much of that disorder was associated with the large number of single male residents and the much larger number of male transients in the city. Single males were disproportionately represented among those arrested for such crimes against public order as gambling, patronization of prostitutes, and drunkenness, partially because their class made them more vulnerable to arrest and partially because they were more likely than others to commit such offenses. By the 1930s gambling, prostitution, and alcohol abuse had been accepted as endemic problems. Fargoans had concluded on the basis of long and sad experience that such problems could not be solved, only controlled. As the *Forum* ruefully put it in 1934, such activities "must be prevented from excessive growth, since to hope that they may be abolished is vain."[2]

Far more disturbing to Fargoans than the activities of those who were expected to behave badly was the apparent rise in child neglect and juvenile delinquency in the city. Indeed, by 1932 Fargoans considered themselves to be suffering from a rising tide of juvenile delinquency. They generally agreed that the source of that problem lay in the ills of the modern age. The "neglected home," highlighted by western North Dakota congressman Usher Burdick in an address to the State Bar Association in 1936, came in for much of the blame, but such environmental factors as indecent magazines and violent and suggestive movies shared responsibility.[3]

Fargoans were willing to treat the disorder coming from adults, but they sought to cure juvenile delinquency. Part of that process involved prophylactic measures designed to shield children from negative influences. But most of it involved the development of organizational and recreational alternatives to antisocial activities. The city, the schools, and such organizations as the Community Welfare Association fought for Fargo's children during the 1930s. In many ways, it was the city's finest hour.

I

America was preoccupied with crime during the 1930s. The activities of major organized crime figures such as Al Capone were followed as avidly as those of sports heroes and movie stars. The exploits of such bank robbers as John Dillinger and Bonnie Parker and Clyde Barrow were widely recounted and frequently admired. And major cases, such as the Lindbergh baby kidnapping, received detailed and sustained attention.

If the headlines in the *Forum* are any indication, Fargo was not immune to this fascination with crime and criminals. In addition to following the activities of criminals nationally, the *Forum* reported visits by such "gentlemen of the underworld" as Bugs Moran, noting that they were "usually free spenders" and thus "not unwelcome guests from a mercenary standpoint." Local angles on national crime stories received extravagant play, as in 1934 when it was revealed that one of the women with Dillinger when FBI agents shot and killed him outside a Chicago theater was former Fargoan Polly Hamilton.[4]

Fear of crime played a role in Fargo life. The national epidemic of bank robberies convinced local bankers to change their hours and install alarm systems connected to the police department, and the city purchased rifles and a machine gun to ensure that the police were not outgunned by bank robbers. Other improvements were instituted at least in part to allow the police to respond more quickly to serious criminal acts. The city increased police mobility by introducing motorcycles and patrol cars in the early thirties, and the installation of two-way radios in cars beginning in 1935 was designed to permit the police to move to crime scenes rapidly.[5]

Fargo was fortunate not to suffer any bank robberies or major kidnappings during the thirties. There were occasional murders, rapes, assaults, and armed robberies, but violent crime was relatively rare. Much more common were auto theft, burglary, and petty larceny, especially shoplifting. Police chief C. W. Albright announced in 1937 that, while there had been no murders or rapes reported in the city during the previous year, the rate of property crimes exceeded national norms and was much above the North Dakota average.[6]

Most of the 2,200 people arrested in Fargo every year were charged with offenses against public order. Transients, especially, were liable to be arrested for vagrancy, panhandling, or riding on trains, charges designed to move them out of town. Also common were arrests for vice-related offenses, such as gambling, prostitution, and drunkenness.[7]

Gambling was common in Fargo and the surrounding area in the thirties, and, indeed, lotteries, punchboards, and other games of chance that promised a big payoff on a small expenditure were popular throughout the country during the Depression. Enforcement of Fargo's laws against gambling was selective, depending largely on the gambler's class. While service clubs and fraternal organizations with a middle-class membership were never disturbed by police, establishments catering to working-class gamblers were raided periodically. Downtown "recreation parlors"—pool halls—along with some cigar stores, groceries, and cafés commonly featured punchboards, pull tabs, slot machines, and even bookmakers who would take bets on baseball games and boxing matches. In September 1930 federal, county, and city officials raided seven downtown establishments, seizing "baseball lottery tickets . . . punch boards" and "several slot machines." Gambling soon resumed at the same sites, however, leading to more raids and prompting Cass County state's attorney A. R. Bergesen to lament that "many men are there gambling away their weekly wages to the detriment of their families."[8]

Prostitution was another offense that appeared frequently in the *Forum* and in police arrest records. At the turn of the century Fargo had hosted a flourishing red-light district between Broadway and the river, but concerted vice campaigns in the teens had destroyed the old-style brothels. By the 1930s most prostitutes plied their trade in one of two locales. A number of African American prostitutes worked out of small houses or shacks in the lower Front Street neighborhood. And several downtown hotels housed white prostitutes. Hotel

managers apparently protected these women and sometimes arranged their li-
aisons. Prostitution was inevitable in a city in which many single men lived and
through which many more passed, but it might have become more prevalent
during the Depression. Two investigators for the *Journal of Social Hygiene,* a
national social work publication, hypothesized that numerous "depression
girls"—"women and girls thought to have become prostitutes because of personal financial distress"—had entered the trade. These investigators catego-
rized Fargo as "bad"—the second-worst category—among the cities whose incidence of prostitution they attempted to measure.[9]

Many of these "depression girls" were probably casual rather than professional prostitutes, supplementing low incomes through occasional assigna-
tions. In her study of single women in Chicago, Joanne Meyerowitz found such
sporadic prostitution to be common, especially among women like waitresses,
who enjoyed numerous opportunities to meet single men. A common charge
in the Fargo police arrest records for the thirties was "resorting to rooms for
immoral purposes." In June 1930 waitress Bessie Steinbach, twenty-two, was
arrested on that charge, along with laborer William Zalusky. The next year
Gordon Shaw, a thirty-nine-year-old salesman, and stenographer Hazel Mat-
tocks, twenty-two, were arrested on the same charge. And in 1938 butcher Dal-
las Warren and WPA worker Mabel DeMarce were charged with resorting to
rooms. While this vague offense could be explained in numerous ways, it is
probable that casual prostitution was involved in at least some cases.[10]

Public attention focused on prostitution in Fargo when clients complained
of being robbed or assaulted by prostitutes or when a disturbance requiring
police intervention arose. In 1934, for example, a cattle buyer from Montana
complained that he was robbed of more than $1,800 at the Riverside Apart-
ments, a notorious prostitutes' haunt downtown. He "went out for a good
time" with Mrs. Helen Lundeen and spent the night in her room. When he
awoke the next morning, Lundeen and his money had both disappeared. And
in 1939 Stepin Fetchit, the stage name for Lincoln Perry, an African American
movie star appearing on stage at the Fargo Theater, was arrested for disorderly
conduct when he discharged a tear gas pen at the home of prostitute Dorothy
Jackson. The actor claimed $100 and an overcoat had been stolen from him
during a drinking party.[11]

Prostitution also came to public attention during the city's periodic anti-
vice campaigns. Officials were especially eager to "clean up" the lower Front
Street area, and nearly every year saw a well-publicized effort. Normally these
campaigns involved rounding up prostitutes, who posted and then forfeited

their bail. Sometimes arrestees were ordered to leave the city, but they usually drifted back within a few weeks, if not days. In 1937 there was a more serious attempt to extirpate prostitution on the main stem, stimulated largely by the FBI's discovery of a large "white slave" ring in the upper Midwest that included two African Americans from Fargo, prizefighter Harlan (Kid) Rippatoe, and the ubiquitous Dorothy Jackson. Even that ambitious endeavor had only a transitory effect.[12]

Anti-prostitution efforts also targeted downtown hotels. In January 1934, Mayor Olsen and State's Attorney Bergesen launched a "vice crusade" that was followed by arrests at the West, Gladstone, and Gordon hotels. The next month the Broadway, Roberts, Tweeden, and Gladstone were all raided. And in the summer of 1936 the Broadway, Roberts, New Palace, Gladstone, Continental, and Tweeden hotels were all targeted. The arrested managers were charged with keeping disorderly houses, and the alleged prostitutes were charged with being residents of disorderly houses.[13]

These campaigns resembled a dance in which both partners knew the steps. They were launched with great fanfare. The police would swoop down on miscreants, always knowing where to go, as observant beat cops should. Those charged would post and forfeit bail, almost as if they were buying a license to operate, and the same people would soon be back in business at the same places. Anti-vice campaigns may have indicated that the city did not approve of prostitution, but they did not demonstrate that it had the will, or even the desire, to extirpate the sex trade. Perhaps officials recognized the inevitability of prostitution in a city inhabited and visited by many unattached men. It was a problem to be managed, certainly, but one unlikely to be solved.

Drunkenness was far and away the most prevalent offense against public order in Fargo, accounting for about half of all arrests in the city during the thirties. Fargo had been dry since 1889, when North Dakota entered the Union with statewide prohibition in place. That was a technicality with little practical application, however, because Minnesota remained wet until 1916, and Moorhead hosted a flourishing liquor trade. While the institution of statewide prohibition in Minnesota and the onset of nationwide prohibition three years later forced adjustments in the liquor business, it hardly destroyed that profitable enterprise, nor did it prevent determined people from acquiring alcohol.

If arrest statistics are any indication, alcohol abuse appeared to become more serious over time. In 1920, 227 people were arrested for public drunkenness in the city. That number rose steadily to more than 900 in 1930 and to just under 1,000 in 1931. In 1935, 1,259 people were arrested for drunkenness, suggesting that, in Fargo as elsewhere, alcohol consumption rose early in the Depression. But numbers alone may actually understate the incidence of alcohol use and abuse, especially when law enforcement was as selective and discretionary as it tended to be in Fargo. The police contended that they were enforcing the laws against public drunkenness more vigorously than they had prior to nationwide prohibition. At the same time, they admitted that many more people drank in their homes than previously and that they never arrested anyone at home unless neighbors complained of loud parties. The police were also reluctant to arrest drunks in cafés, though at times they warned they would begin doing so if revelers became too raucous. At other times they announced they did not intend to enforce the law at all. On New Year's Eve of 1931, for example, police "indicated that if celebrators kept within reason they would not be disturbed." As one officer put it, "if anyone has any money left with which to buy liquor they deserve it." Further compromising the validity of arrest statistics was the reality that poor and working-class Fargoans were disproportionately represented among those charged with drunkenness. More affluent and prominent drunks were commonly taken home by police instead of being charged, or their families were allowed to come to the station to retrieve them.[14]

There were numerous sources of supply to meet a demand that the *Forum* estimated in 1931 to be five hundred gallons a week. For those who could afford it, Canadian whiskey was available, as was "Cuban whiskey" from Chicago. Several drugstores carried liquor that was passed discreetly to affluent buyers. More common drinkers could obtain alcohol at any number of places. Cafés, cigar stores, and recreation parlors frequently had it available or could tell a buyer who was selling and where. A person desiring a drink could usually buy alcohol at the fairgrounds, at baseball games and boxing matches, and at dances, especially those held outdoors at the Tea Garden in Island Park. Clerks at downtown hotels and taxi drivers could usually be prevailed upon to introduce buyers and sellers. Outside of town, alcohol flowed at unlicensed barn dances, "beer farms," and roadhouses like the El Patio, Red Rooster, and Golden Bubble west of town or the Venice Gardens in Little Italy, east of Moorhead at Dilworth.[15]

Most alcohol consumed in Fargo was retailed by bootleggers, some of whom manufactured it at home but most of whom purchased supplies from stills in the countryside. Distilled alcohol came in gallon tins, but "hip pocket" bootleggers broke these down into half-pint bottles, which were much cheaper and more convenient for customers. Fargo drinkers usually "spiked" soft drinks or mixed alcohol with malt to produce "North Dakota champagne." Bootlegging was generally a working-class enterprise, and Fargoans who grew up in working-class neighborhoods invariably remembered neighbors who engaged in the liquor trade. In many parts of the country bootlegger numbers surged in the early years of the Depression as the jobless searched for means of supplementing their incomes, and in Fargo established bootleggers certainly complained of heightened competition. It was also one of those rare enterprises open to men and women on an equal basis. The regular appearance in police arrest records of such names as Signe Burgess, Lillian LaCroix, and Betty Nedtvedt indicates that females were well represented among Fargo bootleggers.[16]

The *Forum*, which periodically printed articles quoting alcohol prices and discussing other developments in the trade, viewed bootlegging as an amusing and even romantic enterprise, but it was hardly a business that made a positive contribution to the community. Because bootlegging was illegal, vendors of alcohol were totally outside the control of law or effective regulation by government. Nobody certified the quality or safety of their product, and there were no controls regarding when, where, or to whom they could sell. Thus, such customers as dangerously intoxicated people and children could, and did, buy alcohol.[17]

Moreover, while the presence of willing sellers and buyers made bootlegging a crime without a victim, criminalization of the alcohol trade made bootleggers especially vulnerable to other criminals. Bootleggers were frequently robbed or hijacked, and they lacked legal recourse when they were. Sometimes they were victims of more serious crimes. In August 1932 Fargo bootlegger Frank Kaiser was kidnapped and held near Detroit Lakes, Minnesota, until his family paid a ransom of $2,500. And in February 1933 bootlegger and fight promoter Tommy O'Loughlin was shot by one of his associates, Jack Kennedy, in a dispute over "the alcohol running racket."[18]

The negative effect of the illicit liquor trade on Fargo was magnified by the fact that the city was an important regional distribution point for alcohol, just as it was for more legitimate products. This meant that the city was home to substantial wholesalers as well as small retailers. Sometimes this led to major busts, as in March 1933 when police seized 2,350 gallons of alcohol that came into town on a Great Northern freight as "roofing compound." But Fargo's significance in the regional alcohol trade also created opportunities for the corruption of police and public officials. Early in April 1930 police caught Fargoans Joe Farrell and John Holzer stealing alcohol from the Fargo Transfer and

Storage Company warehouse. As the case unfolded, it was revealed that the alcohol belonged to Fargo "rum runner" Arthur (Red) Barenson, who moved his product in and out of town with a "fleet" of Reo trucks and with the full knowledge and complicity of Fargo Transfer and Storage owners L. C. Quinn and George J. McCabe. It also came to light that Fargo police chief Ed Madison had inspected a Reo filled with alcohol a few days before and had allowed it to proceed. Suspecting corruption, police commissioner A. T. Peterson charged Madison with negligence, but the City Commission cleared the chief by a three-to-one vote. Peterson kept after Madison, however, eventually forcing him to resign in May. Peterson turned out to be the least of Madison's problems. In September the federal government indicted the former chief for having "aided and abetted in the transportation . . . of liquor." Despite the testimony of policeman Walter Olson, who claimed that Madison and Barenson were intimates, the jury could not agree that the former was guilty. In December 1931 a second jury acquitted Madison.[19]

The Madison case was hardly the only episode suggesting that police were corrupted by the liquor trade and other illicit enterprises. In July 1929 city attorney M. W. Murphy noted that lower Front Street vice interests bragged publicly that they were "receiving protection" from the police. And in 1938 policewoman Mary Maid and the local chapter of the American Crime Control League charged police chief C. W. Albright and police commissioner W. W. Fuller with protecting gambling, prostitution, and underage drinking in the city. Maid was fired, and the complaint was withdrawn under pressure.[20]

As Maid's dismissal illustrated, law enforcement in the city was complicated by the manner in which police officers were employed and compensated. Fargo police were political appointees who served at the pleasure of the City Commission, and they lacked a pension plan, realities that might have diminished their professionalism and increased their vulnerability to corruption. While critics suggested professionalizing and depoliticizing the police, the City Commission appeared to be content with the existing arrangements.[21]

The corruption, hypocrisy, and ineffectiveness of prohibition engendered increasing public disillusionment with it, in Fargo and elsewhere. The churches, the Parent Teacher Association, and the Women's Christian Temperance Union continued to support it, but a *Literary Digest* poll in April 1932 showed more than three-fourths of Fargoans opposed. Early in 1933 a resident of the lower Front Street area pronounced prohibition in Fargo a failure with disastrous consequences, noting that "it has changed a neighborhood of quiet and respectable folk to one of bootleggers and drunks. . . . How many drys have had the pleasure of being awakened at all hours of night by men and women demanding liquor? . . . How many drys have gone to our local dance halls and viewed the proceedings there? . . . Cannot one see plenty of intoxicated folks in our cafes?" Minnesota's early decision to take advantage of federal legalization of 3.2 beer increased disenchantment with prohibition in Fargo, where it was seen as a drag on business that diminished potential tax revenues. As one *Forum* reader put it, maintaining prohibition meant "the fruitless spending of public money for enforcing an unenforceable law and the draining of North Dakota money into the pockets of the bootlegger and the neighboring state, instead of into the tax funds of North Dakota to help relieve overburdened taxpayers."[22]

The introduction of legal beer in Moorhead effectively demonstrated that many Fargoans had a taste for alcohol, even at a 3.2 percent level. When the beer parlors opened for the first time on April 8 they were filled with North Dakotans, some from as far away as Valley City, sixty miles to the west. The first Saturday of beer sales was "a gala night in Moorhead as curious North Dakotans by hundreds [*sic*] swarmed over the border to help inaugurate the return of the beverage and all dispensaries were crowded until the closing hour at midnight." On April 30 the *Forum* noted that 100,000 gallons of beer had been sold in Moorhead in about three weeks, or "nearly 50,000 glasses of the 10 ounce size" per day. This was quite an impressive total in a city whose 1930 population was under 7,700.[23]

Some observers hoped Minnesota's initiative would make prohibition more enforceable in North Dakota, and the "very depressed" business in Fargo speakeasies during the first weekend of legal beer sales provided support for that view. It soon became apparent, however, that Minnesota's action exacerbated North Dakota's enforcement problems. Numerous North Dakotans were arrested crossing the Red in vehicles filled with beer they intended to sell in their localities. In order to meet the Moorhead competition, more than thirty Fargo cafés and pool halls began offering beer to their customers, in blatant disregard for North Dakota law. In June the North Dakota Conference of Organizations Supporting the 18th Amendment censured law enforcement officials for allowing beer to be "sold openly" in Cass County. The City Commission, police, sheriff's office, and state's attorney issued a statement in which they claimed to "have concentrated on alcohol and other hard liquors," which continued to be sold despite the availability of beer. They added that enforcing the law against beer sales was virtually impossible in light of prevailing public sentiment. The officials noted that "to date not a single complaint has been filed by a citizen of this county as to sale of beer" and that "past experience in this county has proved the extreme difficulty of getting jury convictions in beer cases. The present economic situation . . . raises the question as to the advisibility of spending the taxpayers' money in prosecuting beer cases with the prospect that so little will be accomplished." Law enforcement had thrown in the towel in the fight against beer.[24]

Passage of an initiated measure by North Dakota voters in the fall of 1933 legalizing the sale of 3.2 beer removed the embarrassment of having an unenforced—and unenforceable—law on the books, but it launched public officials and alcohol vendors onto uncharted waters. Because the alcohol trade had been illegal since statehood, officials in North Dakota had never attempted to regulate it and vendors had never had to operate under any rules but their own. In October the City Commission wrote an ordinance setting license fees for on- and off-sale establishments, mandating a closing time of midnight, confining beer parlors to the downtown area and adjacent neighborhoods, and prohibiting sales to "a minor, incompetent person, Indian or habitual drunkard." Because there was substantial revenue to be raised, the city passed out licenses liberally—forty-three within the first two months after the ordinance was written.[25]

Problems developed almost immediately. Parlor operators sold to minors, and in dance halls where beer was sold licentious behavior was observed. Moreover, closing time saw numerous drinkers flock to cafés, where they purchased bootleg alcohol, spiked drinks, and engaged in rowdy behavior and "drunken and profane conversation." The City Commission sought to address two of these problems by allowing the beer parlors to remain open twenty-four hours a day except on Sundays, when they were required to be closed between 3 A.M. and 1 P.M. In return for their much more liberal hours, vendors agreed not to sell to minors and to prohibit spiking in their establishments. A few months later the sale of beer in dance halls was prohibited. Critics pointed out that allowing beer sales twenty-four hours a day did not raise the moral tone of the city, nor was it a solution to the evils of drink. But the commission was feeling its way along in a situation where it was guided by public demand and economic interest but not by precedent. The commission had clearly given up on preventing drinking or even controlling it very rigorously. Now it was just hoping to confine it to discrete spaces within the community.[26]

As the spiking issue demonstrated, the availability of beer did not mean that there was no longer a demand for illegal liquor. Indeed, the repeal of the Eighteenth Amendment made liquor more readily available than it had been before, including in dry or partially dry states such as North Dakota. Lodges and fraternal organizations, as well as some cafés, offered liquor to members or patrons. Authorities sometimes cracked down on the latter but allowed the former to operate with impunity, illustrating the enduring class bias embedded in the city's alcohol control and law enforcement generally.[27]

In November 1936 North Dakota voters legalized liquor sales in the state through another initiated measure. By that time the City Commission had some experience with the regulation of alcohol, and its ordinance showed it. Only fifteen on-sale and ten off-sale permits were issued, with license fees set at $1,000 for the former and $500 for the latter. Minors were not allowed on the premises, and dancing was not permitted. In partial tribute to the mores of a bygone day, the commission required that "no woman [was to] be served at a bar. Those who cater to the woman trade to provide tables and chairs [*sic*]." Like the beer parlors, liquor establishments were confined to the center of the city, and none could be within 150 feet of a school or a church. Lodges and clubs, which catered to middle-class and affluent members, could buy a license for $300 and could allow dancing. In contrast to less affluent drinkers, the elite could presumably control themselves.[28]

Rules governing alcohol sales were soon tightened further. In the fall of 1937 the City Commission decided to close beer parlors at midnight because customers of liquor establishments with midnight closings were adjourning to 3.2 establishments and causing trouble. And in 1938 the state supreme court decided that 3.2 beer was intoxicating and ruled that beer parlors must therefore be closed all day on Sunday under the state's blue law. By that point, through trial and error the city had developed a workable set of regulations for alcohol sales, though bootleggers continued to operate, minors continued to acquire alcohol, and public drunkenness and drunk driving remained major problems. Fargoans had surrendered the prohibitionists' elusive dream that alcohol use could be ended. It was enough, most had apparently concluded, that it be controlled and contained.[29]

II

It was implicitly understood in Fargo and elsewhere during the 1930s that threats to public order came disproportionately from those detached from conventional families. Transients and resident single men, who lacked strong family connections or any at all, filled police arrest records chronicling drunkenness, gambling, and patronization of prostitutes. The family was the foundation of social order; it followed that absence of family ties and responsibilities went hand in hand with social disorder.

The indispensability of strong, conventional families to a good and orderly society was almost universally assumed during the 1930s, but this essential institution seemed increasingly embattled. Divorce, self-indulgent behavior, and changing conceptions of women's rights and roles had all challenged traditional understandings of how families should function. Then the Depression occurred and threatened the family in new and troubling ways, prompting observers to devote a great deal of attention to analyzing the effects of hard times on family structures and relationships.

Some argued that the Depression had been good for families because it brought members closer together and enhanced their appreciation of the essential elements of life. First lady Eleanor Roosevelt concluded in 1933 that "the economic conditions of the last few years have . . . had one good effect at least. They have drawn children and parents . . . more closely together." Loring Schuler, editor of the *Ladies' Home Journal,* agreed, observing in 1932 that "home has been brought to new importance by depression. The restless clamor for 'freedom' has given way to a new realization that the creation of a satisfying home life is the truest expression of individuality." At least some Fargoans concurred with Roosevelt and Schuler. Responding to an invitation by the *Forum* to reflect on the year just passed on New Year's Day of 1933, Fargo PTA president Mrs. W. H. Carlson stated her belief that "the home is coming back to its rightful place. . . . Character is being built on a higher plane. The family is learning perseverance, thrift, fairness, consideration for others, originality in thinking and planning . . . and our spiritual life is actually beginning to grow because of it."[30]

Others were less sanguine about the effects of the Depression on the family. Journalist and cultural critic Frederick Lewis Allen wrote in the *Ladies' Home Journal* a month after Schuler's uplifting assessment, "fear and worry are poisoning many family relationships nowadays. The husband becomes irritable and takes out his troubles upon his wife, the wife nags and complains at what she imagines to be her husband's failure to provide, [and] the children lose respect and affection for both parents." Observers considered the humiliations of unemployment and relief to be especially devastating for families. As nationally renowned social worker and activist Lillian Wald put it in 1933, when "one sums up the effects of unemployment on the individual . . . it seems . . . that the loss of the dignity . . . is the first and most tragic. With this is bound up the loss of home, of ties, of position." Social scientists who studied the family connected male loss of dignity to alcoholism, desertion, sexual impotence, and even suicide. But the larger threat looming over fathers' decline was that of the accelerated disintegration of the traditional patriarchal family structure to which Americans were accustomed. Already besieged by emancipated wives and restive children, men who could no longer support their families frequently suffered a loss of respect and control, particularly when wives and children assumed the breadwinning role. Americans worried that families without strong fathers and husbands portended disaster for the nation.[31]

The impact of the Depression on children was a major concern. Hard times affected children in a paradoxical way, simultaneously hastening and delaying maturity. Children were often expected to work, sometimes because their income was needed and sometimes because the Depression put a premium on early acquaintance with the habits of labor. In Fargo, girls such as Avis Gjervold and Dorothy Berglund babysat or cleaned houses. Boys enjoyed more freedom to roam the streets and thus held a wider variety of jobs. Darrow Beaton and Ed Graber sold the *Forum* on downtown corners. Arthur Christianson and Seymour Olson had *Saturday Evening Post* routes. Warner Litten and Robert Pettitt delivered groceries. And Paul Gallagher worked as a stockboy at a haberdashery. These were usually jobs that could be done before or after school, but some Fargo children found that work interfered with education. Discussing truancy in 1931, Fargo Public Schools' home visitor Christine MacKerracher noted that "many of the boys and girls who fail to appear for classes are earning nickels and dimes to help feed hungry brothers and sisters."[32]

Most working children were not truants, of course, and the lessons they learned in the workplace were sometimes valuable supplements to the lessons they learned in school. The *Forum,* which employed four hundred "newsies" as street vendors and in door-to-door delivery, emphasized that its youthful employees learned initiative, courtesy, and promptness on the job. Less positively, they also earned money to use for their own purposes and developed a spirit of independence that could cause friction in the family. Moreover, those who worked downtown corners enjoyed the freedom to roam the city after dark, and they sometimes developed associations of which their parents were not aware and may not have approved. The Parent Teacher Association became concerned about the moral dangers confronting working children, arguing to the City Commission in November 1934 that allowing the very young to sell newspapers, magazines, and cheap merchandise on the streets "really made beggars of children." The City Commission responded by banning street sales by children under twelve.[33]

At the same time children were expected to begin learning adult responsi-bilities in the world of work their full entry into that world was delayed by pro-longed schooling. High school and even college enrollments rose during the thirties as parents and children concluded that education presented a rela-tively attractive alternative to the dismal job market. Paying for education was a problem, and most students at Concordia College, Moorhead State Teach-ers College, and the North Dakota Agricultural College sought part-time work to help them earn board and room and cover expenses for tuition and books. Their search for employment brought protests from local people, such as L. J. Peart of the Fargo Trades and Labor Assembly and the Unemployed Exchange, who complained that "these jobs obtained for students compete directly with the man who is the head of a family faced with the prospect of applying for relief . . . or watching his family do without those things they must have to sustain a bare living." Such complaints had no noticeable effect on either the desire of students to seek work or the willingness of employers to hire them.[34]

As long as young people would—or could—remain in school, they were sheltered to some degree from the vicissitudes of the world. Those who left school surveyed a bleak prospect in which few opportunities existed for the sort of employment that would allow one to embark on adult life. Many in-habited what the Lynds called the "jobless and schoolless population, an idle in-between age group." Lacking experience, few could get decent jobs. Many lived at home, scraping along on part-time work, and those from poor families could sometimes join the Civilian Conservation Corps or obtain other relief. Between 200,000 and 500,000 young people, mostly boys, became transients, exposing themselves to the hazards of the road and learning behaviors that deeply disturbed observers. Some members of what one commentator called the "lost generation" seemed to become bitter and cynical and were consid-ered potentially vulnerable to the appeals of fascism or communism.[35]

Anxieties about young people evaporated during World War II, when the lost generation was found by defense contractors and the military. The youth-ful cynicism and hopelessness that troubled observers rapidly disappeared and was generally forgotten. Certainly, Fargoans who were children and youths during the Depression recalled an idyllic childhood, not a bitter one. They re-membered warm homes, caring, involved parents, and supportive neighbor-hoods. Males, especially, reflected on a relatively safe community in which chil-dren enjoyed remarkable freedom. Men such as Steve Gorman and Tod Gunkleman remembered long summer days of pick-up baseball games and exploration of the fields north of town with neighborhood friends. John Q. Paulsen remembered "hooking" cars in the winter and skating in neighbors' flooded yards. Bob Mason and Jim Pastoret recalled summer bike rides to the river to swim. A more adventurous Charlie Hauser visited the transients in the downtown jungle. And Robert Litherland had no fear, even at ten or twelve years of age, of crossing the footbridge from Moorhead to Fargo at night and listening to the music outside the Crystal Ballroom.[36]

Unfortunately, not all young Fargoans enjoyed the warm and carefree childhood of nostalgic memory. Some children were neglected or abused. In February 1932 police arrested a fifteen-year-old boy for stealing milk bottles. He was attempting to support himself while his mother was out of town working on a farm. Two of his friends, one fifteen and one sixteen, were found sleeping in the hallway of a downtown office building. Social service agencies were well aware that some parents could not keep their children at all. In the days before the Aid for Dependent Children program, St. John's Orphanage and the North Dakota Children's Home provided temporary shelter for numerous children whose parents could not care for them, and it was not uncommon to see ads such as the following in the *Forum:* "Wanted—Home for 1½-year old boy by Sept. 1." The County Welfare Board frequently addressed problems of child neglect and mistreatment. On September 29, 1935, for example, it heard one case of a girl social workers believed had been impregnated by her father and another in which the father terrorized his family and "kept company with other women." Additionally, his wife left their three daughters, aged four to nine, home alone when she "went to shows continually." Nor was child neglect confined to the people who came under the purview of welfare agencies. In April 1933 a letter writer complained to the *Forum* that mothers, many of them affluent, habitually left their children in downtown movie theaters all day and into the night: "Saturday, hundreds of children come in when the doors open and remain indefinitely, even as late as the closing hour at night. . . . Just so long as a theater is considered a safe parking spot for children while their busy mothers attend to other duties, just so long will present conditions continue." One wealthy Fargoan remembered ruefully that his parents were so busy with social and organizational commitments that he "was basically raised by the maids." He would not have been considered neglected, but his hardly qualified as an ideal family, either.[37]

Sometimes the line between the freedom cherished by Fargo children and parental neglect was difficult to draw. Consider these three incidents, all of which occurred within a few blocks of one another in south Fargo in the late spring of 1936. In early May Jimmy Meath, three, and David Anderson, two and a half, decided to walk to the river, a mile away from their homes, to fish. David fell in and drowned, and Jimmy walked home to report, "Davey's in the river." The children had not been missed. A month later Donna Marie Diemert, four, who lived a block west of Jimmy and David, was crushed beneath the wheels of a fruit truck when she fell from her perch on the running board. The driver, who had just made a delivery at the Oakland Market, had previously asked parents to keep their children from riding his bumpers and running boards. On June 16 Richard Warner, seven, of 1413 Eighth Street South, died of internal injuries he sustained when he flew over the handlebars of his bicycle. He and his friend, Richard Goldberg, also seven, were riding their bikes in the evening thirteen blocks from the Warner home. Living in a relatively safe city in which children were expected to make their own fun, many Fargoans would not have seen parental neglect in these incidents, but some did. Charles Dawson, who demonstrated an abiding concern for the children of the city, was moved by Donna Marie Diemert's death to write the *Forum* that "it is not the duty of the police department to prevent children from playing in the streets and from the careless crossing of streets and from hooking on to automobiles. This in my opinion is the plain duty and definite responsibility of parents." But were the parents listening?[38]

Child neglect was a matter that was open to interpretation. Crime by children was easier to define and more disturbing. Much of the juvenile crime in the city during the Depression was of the petty variety, and some might even come under the heading of "making one's own fun." It tended to be seasonal, flowing in summer and during the Christmas holidays and ebbing when school was in session. Vandalism was a chronic problem. Children with air rifles and even .22s prowled the riverbank and the parks, warring on birds and squirrels. Slingshot- and gun-wielders broke residential and business windows and street and porch lights, and most Christmases witnessed destruction of lawn displays. Shoplifting and other forms of petty larceny were also common and were seldom punished, especially when perpetrators were children of customers or neighbors. Usually such offenses were merely annoying, but at times they became something more. In October 1931, for example, several cafés, confectioneries, and drugstores complained of being "raided" by Fargo high school students after a football game with Moorhead: "Swarms of young people ... roamed through the shops" and "on the way out, some of them 'swiped' candy from the counters, grabbed bottles of ginger ale, 'lifted' magazines from racks and fled down the street." Possession of alcohol and public drunkenness were common juvenile offenses, and sexual delinquency appeared on occasion. In 1931 there was a particularly noteworthy case in which a thirteen-year-old girl met a federal prohibition agent, C. A. Thoreson, in a Fargo café. The agent took her to a dance in Argusville, and when they got back to town she suggested they get a hotel room. Thoreson, whom the *Forum* described without apparent irony as an "undercover man," was convicted of statutory rape.[39]

Young Fargoans also committed more serious crimes. Automobile theft was especially common. Youthful thieves were usually just joy riders who abandoned stolen autos, but sometimes they stripped parts from cars or attempted to sell the vehicles. Children were also implicated in such serious property crimes as breaking and entering, burglary, and robbing boxcars. In July 1930 four boys and one girl, aged nine to thirteen, were arrested for breaking into Northern Pacific boxcars and stealing goods. And in the summer of 1933 two boys, thirteen and fourteen, were arrested for burglarizing Scheel's Hardware and stealing firearms. Child criminals in Fargo were usually unarmed but not always. In March 1930 police took a .38 caliber revolver from two boys, fourteen and thirteen, who were burglarizing a farm implement company. And early in 1932 two "boy bandits" robbed a north side grocer using a handgun. The youth and the organization of some juvenile offenders were sobering. In March 1932 police arrested four boys aged ten to fourteen for having "ransacked six downtown offices and four apartments." The "brains of the gang" was a twelve-year-old who had already been incarcerated for two years at the state training school in Mandan. A few months later police arrested another ring of thieves, made up of six boys twelve and under, who had broken into the National Guard Armory as well as a number of stores. Small wonder that district judge Daniel Holt, having heard forty-seven juvenile cases involving children as young as eight in less than five months, concluded in May 1932 that Fargo was "a city rife with juvenile crime."[40]

Holt's impression was that juvenile delinquents usually came "from homes where parental discipline has broken down," and most other observers agreed that parents deserved much of the blame for the failings of children. Policewoman Alice Duffy claimed "that the modern home has fallen down on its job" and condemned "fathers who deal with or handle . . . contraband and the mother who dresses like an abandoned woman . . . setting a bad example for children." Police chief Ed Madison agreed, noting that the job of policing the city was complicated because parents could not or would not keep their children off the streets late at night. An NDAC master's degree candidate studying inmates at the state reformatory concluded that delinquents were most likely to come from families of "common occupation" in which "mothers worked" and "parents were too busy" to manage their children properly. And John C. Pollock, juvenile commissioner for eastern North Dakota, blamed most juvenile delinquency on "careless parents."[41]

While feckless fathers and working mothers received most of the blame, environmental factors were also attacked for encouraging juvenile delinquency. Duffy believed automobiles, cigarettes, dance halls, and especially movies had a bad influence on children, noting that "youngsters who have come to her attention have all too often traced their inspiration to [gangster] movies." Motion pictures had been controversial in Fargo for some time. Evangelical Norwegian Lutheran churches condemned them generally and urged parishioners not to attend. North Dakota blue laws prohibited the showing of movies on Sundays, and several bitter fights to change the law featured moralists denouncing motion pictures for their celebrations of sex and violence and their encouragement of disrespect for authority. Movies were too popular with children and their parents, however, for anti-motion picture forces to have their way, a reality illustrated in September 1933 when six police officers were required to manage a crowd of children who came to the Fargo Theater for an appearance by cowboy star Tom Mix. In place of abolition, the Parent Teacher Association urged reform, launching a campaign in the spring of 1933 for more wholesome films and less sensational movie advertising. At the same time, the PTA, several churches, and the state's attorney's office moved to extirpate "indecent and immoral magazines . . . from Fargo news stands."[42]

Fargo's juvenile delinquency crisis climaxed on Halloween of 1933. Halloween was traditionally an occasion for pranks, rowdiness, and petty vandalism, mainly by boys, and the community usually indulged youthful depredations when they were kept within reasonable bounds. Halloween seemed to become progressively more destructive, however, with that of 1932 declared by Police Chief Albright to be "the worst in recent years." In addition to the customary Halloween disorder, youthful vandals threw "bricks through windows in homes . . . [and] stones at passing automobiles" and broke the windows out of parked cars. The next year was even worse. Along with the regular fare of breaking windows and pulling down fences, boys on the south side shot out porch lights with .22s and broke nearly every globe on Eighth Street South's great white way. West of downtown, Halloween celebrants burned a vacant house to the ground, and a policeman attempting to break up a fight between two rival gangs of boys was injured by thrown rocks. It took city crews two days to clear the streets of "miscellaneous goods of all kinds, garbage cans,

[and] pieces of fencing." More disturbing even than what was done was who was doing it. The *Forum* noted that the six boys arrested were all "sons of prominent families" from south Fargo. Such observers as Holt, Pollock, and Duffy were used to defining juvenile delinquency as a working-class phenomenon, and many Fargoans undoubtedly took comfort in the smug assumption that it was yet another of their less-affluent neighbors' many failings. Thus the involvement of "sons of prominent families" was something new and ominous to contemplate.[43]

Police commissioner W. W. Fuller concluded that the city could not stand another Halloween like that of 1933, and he offered two options. One was police maintenance of public order: "If we have to put on a force of 200 men, we can thoroughly police the city, but that undoubtedly would mean many heartaches as parents found their children hauled into the police station to answer to a charge of malicious destruction of property." The alternative was "that parents of the city of Fargo, with whom rests the right answer to this problem, will work out a different solution," even if that meant "sacrifice[ing] one night in a year, stay[ing] at home on Halloween and see[ing] that their children are not out destroying somebody's property."[44]

As Fuller suggested, Fargo had the means to deal with youthful miscreants when it so desired. Often it did not, and it was common for police to throw a scare into young offenders or turn them over to parents instead of arresting them, especially when they were from prominent and established families. Fargo was, after all, a relatively small city, and one in which beat cops came to know many parents and children. Young people arrested for offenses in the city went into the juvenile justice system, which sounds harsher to the modern ear than it actually was. Minor offenses such as shoplifting or joy riding, along with cases of child neglect and abandonment, were addressed by John C. Pollock, juvenile commissioner for eastern North Dakota, in a hearing rather than a trial setting. In common with most juvenile justice officials of his generation, Pollock believed that youthful offenders were usually good kids who had made a mistake and needed guidance, not desperadoes who required punishment. Pollock normally released juveniles to their parents, almost always with the stipulation that they report to policewoman Alice Duffy for a designated period of time. Duffy had the title of policewoman, but she came from a social work background and defined her role as a helper of vulnerable people rather than a dispenser of punishment. Duffy became a surrogate parent for many Fargo children. In addition to looking after single girls new to the city, she patrolled dance halls to insure decorum, assigned corners to paper boys working downtown, and made numerous suggestions regarding public policy, as in 1934 when she urged the City Commission to prohibit children under twelve from selling magazines or merchandise on the streets. Every year she supervised "several hundred probationers," who visited her office in the Riley Building across from city hall, where she would "tutor them on the laws of Fargo," as one boy who had burned down a haystack put it. She was determined and stern and a little frightening, but, as Irene Fraser remembered, "she was a great friend to kids." More serious offenses than those handled regularly by Pollock and Duffy, such as burglary or robbery, were tried in county or district court. While judges could and sometimes did sentence juveniles to the state training school in Mandan, they, too, frequently released children to parents and to Duffy, especially first offenders, prescribing incarceration only as a last resort. As judge M. J. Englert of Valley City, who frequently heard Fargo cases, put it in April 1932, "I hate to sentence a boy to the training school. . . . Many times they come out worse than they went in. Once a child is sent to a training school, his or her record is marred for life."[45]

Most Fargoans were unwilling to consign the problem of juvenile delinquency to the police and the juvenile justice system, however compassionate and caring those entities might be. Children were different from the drunks and gamblers downtown. They could be redeemed by a caring and engaged community, not just managed or contained. Hence, the community embraced the spirit of Police Commissioner Fuller's second option, developing a solution to the problem that did not depend on law enforcement.

The specific problem of Halloween was addressed by the Junior Chamber of Commerce, which assumed reasonably enough that if children were given a constructive alternative to destructive behavior they would choose it. In 1934 the Jaycees hosted three events, two parties for younger children and a dance for older ones, that were credited with "giving the community its sanest Halloween in the memory of this generation." The Jaycees continued their project, receiving funding from the City Commission and adding a parade and a fourth party, this one for children in their early teens. In 1938, 2,700 children attended Jaycee Halloween parties. Building on its insight that busy children are less likely than idle ones to get into trouble, the Junior Chamber in 1936 enlisted youth in Clean-up Week, an annual May event during which householders were urged to do spring cleaning and beautification and clear trash and junk from their lots.[46]

Others in town also began to see that much of the problem of juvenile delinquency could be traced to the traditional, laissez-faire notion that kids should be allowed to make their own fun. Too often, making their own fun had led children into destructive or criminal acts. More structured, adult-directed alternatives for children seemed to be the answer, not just at Halloween or during Clean-up Week but all year round. That was the assumption of the Community Welfare Association, which took up the problem of juvenile delinquency early in 1934.

The juvenile crisis came at an opportune time for the Community Welfare Association, which faced a crisis of its own in 1933. In the early thirties the deepening Depression had led the association to emphasize welfare activities, but the onset of federally funded relief made local aid agencies appear irrelevant and prompted some to ask whether the Community Chest should even continue to exist. The juvenile delinquency crisis allowed the association to focus on a genuine local problem the federal government was not addressing, thereby maintaining social relevance and public support. In the spring of 1934 the association undertook a study of juvenile delinquency, aided by Alice Duffy, John C. Pollock, Mary Snyder of the PTA, and several representatives of chest agencies serving children and youth. A community survey identified the major behavioral problems of young people as vandalism, profanity, drinking, and joy riding and criticized a "lack of parent interest" in children's activities overall. The association concluded that the "PREVENTION OF DELINQUENCY in our community" required a greater emphasis on such agencies as the YMCA, YWCA, Boy Scouts, and Camp Fire Girls, including a commitment to making "resources available for boys and girls who cannot afford the opportunity of boy scouts, Y's etc." The association organized a special youth department to dramatize its commitment to children, and it began to shift resources to "character-building" agencies, emphasizing in subsequent years that "building character and ideals of good citizenship in young people, [and] fortifying them against the temptations that beset youth and lead young people to the courts and to the prisons" had become a primary goal of the chest.[47]

Other agencies also studied the condition of Fargo's young people. In November 1933 the PTA, with the encouragement of the YMCA and the school board, announced creation of the Citizens' Committee on Leisure Time. The committee, composed of such socially minded Fargoans as Anna Stevens, George Soule, Alma Trubey, and Masonic Temple librarian Clara Richards, focused initially on unemployed women and girls, regarding whom it seemed to be guided by the axiom that an idle mind is the devil's playground. "Unless the individual is blessed with a hobby or some other constructive pursuit during his free hours and days, he is apt to turn to a negative . . . mode of life," the committee explained, "he may easily lose his capacity for straight thinking on economic and political questions. He turns radical. . . . [or] he turns criminal because there he sees the possibility of some immediate result from . . . anti-social activity." While the Citizens' Committee was created with the increasingly restive unemployed in mind, it was inevitable that it would also address the problem of misuse of free time by the young, especially in light of its creation within a week of the destructive Halloween of 1933. The Citizens' Committee added its voice to the city's growing chorus that children could no longer be trusted to make their own fun and that more and better organized recreation was needed.[48]

Organized recreation for adults and young people existed in Fargo, and such annual events as the Ice Carnival drew hundreds of participants, but budget cuts, especially by the park board, had diminished recreational opportunities at the very time such activities seemed essential. To fill the void left by the park board, the city turned to federal relief agencies, first FERA and then the WPA and the National Youth Administration.

Because it was conceived as a permanent agency, the WPA was able to develop an especially energetic recreational program, partly in response to community needs and partly to generate relief jobs beyond the old standards of public works and the sewing room. The WPA opened several "putter" or "arts and crafts" shops, where relievers taught furniture repair, sewing, dressmaking, woodworking, and other crafts. These were open to anyone but were patronized mainly by boys. Of the seven hundred visitors to putter shops during one week early in 1937, for example, nearly six hundred were boys. When the Kiwanis dropped its annual Christmas toy project the WPA took it over, enlisting boys and girls to repair toys and sew doll dresses. The WPA also launched craft competitions, as in 1937 when it obtained the cooperation of lumber dealers in sponsoring a birdhouse contest. Also that year the WPA recreation department initiated a "backyard playground" project aimed at getting parents to install inexpensive play equipment in their yards to keep children out of the streets and to "help children and parents learn to play together." Labor from the WPA and the NYA eventually allowed the park board to develop a summer recreational program far beyond anything it had offered even before the Depression. In 1936 alone children in Fargo parks could attend such imaginative events as Doll Buggy Parade Day, a watermelon feast, a freckle contest, and a Queen of the Playgrounds Pageant.[49]

Organized recreation was one part of the answer to the juvenile problem. Places to play was another. Playgrounds existed in parks and on school grounds, but they were not readily available everywhere and were nonexistent downtown. As part of its 1934 study of juvenile delinquency, the Community Welfare Association discovered that in neighborhoods where arrests of juveniles were numerous, relatively few playgrounds existed. The association suggested that this was an oversight, though it was probably an indication of chronic underinvestment in public facilities in working-class neighborhoods. Supporting rectification of this problem, the *Forum* bemoaned the fact that too many children had to "find some sport in a street or alley" and warned that "bottled up energy is almost certain to break out in vandalism" such as the "widespread destruction of property last Hallowe'en." The Community Welfare Association followed up this early study in 1938 with a campaign for playground construction. Association executive secretary R. L. Sheetz approached both the City Commission and the park board, brandishing maps demonstrating a high incidence of juvenile delinquency in neighborhoods lacking playgrounds. Sheetz argued that a playground could be built for $200 per child, while it cost $536 to keep a child in Mandan for a year. "It isn't that these children are innately bad, or that their families want them to be bad," Sheetz told the park board, "the point is that they live in areas where there just aren't any facilities for constructive recreation." Sheetz's argument convinced city officials to authorize construction of a playground at the old Washington School site in the lower Front Street area, using WPA labor.[50]

The Community Welfare Association concluded by 1938 that playgrounds and organized recreation were necessary solutions to the youth problem but not sufficient by themselves. The association believed it was also necessary that character-building agencies "revamp their programs to deal with youths' problems more effectively," that churches and service clubs address juvenile delinquency more aggressively, and, most notably, that "settlement or neighborhood houses" be built in areas with a high incidence of juvenile delinquency. But the construction of playgrounds and other recreational facilities—concrete representations of community concern—seemed to capture the popular imagination and mobilize the city's energy in a way other innovations did not.[51]

Playgrounds were but one of the products of the effort to enhance recreational facilities for Fargo youth. In 1937 the city undertook construction of a winter sports building in Island Park. This was a cooperative endeavor in which the park board supplied the land, the WPA provided the labor, and entrepreneurs R. E. Chinn and John Saul, managers of the civic auditorium, furnished the materials in return for a twenty-year lease. While the new Ice Arena was used for a variety of commercial endeavors and community programs, its backers stressed that it would provide enhanced recreational opportunities for youth.[52]

WPA workers on the girders for the ice arena, 1938

More directly targeted at children than the Ice Arena was an outdoor swimming pool at Island Park. Fargo opened pools for summer use at Central High School and Roosevelt Junior High, but boys preferred swimming outdoors in the river, especially above the south dam, where the park board stationed a lifeguard. Swimming in the river was relatively safe, but some parents considered it unhealthy. John Q. Paulsen, for example, "caught hell for it" when his parents discovered he had been bathing above the dam. Bob Mason's parents were more tolerant, though he remembered, "you'd come out of that river and your skin would just crawl." City health officer B. K. Kilbourne judged that swimming in the river was "O.K. . . . if you don't swallow too much water," noting that "sewage is dumped in the water . . . at Wahpeton and Breckinridge [about fifty miles south of Fargo]" but that by the time it reached the city the river had "been well purified." Water quality deteriorated rapidly when the river stopped flowing, however, and there were few summers in the dry thirties when the park board did not prohibit swimming for at least a few weeks.[53]

As early as 1932 observers had emphasized the need for more adequate outdoor swimming facilities, and in 1937 the Junior Chamber of Commerce took the lead in providing them. In the early spring of that year, the Jaycees announced a campaign to raise $22,000 for materials for a proposed pool, some of which was to be contributed through private subscription and some of which was to come from door-to-door sales of tiny cement bags by schoolchildren. The park board agreed to contribute land and the WPA offered labor to build the facility. By 1939 it was apparent that the material costs of a pool that would accommodate 830 swimmers and seat 800 spectators would exceed what the Jaycees had been able to raise and local governmental units had been willing to contribute. Pool backers supported a $30,000 bond issue, arguing that the facility would provide "a recreation center under careful supervision" that would prevent juvenile delinquency. The Jaycees used a number of publicity devices, including a parade and a "straw vote" by children that overwhelmingly supported the pool. Responding to these promptings, the normally tax-shy voters approved the bond issue in May by a margin of better than two to one. Construction proceeded, and the Island Park pool opened in the summer of 1940.[54]

The Island Park pool project provided eloquent testimony that the Fargo can-do, volunteer spirit had survived the Depression bruised but intact. It also demonstrated the willingness of many people—the Jaycees, local government, the WPA, and, not least, the voters—to work together on behalf of Fargo youth. And, perhaps most important, it showed the city's desire to deal positively with the problem of juvenile delinquency by providing healthy, supervised recreation as an alternative to antisocial behavior by the city's children.

The emphasis on recreational solutions for the problem of juvenile misbehavior did not mean that prophylactic measures disappeared. The PTA continued its crusade against indecent literature and movies and launched a drive for better enforcement of the curfew for children under sixteen. And the Women's Christian Temperance Union urged the Board of Education to introduce Bible reading in the schools and to be on the lookout for marijuana smoking by high school students because "these cigarettes sometimes cause insanity, loss of memory, perverted sexual[ity], and . . . lead to murders and other crimes." But the main thrust of child protection and anti–juvenile delinquency efforts after 1933 was clearly toward the provision of supervised recreation.[55]

The anti–juvenile delinquency campaign that unfolded in Fargo in response to the crisis of the early thirties tells a good deal about the city and its

Spectators and swimmers at the Island Park pool, conceived by the Junior Chamber of Commerce and built with WPA labor

assumptions about its young people. The widespread desire "to do something in a really constructive and tangible way" for the city's children, in Charles Dawson's words, illustrates the same sort of paternal concern that Fargoans expressed for young women and sometimes for the poor. Further, it embodies the assumptions that something positive *could* be done and that children were fundamentally good and would usually grasp positive alternatives to delinquent behavior if given the chance. While adults such as the single men on lower Front might be lost and could only be controlled, the young were still redeemable by caring, public-spirited people with well-conceived programs. It also indicates the expanding consensus that what many children valued most in Fargo—freedom to do as they liked with relatively little adult supervision—was potentially dangerous. And, finally, it demonstrates an unwillingness on the part of Fargoans to be victims of forces beyond their control and a belief that they had the means and the intelligence and the will to overcome challenges. It expressed the spirit of a confident city, continuing to manifest itself despite the travails of the Depression.[56]

CONCLUSION

"Fargo . . . is the center of a highly prosperous area, in the fertile valley of the Red River. . . .
    "Its strategic location, transportation facilities, extremely favorable freight rates, and
increasingly wealthy trade area, have contributed to its steady growth in population and . . .
property values."
    "Report on the Development of a Six-Year Program for Municipal Improvements
    1939-1940 Through 1944-1945," December 9, 1939

"Children, unborn at the time of the dedication, one day will sing the praises of the pool
and the public spirited citizens who built it for the healthful pleasure of youth."
    Fargo Forum, *August 18, 1940*

WE LIKE TO MEASURE LIFE by dates and events. Perhaps doing so imparts a
sense of certainty to lives that are uncertain or provides the illusion of borders
and boundaries on the unboundable flow of time. Hence, we like to mark the
start of the Great Depression with the stock market crash and end it with the
attack on Pearl Harbor, which, conveniently, also denotes the beginning of
World War II. One door closes, and another opens.

But while dates or events assume great significance in retrospect, they did
not always mean what we think they should have meant to the people who
lived through them. Pearl Harbor might have marked the definitive passage
from one era to another, but it did not signify the end of the Depression to Fargoans. Indeed, there was no single event that denoted the Depression's end,
no specific point at which the mayor or the *Forum* said, "that's it; it's over."
The city drifted into the Depression with the rest of the country, bumped along
the bottom for a while, then drifted out.

National statistics on industrial production, unemployment, commodity
prices, and the like indicated in 1939 that the economy still had not attained
1929 levels, but in Fargo, at least, the public had grown tired of the Depression.
Indeed, local impatience with hard times and the steps taken to counter them
had been noticeable as early as 1934, when it became apparent that things had
stopped getting worse and worse. Perhaps it is not even quite accurate to say

that Fargoans were growing tired of the Depression. Perhaps they had just become accustomed to it. Hard times had become part of people's thinking. They had adjusted to it, learned to live with it, and made it part of a new social and personal equation.

City fathers had stopped dwelling on the implications of economic hardship. In the context of the times, Fargo was getting along fine. When city planners discussed Fargo and its future in 1939, they used such terms as "highly prosperous," "increasingly wealthy," and "growth in population and . . . property values." Fargo's main problems had always been problems of growth. Public officials had always worried about providing adequate recreational and transportation infrastructure, abundant water and efficient sewage disposal, sufficient housing and public buildings. These were precisely the problems the authors of the six-year plan highlighted in 1939. Coping with economic depression or human misery was not mentioned.[1]

The six-year plan was hardly the only sign that Fargo's focus had returned to coping with growth. The City Commission was turning to new problems unrelated to hard times. In October 1939 the commission passed a smoke abatement ordinance designed to address a chronic problem that accompanied coal-burning furnaces, and commissioner Hugh Corrigan announced a campaign to eradicate rats in Fargo. The focus on smoke and rats signaled a reinvigoration of the quality-of-life innovations forward-looking Fargoans had traditionally advanced in their attempt to make their growing city more livable.[2]

In focusing on growth and the quality of life, city fathers were dealing with immediate problems as well as anticipated ones. The 1940 census counted 32,580 people in the city, a 12 percent increase over the 1930 population. Fargo continued to be a regional magnet for young people searching for economic opportunity, and there were numerous indications they had come to the right place. The *Forum* reported that the value of new construction in the city reached $889,000 in 1939, up impressively from the Depression low of $92,000 in 1933, if still substantially below pre-Depression levels. And bank debits—an indication of business activity—reached $218.2 million in 1939, an all-time record. In per capita terms, Fargo's bank debits were second only to those of Bartlesville, Oklahoma, an oil boomtown. When the *Forum* suggested that "business men of the community have every reason to feel encouraged," it was no longer whistling through the graveyard, as it had in 1932 and 1933. Now it was making a judgment based on solid evidence.[3]

Shrinking relief rolls, locally and throughout the state, further strengthened the impression that the Depression was more a memory than a reality. An improving local economy, the shift of many reliefers to Aid for Dependent Children and Old-Age Assistance, tightened program requirements, and federal budget cuts conspired to diminish WPA rolls dramatically. It was heartening to see fewer people on relief, though it was also somewhat misleading, as the city was reminded at Christmas when 800 people appeared at the Avalon Ballroom for WDAY-*Forum* food baskets when organizers had planned for only 650. Nor did smaller contingents of reliefers mean that work was plentiful, as was revealed by the 1940 census, which reported 16 percent of men and 10 percent of women unemployed. But fewer people were on the WPA rolls, with the result that those who remained were increasingly stigmatized and even demonized. Sentencing two WPA workers to prison for relief fraud, district judge M. J. Englert opined in December 1939 that "there are altogether too many who are ready and willing to stick their hands in the public pocket, and I think it is time we sit down on them. Too many . . . are ready to take everything they can get." Englert concluded, "it has come to the point where all pride is lost." And so those on relief completed the transition, initiated in the Depression's earliest days, from neighbors in need, to slackers and chiselers, to losers and con artists lacking the barest elements of self-respect. They had become aliens in their native land.[4]

Shrinkage in the highly visible WPA helped obscure the degree to which the city had come to depend, directly or indirectly, on the federal government and its social programs. It was the federal government that had relieved the burden on local private and public agencies for providing aid to populations in need. Such programs as Old-Age Assistance and Aid for Dependent Children diminished pressures on county government and property tax payers, and institutions rooted in a commitment to local responsibility for the helpless, such as the poor farm and the North Dakota Children's Home, could foresee their demise.

Federal programs that transferred funds of any kind into North Dakota inevitably strengthened its largest and most powerful trade center. While Fargo did not benefit directly from federal agricultural programs, for example, money in farmers' pockets meant business for the city. As the major retail, wholesale, and service center for an expansive rural hinterland, Fargo stood to profit whenever "farmer buying power has been enhanced . . . by a big influx of cash from the federal . . . parity and conservation payments." Indeed, Fargo was more dominant economically in 1940 than it had been in 1930, and much of the credit went to the federal government. Federal programs did not turn losers into winners or winners into losers. Most federal activity strengthened those that were already relatively strong, and Fargo was included among them.[5]

The federal government had further enhanced the position of the Queen City of the Northwest by improving the public infrastructure and the quality of life in Fargo. Paved streets, new bridges and viaducts, a new sewage disposal plant, and numerous recreational facilities were testimony to the local effects of the Public Works Administration and New Deal relief agencies. Certainly unmet needs remained, most notably for a new city hall, library, and auditorium. Ironically, those facilities were built in the early 1960s when a new federal program, Model Cities, provided the money to raze the area east of downtown and west of the river.

Fargo had adjusted to the increased federal presence in local life and in the local economy quickly and with little reflection. The federal government was commonly viewed as another customer to be courted. It spent money in the city and provided employment just as a railroad, creamery, or large retailer would. When the federal government's local activities were new they were understood to be short-term boons inspired by economic emergency, but within a very few years they came to be seen as entitlements and were taken for granted. Fargoans sometimes forgot that the federal government had played any role at all in helping them cope with the Depression or in improving their city, an ironic effect, in part, of the dependence of so many federal programs on local initiative and volunteerism. Celebrating the opening of the Island Park pool in August 1940, the *Forum* predicted that "children, unborn at the time of the dedication, one day will sing the praises of the pool and of the public spirited citizens who built it for the healthful pleasure of youth." Already the WPA architects and engineers who designed it and workers who constructed it were slipping out of civic memory, obscured by the Jaycees, the City Commission, and local voters who approved the bond issue. Fargo took comfort in the belief it was going it alone.[6]

So Fargoans were ready to move on by the time the new decade dawned, or, more accurately, to return to the patterns of life and thinking that had characterized them before the Depression slowed the Queen City's inexorable march to greatness. They were eager to put the unpleasantries of relief, hardship, radicalism, and class conflict behind them and embrace a future similar to the idealized past in some essential ways, a future of social harmony and economic growth and progress, based on independence, self-reliance, and neighborliness. But the Depression changed the city and its people. Individuals were seared by the experience of hardship and the specter of dependency, developing habits they carried through the rest of their lives. Neighborliness and pleasant relations between employers and employees broke down, leaving an aftertaste of bitterness and suspicion. And what had been a generous and caring community demonstrated a capacity for churlishness and cruelty. Moreover, cultural changes continued to have an impact on the city, whether it welcomed them or not. Some children became more independent and affluent, and child-rearing standards slowly became more permissive. Women behaved less in accordance with traditional standards and were more likely to work after marriage and to encroach on traditionally male social and political preserves. The Depression did not change everything, or even anything very much, but Fargo would never again be the same as it was in 1929. After all, there was that new pool to control the kids, built with federal help, and boys and girls were swimming together. Re-creating the comfortable past simply was not possible, even in a city proud of going it alone.

NOTES TO PREFACE

1. Kennedy, *Freedom from Fear.*
2. Tweton, *New Deal at the Grass Roots;* Grant, *Down and Out on the Family Farm.*
3. Cohen, *Making a New Deal;* Murphy, *Mining Cultures;* Lynd and Lynd, *Middletown in Transition.*
4. Danbom, "'Cast Down Your Bucket Where You Are.'"

NOTES TO INTRODUCTION

1. "Fargo Grows," editorial, *Fargo Forum* 54, Jan. 1, 1932, p16.
2. U.S. Department of Commerce, Bureau of the Census, *Fifteenth Census: 1930,* Vol. 3.2, 418; U.S. Department of Commerce, Bureau of the Census, *Fourteenth Census: 1920,* Vol. 1, 270.
3. For Fargo's similarity to other American cities in this regard, see Wiese, "The Other Suburbanites." For one local suburb, see "Community of Golden Ridge Gives Promise of Expansion," *Fargo (Sunday) Forum* 24, Mar. 14, 1932, p12, 16.
4. U.S. Department of Commerce, Bureau of the Census, *Sixteenth Census: 1940,* Vol. 2.5, 435; Interview with Frieda Oster (pseud.), West Fargo, ND, Apr. 8, 1999; interview with Lucille Duval, Fargo, ND, July 18, 1998; interview with Avis Gjervold, Fargo, ND, Sept. 30, 1997.
5. "Topics of the Week," editorial, *Fargo (Sunday) Forum* 22, Dec. 8, 1929, p24.
6. "City Has Little Overcrowding," *Fargo Forum* 57, Apr. 24, 1935, p1, 5; "3,107 Fargoans Operating Cars," *Fargo Forum* 53, May 22, 1931, p16; "Cross-Sectioning Another Market," 22.
7. U.S. Department of Commerce, Bureau of the Census, *Fifteenth Census: 1930,* Vol. 3.2, 433.
8. "Hector Gives Airport to City," *Fargo Forum* 53, Apr. 6, 1931, p1, 10; "Pick Fargo as

Key Air Center," *Fargo Forum* 53, May 12, 1931, p1; "Throngs See Airport Opening," *Fargo Forum* 53, May 27, 1931, p1, 18. For airport development nationally, see Bednarek, *America's Airports.*
9. Dakota Alpha Chapter of Pi Gamma Mu, "Economic and Social Development of Fargo, North Dakota," n.d., 80, North Dakota Institute for Regional Studies (hereafter NDIRS); "City Audit Reveals Errors," *Fargo Forum* 52, Mar. 6, 1930, p1, 11.
10. Minutes of the Regular Meeting of the Board of City Commissioners of Fargo, Aug. 5, 1929, mss. 42, box 14, M-735, NDIRS; Minutes of the Regular Meeting of the Board of City Commissioners of Fargo, Sept. 21, 1931, mss. 42, box 15, N-306, NDIRS.
11. U.S. Department of Commerce, Bureau of the Census, *Fifteenth Census: 1930,* Vol. 3.2, 418.
12. Police Records, 1930–46, mss. 133, NDIRS; "Fargo Chinese Concerts Pass as Café Closes," *Fargo (Sunday) Forum* 23, Feb. 1, 1931, p9.
13. "Harlem Club Party Theme," *Fargo (Morning) Forum* 27, Jan. 1, 1935, p12; "Band to Give Minstrel Show," *Fargo (Sunday) Forum* 27, Jan. 13, 1935, p9; "Central Students Pillage Attics for 'Sock' Day Garb," *Fargo Forum* 53, May 1, 1931, p16; "News About Town," *Fargo Forum* 54, Jan. 15, 1932, p12; "Brevities Acts Are Shaping Up," *Fargo Forum* 57, Mar. 28, 1935, p7; Stott's Briquet ad, *Fargo Forum* 54, July 13, 1932, p2; Fargo Theater ad, *Fargo Forum* 52, July 28, 1930, p9; "They're Harlem Gen'men," *Fargo (Sunday) Forum* 26, Mar. 11, 1934, p10.
14. "Death Ends 84-Year Life for 'Colonel' Plummer," *Fargo Forum* 53, June 25, 1931, p1, 7; "Condition of Front St Hit," *Fargo (Sunday) Forum* 21, July 31, 1929, p1; "Darty May Maintain County Jail Sojourn," *Fargo Forum* 52, Nov. 1, 1930, p6; anonymous interview in

author's possession; "Negro Celebrates Joe's Win; Police Rescue Him from Mob," *Fargo Forum* 57, Sept. 25, 1935, p1.

15. "Fargo Hebrew Congregation Organized in 1896; Serves 100 Local Families," *Fargo Forum* 59, Mar. 25, 1937, p11. A nice overview of the Jewish experience in the Upper Midwest is Schloff, *"And Prairie Dogs Weren't Kosher."* See also Lazar, "Jewish Communal Life in Fargo."

16. Harry Lashkowitz to Alfred K. Stern, May 2, 1929, Harry Lashkowitz Papers, mss. 161, box 34, folder 9, NDIRS; interview with Ruth Landfield, Fargo, ND, Sept. 9, 1997; interview with Joseph Paper, Fargo, ND, Oct. 11, 1998; interview with Edward Stern, Fargo, ND, July 22, 1997.

17. Paper interview; anonymous interview in author's possession; "Fargoan Discovers Germany of Four Years Ago Has Vanished: Finds People Lauding Adolf Hitler," *Fargo (Sunday) Forum* 28, Sept. 13, 1936, p13. For other tributes to Hitler and the Nazis, see, for example, "Barber Finds Germany Is Better than Ever Before," *Fargo (Sunday) Forum* 28, Sept. 22, 1935, p13; and "Berlin Woman Lauds Hitler, and His Program in Germany," *Fargo (Sunday) Forum* 28, Dec. 22, 1935, p13, 20.

18. Interview with Eloise Clower, Fargo, ND, Oct. 28, 1997; interview with Gladys Carney, Fargo, ND, June 15, 2000; interview with Monsignor Anthony Peschel, Arthur, ND, Aug. 18, 1998; interview with Tod Gunkleman, Fargo, ND, Oct. 26, 1999; interview with Evelyn Fisher, Fargo, ND, Mar. 14, 2000; interview with Alden Hvidston, Moorhead, MN, Mar. 9, 2000.

19. "Amphion Back in Home Cities," *Fargo Forum* 57, May 6, 1935, p1, 7; "Amphion, 70 Strong, Home Jubilant but Weary After Triumphant Tour," *Fargo Forum* 59, Apr. 28, 1937, p1.

20. U.S. Department of Commerce, Bureau of the Census, *Fifteenth Census: 1930,* Vol. 3.2, 427.

21. For the Fargo demonstration project, see Harvey and Abrams, *"For the Welfare of Mankind."* See also "Fargo Death Rate Falls Far Below U.S. Average," *Fargo Forum* 53, Jan. 26, 1931, p8.

22. "Cross-Sectioning Another Market."

23. "City Has Little Overcrowding," *Fargo Forum* 57, Apr. 24, 1935, p1, 5.

24. U.S. Department of Commerce, Bureau of the Census, *Fifteenth Census: 1930,* Vol. 3.2, 433.

NOTES TO CHAPTER 1

1. "Fargo Industry to Be Checked," *Fargo (Morning) Forum* 22, Dec. 12, 1929, p7.

2. "Garbage Land Petition Filed," *Fargo Forum* 52, Jan. 13, 1930, p8.

3. "Topics of the Week," *Fargo (Sunday) Forum* 22, Nov. 24, 1929, p22; P. H. Steadman, "It Will Revitalize Agriculture," *Fargo (Morning) Forum* 22, Nov. 7, 1929, p8. The deterioration of the stock market did not merit front-page coverage in the *Forum* until October 20. The relative disinterest in the stock market and lack of involvement in it was not unique to Fargo; see Morgan, "Fort Wayne and the Great Depression."

4. Lorne Wilde, "Fargo Building Program High," *Fargo Forum* 58, Jan. 1, 1936, p1, 14; "Kettle Bells Sing Opening of Drive for Cheer Funds," *Fargo (Sunday) Forum* 22, Dec. 8, 1929, p1; "Many Families Are Destitute," *Fargo (Morning) Forum* 22, Dec. 12, 1929, p2; "Garbage Land Petition Filed," *Fargo Forum* 52, Jan. 13, 1930, p8.

5. "Part Payment Buying Grows," *Fargo (Morning) Forum* 22, Oct. 20, 1929, p15; "Retail Credit Business Here Yearly Totals 20 Millions," *Fargo (Sunday) Forum* 22, Sept. 22, 1929, p13.

6. For the continuing importance of credit, see "The Anticipated Dollar." Interview with John Alsop, Fargo, ND, Nov. 20, 1997; interview with Dora Snyder, Fargo, ND, Aug. 6, 1998. For a recent study of the effects of installment buying on the Depression, see Olney, "Avoiding Default." Gjervold interview; interview with Sophie Dizek, Fargo, ND, Aug. 4, 1998. For the travails of small groceries elsewhere, see Hallgren, "Mass Misery in Philadelphia," and Cohen, *Making a New Deal,* 234–35. Interview with Jim Pastoret, Fargo, ND, Aug. 4, 1998; "Necessary to Raise $75,000 for St. Luke's Hospital Needs," *Fargo (Sunday) Forum* 23, Dec. 7, 1930, p1, 6; Melvin A. Hildreth to Jesse A. Miller, Mar. 6, 1933, Melvin A. Hildreth Papers, mss. 654, box 11, folder 3, NDIRS. For the expansion of credit nationally during the Depression, see Marcosson, "99% Honest."

7. Minutes of the Special Meeting of the

Board of Directors of the Lutheran Hospital Association held Dec. 9, 1930, Meritcare Medical Records, mss. 5 4975 5153, box 4, Northwest Minnesota Regional Historical Center (hereafter NMRHC); "Bakery Cuts Bread Price," *Fargo Forum* 52, May 1, 1930, p1; "Meats Go Back to Levels of Pre-War Times in Local Shops," *Fargo Forum* 52, July 29, 1930, p1; "Bricklayers Slash Wages," *Fargo (Sunday) Forum* 24, Apr. 10, 1932, p1.

8. "Business Unusually Good in Fargo and Moorhead," *Fargo Forum* 53, Dec. 25, 1930, p1, 7; the *Forum* estimated that 1931 prices were 30 percent below 1930 levels in "Fargo Merchandise Sales Largest in 1931," *Fargo Forum* 54, Jan. 1, 1932, p1; "Black's Marks 20th Anniversary Thursday," *Fargo Forum* 54, June 9, 1932, p9.

9. "Sale Extended Three Days; Prizes To All Salesgirls," "The Herbstory" 1 (Mar. 17, 1930): 1.

10. "Saturday Night Shopping Goal of Business Group," *Fargo Forum* 53, Aug. 31, 1931, p2; "Scouts Know Their Fargo," *Fargo Forum* 53, Sept. 25, 1931, p5; Minutes of the Meeting of the Board of City Commissioners of Fargo, May 9, 1932, mss. 42, box 15, p376–80, NDIRS; "City Daylight Savings Plan Starts Bitter Debate," *Fargo Forum* 54, May 12, 1932, p1, 2.

11. For a national perspective, see Barnes, "Business Looks at Unemployment." "Building Opportunity," editorial, *Fargo Forum* 53, Mar. 9, 1931, p4; "Hanna Heads Dollar Drive," *Fargo Forum* 54, Feb. 12, 1932, p7; "Bonds Fail to Bring Buyers," *Fargo Forum* 54, Mar. 10, 1932, p5; Scroggs, "Our 'Orgy of Saving.'"

12. "Trio of Local Vendors Fined," *Fargo Forum* 53, Jan. 17, 1931, p1; "3 Arrested for Keeping Stores Open on Sunday," *Fargo Forum* 53, June 18, 1931, p1.

13. "Anti-Peddler Drive Begins," *Fargo Forum* 52, Mar. 18, 1930, p7; "Patronize the Home Folks," editorial, *Fargo Forum* 53, Sept. 9, 1931, p4; Regular Meeting of the Board of City Commissioners of Fargo, Sept. 8, 1931, mss. 42, box 15, N-301, NDIRS; "Transient Fee on 1st Reading," *Fargo Forum* 54, Mar. 7, 1932, p3; "Meat Dealers, 'Peddlers' War," *Fargo Forum* 55, Dec. 28, 1932, p3; Minutes of the Regular Meeting of the Board of City Commissioners, Feb. 19, 1934, mss. 42, box 15, N-639, NDIRS.

14. "City Mart to Open July 1," *Fargo Forum* 55, June 27, 1933, p1; Minutes of the Regular Meeting of the Board of Commissioners, Oct. 22, 1934, mss. 42, box 15, N-776, NDIRS.

15. "Board to Talk Teachers' Pay," *Fargo Forum* 54, Mar. 1, 1932, p8; "Christmas and What It Means," "The Herbstory" 1 (Dec. 1930): 2.

16. "Report of the Activities of the Chamber of Commerce of Fargo, North Dakota, 1930," Fargo Chamber of Commerce Records, mss. 10484, Annual Reports, 1930–35 File, p28, State Historical Society of North Dakota (hereafter SHSND); Classifieds, *Fargo Forum* 53, Dec. 22, 1930; interview with Richard Hilber by Mary Jo Vrem-Ydstie, Fargo, ND, 1974, File OGL#259, Chester Fritz Library, University of North Dakota (hereafter UND); "Six-Hour Day Is Favored Here," *Fargo Forum* 53, Dec. 3, 1930, p2; "Labor Exodus Toward North," *Fargo Forum* 54, Aug. 23, 1932, p3.

17. For the national collapse in construction, see Flynn, "Mobilizing Deflation," and Holden, "The Crisis in Real Estate." "Fargo to Get 6 Story Building," *Fargo Forum* 52, May 16, 1930, p1. As measured by building permits issued, construction spending in Fargo fell from nearly $2 million in 1929 to just over $96,000 in 1933, Lorne Wilde, "Fargo Building Program High," *Fargo Forum* 58, Jan. 1, 1936, p1, 14.

18. A. T. Cole, "Do That Job Now," *Fargo Forum* 52, Oct. 7, 1930, p2; "Asks Fargoans to Dig Up Jobs," *Fargo Forum* 52, Oct. 10, 1930, p5; "Legion Pledges Laborless Aid," *Fargo Forum* 52, Nov. 14, 1930, p6; "Report of the Activities of the Chamber of Commerce of Fargo, North Dakota, 1930," Fargo Chamber of Commerce Records, mss. 10484, Annual Reports, 1930–35 File, p28, SHSND; "Fargo P. O. to Employ 50 for Yule Tide Rush," *Fargo Forum* 53, Dec. 3, 1930, p1.

19. Minutes of the Regular Meeting of the Board of City Commissioners of Fargo, Nov. 10, 1930, mss. 42, box 15, N-192, NDIRS; Minutes of the Regular Meeting of the Board of City Commissioners of Fargo, Jan. 5, 1931, mss. 42, box 15, N-203, NDIRS; Minutes of the Regular Meeting of the Board of City Commissioners of Fargo, Apr. 13, 1931, mss. 42, box 15, N-236, NDIRS. For the strength of city fi-

nances, see, for example, "Fargo Finances Showing Gain Over 1929 Figures," *Fargo Forum* 53, Dec. 3, 1930, p5, and "Fargo Cuts Bonded Debt to $21,000," *Fargo Forum* 54, Jan. 14, 1932, p1.

20. "Reconstruction, Raising of Red River Dam Ordered," *Fargo Forum* 52, Jan. 6, 1930, p1, 10; Minutes of the Regular Meeting of the Board of Commissioners of Fargo, Dec. 29, 1930, mss. 42, box 15, N-202, NDIRS; "Grim Battle to Help Jobless Is Launched by 'Fighting 62,'" *Fargo Forum* 54, Feb. 26, 1932, p1, 9. The 1930 census showed more than 6,600 families in the city and more than 12,300 employed men and women. Thus, five to six hundred unemployed "heads" of families would translate to four to five percent of the workforce, or seven to nine percent of heads of families.

21. "Demand Assessor Report Adoption," *Fargo Forum* 53, June 16, 1931, p1, 10; "100 Urged to Press Recall," *Fargo Forum* 53, Aug. 21, 1931, p3; "Withdrawals Nullify Recall Petitions," *Fargo Forum* 53, Oct. 29, 1931, p1. Charles Swanee, "Better Late than Never," *Fargo Forum* 53, July 18, 1931, 2; Jennie DeOtle, "Against Tax Frills," *Fargo Forum* 53, July 28, 1931, p2.

22. For the tax revolt nationally, see Beito, *Taxpayers in Revolt,* and Harrows, "The Coming Tax Rebellion."

23. "Taxpayers Unit to Stage City Campaign for New Members," *Fargo Forum* 54, Jan. 29, 1932, p1, 7; "Taxes Imperil Home Owners," *Fargo Forum* 54, June 22, 1932, p10; "Taxpayers' Four Acts Pass with Union's Two," *Fargo Forum* 54, July 2, 1932, p2; "City, Schools Make Drastic Budget Slashes," *Fargo Forum* 54, July 19, 1932, p1, 8. Minutes of the Meeting of the Board of City Commissioners of Fargo, Dec. 19, 1932, mss. 42, box 15, p456–58, NDIRS, indicates that $38,000 in delinquent taxes were owed to the city at that time.

24. "Fargo Budget Carries $100,000 Waterworks Project," *Fargo Forum* 54, July 27, 1932, p1, 9; Lorne Wilde, "Pollution of River Is Fargo's Civic Disgrace," *Fargo Forum* 54, Sept. 15, 1932, p1; Rhodes Arnold, "A Reasonable Rebel," unpublished manuscript in author's possession, p18; P. Jensen, "The Dam—No, No!" *Fargo Forum* 53, Nov. 13, 1931, p8; "River Sewage Data Compiled,"

Fargo Forum 54, Aug. 16, 1932, p2; interview with Seymour Olson, Fargo, ND, Oct. 22, 1998.

25. "Anders Describes Plans for Proposed 'By-pass,'" *Fargo Forum* 53, July 13, 1931, p2; "$500,000 Sewage Plant Bonds Asked," *Fargo Forum* 54, Aug. 22, 1932, p1; "Labor Backing Sewage Plant," *Fargo Forum* 54, Aug. 19, 1932, p2; "Legion Posts of Two Cities Ask Action on Sewage Plants," *Fargo Forum* 54, Aug. 2, 1932, p1, 10; "City to Vote on $400,000 Sewer Bond," *Fargo Forum* 54, Oct. 10, 1932, p1; "Sewer Bond Issue Defeated," *Fargo Forum* 54, Nov. 9, 1932, p1; E. C. Furcht, "The Other Side," *Fargo Forum* 55, Nov. 21, 1932, p5.

26. K. H. Mallarian, "He Wants Publicity," *Fargo Forum* 53, July 25, 1931, p3; Minutes of the Meeting of the Board of Park Commissioners, Aug. 4, 1931, book 4, p77–78, Fargo Park District; Minutes of the Meeting of the Board of Park Commissioners, Mar. 16, 1932, book 4, p115, Fargo Park District; "Fargo Supervised Play Set on Every Other Day," *Fargo Forum* 54, Apr. 6, 1932, p7; "Too Late, Paying For Playing," *Fargo Forum* 54, Apr. 12, 1932, p5.

27. "Local Schools Overcrowded," *Fargo Forum* 52, May 22, 1930, p5; "Fargo Votes $150,000 Bond Issue for New 11 Room School," *Fargo Forum* 52, June 26, 1930, p3; "Salary Raise for Teachers Is Deferred Year by Board," *Fargo Forum* 53, Mar. 18, 1931, p1; "Fargo School Board Budget Pared Down to $468,500 Total," *Fargo Forum* 53, July 18, 1931, p1; "Fargo School Teachers Get 8 Per Cent Cut to Begin in Fall," *Fargo Forum* 54, Mar. 3, 1932, p1, 2; "School Board Hits at Critics," *Fargo Forum* 54, Mar. 11, 1932, p2; "City, Schools Make Drastic Budget Slashes," *Fargo Forum* 54, July 19, 1932, p1. For the public school situation nationally, see Tyack, Lowe, and Hansot, *Public Schools in Hard Times,* and Moreo, *Schools in the Great Depression.*

28. "Teachers' Pay Cut Attacked," *Fargo Forum* 54, Mar. 4, 1932, p1; H. A., "Salary Cuts Hurt Merchants," *Fargo Forum* 54, Mar. 25, 1932, p5; A. B., "The Teacher Pay Cuts," *Fargo Forum* 54, Mar. 21, 1932, p3.

29. The story of the Cass County poor farm is told in Hoffbeck, "The Cold Charity of the Poorhouse." Among the works detailing the mothers' pension movement nationally are Abramovitz, *Regulating the Lives of Women;* Gordon, *Pitied But Not Entitled;* and Sealan-

der, *Private Wealth and Public Life.* Mothers' pensions in Cass County averaged seven to eight dollars per child per month in 1929 and 1930.

30. Singleton, *The American Dole,* 27–48.

31. "Nonresident Poor," editorial, *Fargo Forum* 52, Jan. 13, 1930, p4; "Action Starts Against Poor," *Fargo Forum* 52, Jan. 31, 1930, p12; "26 Ordered from County," *Fargo Forum* 52, Feb. 4, 1930, p8; interview with Naomi Larson, Fargo, ND, May 11, 1999. In North Dakota, one had to live in a county for one year to be considered a resident for relief purposes.

32. "$131,000 Cost of Caring for County's Poor in Last Year," *Fargo Forum* 53, July 21, 1931, p1; "Cass Installs Bid System to Trim Costs of Care for Poor," *Fargo Forum* 53, Oct. 7, 1931, p1, 10; "No County Help for Radio, Car Owners, Board Decrees," *Fargo Forum* 53, Sept. 18, 1931, p1.

33. "$13,560 Spent on Cass Poor," *Fargo Forum* 54, Feb. 4, 1932, p5; "Find Huge Waste in Cass Poor Aid," *Fargo Forum* 54, Feb. 16, 1932, p1, 7.

34. Proceedings of the Board of County Commissioners of Cass County, North Dakota, Feb. 16, 1932, p7, Cass County Auditor's Office.

35. "Find Huge Waste in Cass Poor Aid," *Fargo Forum* 54, Feb. 16, 1932, p1, 7; Fargo Council of Welfare Agencies Meeting, 1, United Way Collection, NDIRS; "'I Won't Work' Men Working," *Fargo Forum* 54, Apr. 12, 1932, p1. For work relief activities in 1932, see Minutes of the Board of Park Commissioners, Mar. 1, 1932, book 4, p110–15, Fargo Park District; "City, County to Join in Public Garden Project," *Fargo Forum* 54, Apr. 18, 1932, p1; "Relief Must Be Worked For," *Fargo Forum* 54, Sept. 7, 1932, p2. For contributions of private agencies nationwide, see Williams, *Federal Aid for Relief.* For work relief in other locales, see Colcord, *Emergency Work Relief.* For the relationship between public and private welfare agencies in another setting, see Traverso, *Welfare Politics in Boston.*

36. "Cass County's Poor to Use Lignite, Board Says," *Fargo Forum* 54, Feb. 17, 1932, p1; Proceedings of the Board of County Commissioners of Cass County, North Dakota, Mar. 1, 1932, p1649, Cass County Auditor's Office; "Cass Contract for Food Let," *Fargo*

Forum 54, Mar. 18, 1932, p1; "Landlords Balk at Plea to Cut Paupers' Rents," *Fargo Forum* 54, Apr. 19, 1932, p1; "Relief Fund Is Exhausted," *Fargo Forum* 54, Mar. 4, 1932, p9. County general assistance spending rose from $45,000 in fiscal 1930 to $75,000 the next year to nearly $120,000 in fiscal 1932. See "Abuses Reduce Relief Funds," *Fargo Forum* 54, Mar. 7, 1932, p3, and "Jump in Poor Aid Cost Faces Budget Framers," *Fargo Forum* 54, July 13, 1932, p1, 8.

37. "Cass Tax Tentatively Set Higher than 1931," *Fargo Forum* 54, July 16, 1932, p1; "Many Are Fined But Few Paid County Courts in Last Decade," *Fargo (Sunday) Forum* 24, Jan. 3, 1932, p1, 8; "Holt to Speed Court Action," *Fargo Forum* 54, July 16, 1932, p2.

38. "Jump in Poor Aid Cost Faces Budget Framers," *Fargo Forum* 54, July 13, 1932, p1, 8; "First Slice Cuts Cass Tax $33,000," *Fargo Forum* 54, July 14, 1932, p1, 10; "Cass Board Closes Doors on Budget Hearing," *Fargo Forum* 54, July 14, 1932, p1, 7.

39. "Cass to Build Barracks for Housing Single Relief Cases," *Fargo Forum* 54, Sept. 6, 1932, p1; "County Relief on New Basis," *Fargo Forum* 54, July 19, 1932, p8; "Cass Poor Aid Expense Is Up," *Fargo Forum* 54, Oct. 5, 1932, p5; "May Ask City Poor Aid Fund," *Fargo Forum* 54, July 25, 1932, p1, 8; Minutes of the Meeting of the Board of City Commissioners, Aug. 15, 1932, mss. 42, box 15, p416–17, NDIRS.

40. For a nice discussion of moral judgments of people seeking public aid, see Katz, *The Undeserving Poor,* 9–10. Singleton, in *The American Dole,* 12, estimates that only one in seven unemployed workers received relief in 1931 and only one in five in 1932.

NOTES TO CHAPTER 2

1. "Chest Spirit Is Symbolized by $100 Check of Group at A. C.," *Fargo Forum* 54, Nov. 11, 1932, p1, 7.

2. "The Challenge," editorial, *Fargo Forum* 53, Oct. 21, 1931, p4.

3. John Alsop interview; interview with Elizabeth Alsop, Moorhead, MN, June 1, 1998; interview with Robert Dawson, Fargo, ND, Oct. 30, 1997; Gunkleman interview.

4. Gunkleman interview.

5. For a similar network in Indianapolis, see Sample, "A Truly Midwestern City."

6. Gunkleman interview. For the development of the service ideal, see Danbom, *"The World of Hope."*

7. For a discussion of national campaigns, see Bird, *The Invisible Scar*, 26. The American Legion was very active in anti-Depression, self-help activities. See, for example, "'Buying Week' Set By Legion," *Fargo Forum* 54, June 24, 1932, p1. For the national origins of the War Against Depression, see Elvins, "Shopping for Recovery."

8. "Business Aid Unit Meeting," *Fargo Forum* 54, Mar. 5, 1932, p1; "Legion Plans Drive for Jobs," *Fargo Forum* 54, Mar. 4, 1932, p3; W. P. Christensen to George Hoenck, Apr. 26, 1932, United Way Collection, NDIRS; "'Marry the Girl' Say Depression Warriors," *Fargo Forum* 54, Mar. 23, 1932, p1; "This Ban on Depression," editorial, *Fargo Forum* 54, Mar. 23, 1932, p4. Leuchtenberg noted the prevalence of military language and imagery in New Deal programs in "The New Deal and the Analogue of War," in Braeman, Bremner, and Walters, eds., *Change and Continuity*. The War Against Depression experience in Fargo and elsewhere suggests that this was one of the areas in which the New Deal represented continuity rather than change.

9. Minutes of the Meeting of the Board of City Commissioners, Mar. 28, 1932, mss. 42, box 15, N-358–59, NDIRS; "Ask Broadway Repaving to Aid Depression War," *Fargo Forum* 54, Mar. 28, 1932, p1, 8; "'War' Campaign Total $211,434," *Fargo Forum* 54, Mar. 30, 1932, p1; "$287,793 Pledged in Depression 'War,'" *Fargo Forum* 54, Mar. 31, 1932, p1; "Fargo's High Record," editorial, *Fargo Forum* 54, Apr. 11, 1932, p4.

10. "We Begin Well," editorial, *Fargo Forum* 54, Mar. 30, 1932, p4.

11. Ferguson, "Charity by Hullabaloo," 739, 745; "We Begin Well," editorial, *Fargo Forum* 54, Mar. 30, 1932, p4.

12. "47 Pledges to NRA Are Filed with Corrigan by Fargo Firms," *Fargo Forum* 55, Aug. 1, 1933, p1; "Fargo Stores to Add Scores of Workers as Result of Code," *Fargo Forum* 55, Aug. 2, 1933, p1; "Fargo Sets Up Campaign Unit," *Fargo Forum* 55, Aug. 4, 1933, p5; "Speakers Limber Up for NRA Campaign in Fargo," *Fargo Forum* 55, Aug. 17, 1933, p1, 3.

13. "City Joins with Nation in Great Recovery Drive Monday," *Fargo Forum* 55, Aug. 23, 1933, p1; "51 Firms Pledge Delegations for NRA Parade," *Fargo Forum* 55, Aug. 25, 1933, p1; "NRA Legions Begin Intensive Canvas of City," *Fargo Forum* 55, Aug. 29, 1933, p1, 7; F. O. Olsen, "A Proclamation," *Fargo Forum* 55, Aug. 29, 1933, p1; "The NRA Parade," editorial, *Fargo Forum* 55, Aug. 30, 1933, p4.

14. "Fargo Making 'Magnificent' Response, Say Drive Workers," *Fargo Forum* 55, Aug. 30, 1933, p1.

15. "Fargo Groups Unite Behind Junior C. C. in Clothing Drive," *Fargo Forum* 56, Jan. 22, 1934, p1.

16. "Clothing Drive Is Set April 23," *Fargo Forum* 55, Apr. 12, 1933, p1; Olivet English Lutheran Church Bulletin, Apr. 16, 1933; "Junior Chamber's Drive Nets 76 Loads of Goods," *Fargo Forum* 55, Apr. 24, 1933, p1.

17. "Fargo Groups Unite Behind Junior C. C. in Clothing Drive," *Fargo Forum* 56, Jan. 22, 1934, p1; "Junior Chamber Drive Brings 2 Carloads of Clothing," *Fargo Forum* 56, Jan. 29, 1934, p1. Another Jaycee clothing drive in 1935 was judged "unusually successful." See "Clothing Drive Here Success," *Fargo (Morning) Forum* 27, Jan. 22, 1935, p2.

18. Fargo's embrace of cooperative individualism and its reliance on local initiative were hardly unique. See, for example, Mullins, *Depression and the Urban West Coast*, and Starr, *Endangered Dreams*.

19. "Service Clubs to Aid Fargo Needy Children," *Fargo (Sunday) Forum* 22, Dec. 19, 1929, p9; "1,000 Children Are Guests of Kiwanis Today at State Show," *Fargo Forum* 54, Dec. 23, 1931, p1, 10; "1,400 Listed for Free Toys," *Fargo Forum* 55, Dec. 19, 1932, p2; "Basket Drive Nears $1,000," *Fargo Forum* 54, Dec. 18, 1931, p1.

20. "September 1932 35th Anniversary of Round Table Club," Round Table Records, mss. 170, box 1, folder 4, p3, NDIRS; "County Begins Clothing Drive to Aid Poor," *Fargo (Sunday) Forum* 25, Sept. 18, 1932, p9; "Charity Clubs Do Big Service," *Fargo (Sunday) Forum* 25, Oct. 16, 1932, p6.

21. "Fargo's Relief Program Carried on Successfully," *Fargo (Sunday) Forum* 25, Jan. 1, 1933, p9; "No Hunger in City; Needy Cared For," *Fargo (Sunday) Forum* 24, Aug. 30, 1931, p9; interview with Charlie Hauser, Fargo, ND, June 23, 1998; "Needy to Be Given Haircuts as Gifts from Union Barbers," *Fargo Forum*

54, Dec. 11, 1931, p14; "This Town We Live In," *Fargo (Sunday) Forum* 29, Dec. 19, 1936, p11; "Cass Charges Get Excursion," *Fargo Forum* 54, Oct. 19, 1932, p5.

22. For orphan asylums and their use by parents in financial difficulty, see Holt, *The Orphan Trains;* Dulberger, *"Mother Donit fore the Best";* Ashby, *Endangered Children;* and Hacsi, *Second Home.*

23. "Superintendent's Report for the Year Ending March 31, 1930," 4, Village Family Service Center; "Annual Report of the North Dakota Children's Home and Aid Society, 1931–1932," 1, Village Family Service Center; "Annual Report of the North Dakota Children's Home and Aid Society, 1932–33," 1, Village Family Service Center. For the plight of orphanages nationwide during the Depression, see Jones, "Crisis of the American Orphanage."

24. For the activities of these agencies, see, for example, "Many Helped by Mission," *Fargo Forum* 52, Mar. 21, 1930, p5, and "Street Corner Worship Small Part of Work Done by Salvation Army: Has Served Fargo Area for 50 Years," *Fargo Forum* 59, Mar. 17, 1937, p8.

25. "Money Paid Out, Oct. 1931," Harry Lashkowitz Papers, mss. 161, box 34, folder 9, NDIRS; Meeting of the Board of Directors of the Catholic Welfare Bureau, Sept. 23, 1931, Catholic Family Services; Annual Report of the Catholic Welfare Bureau for 1934, Catholic Family Services; Peschel interview. See also Norman, *History of Catholic Family Service,* and Brown and McKeown, *The Poor Belong to Us.*

26. Minutes of Meeting of the Board of Trustees, Community Welfare Association, Fargo, N.D., Dec. 22, 1930, p2, United Way Collection, NDIRS. For some background on the Community Chest nationally, see Bucki, *Bridgeport's Socialist New Deal.*

27. W. P. Christensen to George Hoenck, Apr. 26, 1932, United Way Collection, NDIRS; Minutes of the Meeting of the Council of Welfare Agencies, Apr. 9, 1930, United Way Collection, NDIRS; letter from R. A. Trubey, Oct. 16, 1937, 1938 and 1939 Scrapbook, United Way Collection, NDIRS.

28. "Final Community Chest Appeal Made over Air," *Fargo (Sunday) Forum* 22, Nov. 28, 1929, p1, 13; "McCracken Named Head of Welfare Agencies Council," *Fargo*

(Sunday) Forum 22, Dec. 5, 1929, p5; Minutes of Meeting of Budget Committee Community Welfare Association, July 11, 1930, United Way Collection, NDIRS.

29. "Relief 'Racketeers,'" editorial, *Fargo Forum* 54, Dec. 3, 1930, p4; Minutes of the Annual Meeting of the Community Welfare Association of Fargo, N. Dak. Jan. 6, 1931, p1, United Way Collection, NDIRS.

30. Schuler, "No Dole."

31. J. A. Burger to Harry Lashkowitz, Sept. 23, 1931, Harry Lashkowitz Papers, mss. 161, box 34, folder 9, NDIRS; "Chest, Relief Drives Merged," *Fargo Forum* 53, Oct. 16, 1931, p1.

32. "Lions Club Hears Plea for Fund Drive Support," *Fargo Forum* 53, Oct. 19, 1931, p1, 10; "Spirit of Gridiron Spurs Chest Campaign Workers," *Fargo Forum* 53, Nov. 12, 1931, p1; "Thousands Will March in Flare-Lit Chest Parade," *Fargo (Sunday) Forum* 24, Nov. 15, 1931, p1; "Fargo Theaters to Give Benefit Shows for Chest," *Fargo Forum* 53, Nov. 13, 1931, p1, 6.

33. Stock, *Main Street in Crisis,* 62; "Community Chest Tops Quota," *Fargo Forum* 54, Nov. 16, 1931, p1; "Fargo Chest Total Is $97,379," *Fargo (Sunday) Forum* 24, Dec. 6, 1931, p1; Annual Report of the Chamber of Commerce, Fargo, North Dakota, 1931, Fargo Chamber of Commerce Records, mss. 10484, Annual Reports, 1930–35 File, p20, SHSND.

34. "City to Require Work of Charity Recipients," *Fargo Forum* 54, Jan. 22, 1932, p1, 7. The crisis of relief and the resultant pressures on public funds early in 1932 were evident in other places as well. See, for example, Cohen, *Making a New Deal,* 223–24, and Koch, "Politics and Relief in Minneapolis," 155.

35. Minutes of the Meeting of the Budget Committee, May 14, 1932, United Way Collection, NDIRS; Minutes of the Meeting of the Board of City Commissioners, July 25, 1932, mss. 42, box 15, p404, NDIRS.

36. "Chest Leaders Undismayed as Daily Returns Continue Slow," *Fargo Forum* 55, Nov. 17, 1932, p1; George C. Hoenck to Max Goldberg, Jan. 16, 1933, Harry Lashkowitz Papers, mss. 161, box 34, folder 9, NDIRS; annual report of president George Hoenck to the Community Welfare Association, Jan. 11, 1933, United Way Collection, NDIRS; "Chest Fund Is Running Low," *Fargo Forum* 55, May 26, 1933, p6. The role of the Reconstruction Fi-

nance Corporation in funding unemployment relief nationally is detailed in Singleton, *The American Dole,* 93–94.

37. "Board of Directors Meeting Held Thursday, Mar. 24, 1933, in the Chamber of Commerce at 1:00 P.M.," 1, United Way Collection, NDIRS.

38. "No One Need Give," 58; "Burger Asks Drive Quotas Be Fulfilled," *Fargo Forum* 56, Nov. 25, 1933, p2; "City Must Do Its Own Share," *Fargo Forum* 56, Nov. 24, 1933, p1, 5; Meeting of the Executive Committee of the Community Welfare Association, Jan. 22, 1934, United Way Collection, NDIRS. For the challenge presented by New Deal relief programs to charities nationally, see Brown, *Public Relief,* 133–34.

39. Joint Meeting of the Board of Directors and Budget Committee Held Thursday Noon, Sept. 14, 1933, United Way Collection, NDIRS; Harold H. Bond to R. L. Sheets [*sic*], Executive Director of the Community Welfare Association, September 28, 1936," United Way Collection, NDIRS; Meeting of the Board of Trustees of the Community Welfare Association, Tuesday, September 28, 1937, United Way Collection, NDIRS; Meeting of the Budget Committee of the Community Welfare Association, Sept. 21, 1937, United Way Collection, NDIRS; Minutes of the Meeting of the Budget Committee of the Community Welfare Association, April 4, 1938, United Way Collection, NDIRS.

40. C. C. Wattam, R. A. Trubey, and Glenn Saylor to the Community Welfare Association, undated, p2–3, United Way Collection, NDIRS.

41. C. C. Wattam, R. A. Trubey, and Glenn Saylor to the Community Welfare Association, undated, p4, United Way Collection, NDIRS: "Hoenck Gets Club Award as Outstanding Fargoan," *Fargo Forum* 55, Dec. 20, 1932, p1; "Hoenck Presented Medal as Outstanding Citizen," *Fargo Forum* 55, Dec. 29, 1932, p1, 2.

42. "Business, Professional Men Pledge Support to Chest Drive," *Fargo Forum* 56, Nov. 17, 1933, p1; "City Must Do Its Own Share," *Fargo Forum* 56, Nov. 24, 1933, p5; O. C. Brown to Harry Lashkowitz, Apr. 10, 1934, Harry Lashkowitz Papers, mss. 161, box 34, folder 9, NDIRS; letter from R. A. Trubey, President, Community Welfare Association,

Oct. 16, 1937, 1938 and 1939 Scrapbook, United Way Collection, NDIRS; "An Opportunity in Building Good Will," 1938 and 1939 Scrapbook, United Way Collection, NDIRS.

43. Meeting of the Board of Directors of the Community Welfare Association Held in the Chamber of Commerce Oct. 13, 1936 at 4:15 PM, United Way Collection, NDIRS; Minutes of the Meeting of the Campaign Committee of the Community Chest, Sept. 22, 1939, 1940 Scrapbook, United Way Collection, NDIRS.

44. For the experience of other places, see Mullins, *Depression and the Urban West Coast,* 91–120; Brown, *Public Relief,* 410; and Murphy, *Mining Cultures,* 161–62, 215–16.

45. "Jobless Unite to Seek Work," *Fargo Forum* 53, Nov. 13, 1931, p5; "Jobless Club Reforms at Y," *Fargo (Sunday) Forum* 25, Dec. 4, 1932, p1; " 'Y' Organizes Jobless Men," *Fargo (Sunday) Forum* 25, Dec. 18, 1932, p11.

46. "Exchange for Jobless Says Families Here Need Clothing," *Fargo (Sunday) Forum* 25, Jan. 22, 1933, p1; "Wheat Ground for Jobless," *Fargo Forum* 55, Jan. 4, 1933, p3.

47. "Fargo Jobless Band to Help Each Other on 'Seattle Plan,'" *Fargo Forum* 55, Jan. 6, 1933, p1, 8; "Jobless Draft Barter Plans," *Fargo (Sunday) Forum* 25, Feb. 19, 1933, p8. For a contemporary view of the Seattle Plan, see Parry, "Republic of the Penniless." For an overview, see "Cooperative Self-Help Activities." Ross, in "The Spread of Barter," counted 159 barter organizations in 127 cities in 29 states.

48. Minutes of the Meeting of the Board of City Commissioners, Jan. 23, 1933, mss. 42, box 15, p465, NDIRS; Minutes of the Board of Education—Fargo, North Dakota, Feb. 8, 1933, Fargo Public Schools; "Barter and Exchange," editorial, *Fargo Forum* 55, Feb. 20, 1933, p4; "Jobless Draft Barter Plans," *Fargo (Sunday) Forum* 25, Feb. 19, 1933, p8.

49. "1,200 Attend Jobless Ball," *Fargo Forum* 55, Jan. 26, 1933, p10; "Jobless Party Set Monday," *Fargo Forum* 55, Feb. 21, 1933, p5; "Jobless to Get Play Proceeds," *Fargo (Sunday) Forum* 25, Apr. 16, 1933, p6.

50. "Exchange Asks Cleaning Jobs," *Fargo Forum* 55, Apr. 12, 1933, p5; Minutes of the Meeting of the Board of City Commissioners, Mar. 27, 1933, mss. 42, box 15, p488, NDIRS; "Urge Drainage Job Be Pushed," *Fargo Forum* 55, Aug. 2, 1933, p10; Minutes of the

Meeting of the Board of Park Commissioners, Aug. 1, 1933, book 4, p218–22, Fargo Park District; "Exchange Asks New Quarters," *Fargo Forum* 56, Dec. 12, 1933, p5. See ad, under "Men Want Work," *Fargo Forum* 55, Feb. 16, 1933, p9: "Wanted–Home owners and general employers to call 7350. Long Fellow [*sic*] school, Fourth av and Tenth st N, for men to do odd jobs of any kind; 350 men in organization, men of Fargo, most of them heads of families preferring work rather than relief."

51. "Fargo Jobless Band to Help Each Other on 'Seattle Plan,'" *Fargo Forum* 55, Jan. 6, 1933, p1, 8; Minutes of the Meeting of the Board of Park Commissioners, Aug. 1, 1933, box 4, p218–19, Fargo Park Board; County Welfare Board Verbatim Minutes, Aug. 17, 1933, p1, Cass County Social Service; County Welfare Board Verbatim Minutes, Aug. 30, 1933, p1, Cass County Social Service.

52. Minutes of the Board of Education—Fargo, North Dakota, Feb. 8, 1933, p37, Fargo Public Schools; "Exchange Asks New Quarters," *Fargo Forum* 56, Dec. 12, 1933, p5.

NOTES TO CHAPTER 3

1. 1935 Report of the Chamber of Commerce, Fargo Chamber of Commerce Records, mss. 10484, Annual Reports, 1930–35 File, p4, SHSND.

2. Interview with Jean-Cameron Shupienis, Fargo, ND, June 24, 1998; Daniel Heitmeyer to Franklin D. Roosevelt, Oct. 8, 1935, New Deal Clergy Letters, Collection 588, folder 7, p1, Chester Fritz Library, UND. Fargo was not the only place where some people found federal relief humiliating; see Murphy, *Mining Cultures*, 215–16.

3. "Fargo-Moorhead United in Inaugural Fete Plans," *Fargo Forum* 55, Mar. 1, 1933, p1; "Fargo-Moorhead Join in Roosevelt Tribute Parade," *Fargo Forum* 55, Mar. 4, 1933, p1; "Fargo-Moorhead Celebration to Mark Roosevelt Inaugural," *Fargo Forum* 55, Feb. 28, 1933, p1.

4. "Fargo, Despite Lack of Cash, Does Business Near Normally," *Fargo Forum* 55, Mar. 6, 1933, p1, 6; "Bank Reopening Will Begin Monday," *Fargo (Sunday) Forum* 25, Mar. 12, 1933, p1, 12; interview with Vivian Westberg, Moorhead, MN, June 14, 2000; "Banks in Fargo Open for Business," *Fargo Forum* 55, Mar. 14, 1933, p1, 9.

5. "Business Here Reflects U.S. Pickup Trend, Merchants Say," *Fargo Forum* 55, Apr. 11, 1933, p1, 9; "New Deal Store Opened Here," *Fargo Forum* 55, Aug. 22, 1933, p3; "Announcing the New Deal Grocery," *Fargo Forum* 56, Mar. 2, 1934, p7; "Nearly 2,000 Dance Here to Raise $500 for Birthday Fund," *Fargo Forum* 56, Jan. 31, 1934, p1, 7; "Who's Afraid of the Big Bad Wolf?" "Herbstory," Dec. 1933, mss. 158, box 1, folder 19, NDIRS.

6. "Bakers Adopt Working Code," *Fargo Forum* 55, July 7, 1933, p7; "Fargo Business Acts to Put NIRA to Work Here," *Fargo Forum* 55, July 27, 1933, p1, 12; "47 Pledges to NRA Are Filed with Corrigan by Fargo Firms," *Fargo Forum* 55, Aug. 1, 1933, p1; "NRA Army Here Is Marshaled," *Fargo Forum* 55, Aug. 11, 1933, p1, 3; "Fargo NRA Army Mobilizing for General Session Wednesday," *Fargo Forum* 55, Aug. 15, 1933, p1; Proceedings of the Board of County Commissioners of Cass County, North Dakota, Feb. 8, 1934, p1865, Cass County Auditor's Office; "Fargo Stores to Add Scores of Workers as Result of Code," *Fargo Forum* 55, Aug. 2, 1933, p1.

7. William D. Toomey to author, June 25, 1997; "Three Named on NRA Board," *Fargo Forum* 55, Oct. 10, 1933, p1; "NRA Board Here Receives 15 Complaints," *Fargo Forum* 26, Nov. 5, 1933, p9.

8. Westberg interview; interview with Birdie Kerr, Fargo, ND, Sept. 15, 1999; Verbatim Minutes of the Cass County Welfare Board, Apr. 18, 1934, p10, Cass County Social Service; M. E. McCurley, "Teachers and the NRA," *Fargo Forum* 55, Aug. 25, 1933, p5. For a view of the wage problem on a national scale, see Coyle, "Public Works: A New Industry."

9. "Fargo Business Acts to Put NIRA to Work Here," *Fargo Forum* 55, July 27, 1933, p1, 12; "Fargo Stores to Add Scores of Workers as Result of Code," *Fargo Forum* 55, Aug. 2, 1933, p1; "Merchants to Abide by NRA," *Fargo Forum* 5, May 31, 1935, p1. For a comprehensive contemporary examination of the flaws in NRA wage and hours provisions, see Hazlitt, "Fallacies of the N.R.A."

10. Donald E. Bird, "NRA vs. Northwest," *Fargo Forum* 55, Aug. 21, 1933, p5. For the problems small businesses faced with the NRA, see Stolberg and Vinton, "The New Deal vs. Recovery," and Cohen, *Making a New Deal*, 236–37.

11. "Cities Must Be Alert to Share in Future, Says Chamber Chief," *Fargo Forum* 55, June 26, 1933, p1, 10.

12. Interview with Margaret Scott, Fargo, ND, Apr. 24, 2000.

13. Campbell, *Growth of American Government.* For a local explanation of the FHA loan program, see "Housing Clinic Opens in Fargo," *Fargo Forum* 58, May 1, 1936, p1, 9.

14. "House to House Canvass Billed to Promote N.D. Building Drive," *Fargo Forum* 56, Oct. 6, 1934, p1, 8; "Local Housing Drive Mapped," *Fargo Forum* 56, Sept. 11, 1934, p1; "Begin Fargo Housing Drive," *Fargo Forum* 56, Oct. 24, 1934, p1; "Fargo Housing Work Lauded," *Fargo Forum* 57, Dec. 13, 1934, p11. For the program on the national level, see Holden, "Federal Aid for the Householder."

15. A recent account of the veterans' experience and the bonus issue is Keene, *Doughboys, the Great War.*

16. "Fargo Legion Demands Cash," *Fargo Forum* 53, Jan. 27, 1931, p10; "Banks Provide Veteran Loans," *Fargo Forum* 53, Mar. 3, 1931, p1; "Vets Mobilize over Nation for 'Bonus March,'" *Fargo Forum* 53, June 2, 1932, p1; "Ailing Bugler Stops Parade," *Fargo (Sunday) Forum* 24, June 26, 1932, p1. In *Doughboys, the Great War,* p181, Keene argues that the veterans' unemployment rate was 50 percent higher than that of other men in their age group.

17. "Vets 'Storm' Office to Make Bonus Applications," *Fargo Forum* 58, Jan. 29, 1936, p1, 5; "Checks for Bonus Bonds Go into Mail Tonight," *Fargo Forum* 58, June 16, 1936, p1, 14; "Up All Night on Bonus Work," *Fargo Forum* 58, June 17, 1936, p1, 6; "Bonus Spur to Fargo's Trade," *Fargo (Sunday) Forum* 28, June 21, 1936, p10.

18. Olson interview; Westberg interview; Toomey to author, June 25, 1997; interview with Ed Graber, Fargo, ND, Oct. 21, 1997; interview with Mary Arvold, Fargo, ND, June 19, 2000.

19. Hauser interview; interview with Sid Cichy, Fargo, ND, Oct. 16, 1997.

20. Interview with Darrow Beaton, Fargo, ND, May 13, 1999; Gjervold interview; Olson interview; interview of Gladys Bartell Welton by Judith M. Welton, Aug. 14, 1974, OGL #259 File, p3, Chester Fritz Library, UND; interview with John Carlson, Fargo, ND, Apr. 24, 2000.

21. For migratory harvest labor, see Higbie, *Indispensable Outcasts,* DePastino, *Citizen Hobo,* and Isern, *Bull Threshers and Bindlestiffs.*

22. "Police Have Quiet Month," *Fargo Forum* 52, Apr. 2, 1930, p5; "Fargo Hobo Hangouts Hum as Hoards Come," *Fargo (Sunday) Forum* 24, July 26, 1931, p8; "This Town We Live In," *Fargo (Sunday) Forum* 25, Sept. 18, 1932, p9.

23. "Fargo Hobo Hangouts Hum As Hoards Come," *Fargo (Sunday) Forum* 24, July 26, 1931, p8; "Fargo Jail to Add Bread, Water Menu for Old Offenders," *Fargo Forum* 52, Sept. 9, 1930, p1.

24. "News About Town," *Fargo Forum* 53, Sept. 7, 1931, p6; "Charge Transient Took $114 from Companion," *Fargo Forum* 54, Sept. 12, 1932, p8; "5 Negroes Held in Theft of $75 from Transient," *Fargo Forum* 55, Oct. 11, 1933, p3; "Arms Broken in Jungle Row," *Fargo Forum* 53, July 22, 1931, p10; "Train Kills Two at West Fargo," *Fargo Forum* 52, Oct. 9, 1930, p1.

25. "Steals Baby's Milk, Will Be Sent to Jail," *Fargo Forum* 53, Oct. 26, 1931, p1; "2 Transients Held By Police," *Fargo (Sunday) Forum* 24, Aug. 2, 1931, p8; "City Scoured for Masked Killer Who Slew Collector, Menaced Fargo Girl," *Fargo Forum* 52, June 20, 1930, p1, 8; "Jail Ex-Convict for Grocer's Murder," *Fargo Forum* 58, Dec. 21, 1935, p1, 8.

26. "Floater Army Is Increased," *Fargo Forum* 52, Mar. 29, 1930, p3; "Efforts to Aid Transient Fail," *Fargo Forum* 52, July 18, 1930, p9; "Mexican Dies Under Freight," *Fargo Forum* 53, Sept. 7, 1931, p1; "Ill Transients County Worry," *Fargo Forum* 54, May 23, 1932, p6.

27. Minutes of Meetings of Budget Committee, undated, United Way Collection, NDIRS; "Fargo Seeks to Curb Professional Panhandler," *Fargo Forum* 54, Sept. 7, 1932, p1; "Fargo 'Cures' Professional Bum Business," *Fargo (Sunday) Forum* 25, Oct. 16, 1932, p9; "Forger Duplicates Fargo Poor Relief Meal Tickets," *Fargo Forum* 55, Dec. 14, 1932, p1, 14; "News About Town," *Fargo Forum* 55, June 1, 1933, p2; Board of Directors Meeting, June 29, 1933, United Way Collection, NDIRS. For an insightful look at the transient situation elsewhere, see Crouse, *The Homeless Transient.*

28. Herbert Smith, a FERA official, ex-

plained the details of the program to the school board. Minutes of the Board of Education—Fargo, North Dakota, Dec. 6, 1933, p93, Fargo Public Schools; "Treatment for Transients," editorial, *Fargo Forum* 56, Dec. 7, 1933, p4. The program on the national level is well explained by Reed, *Federal Transient Program;* Elizabeth Wickenden, "Reminiscences of the Program for Transients and Homeless in the Thirties," 80–87, in Beard, ed., *On Being Homeless;* and Kusmer, *Down and Out, On the Road,* 201–20. For a popular contemporary analysis, see Mitchell, "Coddling the Bums."

29. Records of Works Progress Administration (hereafter WPA), Record Group 69, box 11, Entry 16, "North Dakota–Statistical" File, National Archives and Records Service (hereafter NARS); "Most Drifters Eager to Work," *Fargo (Sunday) Forum* 26, Feb. 22, 1934, p9; "Transient Treatment," editorial, *Fargo Forum* 56, Jan. 22, 1934, p4; "Newsman Acts as Transient; Finds Food at Station Good," *Fargo (Sunday) Forum* 26, Mar. 4, 1934, p9, 15; "Transients to Present Plays," *Fargo (Sunday) Forum* 27, Nov. 18, 1934, p11; "Transients' Square Club Gives Program at C.C.," *Fargo Forum* 56, June 14, 1934, p1; "Transient Bureau Team Beats Alpha Sigma Tau," *Fargo Forum* 56, June 1, 1934, p14.

30. Minutes of the Special Meeting of the Board of Commissioners of the City of Fargo, Feb. 8, 1935, p14, City Auditor's Office; 1934 Report of the Chamber of Commerce, Fargo Chamber of Commerce Records, mss. 10484, Annual Reports, 1930–35 File, p5, SHSND; "Restoration of Wanderers to Homes Is Goal of U.S. Relief," *Fargo Forum* 56, Apr. 28, 1934, p1, 9; Minutes of the Council of Welfare Agencies Meeting, Jan. 17, 1935, p1, United Way Collection, NDIRS.

31. Minutes of the Regular Meeting of the Board of City Commissioners, July 30, 1934, mss. 42, box 15, N-719, NDIRS; Minutes of the Adjourned Regular Meeting of the Board of Commissioners of the City of Fargo, Sept. 6, 1935, p167, City Auditor's Office; "Will Not Force Dill Hall Plan," *Fargo Forum* 57, Feb. 7, 1935, p1, 11; Minutes of Welfare Board, Jan. 16, 1935, p7, Cass County Social Service.

32. Records of WPA, Record Group 69, box 217, Entry 10, North Dakota Transients January 1935 File, NARS; "News About Town,"

Fargo Forum 57, Dec. 11, 1934, p2; Minutes of the Special Meeting of the Board of Commissioners of the City of Fargo, Feb. 8, 1935, City Auditor's Office.

33. Records of WPA, Record Group 69, box 219, Entry 10, 420 North Dakota Transients August, September 1935 File, and box 221, Entry 10, North Dakota Complaints S-T File, NARS.

34. "New Transient Problem Seen," *Fargo Forum* 57, Sept. 15, 1935, p7; Norman Lewellyn, "Cites Value of Transient Bureau," *Fargo Forum* 57, Aug. 17, 1935, p3; Reade, "Back to Panhandling."

35. "Board Acts as Citizens Complain of Transients," *Fargo Forum* 57, July 29, 1935, p1, 7.

36. Reade, "Back to Panhandling"; Crouse, *The Homeless Transient,* 182–83; Case Number 29813, "Five Weeks In a Transient Camp." Webb, in *The Transient Unemployed,* estimated a population of 500,000 true transients and another one million resident homeless.

37. Springer, "Men Off the Road."

38. "New Transient Problem Seen," *Fargo Forum* 57, Sept. 15, 1935, p7; "Transient Order Arouses Protest."

39. The operation of the Emergency Relief Construction Act is well covered by Singleton, *The American Dole,* 93–107.

40. The operation of New Deal relief programs is explained in Brown, *Public Relief,* and in Williams, *Federal Aid for Relief.*

41. Tweton, *New Deal at the Grass Roots,* 167; "Roosevelt and Relief," editorial, *Fargo Forum* 55, June 19, 1933, p1.

42. "Monthly Summary, Cass County Relief, June, 1934," Harry Lashkowitz Papers, mss. 161, box 31, folder 12, p3, NDIRS; "City, Cass Have High Ratio of Relief List on Work Projects," *Fargo (Sunday) Forum* 26, June 10, 1934, p11.

43. "Relief Outlay in Cass Falls as CWA Crews Go to Projects," *Fargo (Sunday) Forum* 26, Dec. 31, 1933, p1, 18; "CWA Stimulus," editorial, *Fargo Forum* 56, Jan. 17, 1934, p4; "New Jobs, Good Holiday Trade Give Reasons for Rejoicing," *Fargo Forum* 56, Dec. 25, 1933, p1, 2; "Half Million Spent in Cass," *Fargo (Morning) Forum* 27, Jan. 2, 1935, p2; interview with Mrs. O. A. Stevens by Mary Jo Vrem-Ydstie, Fargo, ND, Aug. 6, 1974, OGL#259, Chester

Fritz Library, UND; "WPA Gives Jobs to 740 in City," *Fargo Forum* 58, Mar. 30, 1936, p1, 6; "$350,000 WPA, PWA Funds Spent in Fargo in 1936," *Fargo Forum* 59, Jan. 1, 1937, p8; "F-M Private Building Hits $900,000," *Fargo (Sunday) Forum* 29, May 30, 1937, p1, 2.

44. Earl Jorgenson, City Auditor, to the Members of the Fargo Taxpaying Campaign Committee, Proceedings of the Board of Commissioners of the City of Fargo, Jan. 2, 1937, p469, City Auditor's Office; Minutes of the Meeting of the Taxpaying Campaign Committee, Proceedings of the Board of Commissioners of the City of Fargo, Aug. 4, 1936, p358, City Auditor's Office; "Tax Sale Failure Reveals Serious Revenue Problem," *Fargo Forum* 56, Dec. 13, 1933, p1, 3.

45. "Shoes Squeak, Coat Tight in Clothing of Local Units," *Fargo Forum* 55, Sept. 20, 1933, p1; "Taxpayers Ask Slash 'To Bone,'" *Fargo Forum* 58, July 17, 1936, p6.

46. "Fargo's Budget Cut $23,919 in Final Figures of City Board," *Fargo Forum* 55, July 27, 1933, p1, 10; Minutes of the Meeting of the Board of City Commissioners, Oct. 4, 1933, mss. 42, box 15, p577–78, NDIRS.

47. "Lack of Funds Brings Drastic Slash in Park Board Activity," *Fargo Forum* 55, May 23, 1933, p1, 2; Minutes of the Meeting of Park Commissioners, July 5, 1933, book 4, p137–46, Fargo Park Board.

48. Minutes of the Board of Education—Fargo, North Dakota, Mar. 17, 1933, p46, Fargo Public Schools; Minutes of the Board of Education—Fargo, North Dakota, July 7, 1933, p69, Fargo Public Schools; "Teachers' Pay Item Is Pared 10 Per Cent in School Budget," *Fargo Forum* 55, Aug. 5, 1933, p1, 2; "School Board May Ask Increase in Levy Limit," *Fargo Forum* 55, Oct. 28, 1933, p3.

49. Minutes of the Board of Education—Fargo, North Dakota, May 3, 1933, p55, Fargo Public Schools; "School Fund Figure Is Cut," *Fargo Forum* 55, Apr. 6, 1933, p3; Minutes of the Board of Education—Fargo, North Dakota, Dec. 7, 1932, p28, Fargo Public Schools; Minutes of the Board of Education—Fargo, North Dakota, Feb. 8, 1933, p38, Fargo Public Schools; Minutes of the Board of Education—Fargo, North Dakota, Apr. 5, 1933, p48, Fargo Public Schools; Minutes of the Board of Education—Fargo, North Dakota, Feb. 6, 1935, p186, Fargo Public

Schools; "Fargo Milk Consumption Is Far Below Standard," *Fargo Forum* 56, July 20, 1934, p4.

50. "Banks to Take Warrants for School Board Up to $100,000," *Fargo Forum* 56, Feb. 20, 1934, p1, 2; "Fargo School Levy Increase Wins Favor by Heavy Margin," *Fargo Forum* 56, Aug. 29, 1934, p1; "School Levy Approval," editorial, *Fargo Forum* 56, Aug. 29, 1934, p4.

51. "School Envoys Plead for Tax Payments to Avoid Closing," *Fargo Forum* 56, Jan. 24, 1934, p1; Minutes of the Board of Education—Fargo, North Dakota, Feb. 7, 1934, p109, Fargo Public Schools; "City Unit Asks $390,050 Fund," *Fargo Forum* 58, July 14, 1936, p1; "Tax Discounts to End Jan. 1," *Fargo Forum* 57, Oct. 4, 1935, p2; "Welford Extends Delinquent Tax Payment Program," *Fargo Forum* 58, Jan. 9, 1936, p1, 6. Tax collections also increased because the Home Owners Loan Corporation and the Farm Credit Administration required payment of outstanding taxes before they would refinance mortgages. See "More People Paying Taxes in Cass than Did Year Ago," *Fargo Forum* 56, Feb. 27, 1934, p1.

52. Records of WPA, Record Group 69, box 221, Entry 10, North Dakota Complaints, N-Q File, NARS.

53. Undated Ledger, County Welfare Board Verbatim Minutes, Apr. 1933–Dec. 1935, Cass County Social Service; "3 Projects to Help Jobless Women in Cass Get Approval," *Fargo Forum* 56, Jan. 3, 1934, p1, 6; "Will Continue FERA Classes," *Fargo Forum* 57, June 5, 1935, p9; "Annual Report of Home Physician N.D. Children's Home Society Ending April 1, 1934," 1, Village Family Service Center; "FERA Factory Open in Fargo," *Fargo (Sunday) Forum* 27, Nov. 25, 1934, p11; "FERA Skating Classes Set," *Fargo (Sunday) Forum* 27, Jan. 6, 1935, p7; "Lights Asked for Air Field," *Fargo Forum* 56, Oct. 8, 1934, p1; "Dolve Club Sponsors Building of Ski Jump with 200 Foot Scaffold," *Fargo (Sunday) Forum* 27, Jan. 13, 1935, p1.

54. Singleton, *The American Dole*, 133; 1933 Report of the Chamber of Commerce, Fargo Chamber of Commerce Records, mss. 10484, Annual Reports, 1930–35 File, p4, SHSND; Minutes of the Regular Meeting of the Board of City Commissioners, Jan. 22, 1934,

mss. 42, box 15, N-629, NDIRS; Minutes of the Adjourned Regular Meeting of the Board of City Commissioners, Mar. 21, 1934, mss. 42, box 15, N-654, NDIRS; Minutes of the Regular Meeting of the Board of City Commissioners, Feb. 13, 1934, mss. 42, box 15, N-637, NDIRS.

55. Fargo Park Board to Alvin L. Arneson, Mar. 16, 1938, p1, "W. P. A. Work in F. P. D." folder, Fargo Park Board. See also "Many Varied Projects of Veterans' CCC Company Adding Outstanding Improvements to Fargo's Rapidly Growing Public Park System," *Fargo (Sunday) Forum* 27, Sept. 23, 1934, p11.

56. "Millions in Fargo Projects," *Fargo (Sunday) Forum* 32, Dec. 1939, p13; "Works Board Okays $150,800 to Replace Fargo Block Paving," *Fargo Forum* 56, Jan. 6, 1934, p1, 3; "Block Paving Vexing Fargo," *Fargo Forum* 55, June 30, 1933, p3; "Car Wheel Hurls Pavement Block Through Window," *Fargo Forum* 54, Aug. 23, 1932, p1; "City Will Ask 8th St Paving," *Fargo Forum* 57, June 24, 1935, p1, 10.

57. "Residents Use Caustic Terms at Parley over River Problems," *Fargo Forum* 55, Jan. 18, 1933, p1, 8; "Court Action on Sewage Is Threatened by Cass Farmers," *Fargo Forum* 55, May 22, 1933, p1; Minutes of the Meeting of the Board of City Commissioners, June 5, 1933, mss. 42, box 15, p524, NDIRS; "City Ordered to Build Sewer Plant," *Fargo Forum* 55, July 31, 1933, p1, 5.

58. "Ickes Approves $512,000 Fund for Fargo Sewage Plant," *Fargo Forum* 55, Sept. 14, 1933, p1, 9; "North Side Residents Fight Sewage Plant Location," *Fargo Forum* 55, Sept. 25, 1933, p1, 3; "City Pushes New Sewage Site Plan," *Fargo Forum* 56, Mar. 21, 1934, p1; "Low Sewage Plant Bid $60,000 Over Estimated Cost," *Fargo Forum* 55, Nov. 13, 1933, p1; "U.S. to Allow $785,000 Fund for Plant at New Location," *Fargo Forum* 56, July 20, 1934, p1; "5 Fargo Firms Lowest Bidders on Building of Sewage Plant," *Fargo Forum* 56, Sept. 28, 1934, p1, 3; "Mayor Turns First Earth at Site of Sewage Plant," *Fargo Forum* 56, Nov. 14, 1934, p1, 7.

59. Minutes of the Regular Meeting of the Board of Commissioners of the City of Fargo, May 2, 1938, p772, City Auditor's Office; Minutes of the Meeting of the Park Board, May 9, 1939, book 6, p86, Fargo Park Board; "News About Town," *Fargo Forum* 59, Mar. 1, 1937,

p7; "Telegraphy Is Taught by WPA," *Fargo (Sunday) Forum* 29, May 30, 1939, p6.

60. "Approve WPA Jobs in Fargo," *Fargo Forum* 58, Nov. 19, 1935, p1; "Fargo Assured Baseball Park," *Fargo Forum* 58, Mar. 3, 1936, p1; "Ask Bids on $69,000 Airport Program," *Fargo Forum* 58, Apr. 16, 1936, p1; Minutes of the Adjourned Regular Meeting of the Board of Commissioners of the City of Fargo, May 26, 1939, City Auditor's Office.

61. "City Could Use 1 Million for Public Works, Tradesmen Say," *Fargo Forum* 55, June 29, 1933, p1; Regular Meeting of the Board of Commissioners of the City of Fargo, Nov. 4, 1935, p201–2, City Auditor's Office; Minutes of the Regular Meeting of the Board of Commissioners of the City of Fargo, Oct. 4, 1937, p661, City Auditor's Office; Minutes of the Adjourned Regular Meeting of the Board of Commissioners of the City of Fargo, Aug. 30, 1938, City Auditor's Office; Maurice H. Aved, "He Asks Defeat for Bond Issue," *Fargo Forum* 57, Oct. 26, 1935, p5.

62. "New WPA Work Required Here," *Fargo (Sunday) Forum* 29, Feb. 21, 1937, p6; Minutes of the Adjourned Regular Meeting of the Board of City Commissioners of the City of Fargo, Dec. 2, 1937, p690, City Auditor's Office.

63. Minutes of the Board of Education, Fargo, North Dakota, Aug. 7, 1935, p12, Fargo Public Schools; "Fargo Schools to Open Sept. 3," *Fargo Forum* 57, Aug. 8, 1935, p5.

64. Records of WPA, Record Group 69, box 2216, 693.1 North Dakota File, and box 2208, North Dakota 641 A-J File, NARS.

65. Minutes of the Adjourned Regular Meeting of the Board of Commissioners of the City of Fargo, July 19, 1935, p127, City Auditor's Office; Minutes of the Board of Education, Fargo, North Dakota, Sept. 7, 1935, p22, Fargo Public Schools; "Launch Campaign for Funds to Complete Baseball Park," *Fargo Forum* 58, June 12, 1936, p1; Minutes of the Meeting of the Board of Park Commissioners, July 25, 1934, book 4, p291, Fargo Park District; Minutes of the Meeting of the Board of Park Commissioners of the City of Fargo, Dec. 7, 1937, p694, City Auditor's Office; Minutes of the Regular Meeting of the Board of Commissioners of the City of Fargo, Jan. 10, 1938, p707, City Auditor's Office.

66. Park Board to Arneson, Mar. 16, 1938, p4, W. P. A. Work in F. P. D. folder, Fargo Park

Board; Minutes of the Meeting of the Board of Park Commissioners, Aug. 6, 1935, book 5, p83, Fargo Park Board; Minutes of the Meeting of the Board of Park Commissioners, Dec. 3, 1935," book 5, p111–12, Fargo Park Board.

67. "Fargo Asks Lower Pay Scale in Public Works," *Fargo (Sunday) Forum* 26, Sept. 3, 1933, p1; "N. D. Labor Groups Flay Chamber Wage Cut Move," *Fargo Forum* 55, Sept. 5, 1933, p1, 2; Minutes of the Special Meeting of the Board of City Commissioners, Feb. 28, 1934, mss. 42, box 15, N-643, NDIRS; "Improved WPA Operation Helps Curtail Relief Here," *Fargo Forum* 59, Jan. 20, 1937, p5; Minutes of the Regular Meeting of the Board of Commissioners of the City of Fargo, Aug. 26, 1935, p155, City Auditor's Office. The technological unemployment about which the Trades and Labor Assembly was concerned is addressed by Bix in *Inventing Ourselves Out of Jobs?*

68. "A Rule of the CCC"; Leighton and Hellman, "Half Slave, Half Free," 346; Minutes of the Meeting of the Board of Park Commissioners, Aug. 7, 1934, book 4, p296, Fargo Park District; interview with Merlin Hvidston, Moorhead, MN, Mar. 9, 2000; "News About Town," *Fargo Forum* 59, Mar. 8, 1937, p6; Police Arrest Record, City of Fargo, 1930–46, mss. 133, book 1, p349, NDIRS; "CCC Lads, Girls Held by Police," *Fargo Forum* 60, May 16, 1938, p1.

69. Park Board to Arneson, Mar. 16, 1938, p4, W. P. A. Work in F. P. D. folder, Fargo Park Board.

70. "Realtors Say Homes Scarce," *Fargo Forum* 53, May 5, 1931, p1; Lorne Wilde, "Fargo Building Program High," *Fargo Forum* 58, Jan. 1, 1936, p1, 14; "Fargo Housing Problem Acute," *Fargo (Sunday) Forum* 28, Oct. 27, 1935, p13, 20; 1938 Annual Report of the Chamber of Commerce, Fargo Chamber of Commerce Records, mss. 10484, Annual Reports, 1936–39 File, p7, SHSND.

71. "Report on the Development of a Six-year Program for Municipal Improvements 1939–1940 Through 1944–1945," Dec. 8, 1939, City of Fargo; "Taxpayers Ask Cass Economy," *Fargo Forum* 55, Feb. 24, 1933, p5; "Cass Budget Raised Despite Protest from Taxpayer Unit," *Fargo Forum* 55, July 26, 1933, p1.

72. "Taxpayers Ask Cass Economy," *Fargo Forum* 55, Feb. 24, 1933, p5; "Cass Budget Raised Despite Protest from Taxpayer Unit," *Fargo Forum* 55, July 26, 1933, p1.

73. Gordon, *Pitied But Not Entitled,* 189; Proceedings of the Board of County Commissioners of Cass County, North Dakota, Jan. 5, 1934, p1858, Cass County Auditor's Office; "No FERA Aid in Medical Work," *Fargo Forum* 56, Nov. 22, 1934, p6.

74. Patterson, *America's Struggle Against Poverty,* 40–41.

75. Minutes of Meeting of County Welfare Board, Washington School, Nov. 7, 1934, County Welfare Board Verbatim Minutes, Apr. 1933–Dec. 1935, p5, Cass County Social Services (under agreement with Cass County Social Services, I do not use clients' real names. Hence, "Bertrand Nichols" is the name I have assigned to this man); Proceedings of the Board of County Commissioners of Cass County, North Dakota, Mar. 20, 1935, 1997–2001, Cass County Auditor's Office.

76. For the Townsend Movement nationally, see Brinkley, *Voices of Protest.*

77. "Clubs to Back Pension Plan," *Fargo Forum* 56, Sept. 10, 1934, p3; Minutes of the Board of Education, Fargo, North Dakota, Sept. 24, 1934, p162–63, Fargo Public Schools; Minutes of the Regular Meeting of the Board of Commissioners, Dec. 24, 1934, mss. 42, box 15, N-813, NDIRS; "Roosevelt an Egotist, Townsend Declares Here," *Fargo Forum* 57, July 30, 1935, p7; "1,000 Attend Club's Rally," *Fargo Forum* 57, Sept. 16, 1935, p6; Proceedings of the Board of County Commissioners of Cass County, North Dakota, Dec. 20, 1934, p1972, Cass County Auditor's Office; "Board Backs Pension Move," *Fargo Forum* 57, Dec. 24, 1934, p10.

78. J. B. Larson, "Getting Nowhere," *Fargo (Morning) Forum* 27, Jan. 26, 1935, p5; Albert Holland, "Says Pension Plan Sure Recovery Aid," *Fargo Forum* 58, Dec. 2, 1935, p5; "News About Town," *Fargo Forum* 57, Dec. 17, 1934, p14.

79. "How N. D. Pension Plan Works," *Fargo Forum* 58, Apr. 8, 1936, p1, 9; "Cass Signs Age Aid Agreement," *Fargo Forum* 58, Apr. 9, 1936, p16; "Cass Average Aid for Aged Needy Is Near $18 Monthly," *Fargo (Sunday) Forum* 29, Sept. 20, 1936, p13.

80. "Pension Clubs Lose Charters," *Fargo*

Forum 60, Nov. 3, 1938, p1, 8; "Old Age Help Changes Poor Farm Population," *Fargo (Sunday) Forum* 30, Feb. 27, 1938, p5.

81. "Aid to Dependent Children's Program," "Lutheran Welfare Messenger" 4 (Aug. 1939): 2–3; Third Biennial Report of the Public Welfare Board of North Dakota, for the Biennial Period Ending June 30, 1940, Public Welfare Board of North Dakota; Welfare Board Meeting, Cass County, Oct. 19, 1938, Brief Minutes, 1936 through 1941, p3, Cass County Social Service. For the transformation of mothers' pensions into ADC, see Brown, *Public Relief*, 30, and Howard, "Sowing the Seeds of 'Welfare.'" The delineation of Bertha Swanson and many others as "unemployable" was standard but not exactly accurate. Many "unemployables" could work and were on work relief, but they usually could not earn enough to support themselves and their families even in times of economic prosperity. Unlike mothers' pensions, ADC funds were available to fathers and other relatives, but as a practical matter the vast bulk of the aid went to mothers with dependent children.

82. "Fargo Looks for Heavy Business Gains After Smashing Advance During March," *Fargo Forum* 56, Apr. 5, 1934, p1, 2; "Federal Force Could Use at Once Most of Another Floor," *Fargo Forum* 56, July 30, 1934, p1; "Fargo Christmas Buying Called Best in Years," *Fargo (Morning) Forum* 27, Dec. 25, 1934, p1; "Check Figures Show Increase," *Fargo (Morning) Forum* 27, Jan. 1, 1935, p9; "Fargo Chamber Reports Show Business Gains for City in 1935," *Fargo (Morning) Forum* 27, Jan. 16, 1935, p1.

83. "Welcome, Mr. President!" *Fargo Forum* 58, Aug. 26, 1936, p4.

NOTES TO CHAPTER 4

1. "Public Assistance," 2 (Mar. 1937), Public Welfare Board of North Dakota.

2. "Public Assistance," 2 (Mar. 1937): 2, (Dec. 1937): 1, Public Welfare Board of North Dakota.

3. Monthly Summary Federal Emergency Relief Administration and Cass County Relief, April 1935 Harry Lashkowitz Papers, mss. 161, box 31, folder 12, p2, NDIRS; Hilber interview; Larson interview.

4. Interested Homemaker, "Urges Persons Visit Government's Projects Before Crit-

icizing Them," *Fargo Forum* 58, Mar. 28, 1936, p5; Minutes of Meeting County Welfare Board, Apr. 11, 1934, Apr. 1933–Dec. 1935, p7, Cass County Social Services.

5. "Survey Fargo Relief Work," *Fargo Forum* 55, Jan. 31, 1933, p1; "Relief Expert Charges Fargo, Cass Work for Needy Lacking," *Fargo Forum* 55, Feb. 11, 1933, p1, 7. For Red Cross work in 1932–33, see Jones and Herrick, *Citizens in Service*, 34–35.

6. Lowitt and Beasley, eds. *One Third of a Nation*, 75; "Need of Close Supervision," editorial, *Fargo Forum* 55, Mar. 10, 1933, p4; "The Need for Co-Ordination," editorial, *Fargo Forum* 55, Feb. 27, 1933, p4.

7. Proceedings of the Board of County Commissioners of Cass County, North Dakota, Apr. 7, 1933, p1781, Cass County Auditor's Office; "Relief Chief Reaches City," *Fargo Forum* 55, May 31, 1933, p7.

8. Proceedings of the Board of County Commissioners of Cass County, Nov. 9, 1933, p1844, Cass County Auditor's Office; "Boards at War on Relief Plan," *Fargo Forum* 55, Nov. 10, 1933, p1; Proceedings of the Board of County Commissioners of Cass County, Mar. 21, 1934, p1879, Cass County Auditor's Office; "300 Men Jam Courthouse to Ask Hendricks Ouster," *Fargo Forum* 56, Mar. 21, 1934, p1; "Cass Welfare Board Given Conference Support," *Fargo Forum* 56, Mar. 23, 1934, p1, 2.

9. "County Relief Board Demand Commissioners Give Attitude," *Fargo Forum* 56, May 16, 1934, p1, 12; "Commissioners Hold Welfare Setup Is Not Satisfactory," *Fargo Forum* 56, May 18, 1934, p1, 9.

10. "Board Stands on Relief Plan," *Fargo Forum* 57, Apr. 25, 1935, p1, 10; Proceedings of the Board of County Commissioners of Cass County, Aug. 6, 1935, p2057, Cass County Auditor's Office; "Welfare Unit Controls Funds," *Fargo Forum* 58, Dec. 5, 1935, p1.

11. "Cass without Welfare Unit," *Fargo Forum* 58, Apr. 11, 1936, p1, 6; "4 Welfare Men Explain Stand," *Fargo Forum* 58, Apr. 13, 1936, p1, 7; "Pollock, Thue, Hunsaker, Named to Welfare Board," *Fargo Forum* 58, Apr. 30, 1936, p11.

12. "Drop 10 From Relief Staff," *Fargo Forum* 57, Sept. 5, 1935, p8; "Asks $124,570 Relief Budget," *Fargo Forum* 57, July 10, 1935, p1, 2.

13. Stevens interview.

14. Individual Record—Poor Relief and Social Welfare Aid, County of Cass, loose sheets from 1935–37, Cass County Social Services; Proceedings of the Welfare Board, June 26, 1935, Apr. 1933–Dec. 1935, p5, Cass County Social Services; Minutes of the Meeting of the County Welfare Board, Apr. 18, 1934," Apr. 1933–Dec. 1935, p11, Cass County Social Services. The continuing importance and nature of local relief is discussed by Grattan, "Who Is on Relief?"

15. Welfare Board Meeting, Sept. 25, 1935, Apr. 1933–Dec. 1935, p20, Cass County Social Services.

16. "Relief Optical Contract Let," *Fargo Forum* 57, Oct. 4, 1935, p12; "'Relief' Teeth Will Be Scarce," *Fargo (Sunday) Forum* 27, Apr. 21, 1935, p13; Minutes of the Meeting of the County Welfare Board, Dec. 12, 1934, Apr. 1933–Dec. 1935, p4, Cass County Social Services; Welfare Board Meeting, Cass County, Aug. 19, 1936, Brief Minutes 1936 through 1941, p5, Cass County Social Services; Welfare Board Meeting, Cass County, Mar. 25, 1936, Brief Minutes 1936 through 1941, p1, Cass County Social Services; Welfare Board Meeting, Cass County, June 16, 1937, Brief Minutes 1936 through 1941, p3, Cass County Social Services. For birth control as a means of trimming relief rolls during the thirties, see Rosen, "Federal Expansion, Fertility Control, and Physicians."

17. "Relief Cases Rent Limited," *Fargo Forum* 55, July 7, 1933, p5; "Homes of 5 Rooms Most Numerous Type in Fargo," *Fargo Forum* 56, May 23, 1934, p7; Minutes of Meeting County Welfare Board, Dec. 19, 1934, Apr. 1933–Dec. 1935, p2, Cass County Social Services; Welfare Board Meeting, Sept. 11, 1935, Apr. 1933–Dec. 1935, p3–4, Cass County Social Services; Welfare Board Meeting, Cass County, May 31, 1939, Brief Minutes 1936 through 1941, p5, Cass County Social Services.

18. "Welfare Board Directs New Cass Relief Setup," *Fargo Forum* 55, June 14, 1933, p8; "Relief Clients Must Plant Gardens or Be Cut Off Rolls," *Fargo Forum* 58, Apr. 20, 1936, p1; "County Boasts Good 'Cellar,'" *Fargo (Sunday) Forum* 28, Nov. 24, 1935, p13; "Relief Office Hours Changed," *Fargo Forum* 55, Sept. 8, 1933, p3; "Allot $26,336 in Project to Better

Housing of Fargo Needy," *Fargo (Sunday) Forum* 27, Dec. 23, 1934, p11.

19. For local responsibility over FERA, see Williams, *Federal Aid for Relief,* 58–66, and Kennedy, *Freedom from Fear,* 172. Local authorities also determined eligibility for the Civilian Conservation Corps.

20. For the divergence between federal and local social work attitudes nationally, see Patterson, *The New Deal and the States,* 63–64, and Braeman, Bremner, and Brody, eds., *The New Deal,* xiii.

21. Welton interview.

22. "Allot Sum to Fix Clothing," *Fargo (Morning) Forum* 27, Jan. 18, 1935, p7; Monthly Summary Federal Emergency Relief Administration and Cass County Relief, February, 1935, Harry Lashkowitz Papers, mss. 161, box 31, folder 12, p5, NDIRS; "Bedding Work Is Authorized," *Fargo Forum* 59, Feb. 4, 1937, p5. For the benefits of work relief for women, see Gordon, *Pitied But Not Entitled,* 191. For another view, see Swain, "'The Forgotten Woman.'"

23. "Nursery School Is Becoming Community Project with Several Agencies Aiding," *Fargo (Sunday) Forum* 29, Dec. 6, 1936, p15; Minutes of the Regular Meeting of the Board of Commissioners, Sept. 10, 1934, mss. 42, box 15, N-744, NDIRS; "Children Learn Manners in New Nursery School," *Fargo (Sunday) Forum* 26, May 20, 1934, p11, 17. For a more detailed look at the nursery school program nationwide, see Rose, *A Mothers' Job,* 144–49.

24. Welfare Board Meeting, Oct. 16, 1935, Apr. 1933–Dec. 1935, p3, Cass County Social Service; Welfare Board Meeting, Oct. 23, 1935, Apr. 1933–Dec. 1935, p1, Cass County Social Services. For the relationship between the WPA and local relief officials nationally, see Singleton, *The American Dole,* 175–84.

25. "Relief Office Cost Down 58%," *Fargo Forum* 58, Apr. 21, 1936, p1, 6; Welfare Board Meeting, Cass County, Jan. 20, 1937, Brief Minutes 1936 through 1941, p5, Cass County Social Services. In 1937 supplementation in Cass County averaged $37.70 per WPA employee, according to "Public Assistance" 3 (Mar. 1938), Public Welfare Board of North Dakota.

26. Welfare Board Meeting, Cass County,

Jan. 20, 1937, Brief Minutes 1936 through 1941, p6, Cass County Social Services; Minutes of Meeting County Welfare Board, Oct. 3, 1934, Apr. 1933–Dec. 1935, p1, Cass County Social Service; Monthly Summary Federal Emergency Relief Administration and Cass County Relief, March 1935, Harry Lashkowitz Papers, mss. 161, box 31, folder 12, p2, NDIRS; "All Veterans Receiving Bonus Off Cass Relief," *Fargo Forum* 58, June 19, 1936, p1.

27. Minutes of the County Welfare Board, Dec. 5, 1934, Apr. 1933–Dec. 1935, p17, Cass County Social Services. Nesbith, "Present Relief Policies," suggests that policies and procedures in Cass were hardly extraordinary in their harshness.

28. "Public Assistance," 2 (May 1937): 14, Public Welfare Board of North Dakota; "County Buying Faces Protest," *Fargo Forum* 55, Feb. 8, 1933, p5; "Relief Cases Rent Limited," *Fargo Forum* 55, July 7, 1933, p5. For some of the conflicts between federal and local standards, see Brown, *Public Relief,* 216, and Bremer, *Depression Winters,* 174–75.

29. Welfare Board Minutes, Apr. 17, 1935, Apr. 1933–Dec. 1935, p1, Cass County Social Services.

30. "Relief 'Luxuries' Said Given by 29 Out of 30 Merchants," *Fargo Forum* 59, Jan. 12, 1937, p1, 12. For an interesting article on the manipulation of grocery vouchers nationally, see "Does the World Owe Me a Living?"

31. "Press Release from R. M. Parkins to Eight Cass County Newspapers, September 18, 1939," Cass County Welfare Board 1934 to 1956 File, Cass County Social Services.

32. Welfare Board Meeting, Cass County, Feb. 15, 1939, p1, Brief Minutes 1936 through 1941, Cass County Social Services; "Liquor Out for Relief Clients," *Fargo Forum* 58, June 11, 1936, p6; "2 Face Charge of Nonsupport," *Fargo Forum* 29, Dec. 30, 1936, p1; "Barmen Put on Spot by Rule," *Fargo (Sunday) Forum* 29, Dec. 30, 1936, p1; Local Survey, Fargo, North Dakota, March 1940, Women's Christian Temperance Union of Fargo-Moorhead Records, S 4860 4932, box 1, folder 5, p4, NMRHC.

33. Almond and Lasswell, "Aggressive Behavior by Clients." For organization among the unemployed, see Rosenzweig, "Organizing the Unemployed," and Brown, *Public Re-*

lief, 263–65. For the growing tendency to see relief as a job, see McGovern, *And a Time for Hope,* 15. For organization regionally, see Koch, "Politics and Relief in Minneapolis," and Tweton, *New Deal at the Grass Roots,* 53–54.

34. A Fargo Holiday Member, "A Holidayer Writes," *Fargo Forum* 56, Mar. 22, 1934, p5.

35. Minutes of Meeting Cass County Welfare Board, Oct. 10, 1934, Apr. 1933–Dec. 1935, p10, 8, Cass County Social Services. For the rising tide of protest after the demise of the CWA, see Singleton, *The American Dole,* 142–44.

36. Minutes of Meeting County Welfare Board, Apr. 11, 1934, Apr. 1933–Dec. 1935, p7, Cass County Social Services; Minutes of Meeting County Welfare Board, Apr. 18, 1934, Apr. 1933–Dec. 1935, p8, Cass County Social Services; "Holiday Group Asks Hoglund's Removal from County Board," *Fargo (Sunday) Forum* 26, Feb. 18, 1934, p1; "Seek Four on Riot Charges," *Fargo Forum* 57, Dec. 15, 1934, 3.

37. Welfare Board Meeting, Jan. 30, 1935, Apr. 1933–Dec. 1935, p4, Cass County Social Services; "County Relief Body Protests," *Fargo Forum* 57, Mar. 2, 1935, p1; Welfare Board Meeting, Mar. 13, 1935, Apr. 1933–Dec. 1935, p3, Cass County Social Services. "Mr. Goldschmitz" was probably Ernest, but was perhaps one of his brothers, Roy. Both were active in Local 173.

38. Welfare Board Meeting, Cass County, Feb. 17, 1937, Brief Minutes, 1936 through 1941, p1, Cass County Social Services.

39. Records of WPA, Record Group 69, box 220, PC 37, Entry 10, North Dakota Complaints D-E File, and box 2209, North Dakota 642 A-Z File, NARS.

40. Welfare Board Meeting, Cass County, Mar. 10, 1937, Brief Minutes, 1936 through 1941, p4, Cass County Social Services.

41. Cordell and Cordell, "Unions Among the Unemployed," 507–8; "22 Clay WPA Pickets Jailed; Work Resumed on Fargo Jobs," *Fargo Forum* 61, July 14, 1939, p1, 2.

42. U.S. Department of Commerce, Bureau of the Census, *Fifteenth Census: 1930,* Vol. 3.2, 418, 427.

43. Sutherland and Locke, *Twenty Thousand Homeless Men,* 34. I conservatively esti-

mated the number of working class, single men in the city at about 900. A Relief Office count in 1935 showed 300 on lower Front Street alone, and it was conducted in May when many had left for farm work. See Welfare Board Meeting, May 22, 1935, Apr. 1933–Dec. 1935, p5, Cass County Social Services.

44. "Laborer Dead After Drinking," *Fargo Forum* 58, Sept. 5, 1936, p1.

45. Minutes of the Regular Meeting of the Board of Commissioners, July 22, 1935, p430, City Auditor's Office; Minutes of Adjourned Regular Meeting of the Board of Commissioners, Sept. 27, 1934, mss. 42, box 15, N-749, NDIRS. Springer, "Step-Children of Relief," demonstrates that Fargo's single men situation was hardly unique. For the development and character of urban main stems, see Kusmer, *Down and Out, On the Road,* 160.

46. Dr. Carl E. Elofson Papers, mss. 1165, box 4, folder 26; box 3, folder 14; box 1, folder 14; box 4, folder 15; box 1, folder 26, all NDIRS.

47. Dr. Carl E. Elofson Papers, mss. 1165, box 4, folder 5, NDIRS.

48. "Agencies Deny Lack of Work," *Fargo Forum* 52, Mar. 12, 1930, 6; Minutes of Regular Meeting of January 5, 1931, mss. 42, box 15, N-203, NDIRS; Proceedings of the Board of County Commissioners, Sept. 4, 1931, p1606, County Auditor's Office.

49. "Jobless Group Assembles to Demand Work or County Aid," *Fargo Forum* 56, Dec. 19, 1933, p1; "Board Clamps Lid on Relief Chiselers," *Fargo Forum* 59, Jan. 21, 1937, p1; Records of WPA, Record Group 69, box 220, PC 37, Entry 10, North Dakota Complaints D-E File, and box 2209, North Dakota 642 A-Z File, NARS.

50. "Barracks Proposed to House County Charges," *Fargo Forum* 54, Feb. 10, 1932, p1; "Cass to Build Barracks for Housing Single Relief Cases," *Fargo Forum* 54, Sept. 6, 1932, p1.

51. Minutes of Meeting County Welfare Board, Aug. 1, 1934, Apr. 1933–Dec. 1935, p9, Cass County Social Services; "$17,908 Paid in March in Cass Relief Work," *Fargo Forum* 56, May 7, 1934, p5; Monthly Summary Federal Emergency Relief Administration and Cass County Relief, Mar. 1935, Harry Lashkowitz Papers, mss. 161, box 31, folder 12, p2, NDIRS; "Homeless Men Civic Problem," *Fargo Forum* 57, June 18, 1935, p1.

52. Minutes of Welfare Board, Jan. 16,

1935, Apr. 1933–Dec. 1935, p6, Cass County Social Services; "Public Assistance" 4 (Aug. 1939): 5, Public Welfare Board of North Dakota; Welfare Board Meeting, Oct. 30, 1935, Apr. 1933–Dec. 1935, p3, Cass County Social Services.

53. Minutes of Meeting County Welfare Board, June 20, 1934, Apr. 1933–Dec. 1935, p4, Cass County Social Services; Welfare Board Meeting, Nov. 16, 1938, Brief Minutes 1936 through 1941, p5, Cass County Social Services.

54. "Relief Bureau Ready Oct. 15," *Fargo Forum* 58, Oct. 1, 1936, p16; Welfare Board Meeting, Oct. 7, 1936, Brief Minutes 1936 through 1941, p2, Cass County Social Services; Welfare Board Meeting, Nov. 18, 1936, Brief Minutes 1936 through 1941, p2, Cass County Social Services; Welfare Board Meeting, Jan. 4, 1939, Brief Minutes 1936 through 1941, p5, Cass County Social Services; Individual Record—Poor Relief and Social Welfare Aid, County of Cass, loose sheets from 1935–37, Cass County Social Services. Fargo's treatment of single men was similar to that in other places. See "Homeless in Winter."

55. Records of WPA, Record Group 69, box 2208, 641 N. Dakota E-S, NARS.

56. Monthly Summary Federal Emergency Relief Administration and Cass County Relief, November 1934, Harry Lashkowitz Papers, mss. 161, box 31, folder 12, p2, NDIRS.

57. Kelley, "Good Men Plowed Under," 136, 135, and 130; Minutes of Meeting County Welfare Board, July 25, 1934, Apr. 1933–Dec. 1935, p1–2, Cass County Social Services; Welfare Board Meeting Minutes, Jan. 30, 1935, Apr. 1933–Dec. 1935, p8, Cass County Social Services.

58. Two anonymous interviews; interview with Robert and Rachel Reynolds, May 9–11, 1974, S 4800 4863, NMRHC; Larson interview; Records of WPA, Record Group 69, box 2215, North Dakota Complaints 662 A-F-2 Jan. 1938 File, NARS.

59. Interview with June Dobervich, Fargo, ND, Oct. 28, 1997; interview with Mavis Nymon, Fargo, ND, Nov. 6, 1997; "Personal," *Fargo Forum* 56, Dec. 18, 1933, p9.

60. Proceedings of Welfare Board, Feb. 13, 1935, Apr. 1933–Dec. 1935, p1, Cass County Social Services; "Shack Colony Is Independent," *Fargo (Sunday) Forum* 28, Apr. 26,

1936, p13; "'Old Ones' Shy at Relief Talk," *Fargo (Sunday) Forum* 28, May 24, 1936, p15; A Citizen, "One Viewpoint," *Fargo Forum* 56, Dec. 11, 1933, p5.

61. Records of WPA, Record Group 63, box 220, PC 37, Entry 10, North Dakota Complaints D-E File, NARS.

62. Welfare Board Meeting, May 8, 1935, Apr. 1933–Dec. 1935, p2, Cass County Social Services; Records of WPA, Record Group 69, box 2208 641 N. Dakota E-S, NARS.

63. Welfare Board Minutes, Apr. 17, 1935, Apr. 1933–Dec. 1935, p2, Cass County Social Services; "Lanier Rakes Aid Chiselers," *Fargo Forum* 57, Apr. 23, 1935, p5.

64. "Single Men to Go Off Relief," *Fargo Forum* 57, July 5, 1935, p1; Welfare Board Proceedings, July 24, 1935, Apr. 1933–Dec. 1935, p2-3, Cass County Social Services; "Harvest Wage Scale Debated," *Fargo Forum* 57, July 29, 1935, p1; "Ruling Sought on Transients," *Fargo Forum* 57, July 25, 1935, p1, 8.

65. "Shortage of Labor Leaving Grain Unshocked, Runck Says," *Fargo Forum* 58, July 21, 1936, p1. For the regional outcry in 1935, see "Harvest: Jobless Would Rather" and Kidney, "Harvest and Relief."

66. Interview with Glenn Smith, Fargo, ND, Oct. 23, 1997; "Relief Workers Shirkers? Take a Look at This," *Fargo (Sunday) Forum* 26, May 27, 1934, p4; Interested Homemaker, "Urges Persons Visit Government's Projects Before Criticizing Them," *Fargo Forum* 58, Mar. 28, 1936, p5.

67. Records of WPA, Record Group 69, box 2208 641 N. Dakota E-S, NARS.

68. Amidon, "Always with Us," 107; Olson interview; Carlson interview; Anderson, "Are the Unemployed a Caste?" See also Gilboy, *Applicants for Work Relief,* and *Fortune*'s "Unemployment in 1937."

69. "Public Assistance" 3 (Dec. 1938): 2, 4; (Jan. 1939): 4; (Oct. 1939): 6, all Public Welfare Board of North Dakota.

70. "Cass Relief Is Complimented," *Fargo Forum* 57, Mar. 8, 1935, p1, 7; "Unfortunate," editorial, *Fargo Forum* 55, Feb. 4, 1933, p4; "Relief Understanding," editorial, *Fargo Forum* 56, Nov. 21, 1933, p4. For attitudes elsewhere, see, for example, Lynd and Lynd, *Middletown in Transition,* 142; Patterson, *American's Struggle Against Poverty;* and Trout, *Boston, the Great Depression,* 87.

71. See, for example, "WPA Worker, Two Women Jailed For Drunkenness," *Fargo Forum* 58, Feb. 7, 1936, p8; "Relief Client with Big Bank Account Arrested," *Fargo Forum* 59, Jan. 25, 1937, p1.

72. "Hats Off to Traill," editorial, *Fargo Forum* 57, Feb. 18, 1935, p4; "Improved Morale Is Result of Cavalier Relief Program," *Fargo Forum* 57, Sept. 28, 1935, p2.

73. "Toy Drive Gets Slow Response," *Fargo (Sunday) Forum* 28, Dec. 8, 1935, p5; "600 Families to Benefit in Christmas Toy Project," *Fargo Forum* 61, Dec. 22, 1938, p3.

74. "Pathos, Joy Mingle as Fargo Gives 'Christmas for All,'" *Fargo (Morning) Forum* 22, Dec. 25, 1929, p1, 5.

75. "Corset Fund for 'Suffering Sister' Goes over Top with More than Dollar to Spare," *Fargo Forum* 58, Aug. 24, 1936, p7; "The Corset Friend Story Is All Laced Up: Suffering Sister Fitted with Garment," *Fargo Forum* 58, Aug. 26, 1936, p1.

NOTES TO CHAPTER 5

1. Lynd and Lynd, *Middletown in Transition,* 7; interview with Darrow Beaton, Fargo, ND, Aug. 16, 2002.

2. Bruce Barton, "We Are Learning the Blessing of Work," *American Magazine* 114 (Oct. 1932): 124; A Loyal Fairmont Employee, "Our Job," and "A Thanksgiving Thought for November 24, 1932," Fairmont Food Papers, S 2691 2674, box 1, Newspaper Articles and Advertisements folder, NMRHC. The emphasis on hard work during the Depression is stressed by Hearn in *The American Dream in the Great Depression,* 66.

3. Flynn, "Starvation Wages." The differential in wage rates between new hires and established employees is emphasized by Simon, "The Supply Price of Labor."

4. For the popularity of small business formation among insecure employees during the Depression, see Bird, *The Invisible Scar,* 45-46, and Wheeler, "What Can You Do to Make Money?"

5. "Report of the President," North Dakota AFL-CIO Records, Collection 10038, box 1, folder 2, p1, SHSND.

6. *Historical Statistics of the United States,* part 1, 243-45; Dale, "Dakota Shifts the Farmers' Burden."

7. *Historical Statistics of the United States.*

8. "Fargo Rentals Drop in Step with Incomes," *Fargo (Sunday) Forum* 27, Apr. 7, 1935, p13; "Cross-Sectioning Another Market," 22. For comparisons of Fargo wages to national averages, see U.S. Department of Commerce, Bureau of the Census, *Fifteenth Census: 1930 Distribution,* Vol. 1.3, p27, 479, Vol. 2, p12, 1117, and *Fifteenth Census: 1929 Manufactures,* Vol. 1, p21, 301.

9. Interview with May Bredeson, Moorhead, MN, Apr. 25, 2000; Oster interview; Westberg interview; Olson interview; interview with Jack McNair, Fargo, ND, Sept. 16, 1997; Hauser interview.

10. Proceedings of the Board of County Commissioners of Cass County, North Dakota, May 11, 1933, p1794–95, Cass County Auditor's Office; Proceedings of the Welfare Board, June 26, 1935, County Welfare Board Verbatim Minutes, Apr. 1933–Dec. 1935, p1, Cass County Social Services; e-mail from Arthur G. Christianson, July 23, 1997; Stevens interview; "Costello Gets Garbage Work," *Fargo Forum* 54, June 13, 1932, p8; Special Meeting of the Board of Directors of the Lutheran Hospital Association, Sept. 14, 1937, Meritcare Medical Records, S 4975 5153, box 4, p139, NMRHC.

11. A number of firms reinstated Christmas bonuses in 1936. See, for example, "Penny Staff to Get Bonus," *Fargo Forum* 59, Dec. 1, 1936, p7, and "Fargo Rentals Drop in Step with Incomes," *Fargo (Sunday) Forum* 27, Apr. 7, 1935, p13. For a national comment on the wage reduction versus cost of living issue, see "Editorial Paragraph."

12. Resolution, North Dakota AFL-CIO Records, Collection 10038, box 1, folder 2, SHSND; "Fargo Asks Lower Pay Scale in Public Works," *Fargo (Sunday) Forum* 26, Sept. 3, 1933, p1; "N.D. Labor Groups Flay Chamber Wage Cut Move," *Fargo Forum* 55, Sept. 5, 1933, p1, 2; Minutes of the County Welfare Board, Apr. 18, 1934, County Welfare Board Verbatim Minutes, Apr. 1933–Dec.1935, p10, Cass County Social Service.

13. "Claim Garbage Men Underpaid," *Fargo Forum* 56, Sept. 10, 1934, p3; Minutes of the Regular Meeting of the Board of Commissioners of the City of Fargo, July 18, 1938, City Auditor's Office.

14. "Waitresses Go to 'School' to Brush Up on Fine Points," *Fargo Forum* 57, June 29, 1935, p5; Minutes of the Board of Education, Fargo, North Dakota, Jan. 4, 1935, p181, Fargo Public Schools.

15. A noteworthy example of job immobility was presented in the spring of 1932, when, for the first time in memory, not a single teacher turned down his or her job for the next school year. See "Mrs. Kjorlie President of Fargo School Board," *Fargo Forum* 54, May 5, 1932, p11.

16. Elizabeth Alsop interview; interview with Anna Jane Schlossman, Fargo, ND, Oct. 9, 1997; Beaton 1999 interview; interview with an anonymous respondent, Fargo, ND, Sept. 23, 1997. Paternal relationships between employers and employees were especially common in relatively small cities and in firms with relatively few employees. See, for example, Clark, "Beckerstown: 1932."

17. "What Is the Herbst S and B Club?" "Herbstory," Mar. 17, 1930, Herbst Company Papers, mss. 158, box 1, folder 17, NDIRS.

18. "Herbstory," Mar. 17, 1930, and Dec. 1933, Herbst Company Papers, mss. 158, box 1, folders 17 and 18, NDIRS.

19. Of 126 employees at Herbst in 1934, 98 were women. See "Believe It or Not!" "Herbstory," Feb. 1, 1934, Herbst Company Papers, mss. 158, box 1, folder 19, NDIRS.

20. Interview with an anonymous respondent, Fargo, ND, June 26, 1998. See also "Radical, Happy Work Side by Side for Scrip," *Fargo (Sunday) Forum* 24, Mar. 6, 1932, p9, 17.

21. The background of union labor in Fargo is detailed in Schroeder, "History of Organized Labor in Fargo." Interview with Robert Carson, Fargo, ND, July 30, 1998; interview with respondent whose identity is not revealed at the author's discretion.

22. "Report of the President," North Dakota AFL-CIO Records, Collection 10038, box 1, folder 2, p1; for labor and the Roosevelt administration, see Bernstein, *Turbulent Years.* For the Minneapolis strike, see Schultz, *Conflict and Change.* For improving economic prospects locally, see, for example, "Fargo Looks for Heavy Business Gains After Smashing Advance During March," *Fargo Forum* 56, Apr. 5, 1934, p1–2, and "Fargo Christmas Buying Called Best in

Years," *Fargo (Morning) Forum* 27, Dec. 25, 1934, p1.

23. Schultz, *Conflict and Change;* Wagner, "'The Greatest Thing I Ever Did'"; Solow, "Class War in Minnesota"; Sannes, "Gas Sunday"; "Communism Is Issue at Trial," *Fargo Forum* 57, Mar. 21, 1935, p1, 8. For the Citizens Alliance, see Millikan, *A Union Against Unions.*

24. "Milk Strikers Accept 10-Day Truce After Day of Turmoil in Fargo Area," *Fargo Forum* 56, Nov. 5, 1934, p1, 7; Police Record, City of Fargo, book 1, p184, NDIRS; Minutes of the Meeting of the Board of City Commissioners, Jan. 3, 1933, mss. 42, box 15, p460, NDIRS.

25. "Governor's Aid Brings Strike Stay," *Fargo Forum* 56, Nov. 14, 1934, p1, 10; "Olson Asks Sensible Strike Settling," *Fargo (Sunday) Forum* 27, Nov. 18, 1934, p1, 2; "Strike Settlement in Sight Today," *Fargo Forum* 57, Nov. 19, 1934, p1, 6.

26. Police Records, City of Fargo, book 1, p186, NDIRS; "Work Resumed, Six Held After Theater Crew Labor Flareup," *Fargo Forum* 57, Nov. 27, 1934, p1, 9.

27. "Announcement," *Fargo Forum* 57, Dec. 6, 1934, p10; "Knerr Plant Men on Strike," *Fargo Forum* 57, Dec. 7, 1934, p8; "Knerr Company Seeks Relief from Union's Drive," *Fargo Forum* 57, Dec. 13, 1934, p11; "Seek Four on Riot Charges," *Fargo Forum* 57, Dec. 15, 1934, p1; "Holiday Group Is Restrained," *Fargo Forum* 57, Dec. 17, 1934, p1; "Sentence Four in Cass Court," *Fargo Forum* 57, Mar. 9, 1935, p5. In *Conflict and Change,* p60, Schultz notes that Minneapolis teamsters also enjoyed support of the Holiday Association.

28. John Alsop interview; "Protest Vote for Workers," *Fargo (Sunday) Forum* 27, Jan. 6, 1935, p1; Martinson, *History of North Dakota Labor.*

29. "Fuel Dealers Veto Election," *Fargo Forum* 57, Dec. 14, 1934, p1, 6; "Labor Hearing Next Week," *Fargo (Morning) Forum* 27, Jan. 3, 1935, p1; "Protest Vote for Workers," *Fargo (Sunday) Forum* 27, Jan. 6, 1935, p1; Sannes, "Gas Sunday," 30; Schultz, *Conflict and Change,* 34.

30. "Coal Promised Despite Fargo Strike," *Fargo (Morning) Forum* 27, Jan. 23, 1935, p1, 3.

31. Citizens Committee, "To the General Public," *Fargo (Sunday) Forum* 27, Jan. 27, 1933, p10.

32. "Coal Promised Despite Fargo Strike," *Fargo (Morning) Forum* 27, Jan. 23, 1935, p1, 3.

33. "Call Day's Truce in Trucker Strike," *Fargo (Morning) Forum* 27, Jan. 24, 1935, p1, 2.

34. "Call Day's Truce in Truckers Strike," *Fargo (Morning) Forum* 27, Jan. 24, 1935, p1, 2; Martinson, *History of North Dakota Labor,* 30; "Strike Finish Fight to Begin Today," *Fargo (Morning) Forum* 27, Jan. 25, 1935, p1; "Coal Strike in Period of Calm but Deliveries Below Normal," *Fargo (Sunday) Forum* 27, Jan. 27, 1935, p1, 7; Citizens Committee, "To the General Public," *Fargo (Sunday) Forum* 27, Jan. 27, 1933, p10. The Minneapolis strikers had also drawn substantial support from the unemployed. See Schultz, *Conflict and Change,* 43.

35. "95 Jailed in Fargo Truck Strike Riot," *Moorhead Daily News* 52, Jan. 28, 1935, p1, 6; "94 of Strikers Bound Over to Trial," *Fargo (Morning) Forum* 27, Jan. 29, 1935, p1, 13.

36. "94 Of Strikers Bound Over to Trial," *Fargo (Morning) Forum* 27, Jan. 29, 1935, p1, 13.

37. "Free Strikers, Defense Asks," *Fargo Forum* 57, Feb. 19, 1935, p1, 3; "Jury Finds All Strike Rioters Guilty," *Fargo Forum* 57, Feb. 20, 1935, p1, 3; "Three Strike Leaders Given 6 Months," *Fargo Forum* 57, Feb. 23, 1935, p1, 8.

38. "Maze of Entanglements Surrounds Strike Issue," *Moorhead Daily News* 52, Feb. 1, 1935, p1; "Sathre Backs Police Strike Action," *Fargo (Morning) Forum* 27, Feb. 1, 1935, p1, 8; "Nine More Held in Strike Case," *Fargo Forum* 57, Feb. 13, 1935, p8; "Riot Sentences Saturday; Six More Drivers Attacked," *Fargo Forum* 57, Feb. 21, 1935, p1, 8; "Strike Pickets Posted on Roads Leading into Fargo," *Fargo Forum* 57, Feb. 25, 1935, p1; "Vandals Spill Kjorlie Fuel," *Fargo Forum* 57, Mar. 6, 1935, p1.

39. "Truck Driver Kills Self as Paralytic Mother Watches," *Fargo Forum* 57, Feb. 9, 1935, p1; Dr. Carl E. Elofson Papers, mss. 1165, box 2, folder 9, NDIRS; Schroeder, "History of Organized Labor in Fargo."

40. "Deputies Given House Censure," *Fargo (Morning) Forum* 27, Feb. 1, 1935, p1, 7; "Fuller Defends Police Action in Strike, Hits Back at Solons," *Fargo (Sunday) Forum* 27, Feb. 3, 1935, p1, 3; "Probers Exonerate Fargo Officers," *Fargo Forum* 57, Mar. 8, 1935, p1, 10; Mangold, "On the Labor Front"; Puner, "Gas Sunday"; Heisler, "The Fargo Cases."

41. "Rule by the Club," *Fargo (Morning) Forum* 27, Jan. 29, 1935, p14.

42. "Pastor Flays Tactics of Strikers and N. D. House," *Fargo Forum* 57, Feb. 4, 1935, p1, 7. The fact that two of the ministers in attendance, A. W. Ratz of First Presbyterian and Glen Lindley of First Congregational, told a public meeting called by Local 173 that "Heitmeyer was presenting his own views and was not speaking for the Fargo-Moorhead Ministerial association" indicates that the city's establishment was not completely united on the strike issue, or at least on the use of force by the authorities. See "Two Strikers Furnish Bond," *Fargo Forum* 57, Feb. 6, 1935, p8.

43. "Three Strike Leaders Given 6 Months," *Fargo Forum* 57, Feb. 23, 1935, p1, 8; "People and Labor Real Winners, Says Bergesen on Trial," *Fargo Forum* 57, Feb. 21, 1935, p8; "What the Verdict Means," editorial, *Fargo Forum* 57, Feb. 21, 1935, p4; "1935 Report of the Chamber of Commerce," Fargo Chamber of Commerce Records, mss. 10484, Annual Reports, 1930–35 File, p6, SHSND.

44. Millikan, *A Union Against Unions*, 25.

45. "What the Verdict Means," editorial, *Fargo Forum* 57, Feb. 21, 1935, p4.

46. "Assembly Ousts Local 173; Leadership Denounced," *Fargo Forum* 57, Mar. 19, 1935, p1, 9; "A Pretention [*sic*] Shattered," editorial, *Fargo Forum* 57, Mar. 19, 1935, p4; Lawrence J. Mero to L. A. Troutman, Mar. 21, 1935, copy, William W. Murrey Papers, mss. 60, box 1, folder 2, NDIRS.

47. Interview with Marion Pressler, Fargo, ND, Aug. 6, 1997; "Fargoans Hear Socialist Talk," *Fargo Forum* 54, Aug. 29, 1932, p2; "Norman Thomas, Wife, Honored by Fargoans," *Fargo Forum* 58, Oct. 8, 1936, p15.

48. "22 in Race for 3 Fargo Posts," *Fargo Forum* 55, Mar. 16, 1933, p1; "Communists to Meet Here," *Fargo Forum* 60, May 13, 1938, p6; "Communist to Speak in City," *Fargo Forum* 61, Sept. 25, 1939, p5; interview with Thomas McGrath, Mar. 30, 1967, S233 230, NMRHC.

49. "The Blame Fixed," editorial, *Fargo Forum* 57, Mar. 9, 1935, p4; "Injunction Proceedings Launched Against Local 173," *Fargo Forum* 57, Mar. 11, 1935, p1, 3. Communism became an issue at the injunction hearing when one of Local 173's attorneys, Francis Heisler of Chicago, was accused of being a Communist. See "Communism Is Issue in Trial," *Fargo Forum* 57, Mar. 21, 1935, p1, 8. Ballou and Hagan were not named in the injunction that was granted. See "Injunction in Strike Given," *Fargo Forum* 57, Mar. 23, 1935, p1, 6. For Steve Hagan's activities at the NDAC, see Danbom, *"Our Purpose Is to Serve,"* 110–14.

50. Sannes, "Gas Sunday," 31; "Communism 'Seeping' into N.D.A.C., Weston Avers," *Fargo Forum* 57, Apr. 23, 1935, p1; "'Red' Activity at A.C. Probed," *Fargo Forum* 57, May 28, 1935, p5.

51. Disinterested, "N.D.A.C. Innocent Victim of Charges," *Fargo Forum* 57, May 4, 1935, p6; Ex-Sophomore, "Communists Called Hopeless Sophomores," *Fargo Forum* 57, May 4, 1935, p6; "Schools Deny 'Red' Charges," *Fargo Forum* 58, May 19, 1936, p1, 12: "NDAC Straw Vote Voids 'Red' Label, Spectrum States," *Fargo (Sunday) Forum* 29, Oct. 18, 1936, p7.

52. "News About Town," *Fargo Forum* 57, Aug. 15, 1935, p14, reported Dunne still in Moorhead; "Pair Convicted in Strike Case," *Fargo Forum* 58, Mar. 30, 1936, p1; "Mrs. Schaffner, Cruden Named," *Fargo Forum* 59, Feb. 2, 1937, p1; Hank Frank, "This Town We Live In," *Fargo (Sunday) Forum* 30, Jan. 23, 1938, p11; "8 Now in Race for City Board," *Fargo Forum* 59, Mar. 3, 1937, p1, 6; "Sutherland Is Only New Man," *Fargo Forum* 59, Apr. 7, 1937, p1, 7.

53. Schroeder, "History of Organized Labor in Fargo," 51.

54. "Argue Barber Action United," *Fargo Forum* 59, Oct. 19, 1937, p6; "3 Barber Shops Leave Union Price Agreement," *Fargo Forum* 60, Dec. 1, 1937, p1, 15; "Judge Enjoins Picketing Here," *Fargo Forum* 60, Dec. 3, 1937, p1.

55. "Strike Halts Some Bakeries," *Fargo Forum* 59, Oct. 6, 1937, p1; "Six Fargoans Held in Strike," *Fargo Forum* 60, Dec. 8, 1937, p8; "3 More Union Members to Post Bond on Riot Counts," *Fargo Forum* 60, Dec. 11, 1937, p1.

56. "Load of Bread Doused with Kerosene in Strike Flareup," *Fargo Forum* 60, Sept. 17, 1938, p1; "Moorhead Man Blown to Death by Bomb Set in Auto," *Fargo Forum* 61, June 10, 1939, p1, 2; "Find Threat Note in Death Car," *Fargo (Sunday) Forum* 31, June 11, 1939, p1, 5; "Lee, Knutson Dazed by Plot to Destroy

Them," *Fargo Forum* 61, June 12, 1939, p1; "Lee Bombing Death Probe Called Officially Closed," *Fargo Forum* 61, Sept. 29, 1939, p6.

57. "Local Armour Protest Made," *Fargo Forum* 61, Aug. 9, 1939, p5; "Strike On at Armour Plant," *Fargo Forum* 61, Aug. 23, 1939, p1, 6; "Warrants Issued as Near-Riot Flares in Armour Strike," *Fargo Forum* 61, Aug. 24, 1939, p1, 12; "Armour Strike 'Break' Comes," *Fargo Forum* 61, Aug. 25, 1939, p1; "Stipulation Brings End to 10-Week Strike at Armour," *Fargo Forum* 61, Nov. 4, 1939, p1.

58. "Truck Strike Here Settled," *Fargo Forum* 59, Oct. 30, 1937, p1; Report of President W. W. Murrey, North Dakota AFL-CIO Records, Collection 10038, box 1, folder 2, p2, SHSND.

NOTES TO CHAPTER 6

1. Mrs. M. C. Osman, "Jobs and Married Women," *Fargo Forum* 54, June 21, 1932, p5; "Femininity Back," editorial, *Fargo Forum* 56, Feb. 21, 1934, p4.

2. U.S. Department of Commerce, Bureau of the Census, *Fifteenth Census: 1930,* Vol. 3.2, 427.

3. U.S. Department of Commerce, Bureau of the Census, *Fifteenth Census: 1930,* Vol. 3.2, 427.

4. Harriet Hatfield is the name I have assigned to an interviewee who asked that her name not be used. Frieda Oster is the name I have assigned to a woman who would like to remain anonymous until after her death, "North Dakota Woman's Diary," mss. 214, NDIRS; Duval interview.

5. Shupienis interview; "North Dakota Woman's Diary," Nov. 30, 1939, mss. 214, NDIRS.

6. U.S. Department of Commerce, Bureau of the Census, *Fifteenth Census: 1930,* Vol. 3.2, 433.

7. Minutes of the Board of Education, Fargo, North Dakota, Sept. 24, 1935, p24–28, Fargo Public Schools; Carney interview; "Term of Office May Be Longer," *Fargo Forum* 53, Oct. 8, 1931, p5; "Save $26,000 in Teacher Wages," *Fargo Forum* 54, Mar. 11, 1932, p6; Minutes of the Board of Education–Fargo, North Dakota, Oct. 7, 1931, p483–84, Fargo Board of Education; Oster in-

terview; interview with Irene Fraser, Fargo, ND, Oct. 21, 1997.

8. Special Meeting of the Board of Directors of the Lutheran Hospital Association, Sept. 14, 1937, Meritcare Medical Records, mss. S 4975 5153, box 4, p139–40, NMRHC; "Ask Two More Caseworkers," *Fargo Forum* 58, May 14, 1936, p8.

9. Carlson interview; North Dakota Woman's Diary, Mar. 17, 1937, and Apr. 1, 1938, mss. 214, NDIRS. The experience of single working women elsewhere was similar. See, for example, Mary W. M. Hargreaves, "Darkness Before the Dawn: The Status of Women in the Depression Years," in Deutrich and Purdy, eds., *Clio Was a Woman;* Meyerowitz, *Women Adrift;* and Garceau, *The Important Things of Life.*

10. "N.D. Women to Work for Less Under Ordered Minimum Scale," *Fargo Forum* 54, Sept. 21, 1932, p1; Workmen's Compensation Bureau, Seventh Biennial Report of the Minimum Wage Department to the Governor of North Dakota for the Biennium Ending June 20, 1932, p3, SHSND; "Workers Don't Get Best Food," *Fargo Forum* 54, Aug. 13, 1932, p2; Report of the Secretary-Treasurer, 1933, North Dakota AFL-CIO Records, Collection 10038, box 1, folder 2, p5, SHSND.

11. "Workers Don't Get Best Food," *Fargo Forum* 54, Aug. 13, 1932, p2; "Cafe Owner Testifies to Dodging Law Since 1929," *Fargo Forum* 54, Aug. 12, 1932, p1, 6; "N. D. Women to Work for Less Under Ordered Minimum Scale," *Fargo Forum* 54, Sept. 21, 1932, p1.

12. Landfield interview; "'Maid's Night Out' Cause for Majority of Trouble with Domestics, Cline Finds," *Fargo (Sunday) Forum* 31, Mar. 12, 1939, p13; Shupienis interview; John Alsop interview; "Employment in February High," *Fargo Forum* 61, Mar. 10, 1939, p5. For a history of domestic service nationally, see Katzman, *Seven Days a Week.*

13. Eva Nelson, "Depressing Years," memoirs, mss. 21, box 1, folder 11, NDIRS.

14. Nelson, "Depressing Years," 3–4; "'Maid's Night Out' Cause for Majority of Trouble with Domestics, Cline Finds," *Fargo (Sunday) Forum* 31, Mar. 12, 1939, p13; interview with Bill Snyder, Fargo, ND, Feb. 20, 2000. Maid's night out also had an effect on affluent families, forcing them to fend for

themselves. In order to lend a hand, the Fargo Country Club declared Thursday "family night" and offered dinner specials.

15. "A Note on the Servant Problem."

16. "Fargo Women Draw Censure," *Fargo Forum* 53, Mar. 12, 1931, p6; "Women Want Work," *Fargo Forum* 55, Nov. 19, 1932, p7; "Women Want Work," *Fargo Forum* 55, Nov. 22, 1932, p11. It is likely that rapid turnover in domestic positions contributed to the severe erosion of maids' wages. Generally, employers offered wages to new hires at substantially lower levels than those obtained by established employees.

17. A Subscriber, "It's Not So Bad," *Fargo Forum* 53, Apr. 3, 1931, p17; "Rather Broad," editorial, *Fargo Forum* 53, Mar. 14, 1931, p4.

18. Catherine Murphy, "Only $3 a Week," *Fargo Forum* 53, Mar. 20, 1931, p10; A Woman Reader, "No Wonder They're Blue," *Fargo Forum* 53, Mar. 24, 1931, p8.

19. O. E. Clauson, "Luther Hall—A Home for Girls: A Prospectus," Minutes of Meeting of Budget Committee, 1936–38, United Way Collection, NDIRS: Norman, *History of Catholic Family Service*, 38.

20. "Inside the Chest: The Y.W.C.A.," *Fargo Forum* 56, Nov. 12, 1934, p6; "Y.W.C.A. Is Boon to Small Salaried Girls," *Fargo (Sunday) Forum* 25, Oct. 9, 1932, p9.

21. "Modernity Keynote of Fargo Woman's Board House Furnishing," *Fargo (Sunday) Forum* 28, Oct. 20, 1935, p9.

22. Annual Report for the Year 1934, Catholic Welfare Bureau, Catholic Family Services. For the North Dakota House of Mercy, see Rebecca Chapek, "History of the North Dakota House of Mercy, 1922–1965," unpublished manuscript, Lutheran Social Service. For treatment of unwed mothers nationwide, especially by the Florence Crittenton Homes, see Aiken, *Harnessing the Power of Motherhood;* Kunzel, *Fallen Women, Problem Girls;* and Morton, *And Sin No More.*

23. Untitled Document, "Child Welfare," Collection 493, p4–5, Chester Fritz Library, UND; Proceedings of the Board of County Commissioners of Cass County, North Dakota, Jan. 18, 1933, p1757, Cass County Auditor's Office; Yearly Report of Activities of the Scandinavian W.C.T.U., Fargo, No. Dak., Sept. 1934 to Aug. 31, 1935, W.C.T.U. Fargo-Moorhead Records, S 4860 4932, box 1,

NMRHC; "News About Town," *Fargo Forum* 56, Jan. 26, 1934, p2.

24. "Care, Guidance for Women in Need Found at Rescue Home," *Fargo Forum* 56, Nov. 21, 1933, p1; "Second Chance Held Out for Girls in Need at Fargo Home," *Fargo Forum* 56, Nov. 23, 1933, p1; Report on Inter Agency Child Welfare Standards Committee and General and Specific Policies of Private Agencies Operating in North Dakota, Oct. 13, 1941, p6–8, Lutheran Social Services; Peschel interview.

25. "North Dakota House of Mercy Regulations," "Child Welfare," mss. 493, Chester Fritz Library, UND; Report on Inter Agency Child Welfare Standards Committee and General and Specific Policies of Private Agencies Operating in North Dakota, Oct. 13, 1941, p6, Lutheran Social Services.

26. Elizabeth Alsop interview.

27. Reckless, "Why Women Become Hoboes," 175; "A Remarkable Man, Finance!" *Fargo (Sunday) Forum* 30, Apr. 3, 1938, p13; "Girl Hurt by Freight Train," *Fargo Forum* 61, June 30, 1939, p6. For discussions of female transience and homelessness, see Schuler, "Homeless Girls," and Le Sueur, "Women Are Hungry."

28. For the plight of independent women, see Pruette, ed., *Women Workers Through the Depression;* Hickey, *Hope and Danger in the New South City;* and Abelson, "'Women Who Have No Men to Work for Them.'"

29. "Exchange Asks New Quarters," *Fargo Forum* 56, Dec. 12, 1933, p5; "Women Want Work," *Fargo Forum* 56, Feb. 17, 1934, p7; A Reader, "What About Girls Who Can't Get Work," *Fargo Forum* 58, Aug. 22, 1936, p5. For the situation confronting female wage earners in Minneapolis, see Faue, *Community of Suffering and Struggle.*

30. LaFollette, *Concerning Women*, 93.

31. "Turmoil of June Further Upset by Lake Dwellers Leaving City for Summer," *Fargo Forum* 54, May 30, 1932, p6; "Fargoans Lured to Warmer Climates, Many Plan Visits to Points in West, South," *Fargo (Morning) Forum* 27, Jan. 27, 1935, p6.

32. Landfield interview; Schlossman interview.

33. Minutes of the Meeting of the Board of Trustees, Community Welfare Association, Fargo, N.D., December 22, 1930, p2, United

Way Collection, NDIRS; "Mrs. Gunkleman Is Named Woman's Crusade Chairman," *Fargo (Sunday) Forum* 29, Aug. 23, 1936, p5.

34. Beaton 1999 interview.

35. Interview with Emily Jackson, Fargo, ND, Oct. 9, 1997; Clower interview; interview with Jocelyn Burdick, Fargo, ND, June 11, 1997; Pastoret interview; Stevens interview.

36. Shupienis interview; interview with Paul Gallagher, Fargo, ND, Dec. 2, 1997.

37. Interview with Katherine Burgum, Fargo, ND, Oct. 16, 1997; interview with Warner Litten, Fargo, ND, June 5, 1997; U.S. Department of Commerce, Bureau of the Census, *Fifteenth Census: 1930,* Vol. 6, 1007; Bredeson interview; Duval interview.

38. For the connection between citizenship and participation in the economy, see Kessler-Harris, *In Pursuit of Equity.*

39. Interview with Jean Guy, Fargo, ND, June 18, 1997; interview with Jacques Stockman, Fargo, ND, May 19, 1999; Dora Snyder interview. For the courage of professional women who wanted both a home and a career, see Glazer and Slater, *Unequal Colleagues.* For growing opportunities for married women in two fields, see Willett, *Permanent Waves,* and Hornstein, "'Rosie the Realtor.'"

40. Graber interview; interview with Jerry Lein, Moorhead, MN, Sept. 10, 1998.

41. Benson, *Counter Cultures.*

42. Matthews, "*Just a Housewife,*" 190; Rinehart, "Cutting Down Expenses."

43. "It's Up to the Women"; "It's Up to the Women: Leaders of Millions." See also Matthews, "*Just a Housewife,*" for the changing expectations of housewives' proper social roles.

44. Litten interview.

45. A Fargo Resident, "No—Give Unmarried Work," *Fargo Forum* 53, Jan. 13, 1931, p5; Also A Reader of the *Fargo Forum,* "Dissatisfied Wives," *Fargo Forum* 53, Feb. 23, 1931, p10; Her Mother, "Just a Gigolo," *Fargo Forum* 53, Apr. 9, 1931, p13; R. E. C., "They Had Their Chance," *Fargo Forum* 54, June 29, 1932, p5. For cultural conservatives' views of working wives, see Lynd and Lynd, *Middletown,* 26–27; Wandersee, *Women's Work and Family Values;* and Dumenil, *The Modern Temper.*

46. One Who Is Not Narrow-Minded, "A Married Woman Answers," *Fargo Forum,* 53,

Apr. 2, 1931, p5; P. H. Redington, "How About the Scrub-Woman," *Fargo Forum* 53, May 19, 1931, p6; Mrs. M. C. Osman, "Jobs and Married Women," *Fargo Forum* 54, June 21, 1932, p5.

47. A Forum Follower, "Women Supplant Men," *Fargo Forum* 53, Feb. 13, 1931, p15; For More Justice, "There's a Remedy," *Fargo Forum* 53, Mar. 27, 1931, p9; A Reader, "A Single Girl Answers," *Fargo Forum* 53, Apr. 9, 1931, p13.

48. "Employment of Married Women in State Offices," Resolutions of the Twentieth Annual Convention of the North Dakota State Federation of Labor, North Dakota AFL-CIO Records, Collection 10038, box 1, folder 2, SHSND; Minutes of the Regular Meeting of the Board of City Commissioners of Fargo, Dec. 21, 1931, mss 42, box 15, N-332, NDIRS; Minutes of the Meeting of the Board of City Commissioners, Feb. 24, 1932, mss 42, box 15, N-351, NDIRS; Proceedings of the Board of County Commissioners of Cass County, North Dakota, June 9, 1932, p1680, Cass County Auditor's Office. For the national controversy regarding the employment of married women, see Chafe, *The American Woman;* Harris, *Beyond Her Sphere;* Scharf, *To Work and to Wed;* Wandersee, *Women's Work and Family Values;* Kessler-Harris, *Out to Work;* and Ware, *Holding Their Own.*

49. Moehling, "Women's Work and Men's Unemployment."

50. Among those who have discussed the motives of working women are Milkman, "Women's Work and Economic Crisis"; Bolin, "The Economics of Middle-Income Family Life"; Helmbold, "Downward Occupational Mobility"; Levine, "Workers' Wives"; and Cross, *An All-Consuming Century.*

51. Westberg interview. For the situation nationally, see National Industrial Conference Board, *Women Workers and Labor Supply,* and Shallcross, *Should Married Women Work?*

52. "Rather Broad," *Fargo Forum* 53, Mar. 14, 1931, p4.

53. "Armour to Ban Working Wives," *Fargo Forum* 55, Nov. 9, 1933, p1; A Subscriber, "The Survival of the Fittest," *Fargo Forum* 53, Mar. 2, 1931, p10; Westberg interview. For a look at the national situation, see Grattan, "Women of the Other Nation."

54. *Polk's Fargo and Moorhead City Directory* 1928: 318, 1932: 327; Police Arrest Records, City of Fargo, 1930–46, mss. 133, book 1, p113, NDIRS. For James Kennedy's contributions to Fargo's built environment, see Roberts, *Fargo's Heritage.*

55. Proceedings of the Board of County Commissioners of Cass County, North Dakota, Feb. 4, 1932, p1644, Cass County Auditor's Office.

56. Minutes of Meeting County Welfare Board, Apr. 18, 1934, County Welfare Board Verbatim Minutes, Apr. 1933–Dec. 1935, p9, Cass County Social Service; Minutes of Meeting of County Welfare Board, July 25, 1934, County Welfare Board Verbatim Minutes, Apr. 1933–Dec. 1935, p3, Cass County Social Service.

57. Minutes of Meeting County Welfare Board, Oct. 3, 1934, County Welfare Board Verbatim Minutes, Apr. 1933–Dec. 1935, p3–7, Cass County Social Service.

58. Nelson, "Depressing Years," 3–4.

59. North Dakota Woman's Diary, June 2, 1939, July 24, 1938, and Aug. 10, 1939, mss. 214, NDIRS. The Fort was a downtown hotel. Wolverton and Sabin are Minnesota towns near Fargo-Moorhead.

60. William C. Sherman, "The Dakota Environment," 4, in Sherman and Thorson, eds., *Plains Folk.*

61. "Alice Duffy Dies at Home," *Fargo Forum* 59, Mar. 15, 1937, p12. For the connections between social work and early policewomen, see Appier, *Policing Women.* For the relationship among women's economic independence, commercial leisure, and personal behavior, see Meyerowitz, *Women Adrift;* D'Emilio and Freedman, *Intimate Matters;* and Jensen, "Sexuality on a Northern Frontier," 136–37.

62. "Mother Taken from Home," *Fargo Forum* 53, Apr. 21, 1931, p10; "Woman Dies in Rooms of Federal Narcotics Agent Here After 'Party,'" *Fargo Forum* 55, Aug. 2, 1933, p1, 2; "Verdict of Jury," Dr. Carl E. Elofson Papers, mss 1165, box 2, folder 18, NDIRS.

63. Lynd and Lynd, *Middletown in Transition,* 280.

64. "What Would You Say About This?" *Fargo Forum* 52, Jan. 29, 1930, p5; "'Ladies that Smoke?—Ladies Don't!' Says Rev. Sains-

bury," *Fargo Forum* 52, Jan. 13, 1930, p1; Contributor J., "Those Smoking Girls," *Fargo Forum* 52, Feb. 4, 1930, p8.

65. Murdock, *Domesticating Drink;* "First Tasters Throng Gleeful Moorhead as Beer Flows Again," *Fargo Forum* 55, Apr. 8, 1933, p3; Local Survey, Fargo, North Dakota, March 1940, Women's Christian Temperance Union of Fargo-Moorhead Records, s 4860 4932, box 1, folder 5, p4, NMRHC. For female drinking practices in another small city, see Murphy, *Mining Cultures,* 62–64.

66. "City Scoured for Masked Killer Who Slew Collector, Menaced Fargo Girl," *Fargo Forum* 52, June 30, 1930, p1, 8; "Murder Searchers Turn to Earlier Fairground Robberies," *Fargo Forum* 52, July 2, 1930, p1; "Fargo Lovers' Lane Doomed by Uncle Sam," *Fargo (Sunday) Forum* 22, Aug. 10, 1930, p1; "Police Ban Night Parking Fearing Murder Repetition," *Fargo Forum* 56, July 17, 1934, p1, 8. For changing courtship practices nationally, see Bailey, *From Front Porch to Back Seat;* and Michael L. Berger, "The Car's Impact on the American Family," 57–74, in Wachs and Crawford, eds., *The Car and the City.*

67. "Exposure Is Death Cause," *Fargo (Sunday) Forum* 22, Nov. 14, 1929, p1; "Baby's Body Is Found in Fargo," *Fargo Forum* 58, May 9, 1936, p1; "Body of Murdered Baby Is Found at City Dump," *Fargo Forum* 59, Mar. 22, 1937, p1; Police Arrest Records, City of Fargo, 1930–46, mss. 133, book 1, p4, NDIRS.

68. "Dimmick Held on Charge of Performing Illegal Operation," *Fargo Forum* 61, Aug. 9, 1939, p1. The Elofson Papers at the NDIRS include a number of autopsies of aborted fetuses.

69. Personal Column, *Fargo Forum* 55, July 15, 1933, p7; North Dakota Woman's Diary, Mar. 16, 1937, mss. 214, NDIRS. For the state of birth control in the thirties, see Gordon, *Woman's Body, Woman's Right.*

70. "Marriages in Cass Drop and Divorces Gain in 20 Years," *Fargo (Sunday) Forum* 22, Jan. 5, 1930, p4; "Pick Homely Girl to Stay Out of Jail, Judge Advises Youthful Wife Seekers," *Fargo Forum* 53, Mar. 11, 1931, p1.

71. Banning, "Brought Up to Do Something"; "For the Business-Woman Housewife: Here Are Some Menus for Busy Days," *Fargo Forum* 59, Sept. 24, 1937, p10.

NOTES TO CHAPTER 7

1. "Fargo Expends $71,740 in '30 to Fight Crime, Law Body Says," *Fargo Forum* 53, Aug. 21, 1931, p1.

2. "The Leisure Problem," editorial, *Fargo Forum* 56, Mar. 21, 1934, p4.

3. "Neglected Homes Breed Crime, Burdick Tells Attorney," *Fargo Forum* 58, Aug. 10, 1936, p6.

4. "This Town We Live In," *Fargo (Sunday) Forum* 26, Dec. 31, 1933, p13; "Polly Hamilton's Family Is Back of Her to Last," *Fargo Forum* 56, July 25, 1934, p1, 9.

5. "Police Given Machine Gun," *Fargo Forum* 55, Sept. 7, 1933, p3; "Banks to Open Hour Later as Safety Move Against Holdups," *Fargo Forum* 56, Mar. 17, 1934, p1, 5.

6. "Fargo Crimes Above Average," *Fargo (Sunday) Forum* 29, Mar. 28, 1937, p13.

7. Police estimated that three-fourths of arrestees were transients. See "50,000 Lawbreakers Have Gone Through Fargo's Jail," *Fargo (Sunday) Forum* 32, Oct. 8, 1939, p15.

8. "Bind 7 Over to District Court," *Fargo Forum* 52, Sept. 15, 1930, p1; "Gambling Out, Says Bergesen," *Fargo (Sunday) Forum* 27, Feb. 4, 1935, p1. For the popularity of gambling nationwide, see Allen, *Since Yesterday,* 151.

9. Johnson and Kinsie, "Prostitution in the United States," 484, 473.

10. Meyerowitz, *Women Adrift;* Police Record, City of Fargo, 1930–46, mss. 133, book 1, p10, 39, 300, NDIRS.

11. "Hold Woman on Larceny Count," *Fargo Forum* 57, Dec. 15, 1934, p1; "Stepin Fetchit Fined, Given Suspended Sentence After One-Man Riot in Fargo," *Fargo Forum* 61, Apr. 25, 1939, p1.

12. "11 Negresses Forfeit Bond," *Fargo Forum* 51, July 24, 1935, p5; "Negroes Forfeit Bonds, Bringing $575 for Fargo," *Fargo Forum* 59, July 10, 1937, p8; "Wide Drive on Vice Rings Is Underway," *Fargo Forum* 59, July 20, 1937, p1; "Fargo Negro Woman Nabbed in White Slave Operations," *Fargo Forum* 59, Aug. 11, 1937, p1.

13. "Mayor Calls Mass Meeting in Fargo Vice Crusade," *Fargo Forum* 56, Jan. 24, 1934, p1; "6 Arrested in Hotel Raid as Fargo Vice War Continues," *Fargo Forum* 56, Jan. 23, 1934, p1; "Officers Strike Thrice, Jail 8 in Vice Crusade," *Fargo Forum* 56, Feb. 19, 1934, p1, 7;

Police Arrest Records, City of Fargo, 1930–46, mss. 133, book 1, p214–16, 259, NDIRS.

14. "Fargo Drunk Arrests Largest in 15 Years," *Fargo Forum* 54, Jan. 1, 1932, p3; "Arrest 2,403 Here in 1935," *Fargo Forum* 58, Jan. 1, 1936, p6; "500 Arrested Annually Here for Drinking," *Fargo (Sunday) Forum* 22, Oct. 27, 1929, p1; "Fargo Braces for Its Annual New Year's Jolt," *Fargo Forum* 54, Dec. 31, 1931, p1; interview with Ervin Morris, Jr., Fargo, ND, Mar. 13, 2000. For a perspective on the upsurge in drinking nationally, see Clark, "Beckerstown: 1932."

15. "Weekly Liquor Sales in Fargo Average 500 Gallons," *Fargo Forum* 24, Aug. 9, 1931, p9, 10; "Al Capone Booze Flows in Fargo Rum Channels," *Fargo (Sunday) Forum* 23, June 7, 1931, p1, 8; "El Patio Raid Nets Bottles," *Fargo Forum* 54, July 5, 1932, p8; "'Red Rooster' Inn Is Raided," *Fargo Forum* 54, Aug. 8, 1932, p1; "2 Little Italy 'Clubs' Closed," *Fargo Forum* 55, Mar. 13, 1933, p1. My discussion of sources of alcohol is also informed by several interviews with sources I have decided not to reveal.

16. "Competition Brings Forth Half Gallon Tins," *Fargo (Sunday) Forum* 24, Feb. 14, 1932, p13; "Alcohol, Beer Seized in Raid on Home Here," *Fargo Forum* 54, Aug. 20, 1932, p1; "Fargo Woman Arrested on Transporting Charge," *Fargo Forum* 55, Nov. 22, 1932, p7. For the Depression and bootlegging, see Murphy, *Mining Cultures,* 60–62, and Childs, "Main Street Ten Years After."

17. "This Town We Live In," *Fargo (Sunday) Forum* 25, Jan. 9, 1933, p8; "Lad, 16, Held for Selling Liquor to Fargo Minors," *Fargo Forum* 52, Feb. 25, 1930, p1.

18. "Fargoan Pays $2,500 Kidnap Ransom," *Fargo Forum* 54, Aug. 30, 1932, p1; "O'Loughlin at Death's Door as Assailant Eludes Hunt," *Fargo Forum* 55, Feb. 3, 1933, p1, 3.

19. "2,350 Gallons of Alcohol, 2 Trucks Taken," *Fargo Forum* 55, Mar. 14, 1933, p1; "Police Seize Huge Rum Cache," *Fargo Forum* 52, Apr. 3, 1930, p1, 6; "Commission Clears Madison," *Fargo Forum* 52, Apr. 7, 1930, p1, 10; "Seek Three More in Rum Probe," *Fargo (Sunday) Forum* 22, Apr. 12, 1930, p1; "Madison Resigns as Fargo Police Chief," *Fargo Forum* 52, May 16, 1930, p1; "Madison Faces

U.S. Rum Count," *Fargo Forum* 52, Sept. 13, 1930, p1; "Disagree on Madison Verdict," *Fargo Forum* 52, Sept. 20, 1930, p1, 7; "Dillage, Madison Free; Jennings Is Guilty," *Fargo Forum* 54, Dec. 16, 1931, p1, 12.

20. "Condition of Front St. Hit," *Fargo (Sunday) Forum* 21, July 31, 1929, p1; "Policewoman's Ouster Asked," *Fargo Forum* 60, July 6, 1938, p1.

21. In 1931 a University of North Dakota study cited political appointments of police and the absence of a pension plan as "impediments to effectively handling crime," but the City Commission did not change the system. See "Report Details Cost of Curbing Crime Here," *Fargo (Sunday) Forum* 24, Sept. 10, 1931, p9, 10.

22. "Fargo Voters More than 76 Per Cent Wet," *Fargo Forum* 54, Apr. 29, 1932, p9; S. B., "Music of the 'Tin,'" *Fargo Forum* 55, Apr. 4, 1933, p5; J. Noren, "Why Perpetuate It?" *Fargo Forum* 55, Apr. 14, 1933, p4.

23. "America Festive as New Beer Flows," *Fargo Forum* 55, Apr. 7, 1933, p1, 6; "Moorhead Beer Sales System Satisfactory, Say Officials," *Fargo Forum* 55, Apr. 10, 1933, p1; "100,000 Gallons of Beer Disposed of in Moorhead," *Fargo (Sunday) Forum* 25, Apr. 30, 1933, p5.

24. "'It Aint [*sic*] Bad,' Is Verdict of 'Leggers on 3.2 Brew," *Fargo Forum* 55, Apr. 10, 1933, p1; "Liquor Truck Is Seized Here," *Fargo Forum* 55, Apr. 21, 1933, p10; "U.S. Agents in Fargo Launch Drive Against Beer Truckers," *Fargo (Sunday) Forum* 25, Apr. 23, 1933, p1; "Law Will Act in Beer Cases If Complaints Are Received," *Fargo Forum* 55, June 9, 1933, p1.

25. "Beer Ordinance on First Reading in Commission," *Fargo Forum* 55, Oct. 2, 1933, p5; "43 Get Fargo Beer Permits," *Fargo Forum* 56, Dec. 5, 1933, p5.

26. "Cafes Warned by Bergeson," *Fargo Forum* 56, Jan. 15, 1934, p1; "Parley Agrees on 24-Hour Beer Sale," *Fargo Forum* 56, Jan. 26, 1934, p1, 2; "Body Blow Is Dealt Spiking," *Fargo Forum* 56, Feb. 23, 1934, p1; "Board Passes Ordinance to Prohibit Beer in Dance Halls," *Fargo Forum* 56, July 9, 1934, p1.

27. "U.S. Cracks Down on N.D. Liquor Sales," *Fargo Forum* 58, Sept. 2, 1936, p1.

28. "Propose Limit of 25 Liquor Vendors," *Fargo Forum* 58, Nov. 14, 1936, p1; "City Draws Stringent Liquor Rules," *Fargo Forum* 58, Nov. 16, 1936, p1.

29. Minutes of the Regular Meeting of the Board of Commissioners of the City of Fargo, Oct. 25, 1937, p676, City Auditor's Office; "Sunday Beer Banned Here," *Fargo Forum* 60, Apr. 12, 1938, p1, 6.

30. Roosevelt, *It's Up to the Women*, 122; Schuler, "A Challenge for Tomorrow"; "Fargo Leaders Survey Year, Find Community Character Strengthened by Time of Trials," *Fargo (Sunday) Forum* 25, Jan. 1, 1933, p1.

31. Allen, "Until Tomorrow," 61; Wald, "The Lean Years," 652. Some of the many studies of families during the Depression by social scientists are Angell, *The Family Encounters the Depression;* Bakke, *Citizens Without Work;* Cavan and Ranck, *The Family and the Depression;* Komarovsky, *The Unemployed Man and His Family;* and Nesbith, "Present Relief Policies."

32. Gjervold interview; interview with Dorothy Berglund, Fargo, ND, May 21, 1999; Beaton 1999 interview; Graber interview; Christianson e-mail; Olson interview; Litten interview; interview with Robert R. Pettit, Fargo, ND, July 28, 1998; Gallagher interview; "Truants Haunt Any Place to Earn Nickels," *Fargo (Sunday) Forum* 13, May 10, 1931, p9.

33. "Many Famous Men Began Their Careers as Newsies," *Fargo (Sunday) Forum* 22, July 20, 1930, p9, 10; Minutes of the Regular Meeting of the Board of Commissioners, Nov. 19, 1934, mss. 42, box 15, p792, NDIRS. Griswold emphasizes the difficulty confronting fathers trying to control employed children, particularly when they were unemployed themselves, in *Fatherhood in America*, 150. For the national controversy over newspaper sales, which employed more children than any other enterprise at the beginning of the Depression, see Postol, "Masculine Guidance," and Baldwin, "'Nocturnal Habits and Dark Wisdom.'"

34. "Costs Keeping Students Home," *Fargo Forum* 53, Sept. 29, 1931, p5; "Students Hit by Depression," *Fargo Forum* 54, May 11, 1932, p6; L. J. Peart, "Students and Workers," *Fargo Forum* 55, Sept. 20, 1933, p5. For increases in school attendance nationally during the Depression, see Tyack, Lowe, and Hansot, *Public Schools in Hard Times.*

35. Lynd and Lynd, *Middletown in Tran-*

sition, 49; Leighton and Hellman, "Half Slave, Half Free"; "200,000 Wandering Boys"; Marcosson, "Our Muddled Youth"; Davis, *The Lost Generation.* For a more recent examination of the effect of the Depression on children and young people, see Elder, *Children of the Great Depression.*

36. Interview with Steve Gorman, Fargo, ND, June 10, 1997; Gunkleman interview; interview with John Q. Paulsen, Fargo, ND, June 7, 2000; interview with Robert Mason, Fargo, ND, Oct. 14, 1997; Pastoret interview; Hauser interview; interview with Robert Litherland, Moorhead, MN, Nov. 13, 1997. The relationship between memory and reality is a complicated one, which I explore in my North Dakota Humanities Committee presentation, "The Past Isn't What We Used to Be."

37. "Youth Tells Police Milk Bottles Stolen in Order to Make Living," *Fargo Forum* 54, Feb. 4, 1932, p1; "Personal," *Fargo Forum* 57, Aug. 29, 1935, p17; Welfare Board Meeting, Sept. 25, 1935, County Welfare Board Verbatim Minutes, Apr. 1933–Dec. 1935, p11–12, 16, Cass County Social Service; D.R.A., "Parking Place?" *Fargo Forum* 55, Apr. 8, 1933, p2; interview kept confidential at the author's discretion. For the problem of child neglect nationally, see Ashby, *Endangered Children.*

38. "Rites for Boy on Wednesday," *Fargo Forum* 58, May 4, 1936, p1; "Officials Hold Driver Blameless in Death of Fargo Child, 4, under Truck," *Fargo Forum* 58, June 4, 1936, p1, 6; "Dickie Warner, Thrown from Bicycle, Is Dead of Injuries," *Fargo Forum* 58, June 17, 1936, p1; Charles A. Dawson, "Keep Children Off Streets—Avoid Death," *Fargo Forum* 58, June 6, 1936, p5.

39. "Fargo Wild Animal Life Falling Before Air Rifles," *Fargo Forum* 52, July 25, 1930, p1; "Slingshot Shooters Damage Plate Glass in Business Houses," *Fargo Forum* 53, Oct. 30, 1931, p5; "Fargo Stores Resent Raids," *Fargo Forum* 53, Oct. 28, 1931, p7; "Boy, 15, Held as Drunk Driver," *Fargo Forum* 57, Oct. 28, 1935, p1; "Thoreson Gets 2-Year Term," *Fargo Forum* 53, Apr. 14, 1931, p12. For the seasonality of juvenile crime, see "School Stems Delinquency," *Fargo (Sunday) Forum* 21, Sept. 20, 1929, p10.

40. "Youths Admit 5 Auto Thefts," *Fargo Forum* 54, Nov. 30, 1931, p1; "Pair Sent to State School," *Fargo Forum* 52, July 24, 1930,

p14; "Three Boys Confess Boxcar Pilfering," *Fargo Forum* 52, July 25, 1930, p1; "Boys Held for Burglary Here," *Fargo Forum* 55, July 10, 1933, p6; "Fargo Youth, 14, Defies Police, Whistles in Cell," *Fargo Forum* 52, Mar. 14, 1930, p1; "Young Bandits Hold Up Grocer," *Fargo Forum* 54, Feb. 26, 1932, p7; "4 Boys Jailed as Theft Gang," *Fargo Forum* 54, Mar. 28, 1932, p1; "Crime Career of Boys Ends," *Fargo Forum* 54, Aug. 16, 1932, p1; "Juvenile Crime Problem in City Grave, Holt Says," *Fargo Forum* 55, May 25, 1932, p1.

41. "Juvenile Crime Problem in City Grave, Holt Says," *Fargo Forum* 55, May 25, 1932, p1; "Modern Home Is Condemned," *Fargo (Sunday) Forum* 21, Sept. 12, 1929, p4; "'Gallivantin' Around Must Stop Says Chief," *Fargo (Sunday) Forum* 21, July 27, 1929, p2; "Children Lack Home Training," *Fargo Forum* 55, June 12, 1933, p3; "Parents Make Boy Criminals," *Fargo Forum* 55, Sept. 26, 1933, p7.

42. "Miss Duffy Is Club Speaker," *Fargo Forum* 54, Mar. 1, 1932, p3; "Luther League Holds Movies Destructive of Morality," *Fargo (Sunday) Forum* 22, June 22, 1930, p1; Mabel E. Bergstrom, "Another Objection," *Fargo Forum* 52, Feb. 14, 1930, p7; "Kids Awed by Tom Mix Here," *Fargo Forum* 55, Sept. 5, 1933, p8; "Fargo P.T.A. Units Map Policy, Elect Officers," *Fargo Forum* 55, Apr. 13, 1933, p1, 7; "Authorities Declare War on 'Indecent' Magazines," *Fargo Forum* 55, Mar. 20, 1933, p1.

43. "Halloween Is 'Destructive,'" *Fargo Forum* 54, Nov. 1, 1932, p1; "'Pranks' Jail Six Fargo Youths," *Fargo Forum* 55, Nov. 1, 1933, p1, 10; "Lose Some Property?" *Fargo Forum* 55, Nov. 2, 1933, p1.

44. "Boys to Face Judge Today," *Fargo Forum* 55, Nov. 2, 1933, p1, 10.

45. Minutes of the Regular Meeting of the Board of City Commissioners, Nov. 26, 1934, mss. 42, box 15, N-798, NDIRS; "Work of Fargo Woman Praised," *Fargo Forum* 57, Oct. 15, 1935, p8; Fraser interview; "Elders Blamed for Boy Crimes," *Fargo Forum* 54, Apr. 1, 1932, p1. For Duffy's career, see "Alice Duffy Dies at Home," *Fargo Forum* 59, Mar. 15, 1937, p12. For the juvenile justice system and its social work roots, see Platt, *The Child Savers.* For informality in the policing of juvenile offenders nationally, see Wolcott, "'The Cop Will Get You.'"

46. "Junior C. of C. Program Gives City Most Quiet Night in Years," *Fargo Forum* 56, Nov. 1, 1934, p1; Minutes of the Regular Meeting of the Board of Commissioners of the City of Fargo, Nov. 2, 1936, p419–20, City Auditor's Office; "Police Chief Praises JCC's Taming of Halloween Spirit," *Fargo Forum* 60, Nov. 1, 1938, p1; "Police Woman Lauds Cleanup," *Fargo Forum* 58, May 9, 1936, p1, 5.

47. "Council of Welfare Agencies Meeting Held Wednesday, May 16th, 1934," United Way Collection, NDIRS; "Youth Welfare Unit Approved," *Fargo Forum* 56, June 7, 1934, p3; "Could You List All of the Things that the Welfare Agencies in Fargo Do to Make This a Better City in Which to Live," 1937 Scrapbook, United Way Collection, NDIRS.

48. Minutes of the Board of Education—Fargo, North Dakota, Nov. 6, 1933, p88, Fargo Public Schools; "Map Plans for Jobless Girls," *Fargo Forum* 56, Nov. 17, 1933, p6; "Survey Begins on 'Free Time,'" *Fargo Forum* 56, Mar. 1, 1934, p1, 8.

49. Minutes of the Regular Meeting of the Board of Commissioners of the City of Fargo, May 2, 1938, p772, City Auditor's Office; "Putter Shops' Name Changed," *Fargo Forum* 59, Feb. 6, 1937, p5; "7 Win Awards on Bird Houses," *Fargo Forum* 59, Apr. 21, 1937, p1; "Fun? It's in Your Yard," *Fargo (Sunday) Forum* 29, May 16, 1937, p1; "Doll Buggies Parade Friday," *Fargo Forum* 58, July 1, 1936, p5; "Young Fargo Feasts," *Fargo Forum* 58, July 18, 1936, p5; "Sun Tan, Lotta Freckles Needed to Enter Contest," *Fargo Forum* 58, July 27, 1936, p1; "Bernice Myhra Proclaimed Queen of the Playgrounds," *Fargo Forum* 58, Aug. 29, 1936, p5.

50. "Youth Recreation Survey Procedure," United Way Collection, NDIRS; "More Play Places Needed," editorial, *Fargo Forum* 56, May 14, 1934, p4; Minutes of the Meeting of the Park Board, July 5, 1938, Proceedings of the Board of Park Commissioners, book 6, p4, Fargo Park District; Minutes of the Regular Meeting of the Board of Commissioners of the City of Fargo, July 11, 1938, p827, City Auditor's Office; "City Playground Asked in War Against Juvenile Delinquency," *Fargo (Sunday) Forum* 31, July 10, 1938, p5.

51. "Delinquency Causes Cited," *Fargo Forum* 60, Aug. 16, 1938, p2.

52. "Winter Sports Drive Revived," *Fargo Forum* 59, June 9, 1937, p3; "WPA Okays Winter Sports Building for Fargo," *Fargo Forum* 59, Oct. 21, 1937, p1, 7; Minutes of the Meeting of the Park Board, Nov. 9, 1937, Proceedings of the Board of Park Commissioners, book 5, p250–53, Fargo Park District.

53. Paulsen interview; Mason interview; "This Town We Live In," *Fargo (Sunday) Forum* 24, June 12, 1932, p9; Minutes of the Meeting of the Board of Park Commissioners, July 27, 1933, Proceedings of the Board of Park Commissioners, book 4, p150, Fargo Park District.

54. "Planning Body Indorses Swimming Pool Project," *Fargo Forum* 59, Mar. 5, 1937, p5; "Schools Begin Pool Campaign," *Fargo Forum* 59, Mar. 15, 1937, p1; Minutes of the Meeting of the Board of Park Commissioners, Mar. 9, 1937, Proceedings of the Board of Park Commissioners, book 5, p191–92, Fargo Park District; "New Pool Site in Island Park," *Fargo Forum* 60, Feb. 22, 1938, p1; Proceedings of the Board of County Commissioners of Cass County, North Dakota, Apr. 19, 1939, p2423, County Auditor's Office; "G. W. Plath Heads Junior Chamber, Smith Honored," *Fargo Forum* 61, May 10, 1939, p5; Minutes of the Adjourned Regular Meeting of the Board of Commissioners of the City of Fargo, May 26, 1939, City Auditor's Office.

55. "Curfew to Be Enforced Here," *Fargo Forum* 61, Nov. 13, 1939, p1; Minutes—Board of Education, June 9, 1937, p179, Fargo Public Schools; Minutes of the Regular Meeting of the Scandinavian W.C.T.U., Apr. 27, 1937, W.C.T.U. Fargo-Moorhead Records, 5 4860 4932, box 1, NMRHC.

56. Charles Dawson to R. L. Sheetz, Sept. 23, 1938, and Minutes of Meetings of Budget Committee, 1936–38, both United Way Collection, NDIRS.

NOTES TO CONCLUSION

1. "Report on the Development of a Six-Year Program for Municipal Improvements 1939–1940 Through 1944–1945," Dec. 8, 1939, p4, City of Fargo, North Dakota.

2. "Fargo Begins Drive on Smoke," *Fargo Forum* 61, Oct. 9, 1939, p1; "Fargo to War on Rats," *Fargo Forum* 61, Oct. 18, 1939, p1. For the smoke abatement campaign nationally, see Stradling, *Smokestacks and Progressives*.

3. U.S. Department of Commerce, Bu-

reau of the Census, *Sixteenth Census: 1940,* Vol. 2.5, 534–36; "Fargo-Moorhead Snapping Out of Home-Building Lull," *Fargo (Sunday) Forum* 32, Dec. 31, 1939, p4; "Fargo's Bank Debits Hit 8-year High," *Fargo (Sunday) Forum* 32, Dec. 31, 1939, p1; "More Encouraging News," *Fargo (Sunday) Forum* 32, Jan. 7, 1940, p18.

4. "Public Welfare Bulletin" 4 (Dec. 1939): 3–4, Public Welfare Board of North Dakota; "Unexpected Requests for Yale Bas-

kets Swamp Workers; 800 Dinners Distributed," *Fargo Forum* 62, Dec. 23, 1939, p1; U.S. Department of Commerce, Bureau of the Census, *Sixteenth Census: 1940,* Vol. 2.5, 536; "Relief Chiselers Go to Prison, Englert Flays Misuse of Aid," *Fargo Forum* 62, Dec. 13, 1939, p1.

5. "More Encouraging News," *Fargo (Sunday) Forum* 32, Jan. 7, 1940, p18.

6. "The New Swimmin' Hole," *Fargo (Sunday) Forum* 33, Aug. 18, 1940, p20.

BIBLIOGRAPHY

ABBREVIATIONS

NARS   National Archives and Records Service, College Park, Maryland

NDIRS   North Dakota Institute for Regional Studies, North Dakota State University, Fargo

NMRHC   Northwest Minnesota Regional Historical Center, Minnesota State University, Moorhead

SHSND   State Historical Society of North Dakota, Bismarck

UND   Elwyn D. Robinson Department of Special Collections, Chester Fritz Library, University of North Dakota, Grand Forks

PRIMARY SOURCES
MANUSCRIPT COLLECTIONS

Anders, Frank. Collection. UND.

Catholic Family Services. Meeting minutes and annual reports. Fargo, North Dakota.

Child Welfare. Collection. UND.

Dakota Chapter of Pi Gamma Mu. "Economic and Social Development of Fargo, North Dakota." NDIRS.

Elofson, Carl E. Papers. NDIRS.

Fairmont Foods. Papers. NMRHC.

Fargo Chamber of Commerce. Annual reports. SHSND.

Herbst Company. "Herbstory" newsletters. NDIRS.

Hildreth, Melvin A. Papers. NDIRS.

Interviews. NMRHC.

Lashkowitz, Harry. Papers. NDIRS.

Lutheran Social Service. "Lutheran Welfare Messenger," meeting minutes, and reports. Fargo, North Dakota.

Meritcare Medical Records. Meeting minutes. NMRHC.

Murrey, William M. Papers. NDIRS.

Nelson, Eva. Memoirs. NDIRS.

New Deal Clergy Letters. Collection. UND.

North Dakota AFL-CIO. Records. SHSND.

North Dakota Business and Professional Women's Federation. Publications. SHSND.

North Dakota Depression Interviews. Collection. UND.

North Dakota Woman's Diary. NDIRS.

Round Table. Records. NMRHC.

United Way of Cass-Clay. Letters, minutes, publications, and reports. NDIRS.

Village Family Service Center. Letters, reminiscences, and reports. Fargo, North Dakota.

W.C.T.U. Fargo-Moorhead Records. Minutes and reports. NMRHC.

GOVERNMENT DOCUMENTS, PUBLICATIONS, AND RECORDS

Cass County Board of Commissioners Meeting Minutes. Cass County Auditor's Office.

Cass County Social Services. Vouchers and miscellaneous documents.

Cass County Welfare Board Minutes. Cass County Social Services.

Fargo Board of Education Minutes. NDIRS.

Fargo City Commission Minutes. NDIRS and City Auditor's Office.

Fargo Park Board. Minutes, correspondence, and miscellaneous documents.

Fargo Police Arrest Records. NDIRS.

Federal Emergency Relief Administration Records. NARS.

Historical Statistics of the United States: Colonial Times to 1970. Washington, DC: U.S. Bureau of the Census, 1975.

North Dakota Public Welfare Board. Annual reports and monthly newsletter.

Pidgeon, Mary Elizabeth. *Women in the Economy of the United States of America: A Summary Report*. Bulletin of the Women's Bureau, No. 155. Washington, DC: GPO, 1937.

"Report on the Development of a Six-Year Program for Municipal Improvements 1939–1940 Through 1940–1945." Fargo, ND: The City, 1939. NDIRS.

U.S. Department of Commerce. Bureau of the

Census. *Fifteenth Census of the United States: 1930.* Vol. 3.2, Population, Vol. 6, Families. Washington, DC: GPO, 1932, 1933.

———. ———. *Fifteenth Census of the United States: 1930 Distribution.* Vol. 1.3, Retail Distribution, Vol. 2, Wholesale Distribution. Washington, DC: GPO, 1932.

———. ———. *Fifteenth Census of the United States: 1929 Manufactures.* Vol. 1, General Report: Statistics by Subjects. Washington, DC: GPO, 1933.

———. ———. *Fourteenth Census of the United States: Taken in the Year 1920.* Vol. 1, Population. Washington, DC: GPO, 1921.

———. ———. *Sixteenth Census of the United States: 1940.* Vol. 2.5, Population. Washington, DC: GPO, 1943.

Webb, John N. *The Transient Unemployed: A Description and Analysis of the Transient Relief Population.* Washington, DC: Works Progress Administration, 1935.

Workmen's Compensation Bureau. "Seventh Biennial Report of the Minimum Wage Department to the Governor of North Dakota for the Biennium Ending June 30, 1932." Bismarck: State of North Dakota, 1932. SHSND.

Works Progress Administration Records. NARS.

NEWSPAPERS
Fargo Forum
Moorhead Daily News

PUBLISHED MATERIAL

Abbott, Edith. "The Crisis in Relief." *The Nation* 137 (Oct. 11, 1933): 400–402.

Adams, James Truslow. "Responsibility under Relief." *Woman's Home Companion* 62 (Oct. 1935): 17–18.

Allen, Frederick Lewis. *Since Yesterday: The Nineteen-Thirties in America, September 3, 1929–September 3, 1939.* New York: Harper and Brothers, 1939.

———. "Until Tomorrow." *Ladies' Home Journal* 49 (Nov. 1932): 8–9, 61, 63–64.

Almond, Gabriel, and Harold D. Lasswell. "Aggressive Behavior by Clients Toward Public Relief Administrators: A Configurative Analysis." *American Political Science Review* 28 (Aug. 1934): 643–55.

Amidon, Beulah. "Always with Us." *Survey Graphic* 25 (Feb. 1936): 107–10, 125–26.

Anderson, Douglas McClure. "Who Gets Relief?" *Atlantic Monthly* 155 (Jan. 1935): 48–55.

Anderson, Nels. "Are the Unemployed a Caste?" *Survey Graphic* 24 (July 1935): 345–47, 365, 367.

Angell, Robert Cooley. *The Family Encounters the Depression.* New York: Charles Scribner's Sons, 1936.

"The Anticipated Dollar." *Fortune* 7 (Jan. 1933): 68–69.

Baker, Newton D. "Can Uncle Sam Do Our Good Neighboring?" *Saturday Evening Post* 207 (Oct. 13, 1934): 23, 74, 77–78, 80.

Bakke, E. Wight. *Citizens Without Work: A Study of the Effects of Unemployment upon the Workers' Social Relations and Practices.* New Haven, CT: Yale University Press, 1940.

"Balleyhoo Housing." *Ladies' Home Journal* 51 (Dec. 1934): 26.

Banning, Margaret Culkin. "Brought Up to Do Something." *Ladies' Home Journal* 52 (Nov. 1935): 18.

———. "You Might as Well Spend It." *Ladies' Home Journal* 52 (Apr. 1935): 24, 117.

Barnes, Julius H. "Business Looks at Unemployment." *Atlantic Monthly* 148 (Aug. 1931): 238–48.

Barton, Bruce. "Out of a Job: What Would You Do?" *American Magazine* 114 (Oct. 1932): 124.

Bauer, W. W. "The Death-Rate in the Depression." *American Mercury* 29 (May 1933): 19–25.

Bernheim, Alfred L. "Are Wages Going Down?" *The Nation* 131 (Nov. 5, 1930): 489–91.

Bigelow, Howard F. "Your Spending Plans for 1931." *Ladies' Home Journal* 48 (Jan. 1931): 65.

Bliven, Bruce. "No Money, No Work." *The New Republic* 65 (Nov. 19, 1930): 12–14.

Block, Edward A. "We Can't Escape the Dole: Why Not Face It Squarely." *The Forum* 87 (Mar. 1932): 130–35.

Brandeis, Elizabeth. *History of Labor in the United States, 1896–1932.* Vol. III, *Labor Legislation.* New York: Augustus Kelley, 1966.

Bromley, Dorothy Dunbar. "Birth Control and the Depression." *Harpers Magazine* 169 (Oct. 1934): 563–74.

Brophy, Loire. *Men Must Work.* New York: D. Appleton–Century Company, 1938.

Brown, Josephine Chapin. *Public Relief, 1929–1939.* New York: Octagon Books, 1971.

Burns, Eveline M. "An Appraisal of Services for the Unemployed." *Annals of the American Academy of Political Social Sciences* 202 (Mar. 1939): 42–52.

Burrows, Edward M. "The Coming Tax Rebellion." *The New Outlook* 161 (Apr. 1933): 40–43.

Cabot, Phillip. "A Challenge." *Atlantic Monthly* 151 (May 1933): 528–38.

Carlson, Avis D. "Deflating the Schools." *Harpers Magazine* 167 (Nov. 1933): 705–14.

Case Number 29813. "Five Weeks in a Transient Camp." *The Commonweal* 22 (Oct. 18, 1935): 599–601.

Cavan, Ruth Shoule, and Katherine Howland Ranck. *The Family and the Depression: A Study of One Hundred Chicago Families.* New York: Arno Press, 1971.

Chase, Stuart. "Laid Off at Forty." *Harpers Magazine* 159 (Aug. 1929): 340–47.

———. "The Nemesis of American Business." *Harpers Magazine* 162 (July 1930): 129–38.

"Children of Depression." *The New Republic* 73 (Dec. 21, 1932): 149.

Childs, Marquis. "Main Street Ten Years After." *The New Republic* 73 (Jan. 18, 1933): 263–65.

Clark, George R. "Beckerstown: 1932. An American Town Faces the Depression." *Harpers Magazine* 165 (Oct. 1932): 580–91.

Clark, Neil M. "What You and I Can Do to Speed Up Business." *American Magazine* 112 (Sept. 1931): 15–17, 81–82.

Colcord, Joanna C. *Emergency Work Relief: As Carried Out in Twenty-Six American Communities, 1930–1931, with Suggestions for Setting Up a Program.* New York: Russell Sage Foundation, 1932.

"Cooperative Self-Help Activities Among the Unemployed—General Summary." *Monthly Labor Review* 36 (Mar.–June 1933): 1229–40.

Cordell, William H., and Kathryn Coe Cordell. "Unions Among the Unemployed." *North American Review* 240 (Dec. 1935): 498–510.

Coyle, David Cushman. "Public Works: A New Industry." *Atlantic Monthly* 152 (Dec. 1933): 756–63.

"Cross-Sectioning Another Market." *Business Week* (Aug. 24, 1935): 22.

Crowther, Samuel. "Cash and Carry: A Survey of Our Five Billion Dollar Chain-Store Industry." *World's Work* 59 (July 1930): 42–46.

———. "Our Extravagant Counties." *Ladies' Home Journal* 49 (Mar. 1932): 8–9, 54.

———. "What *You* Can Do to Help Restore Normal Living and Buying—in Other Words, Prosperity." *Ladies' Home Journal* 49 (Mar. 1932): 3, 120–21.

———. "Why Traitor Dollars Prolong the Depression." *Ladies' Home Journal* 49 (Feb. 1932): 21, 114, 116.

Dale, Alfred S. "Dakota Shifts the Farmer's Burden." *New Republic* 76 (Aug. 16, 1933): 16–17.

Davis, Elmer. "Can Business Manage Itself?" *Harpers Magazine* 162 (Mar. 1931): 385–96.

———. "Happy Days Will Come Again: A Prospectus for the Next Boom." *Harpers Magazine* 163 (Oct. 1931): 513–22.

Davis, Maxine. *The Lost Generation: A Portrait of American Youth Today.* New York: Macmillan, 1936.

———. "200,000 Vagabond Children." *Ladies' Home Journal* 49 (Sept. 1932): 8–9, 46, 48, 50.

"Does the World Owe Me a Living?" *Scribner's Magazine* 95 (June 1934): 425–28.

Douglas, Lewis W. "There Is One Way Out." *Atlantic Monthly* 156 (Sept. 1935): 267–72.

Duffus, R. L. "Relief by Guess." *New Republic* 68 (Oct. 7, 1931): 196–99.

"Editorial Paragraph." *The Nation* 133 (Oct. 14, 1931): 375–76.

Epstein, Abraham. "Do the Rich Give to Charity?" *American Mercury* 23 (May 1931): 22–30.

———. "Faith Cures for Unemployment." *American Mercury* 22 (Jan. 1931): 94–103.

———. *Insecurity: A Challenge to America: A Study of Social Insurance in the United States and Abroad.* New York: Azathon Press, 1968.

Ernst, Edward G., and Emil M. Hartl. "Chains versus Independents. IV. The Fighting Independents." *The Nation* 131 (Dec. 3, 1930): 606–8.

"Exploiting the Unemployed." *The New Republic* 62 (Mar. 12, 1930): 85–87

Ferguson, Charles W. "Charity by Hullabaloo: The Pathology of the 'Nation-Wide Drive.'" *Harper's Monthly Magazine* 164 (May 1932): 739–45.

Flynn, John T. "Mobilizing Deflation." *The Forum* 83 (Feb. 1930): 65–69.

———. "Starvation Wages: The Plight of the Employed." *The Forum* 89 (June 1933): 327–31.

Foster, William Trufant. "Better than the Bonus: Why Not Self-Liquidating Relief?" *The Forum* 88 (Aug. 1932): 88–92.

Foster, William Trufant, and Waddill Catchings. "In the Day of Adversity." *Atlantic Monthly* 148 (July 1932): 101–6.

———. "Must We Reduce Our Standard of Living?" *The Forum* 85 (Feb. 1931): 74–79.

Fowler, Cedric. "The Youth Ticket." *The New Outlook* 165 (Jan. 1935): 39–42.

Friday, David. "1933: The Government's Key to Economic Recovery." *Atlantic Monthly* 151 (Jan. 1933): 108–13.

Gilboy, Elizabeth W. *Applicants for Work Relief: A Study of Massachusetts Families under the FERA and WPA.* Cambridge, MA: Harvard University Press, 1940.

Gill, Corrington. "A Study of Three Million Families on Relief in October 1933." *Annals of the American Academy of Political and Social Science* 176 (Nov. 1934): 25–36.

Grattan, C. Hartley. "The Road to Destitution: Why Twenty Million Need Relief." *Harpers Magazine* 171 (June 1935): 80–91.

———. "Who Gets Supplementary Relief?" *The Nation* 141 (July 31, 1935): 125–26.

———. "Who Is on Relief?" *Scribner's Magazine* 97 (June 1935): 24–30.

———. "Women of the Other Nation." *New Outlook* 165 (Feb. 1935): 17–21.

Hackett, Catherine. "Why We Women Won't Buy." *The Forum* 88 (Dec. 1932): 343–48.

Hallgren, Mauritz A. "Billions for Relief." *The Nation* 135 (Nov. 30, 1932): 521–22.

———. "Easy Times in Middletown." *The Nation* 132 (May 6, 1931): 497–99.

———. "Help Wanted—For Chicago." *The Nation* 134 (Mar. 11, 1932): 534–36.

———. "Mass Misery in Philadelphia." *The Nation* 134 (Mar. 9, 1932): 275–77.

Harrison, Leonard V., and Elizabeth Laine. *After Repeal: A Study of Liquor Control Administration.* New York: Harper and Brothers, 1936.

Harrows, Edward M. "The Coming Tax Rebellion." *The New Outlook* 161 (Apr. 1933): 40–43.

"Harvest: Jobless Would Rather Reap Relief

Doles than Wheat." *Newsweek* 6 (July 27, 1935): 9.

Hazlitt, Henry. "The Fallacies of the N.R.A." *American Mercury* 30 (Dec. 1933): 415–23.

———. "These Economic Experiments." *American Mercury* 31 (Feb. 1934): 138–48.

Heffernan, Joseph L. "The Hungry City." *The Atlantic Monthly* 149 (May 1932): 538–46.

Heisler, Francis. "The Fargo Cases." *The Nation* 141 (Aug. 7, 1935): 157.

Heywood, Johnson. "Taking the Starch Out of White-Collar Workers." *World's Work* 60 (Sept. 1931): 58–59, 74.

Holden, Arthur C. "The Crisis in Real Estate." *Harper's Magazine* 163 (Nov. 1931): 671–79.

———. "Federal Aid for the Householder." *The Forum* 92 (Oct. 1934): 244–46.

Holt, Byron W. "Should Wages Be Cut? Yes!" *The Forum* 86 (Sept. 1931): 182–83.

"Homeless in Winter." *The Survey* 72 (Oct. 1936): 302.

"Hungry Children." *Ladies' Home Journal* 51 (June 1934): 30.

Hutchins, Grace. *Women Who Work.* New York: International Pamphlets, 1932.

"It's Up to the Women." *Ladies' Home Journal* 49 (Jan. 1932): 3.

"It's Up to the Women: Leaders of Millions of Women Support the Seven-Point Plan for Normal Living." *Ladies' Home Journal* 49 (Feb. 1932): 6–7, 52.

"It's Up to the Women: The Movement Started by the Journal Is Sweeping the Country." *Ladies' Home Journal* 49 (Apr. 1932): 12.

"It's Up to the Women: Rochester Plan and Other Concrete Suggestions to Help Improve Business." *Ladies' Home Journal* 49 (Mar. 1932): 13, 141–42.

Johnson, Bascom, and Paul M. Kinsie. "Prostitution in the United States." *Journal of Social Hygiene* 19 (Dec. 1933): 467–91.

Kazarian, John. "The Starvation Army." *The Nation* 136 (Apr. 12, 1933): 396–98.

Kelley, Hubert. "Good Men Plowed Under." *American Magazine* 120 (Nov. 1935): 16–17, 130–36.

Kelly, Alice D. "These Downtrodden Men." *Harpers Magazine* 162 (Apr. 1931): 558–65.

Kidney, Daniel M. "Harvest and Relief." *Survey Graphic* 24 (Sept. 1935): 420–25, 461, 464.

Kinder, F. S. "The Slump and Installment Buying." *The New Republic* 65 (Nov. 19, 1930): 20.

Kiplinger, W. M. "Indirect Relief: What Is Its Relation to the Breadline." *The Forum* 87 (June 1932): 349–52.

Komarovsky, Mirra. *The Unemployed Man and His Family—The Effects of Unemployment upon the Status of the Man in Fifty-Nine Families.* New York: Octagon Books, 1971.

LaFollette, Suzanne. *Concerning Women.* New York: Albert and Charles Boni, 1926.

Lawrence, Joseph Stagg. "We've More than Paid the Price." *World's Work* 60 (Oct. 1931): 28–32.

Leach, Henry Goddard. "Depression Brides: A Forward by the Editor." *The Forum* 87 (May 1932): 257–58.

———. "Editor's Forward." *The Forum* 87 (Dec. 1932): 1.

Leary, John J., Jr. "If We Had the Dole." *American Magazine* 112 (Dec. 1931): 11–13, 82, 84, 86.

Leighton, George R. "Doing Business Without Money." *Harper's Magazine* 167 (July 1933): 155–69.

———. "They Call It Barter." *Harper's Magazine* 167 (Aug. 1933): 314–24.

Leighton, George R., and Richard Hellman. "Half Slave, Half Free: Unemployment, the Depression, and American Young People." *Harper's Magazine* 171 (Aug. 1935): 342–53.

Le Sueur, Meridel. "Women Are Hungry." *American Mercury* 31 (Mar. 1934): 316–26.

Levinson, Edward. "Strikebreaking Incorporated: The Story of a Lucrative American Industry." *Harpers Magazine* 171 (Nov. 1935): 719–30.

Lindeman, Edward C. "Social Workers in the Depression." *The Nation* 138 (Mar. 7, 1934): 274–75.

Lonigan, Edna. "Prices Must Come Down!" *The New Republic* 68 (Sept. 23, 1931): 142–46.

Lubin, Isador. "What Delays Revival." *The New Republic* 67 (June 10, 1931): 92–93.

Lutz, Alma. "Women and Wages." *The Nation* 137 (Oct. 17, 1934): 440–41.

Lynd, Robert S., and Helen Merrell Lynd. *Middletown: A Study in American Culture.* New York: Harcourt, Brace and World, Inc., 1929.

———. *Middletown in Transition: A Study in Cultural Conflicts.* New York: Harcourt, Brace and Company, 1937.

Mack, Gertrude. "Rising Above the Market." *The Forum* 85 (Apr. 1931): 228–33.

McKnight, Edna C. "Jobs—For Men Only?" *Outlook and Independent* 159 (Sept. 2, 1931): 12–13, 18.

Mangold, William B. "On the Labor Front." *The New Republic* 82 (Mar. 27, 1935): 186–87.

"Man Out of Work. By His Wife." *Harpers Magazine* 161 (July 1930): 195–201.

"The March of Events." *World's Work* 59 (Dec. 1930): 17.

"The March of Events." *World's Work* 60 (Feb. 1931): 17.

Marcosson, Isaac F. "99% Honest." *American Magazine* 122 (Dec. 1936): 18–19, 129–31.

———. "Our Muddled Youth." *American Magazine* 122 (Sept. 1936): 24–26, 109–12.

Martin, James R. "'Buy Now'—on $30 a Week." *The Nation* 137 (Nov. 1, 1933): 502–3.

"The Meaning of Barter Exchanges." *The New Republic* 73 (Jan. 4, 1933): 202–3.

"Middletown—Ten Years After." *Business Week* (June 9, 1934): 12–13.

Mitchell, James P. "Coddling the Bums." *The Nation* 139 (Aug. 22, 1934): 214–16.

Mitchell, Jonathan. "Alms-Giver: Harry L. Hopkins." *The New Republic* 82 (Apr. 10, 1935): 235–38.

Moorhead, Frank G. "Broke at Fifty-Five." *The Nation* 132 (May 13, 1931): 528–30.

M. S. D. "Should I Take a Job When My Husband Has One Too?" *American Magazine* 115 (Feb. 1933): 134.

National Industrial Conference Board. *Women Workers and Labor Supply.* New York: National Industrial Conference Board, 1936.

Nesbith, Florence. "Present Relief Policies and Their Effect on Family Relationships." *Journal of Home Economics* 27 (Dec. 1935): 625–31.

"No One Has Starved." *Fortune* 6 (Sept. 1932): 18–29, 80, 82, 84, 86, 88.

"No One Need Give." *Fortune* 8 (Nov. 1933): 58–61, 102.

"A Note on the Servant Problem." *Fortune* 6 (Dec. 1932): 49.

"Only Once Every 142 Years." *Fortune* 11 (June 1935): 76–79, 168, 170, 172, 174, 176–78, 180–81.

"On the Dole: 17,000,000." *Fortune* 10 (Oct. 1934): 54–62, 146–58, 182.

"Open Letter from a Congregation." *The Christian Century* 55 (June 15, 1938): 761–62.

Orsino, F. E. "The Plight of the Landlords." *The Forum* 88 (Oct. 1932): 220–24.

"Our Frolicking City Fathers." *World's Work* 61 (Apr. 1932): 44–47.

Parry, Tom Jones. "The Republic of the Penniless." *Atlantic Monthly* 150 (Oct. 1932): 449–57.

Parsons, G. L. "Part-Time Occupations for Women." *Ladies' Home Journal* 48 (Mar. 1931): 120, 127.

"People Do Starve." *The New Republic* 72 (Oct. 5, 1932): 192–94.

"Permanent Prosperity: An Editorial Presenting the Third Step in a Far-Reaching Program for the American Home." *Ladies' Home Journal* 49 (Apr. 1932): 3.

"Pocketbook Patriotism." *Ladies' Home Journal* 49 (Feb. 1932): 3.

Polk's Fargo and Moorhead City Directories. St. Paul, MN: R. L. Polk and Company, 1928, 1932.

Potter, Ellen C. "Mustering Out the Migrants." *The Survey* 69 (Dec. 1933): 411–12.

———. "The Problem of the Transient." *Annals of the American Academy of Political and Social Science* 176 (Nov. 1934): 66–73.

"The Price Merry-Go-Round." *World's Work* 61 (Jan. 1932): 47–50.

"A Program for 1934." *Ladies' Home Journal* 51 (Jan. 1934): 20.

Pruette, Lorine, ed. *Women Workers Through the Depression: A Study of White Collar Employment Made by the American Woman's Association.* New York: Macmillan, 1934.

Puner, Samuel Paul. "Gas Sunday." *The Nation* 141 (July 3, 1935): 20.

Reade, J. O. "Back to Panhandling." *The New Republic* 84 (Oct. 9, 1935): 237–38.

Reckless, Walter C. "Why Women Become Hoboes." *American Mercury* 31 (Feb. 1934): 175–80.

Reed, Ellery F. *Federal Transient Program: An Evaluative Survey, May to July, 1934.* New York: Committee on Care of Transient and Homeless, 1934.

Rinehart, Mary Roberts. "Cutting Down Expenses." *Ladies' Home Journal* 48 (Dec. 1931): 25.

———. "The Family Pays the Bill." *Ladies' Home Journal* 52 (Mar. 1935): 25, 58.

———. "Put Your Money to Work and Other Thoughts." *Ladies' Home Journal* 49 (Feb. 1932): 20, 116, 119.

———. "Thoughts." *Ladies' Home Journal* 49 (Mar. 1932): 25, 126, 128.

———. "The Wife Who Earns." *Ladies' Home Journal* 48 (July 1931): 23.

———. "Women and Money." *Ladies' Home Journal* 48 (Sept. 1931): 71.

———. "Your Child and the Movies." *Ladies' Home Journal* 48 (Apr. 1931): 8–9, 96.

Rogers, H. O. "The Vanishing Job." *The Nation* 132 (Apr. 8, 1931): 375–77.

Roland, Louis. "White Collar Unemployment." *Outlook and Independent* 156 (Nov. 12, 1930): 440.

Roosevelt, Eleanor. *It's Up to the Women.* New York: Frederick A. Stokes Company, 1933.

———. "Servants." *The Forum* 83 (Jan. 1930): 24–28.

Ross, Malcolm. "The Spread of Barter." *The Nation* 136 (Mar. 1, 1933): 228–29.

"A Rule of the CCC." *The Survey* 71 (Aug. 1935): 240.

Ryerson, Edward L., Jr. "Out of the Depression." *The Survey* 70 (Jan. 1934): 3–7.

"Scarcity Diets." *Ladies' Home Journal* 51 (Nov. 1934): 26.

Schnurmann, Paul. "No Fun to Be Single." *The Nation* 138 (Jan. 10, 1934): 47.

Schroeder, James Price. "A History of Organized Labor in Fargo, North Dakota." Master's thesis, University of North Dakota, 1939.

Schuler, Loring A. "A Challenge for Tomorrow." *Ladies' Home Journal* 49 (Oct. 1932): 20.

———. "Child Labor." *Ladies' Home Journal* 48 (Apr. 1931): 30.

———. "Christmas." *Ladies' Home Journal* 49 (Dec. 1932): 20.

———. "Family Spending and Saving." *Ladies' Home Journal* 47 (Dec. 1930): 24.

———. "Homeless Girls." *Ladies' Home Journal* 50 (July 1933): 20.

———. "No Dole." *Ladies' Home Journal* 48 (Nov. 1931): 28.

———. "Part-Time Jobs." *Ladies' Home Journal* 49 (July 1932): 20.

———. "Wages." *Ladies' Home Journal* 48 (Apr. 1931): 30.

Schuler, Myra Blake. "X Stands for Women's Exchange." *Ladies' Home Journal* 49 (Aug. 1932): 41.

Scroggs, William O. "Balancing Production and Consumption." *Outlook and Independent* 156 (Dec. 24, 1930): 664.

———. "Chain Stores and Politicians." *Outlook and Independent* 156 (Nov. 1930): 386.

———. "Our 'Orgy of Saving.'" *Outlook and Independent* 157 (Feb. 4, 1931): 182.

———. "Shall We Cut Wages?" *Outlook and Independent* 158 (May 6, 1931): 19–20.

———. "What About Wages?" *Outlook and Independent* 157 (Jan. 28, 1931): 144.

Shallcross, Ruth. *Should Married Women Work?* New York: Public Affairs Committee of the National Federation of Business and Professional Women's Clubs, 1940.

Sherlock, Chelsa C. "Why You Should Build Your Home This Spring." *Ladies' Home Journal* 47 (Mar. 1930): 32, 168, 170.

"Single Men Are Hoboes." *The New Republic* 76 (Oct. 18, 1933): 268.

Slichter, Sumner. "Doles for Employers." *The New Republic* 65 (Dec. 31, 1930): 181–83.

Smith, Edgar Lawrence. "The Break in the Credit Chain." *Atlantic Monthly* 145 (Jan. 1930): 108–13.

Sokolsky, George E. "The Political Burden of Relief." *Atlantic Monthly* 158 (Sept. 1936): 331–40.

Solow, Herbert. "Class War in Minnesota." *The Nation* 139 (Dec. 26, 1934): 743–44.

Soule, George. "After Revival, What?" *Harper's Magazine* 166 (Dec. 1932): 94–101.

Sparkes, Boyden. "The New Deal for Transients." *The Saturday Evening Post* 208 (Oct. 19, 1935): 90–95.

Sprague, Jesse Rainsford. "Panic and Time Payments." *Harper's Monthly Magazine* 162 (Apr. 1931): 612–21.

Spreckels, Rudolph. "Should Wages Be Cut? No!" *The Forum* 86 (Sept. 1931): 180–82.

Springer, Gertrude. "Men Off the Road." *Survey Graphic* 23 (Sept. 1934): 420–28, 448.

———. "Step-Children of Relief." *The Survey* 69 (June 1933): 212–13.

Stark, Louis. "Jobs for Jobless." *Outlook and Independent* 156 (Nov. 12, 1930): 414–16, 436–38.

———. "Old at Forty." *Outlook and Independent* 153 (Sept. 4, 1929): 3–6, 38–39.

Stevens, Laura Turnidge. "We Haven't Saved

a Cent." *The Nation* 133 (Sept. 16, 1931): 281–83.

Stolberg, Benjamin, and Warren Jay Vinton. "The New Deal vs. Recovery." *American Mercury* 33 (Dec. 1934): 385–97.

Sutherland, Edwin H., and Harvey J. Locke. *Twenty Thousand Homeless Men: A Study of Unemployed Men in the Chicago Shelter.* Chicago, IL: J. B. Lippincott Company, 1936.

"They'd Rather Live on Relief." *The Nation* 141 (Aug. 7, 1935): 144.

Tilden, Freeman. "The Corner Grocer Talks About Chain-Store Competition." *The World's Work* 59 (Apr. 1930): 61–63.

"Transient and Homeless Population in 12 Cities." *Monthly Labor Review* 45 (Oct. 1937): 868–70.

"Transient Order Arouses Protest." *The Survey* 71 (Oct. 1935): 310–11.

"200,000 Wandering Boys." *Fortune* 7 (Feb. 1933): 46–47.

"Unemployment in 1937." *Fortune* 16 (Oct. 1937): 99–107, 188, 191–92, 194, 197.

Wald, Lillian D. "The Lean Years." *Atlantic Monthly* 152 (Dec. 1933): 650–59.

Walker, Charles R. "Relief and Revolution." *The Forum* 88 (Aug. 1932): 73–78.

———. "Relief and Revolution: The Prospect for Next Winter." *The Forum* 88 (Sept. 1932): 152–58.

"The Week." *The New Republic* 68 (Sept. 16, 1931): 111.

Wheeler, Edgar C. "What Can You Do to Make Money?" *American Magazine* 114 (July 1932): 44–45, 70, 72.

Williams, Edward Ainsworth. *Federal Aid for Relief.* 1939. Reprint, New York: AMS Press, 1968.

Wilson, Edmund. "Hull-House in 1932: III." *The New Republic* 73 (Feb. 1, 1933): 317–22.

"Without Generosity." *Ladies' Home Journal* 51 (Sept. 1934): 24.

Wolfe, W. Béran. "Psycho-Analyzing the Depression." *The Forum* 87 (Apr. 1932): 209–14.

SECONDARY SOURCES

Abelson, Elaine S. "'Women Who Have No Men to Work for Them': Gender and Homelessness in the Great Depression." *Feminist Studies* 29 (Spring 2003): 104–27.

Abramovitz, Mimi. *Regulating the Lives of Women: Social Welfare Policy from Colonial*

Times to the Present. Boston, MA: South End Press, 1988.

Aiken, Katherine G. *Harnessing the Power of Motherhood: The National Florence Crittenton Mission, 1883–1925.* Knoxville: University of Tennessee Press, 1998.

Alexander, Ruth M. *The "Girl Problem": Female Sexual Delinquency in New York, 1900–1930.* Ithaca, NY: Cornell University Press, 1995.

Appier, Janis. *Policing Women: The Sexual Politics of Law Enforcement and the LAPD.* Philadelphia, PA: Temple University Press, 1998.

Argersinger, Jo Ann E. *Toward a New Deal in Baltimore: People and Government in the Great Depression.* Chapel Hill: University of North Carolina Press, 1988.

Asbury, Herbert. *The Great Illusion: An Informal History of Prohibition.* Garden City, NJ: Doubleday and Company, 1950.

Ashby, LeRoy. *Endangered Children: Dependency, Neglect, and Abuse in American History.* New York: Twayne Publishers, 1997.

Bailey, Beth L. *From Front Porch to Back Seat: Courtship in Twentieth-Century America.* Baltimore, MD: Johns Hopkins University Press, 1988.

Baldwin, Peter C. "'Nocturnal Habits and Dark Wisdom': The American Response to Children in the Streets at Night, 1880–1930." *Journal of Social History* 35 (Spring 2002): 593–611.

Barker, Neil. "Portland's Works Progress Administration." *Oregon Historical Quarterly* 101 (Winter 2000): 414–41.

Baron, Ann, ed. *Work Engendered: Toward a New History of American Labor.* Ithaca, NY: Cornell University Press, 1991.

Beard, Rick, ed. *On Being Homeless: Historical Perspectives.* New York: Museum of the City of New York, 1987.

Bednarek, Janet R. Daly. *America's Airports: Airfield Development, 1918–1947.* College Station: Texas A&M University Press, 2001.

Beito, David T. *Taxpayers in Revolt: Tax Resistance During the Great Depression.* Chapel Hill: University of North Carolina Press, 1989.

Benson, Susan Porter. *Counter Cultures: Saleswomen, Managers, and Customers in American Department Stores, 1890–1940.* Urbana: University of Illinois Press, 1986.

Bergman, Andrew. *We're in the Money: Depression America and Its Films.* New York: New York University Press, 1971.

Bernstein, Irving. *Turbulent Years: A History of the American Worker, 1933–1941.* Boston, MA: Houghton Mifflin Company, 1970.

Biles, Roger. *Memphis in the Great Depression.* Knoxville: University of Tennessee Press, 1986.

Bird, Caroline. *The Invisible Scar.* New York: David McKay, 1966.

Bix, Amy Sue. *Inventing Ourselves Out of Jobs? America's Debate over Technological Unemployment, 1929–1981.* Baltimore, MD: Johns Hopkins University Press, 2000.

Blackwelder, Julia Kirk. *Now Hiring: The Feminization of Work in the United States, 1900–1995.* College Station: Texas A&M University Press, 1997.

Blewett, Mary H. *Men, Women, and Work: Class, Gender, and Protest in the New England Shoe Industry, 1780–1910.* Urbana: University of Illinois Press, 1988.

Bolin, Winifred D. Wandersee. "The Economics of Middle-Income Family Life: Working Women During the Great Depression." *Journal of American History* 65 (June 1978): 60–74.

Braeman, John, Robert H. Bremner, and David Brody, eds. *The New Deal: The State and Local Levels.* Columbus: Ohio State University Press, 1975.

Braeman, John, Robert H. Bremner, and Ron Walters, eds. *Change and Continuity in Twentieth-Century America.* Columbus: Ohio State University Press, 1964.

Breen, William J. *Labor Market Politics and the Great War: The Department of Labor, the States, and the First U.S. Employment Service, 1907–1933.* Kent, OH: Kent State University Press, 1997.

Bremer, William W. *Depression Winters: New York Social Workers and the New Deal.* Philadelphia, PA: Temple University Press, 1994.

Brinkley, Alan. *Voices of Protest: Huey Long, Father Coughlin and the Great Depression.* New York: Vintage Books, 1983.

Brown, Dorothy M., and Elizabeth McKeown. *The Poor Belong to Us: Catholic Charities and American Welfare.* Cambridge, MA: Harvard University Press, 1997.

Bucki, Cecelia. *Bridgeport's Socialist New*

Deal, 1915–36. Urbana: University of Illinois Press, 2001.

Campbell, Ballard C. *The Growth of American Government: Governance from the Cleveland Era to the Present.* Bloomington: Indiana University Press, 1995.

Chafe, William H. *The American Woman: Her Changing Social, Economic, and Political Roles, 1920–1970.* New York: Oxford University Press, 1972.

———. "Flint and the Great Depression." *Michigan History* 53 (Fall 1969): 225–39.

Chauncey, George. *Gay New York: Gender, Urban Culture, and the Making of the Gay Male World, 1890–1940.* New York: Basic Books, 1994.

Chudacoff, Howard P. *The Age of the Bachelor: Creating an American Subculture.* Princeton, NJ: Princeton University Press, 1999.

Cohen, Lizabeth. *Making a New Deal: Industrial Workers in Chicago, 1919–1939.* Cambridge, MA: Cambridge University Press, 1990.

Cross, Gary. *An All-Consuming Century: Why Commercialism Won in Modern America.* New York: Columbia University Press, 2000.

Crouse, Joan M. *The Homeless Transient in the Great Depression: New York State, 1929–1941.* Albany: State University of New York Press, 1986.

Danbom, David B. "'Cast Down Your Bucket Where You Are': Professional Historians and Local History." *South Dakota History* 33 (Fall 2003): 263–73.

———. "*Our Purpose Is to Serve*": The First Century of the North Dakota Agricultural Experiment Station. Fargo: NDIRS, 1990.

———. "*The World of Hope*": Progressives and the Struggle for an Ethical Public Life. Philadelphia, PA: Temple University Press, 1987.

D'Emilio, John, and Estelle B. Freedman. *Intimate Matters: A History of Sexuality in America.* New York: Harper and Row, 1988.

DePastino, Todd. *Citizen Hobo: How a Century of Homelessness Shaped America.* Chicago, IL: University of Chicago Press, 2003.

Deutrich, Mabel E., and Virginia C. Purdy, eds. *Clio Was a Woman: Studies in the History of American Women.* Washington, DC: Howard University Press, 1980.

Dighe, Ranjit S. "Efficiency Wages, Insiders and Outsiders, and the Great Depression." *Essays in Economic and Business History* 21 (2003): 71–88.

Dulberger, Judith A. *"Mother Donit fore the Best": Correspondence of a Nineteenth-Century Orphan Asylum.* Syracuse, NY: Syracuse University Press, 1996.

Dumenil, Lynn. *The Modern Temper: American Culture and Society in the 1920's.* New York: Hill and Wang, 1995.

Elder, Glen H., Jr. *Children of the Great Depression: Social Change in Life Experiences.* Chicago, IL: University of Chicago Press, 1974.

Elvins, Sarah. "Shopping for Recovery: Local Spending Initiatives and the Great Depression in Buffalo and Rochester, New York." *Journal of Urban History* 29 (Sept. 2003): 670–92.

Faue, Elizabeth. *Community of Suffering and Struggle: Women, Men, and the Labor Movement in Minneapolis, 1915–1945.* Chapel Hill: University of North Carolina Press, 1991.

Feldstein, Ruth. *Motherhood in Black and White: Race and Sex in American Liberalism, 1950–1965.* Ithaca, NY: Cornell University Press, 2000.

Flannigan, Lillian Frances Paddock. "As We Lived It: The Paddock Family and the Great Depression in Wilmington, Delaware." *Delaware History* 27 (Spring–Summer, Fall–Winter 1997): 129–63, 245–77.

Friedlander, Judith, Blanche Wiesen Cook, Alice Kessler-Harris, and Carroll Smith-Rosenberg, eds. *Women in Culture and Politics: A Century of Change.* Bloomington: Indiana University Press, 1986.

Gamber, Wendy. *The Female Economy: The Millinery and Dressmaking Trades, 1860–1930.* Urbana: University of Illinois Press, 1997.

Garceau, Dee. *The Important Things of Life: Women, Work, and Family in Sweetwater County, Wyoming, 1880–1929.* Lincoln: University of Nebraska Press, 1997.

Glazer, Penina Migdal, and Miriam Slater. *Unequal Colleagues: The Entrance of Women into the Professions, 1890–1940.* New Brunswick, NJ: Rutgers University Press, 1987.

Gordon, Linda. *Pitied But Not Entitled: Sin-*

gle Mothers and the History of Welfare, 1890–1935. New York: Free Press, 1994.

——. Woman's Body, Woman's Right: Birth Control in America. New York: Penguin Books, 1974.

Grant, Michael Johnston. Down and Out on the Family Farm: Rural Rehabilitation in the Great Plains, 1929–1945. Lincoln: University of Nebraska Press, 2002.

Green, Elna C., ed. The New Deal and Beyond: Social Welfare in the South Since 1930. Athens: University of Georgia Press, 2003.

Griswold, Robert L. Fatherhood in America: A History. New York: Basic Books, 1993.

Hacsi, Timothy A. Second Home: Orphan Asylums and Poor Families in America. Cambridge, MA: Harvard University Press, 1997.

Harris, Barbara J. Beyond Her Sphere: Women and the Professions in American History. Westport, CT: Greenwood Press, 1978.

Harvey, A. McGehee, and Susan L. Abrams. "For the Welfare of Mankind": The Commonwealth Fund and American Medicine. Baltimore, MD: Johns Hopkins University Press, 1986.

Hearn, Charles R. The American Dream in the Great Depression. Westport, CT: Greenwood Press, 1977.

Helmbold, Lois Rita. "Downward Occupational Mobility During the Great Depression: Urban Black and White Working Class Women." Labor History 29 (Spring 1988): 135–72.

Hickey, Georgina. Hope and Danger in the New South City: Working-Class Women and Urban Development in Atlanta, 1890–1940. Athens: University of Georgia Press, 2003.

Higbie, Frank Tobias. Indispensable Outcasts: Hobo Workers and Community in the American Midwest, 1880–1930. Urbana: University of Illinois Press, 2003.

Hoffbeck, Steven R. "The Cold Charity of the Poorhouse: The Cass County Hospital and Poor Farm, Fargo." Unpublished paper, in author's possession.

Hoffschwelle, Mary S. "Organizing Rural Communities for Change: The Commonwealth Fund Child Health Demonstration in Rutherford County, 1923–1927." Tennessee Historical Quarterly 53 (Fall 1994): 154–65.

Holt, Marilyn Irvin. The Orphan Trains: Placing Out in America. Lincoln: University of Nebraska Press, 1992.

Hornstein, Jeffrey M. "'Rosie the Realtor' and the Re-Gendering of Real Estate Brokerage, 1930–1960." Enterprise and Society 3 (June 2002): 318–51.

Howard, Christopher. "Sowing the Seeds of 'Welfare': The Transformation of Mothers' Pensions, 1900–1940." Journal of Policy History 4 (1992): 188–227.

Hunnicutt, Benjamin Kline. Kellogg's Six Hour Day. Philadelphia, PA: Temple University Press, 1996.

Isern, Thomas D. Bull Threshers and Bindlestiffs: Harvesting and Threshing on the North American Plains. Lawrence: University Press of Kansas, 1990.

Jensen, Joan M. "Sexuality on a Northern Frontier: The Gendering and Disciplining of Rural Wisconsin Women, 1850–1920." Agricultural History 73 (Spring 1999): 136–67.

Jones, John Finbar, and John Middlemist Herrick. Citizens in Service: Volunteers in Social Welfare During the Depression, 1929–1941. East Lansing: Michigan State University Press, 1976.

Jones, Marshall B. "Crisis of the American Orphanage, 1931–1940." Social Service Review 63 (Dec. 1989): 613–29.

Katz, Michael B. The Undeserving Poor: From the War on Poverty to the War on Welfare. New York: Pantheon Books, 1990.

Katzman, David M. Seven Days a Week: Women and Domestic Service in Industrializing America. New York: Oxford University Press, 1978.

Keene, Jennifer D. Doughboys, the Great War, and the Remaking of America. Baltimore, MD: Johns Hopkins University Press, 2001.

Kennedy, David M. Freedom from Fear: The American People in Depression and War, 1929–1945. New York: Oxford University Press, 1999.

Kessler-Harris, Alice. In Pursuit of Equity: Women, Men, and the Quest for Economic Citizenship in 20th-Century America. New York: Oxford University Press, 2001.

——. "In the Nation's Image: The Gendered Limits of Social Citizenship in the Depression Era." Journal of American History 86 (Dec. 1999): 1251–79.

——. Out to Work: A History of Wage-Earning Women in the United States. New York: Oxford University Press, 1982.

——. *A Woman's Wage: Historical Meanings and Social Consequences*. Lexington: University Press of Kentucky, 1990.

Koch, Raymond L. "Politics and Relief in Minneapolis During the 1930's." *Minnesota History* 41 (Winter 1968): 153–70.

Kunzel, Regina G. *Fallen Women, Problem Girls: Unmarried Mothers and the Professionalization of Social Work, 1890–1945*. New Haven, CT: Yale University Press, 1993.

Kusmer, Kenneth L. *Down and Out, On the Road: The Homeless in American History*. New York: Oxford University Press, 2002.

LaRossa, Ralph. *The Modernization of Fatherhood: A Social and Political History*. Chicago, IL: University of Chicago Press, 1997.

Lazar, Robert. "Jewish Communal Life in Fargo, North Dakota: The Formative Years, 1881–1917." *Western States Jewish History* 35 (Winter 2003): 182–91.

Levine, Susan. "Workers' Wives: Gender, Class, and Consumerism in the 1920s United States." *Gender and History* 3 (Spring 1991): 45–64.

Lindenmeyer, Kristi. *"A Right to Childhood": The U.S. Children's Bureau and Child Welfare, 1912–46*. Urbana: University of Illinois Press, 1997.

Longmore, Paul H., and David Goldberger. "The League of the Physically Handicapped and the Great Depression: A Case History in the New Disability History." *Journal of American History* 87 (Dec. 2000): 888–922.

Lowitt, Richard, and Maurine Beasley, eds. *One Third of a Nation: Lorena Hickok Reports on the Great Depression*. Urbana: University of Illinois Press, 1981.

McElvaine, Robert S. *The Great Depression: America, 1929–1941*. New York: Times Books, 1984.

McGovern, James R. *And a Time for Hope: Americans in the Great Depression*. Westport, CT: Praeger, 2000.

McShane, Clay. *Down the Asphalt Path: The Automobile and the American City*. New York: Columbia University Press, 1994.

Marchand, Roland. *Advertising the American Dream: Making Way for Modernity, 1920–1940*. Berkeley: University of California Press, 1985.

Margolin, Leslie. *Under the Cover of Kindness: The Invention of Social Work*. Charlottesville: University Press of Virginia, 1997.

Martinson, Henry R. *History of North Dakota Labor*. Fargo, ND: Henry R. Martinson, 1970.

Matt, Susan. *Keeping Up with the Joneses: Envy in American Consumer Society, 1890–1930*. Philadelphia: University of Pennsylvania Press, 2003.

Matthews, Glenna. *"Just a Housewife": The Rise and Fall of Domesticity in America*. New York: Oxford University Press, 1987.

May, Elaine Tyler. *Homeward Bound: American Families in the Cold War Era*. New York: Basic Books, 1988.

Meyerowitz, Joanne J. *Women Adrift: Independent Wage Earners in Chicago, 1880–1930*. Chicago, IL: University of Chicago Press, 1988.

Milkman, Ruth. *Gender at Work: The Dynamics of Job Segregation by Sex During World War II*. Urbana: University of Illinois Press, 1987.

——. "Women's Work and Economic Crisis: Some Lessons of the Great Depression." *Review of Radical Political Economics* 8 (Spring 1976): 73–97.

Millikan, William. *A Union Against Unions: The Minneapolis Citizens Alliance and Its Fight Against Organized Labor, 1903–1947*. St. Paul: Minnesota Historical Society Press, 2001.

Mintz, Steven, and Susan Kellogg. *Domestic Revolutions: A Social History of American Family Life*. New York: Free Press, 1988.

Moehling, Carolyn M. "Women's Work and Men's Unemployment." *Journal of Economic History* 61 (Dec. 2001): 926–49.

Moore, Mark H., and Dean R. Gerstein, eds. *Alcohol and Public Policy: Beyond the Shadow of Prohibition*. Washington, DC: National Academy Press, 1981.

Moreo, Dominic W. *Schools in the Great Depression*. New York: Garland, 1996.

Morgan, Iwan. "Fort Wayne and the Great Depression: The Early Years, 1929–1933." *Indiana Magazine of History* 80 (June 1984): 122–45.

Morton, Marian J. *And Sin No More: Social Policy and Unwed Mothers in Cleveland, 1855–1990*. Columbus: Ohio State University Press, 1993.

——. "The Transformation of Catholic Orphanages: Cleveland, 1851–1996." *Catholic Historical Review* 88 (Jan. 2002): 65–89.

Mullins, William H. *The Depression and the*

Urban West Coast, 1929–1933: Los Angeles, San Francisco, Seattle, and Portland. Bloomington: Indiana University Press, 1991.

Murdock, Catherine Gilbert. *Domesticating Drink: Women, Men, and Alcohol in America, 1870–1940.* Baltimore, MD: Johns Hopkins University Press, 1998.

Murphy, Mary. *Mining Cultures: Men, Women, and Leisure in Butte, 1914–41.* Urbana: University of Illinois Press, 1997.

Norman, Ernest. *A History of Catholic Family Service: Social Ministry in North Dakota.* Fargo, ND: Catholic Family Service, 1998.

Nye, Ronald L. "The Challenge of Philanthropy: Unemployment Relief in Santa Barbara, 1930–1932." *California Historical Quarterly* 56 (Winter 1977–78): 310–27.

Olney, Martha L. "Avoiding Default: The Role of Credit in the Consumption Collapse of 1930." *Quarterly Journal of Economics* 114 (Feb. 1999): 319–35.

Patterson, James T. *America's Struggle Against Poverty, 1900–1994.* Cambridge, MA: Harvard University Press, 1994.

———. *The New Deal and the States: Federalism in Transition.* Westport, CT: Greenwood, 1969.

Platt, Anthony M. *The Child Savers: The Invention of Delinquency.* Chicago, IL: University of Chicago Press, 1977.

Plesur, Milton, ed. *An American Historian: Essays to Honor Selig Adler.* Buffalo: State University of New York, 1980.

Postol, Todd Alexander. "Masculine Guidance: Boys, Men, and Newspapers, 1930–1939." *Enterprise and Society* 1 (June 2000): 355–90.

Roberts, Norene A. *Fargo's Heritage.* Fargo, ND: Fargo Heritage Society, 1983.

Rose, Elizabeth. *A Mother's Job: The History of Day Care, 1890–1960.* New York: Oxford University Press, 1999.

Rose, Nancy E. *Put to Work: Relief Programs in the Great Depression.* New York: Monthly Review Press, 1994.

———. *Workfare or Fair Work: Women, Welfare, and Government Work Programs.* New Brunswick, NJ: Rutgers University Press, 1995.

Rosen, Robyn L. "Federal Expansion, Fertility Control, and Physicians in the United States: The Politics of Maternal Welfare in the Interwar Years." *Journal of Women's History* 10 (Autumn 1998): 53–73.

Rosenzweig, Roy. "Organizing the Unemployed: The Early Years of the Great Depression, 1929–1933." *Radical America* 10 (July–Aug. 1976): 37–60.

Sample, Bradford. "A Truly Midwestern City: Indianapolis on the Eve of the Great Depression." *Indiana Magazine of History* 97 (June 2001): 127–47.

Sannes, Erling N. "Gas Sunday: Organizing Fargo, North Dakota Teamsters in 1935." *Journal of the West* 35 (Apr. 1, 1996): 29–32.

Scanlon, Jennifer. *Inarticulate Longings: The Ladies' Home Journal, Gender, and the Promises of Consumer Culture.* New York: Routledge, 1995.

Scharf, Lois. *To Work and to Wed: Female Employment, Feminism, and the Great Depression.* Westport, CT: Greenwood Press, 1980.

Schloff, Linda Mack. *"And Prairie Dogs Weren't Kosher": Jewish Women in the Upper Midwest Since 1855.* St. Paul: Minnesota Historical Society Press, 1996.

Schultz, Robert T. *Conflict and Change: Minneapolis Truck Drivers Make a Dent in the New Deal.* Prospect Heights, IL: Waveland Press, 2000.

Sealander, Judith. *Private Wealth and Public Life: Foundation Philanthropy and the Reshaping of American Social Policy from the Progressive Era to the New Deal.* Baltimore, MD: Johns Hopkins University Press, 1997.

Sherman, William C., and Playford V. Thorson, eds. *Plains Folk: North Dakota's Ethnic History.* Fargo: NDIRS, 1988.

Simon, Curtis J. "The Supply Price of Labor During the Great Depression." *Journal of Economic History* 61 (Dec. 2001): 877–903.

Singleton, Jeff. *The American Dole: Unemployment Relief and the Welfare State in the Great Depression.* Westport, CT: Greenwood Press, 2000.

Sorin, Gerald. *Tradition Transformed: The Jewish Experience in America.* Baltimore, MD: Johns Hopkins University Press, 1997.

Stansell, Christine. *City of Women: Sex and Class in New York, 1789–1860.* Urbana: University of Illinois Press, 1986.

Starr, Kevin. *Endangered Dreams: The Great Depression in California.* New York: Oxford University Press, 1996.

Sternsher, Bernard, ed. *Hitting Home: The*

Great Depression in Town and Country. Chicago, IL: Ivan R. Dee, 1989.

Stock, Catherine McNicol. *Main Street in Crisis: The Great Depression and the Old Middle Class on the Northern Plains.* Chapel Hill: University of North Carolina Press, 1992.

Storrs, Landon R. Y. *Civilizing Capitalism: The National Consumers' League, Women's Activism, and Labor Standards in the New Deal Era.* Chapel Hill: University of North Carolina Press, 2000.

Stradling, David. *Smokestacks and Progressives: Environmentalists, Engineers, and Air Quality in America, 1881–1950.* Baltimore, MD: Johns Hopkins University Press, 1999.

Swain, Martha H. "'The Forgotten Woman': Ellen S. Woodward and Women's Relief in the New Deal." *Prologue* 15 (Winter 1983): 200–213.

Thornton, Mark, and Chetley Weise. "The Great Depression Tax Revolts Revisited." *The Journal of Libertarian Studies* 15 (Summer 2001): 95–105.

Tidd, James Francis, Jr. "Stitching and Striking: WPA Sewing Rooms and the 1937 Relief Strike in Hillsborough County." *Tampa Bay History* 11 (Spring–Summer 1989): 5–21.

Trattner, Walter I., ed. *Social Welfare or Social Control? Some Historical Reflections on Regulating the Poor.* Knoxville: University of Tennessee Press, 1983.

Traverso, Susan. *Welfare Politics in Boston, 1910–1940.* Amherst: University of Massachusetts Press, 2003.

Trout, Charles H. *Boston, the Great Depression, and the New Deal.* New York: Oxford University Press, 1977.

Tweton, D. Jerome. *The New Deal at the Grass Roots: Programs for the People in Otter Tail County, Minnesota.* St. Paul: Minnesota Historical Society Press, 1988.

Tyack, David, Robert Lowe, and Elisabeth Hansot. *Public Schools in Hard Times: The Great Depression and Recent Years.* Cambridge, MA: Harvard University Press, 1984.

Van Sickle, Frederick Mercer. "A Special Place: Lake Forest and the Great Depression, 1929–1940." *Illinois Historical Journal* 79 (Summer 1986): 113–26.

Wachs, Martin, and Margaret Crawford, eds. *The Car and the City: The Automobile, the Built Environment, and Daily Urban Life.* Ann Arbor: University of Michigan Press, 1992.

Wagner, Jonathan F. "'The Greatest Thing I Ever Did Was Join the Union': A History of the Dakota Teamsters During the Depression." *Great Plains Quarterly* 8 (Winter 1988): 16–28.

Wandersee, Winifred D. *Women's Work and Family Values, 1920–1940.* Cambridge, MA: Harvard University Press, 1981.

Ware, Susan. *Holding Their Own: American Women in the 1930s.* Boston, MA: Twayne Publishers, 1982.

Wenger, Beth D. *New York Jews and the Great Depression: Uncertain Promise.* New Haven, CT: Yale University Press, 1996.

Westin, Jeane. *Making Do: How Women Survived the '30s.* Chicago, IL: Follett, 1976.

Wiese, Andrew. "The Other Suburbanites: African American Suburbanization in the North Before 1950." *Journal of American History* 85 (Mar. 1999): 1495–524.

Willett, Julie A. *Permanent Waves: The Making of the American Beauty Shop.* New York: New York University Press, 2000.

Wolcott, David. "'The Cop Will Get You': The Police and Discretionary Juvenile Justice, 1890–1940." *Journal of Social History* 35 (Winter 2001): 349–71.

Going It Alone was designed and set in type by Will Powers at the Minnesota Historical Society Press. The text typeface is Bulmer. Printed by Thomson-Shore, Inc., Dexter, Michigan.